MANY MIRRORS

MANY MIRRORS

Body Image and Social Relations

edited by

Nicole Sault

Rutgers University Press   New Brunswick, New Jersey

Library of Congress Cataloging-in-Publication Data

Many mirrors : body image and social relations /
[edited by] Nicole Sault.
p. cm.
Includes bibliographical references (p.   ) and index.
ISBN 0-8135-2079-7 (cloth)—ISBN 0-8135-2080-0 (pbk.)
1. Body, Human—Social aspects—Cross-cultural studies.   2. Body
image—Cross-cultural studies.   3. Feminine beauty (Aesthetics)—
Cross-cultural studies.   I. Sault, Nicole Landry.
GN298.M36 1994
306.4—dc20   93-37997
                                                                                 CIP

British Cataloging-in-Publication information available

To
Helen Vail Muller
and
Helen Muller Drachkovitch

I recalled a time when I was eight years old: I came home from school, devastated because friends on the playground were making fun of my naturally curly hair when straight hair was in. They called me a "witch." Mother took me by the hand into the bathroom and sat me in front of the mirror.

"Tell me what you see," she said.

I couldn't look.

She took her hand and lifted my chin. "Tell me what you see."

I looked in the mirror, and she said, "I see a beautiful girl with green eyes. I want you to stay here until you see her too."

From *Refuge: An Unnatural History of Family and Place,*
by Terry Tempest Williams (Pantheon Books, 1991)

CONTENTS

FOREWORD

PEGGY REEVES SANDAY

Anthropology is notorious for its strange cases and even stranger comparisons. Why is beauty defined as thin in the United States and plump in Jamaica? Why would a Rashaayda Bedouin woman tattoo her thigh with a camel brand? What does this have to do with women in the United States becoming bodybuilders or applying cosmetics? Why do Americans split body from self and look back on the body as if it were a foreign territory to be conquered, controlled, and shaped—a stage on which power is sometimes forcibly applied and always negotiated?

This book addresses these and many other questions. By describing the myriad ways in which the body occupies center stage in the drama of social relations, this book contributes to the rich tradition of the anthropological study of the body. The individual case studies are tied by a common thesis. Body and society are reciprocal mirrors, each reflecting the consequences of the other's conscious wishes and repressed desires. It is through the body image that human beings become not only self-aware but socially aware. Through the ways the women and men described in these pages learn to control, repress, or express themselves in terms of their bodies, the reader learns about the constant and variable factors by which people place themselves or are placed by others on the stage of human interaction.

Each chapter describes some aspect of the mirroring process by showing how people make themselves or are forcibly made into a particular social image. The topics range from marking or altering the body to the social and bodily meanings of rape, childbirth, and aging. In her comprehensive introduction, Nicole Sault surveys the literature on the body as metaphor and model and provides a framework that connects the seemingly unrelated practices discussed by the authors. Power and control—who has it and how it is applied in the breaching and setting of boundaries—is a major theme. How self-awareness and the presentation of self are stamped by social expectations is another.

Control is an issue that predominates in all the discussions, and rebellion is the subtext, especially for women and girls. They wrestle with control as they display their power through bodybuilding, dramatize different roles with cosmetics, separate from the physical pain of childbirth by retreating into the mind, or act out the messages of rape trauma to protect against further assaults. When the mind is numbed, the memory of abuse is represented in bodily reactions, reminding us that memory is lodged throughout the whole body.

These case studies compel us to expand the notion of *internalized oppression* from a state of mind to include bodily actions and reactions. When we internalize male dominance and racism, this oppression is expressed through the body, since it affects the whole person. Sometimes, in rebelling against passive female roles, women may even adopt standard male roles in their bodily practices.

By placing the themes of the book in the context of the literature, Sault provides an important educational service for students of the body. Taken together these themes broaden and expand the anthropological paradigm initiated by Mary Douglas, Edith Turner, and Victor Turner, who showed so vividly how the social is written in, on, and through the body. By expanding the discussion of body image to include women and girls in the United States as well as other countries, the book also contributes to feminist theory cross-culturally.

As Clifford Geertz demonstrated how Balinese men find in the cockfight a representation of masculine temperament and a chance to enact status concerns, we can find in the descriptions provided here both a representation of the culturally prescribed temperament for American women and a reflection of the hierarchical, controlling relationship between those who represent and define body image and those who accept or resist these representations and redefine their meaning. This rich group of essays illuminates the ways in which people respond to and are shaped by experience, trauma, and ideals. It is a key book for those interested in gender studies and the use of the body as both the medium and the message.

ACKNOWLEDGMENTS

A book is the work of many people. This particular book came about through the contributions of my colleagues, friends, and family, and there are many to whom I express my gratitude. Foremost among them is Peter C. Reynolds, whose insights inform the pages of this book. He tirelessly read each draft and kept his fine sense of humor throughout. My thanks go to Cathy Winkler, Mitch Allen, Peggy Sanday, and Carole Browner. Each of them has provided valuable criticism, advice, and enthusiasm. Those who know Cathy Winkler are blessed by her joyful understanding. For anyone writing a book in anthropology, Mitch Allen is a treasure. Peggy Sanday has a courage and clarity that few can hope to attain. Carole Browner is a person of undaunted and generous spirit; she is a beacon for all those around her. Since I began graduate studies in anthropology, Fadwa El Guindi has influenced my work over the years, and I continue to be impressed by the depth of her ability to address issues from a truly cross-cultural perception as well as greatness of heart. My work has benefited greatly from Dwight Read's fine logic and insight. Helga Wild and Niklas Damiris carried our discussions into the early hours and provided not only key references but a greater awareness of rhythm. My colleagues at Santa Clara University are important in numerous ways, and some have been especially supportive of this book, including Alma M. Garcia, Diane Jonte-Pace, Maryellen Mori, and Darlene Rodrigues. I am fortunate to be working with Marlie Wasserman at Rutgers University Press, an editor whose high reputation is well deserved. This book has benefited greatly from careful and patient editing by Anne Knight and Kathryn Gohl. Living in Mexico has informed who I am and what I write, for my view of the world has been enriched by many families throughout the country. Certain individuals in Oaxaca and Mexico City deserve special thanks; they include Juana Ramos Gonzalez, Manuel Reyes Méndez, María de los Angeles Romero Frizzi, Manuel Esparza Camargo, Cecil Welte, Mario Antonio Barrón y Sierra, and Esperanza Soto de Petit. Finally, *Many Mirrors* is dedicated to my mother and my grandmother, who made this book possible in innumerable ways.

Nicole Sault
Santa Clara, California
August 1993

MANY MIRRORS

INTRODUCTION

The Human Mirror

NICOLE SAULT

C ontemporary Western culture teaches us to think of the body as an object with a material reality that is physically observable, but anthropology shows that we perceive our bodies through a culturally constructed body image that shapes what we see and experience. As we negotiate social relationships, our sense of a body image develops, for the two are reciprocally related. This book explores the dynamic interaction that occurs between social behavior and symbolic meaning as people attempt to alter and control themselves and others by changing their body images.

The human body is a topic of interest to scholars in many fields, but anthropologists' special contribution in this area is to provide a cross-cultural perspective that includes the beliefs and values of people from societies throughout the world and throughout history. Anthropology can show how body-related beliefs and behaviors vary from one society to another and can elucidate the underlying assumptions within each culture. Using the comparative perspective of anthropology to examine the body image within a system of culturally defined social relations, this book asks us to rethink our most basic ideas about body, self, and other.

What if we had no mirrors, photographs, or videos to show us how we look? How would we see ourselves? Despite the fact that we have material objects to show us reflections of our selves, we are also social mirrors to each other, and we rely on the reactions of others to learn how we look and who we are. As we alter our bodies, we express our social identity and relationships, shaping and being shaped by others in ways that communicate our changing status over time.

This introduction describes perceptions of the body and ways of assigning meaning according to distinct views of the world that incorporate healing systems and strategies for control. I discuss the body image in terms of historical and current practices, including material from psychology and feminist studies as well as the anthropological literature, and then draw on these sources to present an alternative conceptual framework. This framework introduces the *body image system* as a way to understand how people in all societies perceive, describe, and alter their bodies.

The book's eleven chapters are grouped into four sections, each portraying a particular stance one may adopt toward the body image in acting upon and reacting to oneself and others. In summarizing the main themes that recur throughout the essays, I describe the ways in which the body image system contributes toward rethinking the many issues that contemporary problems have generated.

"Good to Think with"

These days the body is a hot topic as a source of both self-discovery and concern. The mass media present body-related issues with a growing sense of urgency, enjoining us to keep our bodies healthy, youthful, and well attired, always reminding us that self-identity is defined by the condition of our bodies. Anthropology holds a special place in these discussions, for anthropologists have long been interested in research on the human body, and the anthropological perspective addresses the cultural premises that underlie our preoccupation with the body.[1] Well-known early anthropologists used the body as a central construct in describing social relations and symbolic systems (Douglas 1970; Durkheim 1954; Firth 1936; Leach 1969; Lévi-Strauss 1966; Mauss 1973; Needham 1973; Turner 1968).

Mauss notes that "the body is the first and most natural tool of man" (1973:75). It is a source of symbols and their classification (Ellen 1977:356). As Lévi-Strauss explains, "The total system of social relations, itself bound up with a system of the universe, can be projected onto the anatomical plane" (1966:168–169). Throughout the world the human body is used to express connection to the land and to define social space. Among the Dogon of West Africa, the layout of a village extends like a person lying down: "the head is the council house, built on the chief square . . . to the east and west are houses for menstruating women; they are round like wombs and represent the hands of the village. The large family houses are its chest and belly; the communal altars at the south of the village are its feet" (Griaule, as quoted in Ellen 1977:359).

Douglas describes the body as a natural symbol that is "good to think with"; used as a cognitive map, it provides many of our richest metaphors (1970:65). She emphasizes the social interactive meaning of the body, as it expresses social situations, contributes to a particular setting, and mediates the social structure (1975:83, 87). The way we perceive the physical experience of the body is constrained by the social body—our culturally constructed reality—for we know our bodies through experiences that are always modified by social categories (1970:65).

Writing in "Body Techniques," Mauss describes the mechanisms and processes that transform the body into an artifact assembled "by and for society" (1973). His student, Needham, argues that the body is used to justify and sustain particular values and social arguments (1973:109). Scheper-Hughes and Lock point out that cultures "reproduce and socialize the kinds of bodies that they need," domesticating the individual body for a particular social and political order (1987:25–26). These authors use this perspective to characterize the current cultural context of medicine. Sickness "is a form of communication," and the medical gaze is "a controlling gaze" (1987:-31,27). A powerful example is Ong's discussion of Cambodian refugees' encounters with Western medicine in California hospitals and clinics (Ong 1990).

Although anthropological interest in the body has been ongoing, research on the body image is relatively recent. Scheper-Hughes and Lock note that the existing literature on body imagery is largely psychiatric and has been "virtually untapped by social and especially medical anthropologists, who could benefit from attention to body boundary conceptions, distortions in body perception, etc." (1987:-16–17). Other areas of anthropology which relate to body image and deserve greater attention include dance, song, rhythm and scent. Royce describes dance as "the human body making patterns in time and space," something unique among the arts and "perhaps older than the arts" (1977:3). The role of the body in dance has still been largely ignored or treated as entertainment (Kaeppler 1978), although the number of studies that give serious attention to dance is growing (Cowan 1990; Ness 1992; Lange 1975; Spencer 1985). The influence of song on the body image is discussed by Kivnick (1990) and Schroeder-Sheker (in Rosenberg 1991), while Kanafani (1983),

Zimmerman (1988), and Wilbert (1987) have examined the cultural significance of smell, perfume, and incense. With this long history of anthropological studies of the body in other societies and our current fascination with body issues, why have we been so slow to analyze the cultural meaning of contemporary body imagery?

The "Savage" Body

Not so many years ago in England, Polhemus called for "an anthropology of the anthropology of the human body," and his call to address this issue is still relevant. He argues that to understand the Western "religious cult" of the human body we must examine the history of this research (Polhemus 1975:13–14). Anthropology began in Europe as the study of "savages," and Polhemus points out that initially anthropological interest in the body was an attempt to make the bizarre "fit into rational, empirical models of human behavior" (1975:15). He suggests that "what worried Westerners most about these savages was that they were 'naked'; that they danced and communicated powerful symbolic statements with their tattooed bodies" (1975:14). The anthropologist's role was "to render the savage understandable," which meant understanding "his nakedness." As Polhemus explains, "If we were to render the savage world safe for Western, verbalizing man, we would have to bring the mysteries of the human body within the boundaries of Western rationality" (1975:15).

There are, however, multiple meanings to the phrase "to render the savage understandable." Early European commentators sought to categorize savage behavior within the European worldview, to surround it with a familiar frame that would make it safe—exotic, but no longer dangerous. It was not enough to subdue a people physically; it was even more important to encapsulate them mentally with European definitions. So in the early period of anthropology, "the savage" was defined by "his nakedness, his scarification, his tattooing, his dancing, and his erotic appeal" (Polhemus 1975:15). Note that these features emphasize the savage as an active *body*, not a mind, much less a soul. After all, what could be expected of "the savage mind"? In the process of conquest, "the savage" was generally portrayed as a male body. After being conquered, "the savage body" was portrayed as female or feminized because it had been dominated. These "savages" were important to Europeans only in relation to themselves. "Savages" had meaning insofar as they defined what being "European" was in relation to what being "European" was not. In this view of the world which separated body from mind, the "other" came to exemplify the "inferior" body in contrast to the "superior" mind of the European. So descriptions of "savages" emphasized their nakedness. "Savages" had to be seen as *naked bodies* without thinking minds, just as Europeans had to be seen as clothed.[2] Thus the quest to "describe" and "understand" the naked "savage" was essential to expanding colonial control by making "the other" safe to think about and act upon.

The legacy of the "savage" naked body has carried over into the present, for the body continues to symbolize "the wild" and "the inferior" which need to be controlled. For example, in a 1990 article from *Omni* magazine reprinted in an introductory anthropology text, a Matses man of the Peruvian Amazon is described in these words: "a young Indian silently appeared at our campsite. He was small and dark-skinned, naked except for an old pair of green swim trunks" (Gorman 1991:214). Why call him "naked" if he is wearing swim trunks? Because his nakedness is what is important to Gorman. Whether clothed or unclothed, the bodies of people in other societies are still portrayed as exotic and colorful examples of curious or bizarre practices that contrast with "correct" Euro-American standards for behavior.

One of the premises of colonization then and now is that a fundamental distinction exists between the ways "savage" and "civilized" people alter their bodies: "savages" go naked and "mutilate" their bodies, whereas "civilized" people cover themselves with removable objects such as clothing and jewelry. "Civilized" people *perceive* their bodies and are aware of the need to be clothed, whereas "savages" *are* their bodies so they do not recognize their nakedness. This polarizing view appears in theories of the body that portray clothing as "normal" and body "mutilations" as abnormal, each explicable according to a different set of causes.

"Savage" Body Parts

The concept of the "savage" body is still with us in a new form that reflects changes in the Western body image. Many contemporary Euro-American societies are characterized by a worldview that defines the body in terms of an isolated, independent individual: "social relations are seen as partitioned, segmented, and situational," and this is re-flected in a particular understanding of the body and the self as "dis-tinct and separable entities" (Scheper-Hughes and Lock 1987:21). Body and self are perceived in opposition to each other, and this en-ables us to think of the body as a separate object. The individual *has* a body, and that body is like a machine that can be broken down into parts.[3] By accepting this mechanical model, people now see them-selves as divided into parts and their bodies as assemblages of func-tionally defined units. In our everyday language we reduce people to body parts, referring to individuals in terms of particular anatomical segments—brain, breasts, genitals, heart, legs, and so on. The "unity of the person" has been fragmented (Martin 1987:19).

Our sense of fragmentation is then turned outward and mirrored in the way we portray people in other societies, recasting "the savage body" in terms of a Euro-American concern with "savage body parts." Ellen observes that discussions of the body in other cultures often focus on *parts* of the body, such as "the mouth, anus, penis and so on," stressing "the function of individual parts rather than the rela-tionships between them" (1977:364). Such an approach ignores "the basic context, perception, and classification of the body" (1977:364). Polhemus argues that by focusing on "feather head-dresses, penis-sheaths, smiles, postures, ear-rings, tattooing, cranial deformation, gestures, etc.," we have "dealt with only bits and pieces of the body instead of the *whole* body" (1975:33). Anthropologists have "studied the body and its aids of adornment and clothing as separate media and not as a total and complete body system." We have supplied "*our own* would-be objective definition of the boundaries of the body and its peripheral media; we should in the future be more sensitive to *native* definitions of the body as a system of meaning" (1975:33). We have "allowed our own condition of social anomie, of formlessness, to creep into our research" (1975:33).

We have given little or no recognition to body parts in relation to the whole person or the person as a member of a social group. Thus in current Euro-American thinking, the naked "savage" has yielded place to the "savage body part." In the "savage body" concept, the person who represents the "other" is defined as a naked body, lacking both mind and soul. In the "savage body parts" concept, however, the person who represents the other is reduced to a specific body part that holds special meaning for the observer. A particular body part is emphasized in order to draw attention to certain curious or bizarre behavior demonstrated by "the other." Mind, soul, the rest of the body, and the person's social group are simply ignored. What remains unspoken is that a particular "savage body part" is significant to the observer for the contrast it provides with the observer's own "normal" body part and related practices.

For example, anthropologists doing research in the Middle East complain that when they give presentations before academic audiences in the United States they are almost inevitably asked about women's veiling or women's genital operations. No matter what the intended subject of the talk, veiling and genital operations eventually become the topic of discussion.[4] Of course one could argue that these are important subjects which give us crucial information about gender roles in Middle Eastern societies. But the focus is on body parts rather than whole people existing within a larger political, social, and cultural context.

Unfortunately, for most people in the United States, Middle Eastern women are defined in terms of their hidden faces and their altered genitals—not as whole bodies or social beings.[5] In this way our own concern with particular issues symbolized by these body parts has obscured our understanding of people in other societies and the issues that are important to them. Despite contemporary recognition of the ways our colonial legacy shapes images of "the other" (Marcus and Fischer 1986; Said 1979), the mass media and academics, including many anthropologists, continue to conceptualize people in terms of "savage body parts." This colonial perspective will persist as long as we refuse to address the cultural context for our own understanding of the body in opposition to the self, and it will continue to influence how power over the body is perceived and defined in Europe and the United States.

Conformity and Control

Scholars in diverse fields are turning their focus toward examining the body as the site of social and political control. Many authors have noted that attitudes toward pregnancy and childbirth reflect a patriarchal and mechanical worldview that is acted out in the delivery rooms of U.S. hospitals and research facilities (Arditti et al. 1985; Arms 1975; Corea 1985; Ehrenreich and English 1978; Martin 1987; Oakley 1984; Spallone and Steinberg 1987). This topic is discussed in the chapter by Robbie E. Davis-Floyd as well as in my own final chapter.

Other authors have focused on the thin-body ideal promoted in the media. Bordo analyzes the "normalizing function" of the American preoccupation with fat, diets, and slenderness. Many struggle to achieve the ideal body, which is firm, tight, "contained," and "bolted down," a body whose smooth boundaries show that the "internal processes" are properly managed (Bordo 1990:90). Our concern about maintaining body boundaries is expressed through images of bodily eruption that frequently appear in science fiction or horror films, for example, the exploding intestines scene in *Alien*. Bordo sees the emphasis on the body boundary as "a metaphor for anxiety about internal processes out of control—uncontained desire, unrestrained hunger, uncontrolled impulse" (1990:89). The new "body management" has ensured "the production of self-monitoring and self-disciplining 'docile bodies' " (1990:85).[6]

Women in particular are trained to adhere to an acute degree of conformity. Whereas men are dissatisfied with areas of their bodies that are "too small," women are concerned about appearing "too large" (Fisher 1968:115). Bordo notes the growing concern with soft protuberances—lumps, bumps, bulges, and flab. As one woman explained: "My body can turn on me at any moment; it is an out of control mass of flesh" (Bordo 1990:89). An obese woman is perceived as more than fat; she is out of control, unrestrained, and immoral (Turner 1984:197).

In print and broadcast advertising, women's struggle to achieve thin bodies is portrayed as liberating and empowering, by using bodily control to achieve greater fitness and health. However, being thin also connotes "fragility, defenselessness, and lack of power" when compared with the muscular bulk of "a decisive male occupation of social space" (Bordo 1990:86). As a woman gains control over her body and shrinks in size, she communicates to those in power that she is managing herself. The lean body in professional dress sends a message of "neutralization," as the businesswoman symbolically declares her "allegiance to the professional, white, male world" (1990:104). She will neither compete for male space nor subvert male control with alternative "female values." Her female energy has been contained within a tightly regulated body boundary.

As various authors have noted, science and medicine present an androcentric view of the world in which men represent Culture, while women are the embodiment of Nature and thus naturally fall under the control of men. Due to their association with Nature, women are also perceived as representing the "Savage." The culturally defined opposition between female Nature and male Culture is restated in terms of another opposition between body and mind.[7] Women are viewed as more body than mind, and the body represents the "other" that must be controlled. Either women's bodies are controlled by men or women themselves must learn to control their own bodies. Otherwise a woman's body may rebel and take over the "true self" that resides in the mind. Martin found that the women she interviewed repeatedly expressed this body/self dichotomy: "Your self is separate from your body. . . . Your body is something your self has to adjust to or cope with. . . . Your body needs to be controlled by your self" (Martin 1987:77).

The Western concept of the unruly body that requires self-control is far from universal and creates problems for many immigrants when they arrive in the United States and are forced to adjust to a new body concept. Ong found that among Khmer women emigrating to the United States from Cambodia, part of the acculturation process involved learning to think of the body as separate from the self (Ong 1990). Like other Buddhists, Khmer women "consider the body to be a sacred container of their life spirits" (1990:11). They do not have a detached attitude toward the body as a separate entity that needs to be managed by the self. Biomedical models with a body/mind split, pelvic exams, surgical procedures, and countless forms to be filled out create a "medical reimaging" that intensifies their sense of displacement and disembodiment and recalls the Khmer experience of interrogations, torture, and warfare (1990:2). Imposing a model of the body as separate from cultural experience is a way of erasing Khmer cultural memory (1990:13). It is also a powerful means of control.

Contrasting Models for Illness and Healing

Meanings attributed to the body or parts of the body reflect attitudes toward the self and the larger society. In Western society, the separate, bounded individual existence of the self is accepted as a natural aspect of objective reality, but this view is actually a relatively recent historical phenomenon (Geertz 1984; Scheper-Hughes and Lock 1987; Webel

1983). Many societies believe the body-self is "fused with or absorbed by the social body," and still other societies perceive the individual as "comprised of a multiplicity of selves" (Scheper-Hughes and Lock 1987:15) or having several souls (Kensinger 1991). How the body is recognized in defining personhood is especially important for understanding illness and healing (Manning and Fabrega 1973; Desjarlais 1992; Taylor 1992).

The Western biomedical model that separates body from self also divides the body, defining it as an aggregation of parts that break down and require repair. The family and the community are not involved in the healing process; the family participates only by visiting the patient and paying the bills. As Scheper-Hughes and Lock explain, in Western biomedicine, "body and self are understood as distinct and separable entities; illness resides in either the body or the mind. Social relations are seen as partitioned, segmented, and situational—generally discontinuous with health or sickness" (1987:21).

By contrast, in the healing systems of many other societies there is no division between body/mind or body/self. The Cashinahua of Peru reject such a separation. When Kensinger repeatedly asked them where thinking occurs, they explained that thinking is not localized in the brain. For the Cashinahua, different kinds of knowledge are associated with the hands, the ears, the genitals, and the skin, but the whole body knows and "a wise person," or *unaya*, has knowledge throughout his or her whole body (Kensinger 1991:44).

The cultural understanding of the body influences how illness and healing are understood, as Scheper-Hughes and Lock explain:

> illness cannot be situated in mind or body alone. Social relations are also understood as a key contributor to individual health and illness. In short the body is seen as a unitary, integrated aspect of self and social relations. It is dependent on, and vulnerable to, the feelings, wishes, and actions of others, including spirits and dead ancestors. The body is not understood as a vast and complex machine, but rather as a microcosm of the universe. (Scheper-Hughes and Lock 1987:21)

Healing is expressed in terms of achieving balance, restoring the soul, or connecting to the land. Sickness may be explained according to an imbalance within a person who has become "too hot" or "too cold." Illness may also occur when a person's body rhythmn is off beat: "a body's veins or 'rivers' (n. *nadi*) beat smooth and rhythmical when healthy, but when the body is sick a ghost causes the pulse to 'come out,' strike eratically" (Desjarlais 1992:39). Sickness often represents a physical manifestation of a deeper spiritual problem with a number of possible sources. It may be explained as the loss of one's soul or souls. It may be caused by angry supernatural beings, human enemies, or the breaking of a taboo (either by the sick person or by a relative). In these cases, illness is a sign of social disequilibrium. Healing requires restoration of balance and integration, not simply within the person, but between the person and other community members or the land. Sometimes this involves confession and forgiveness or atonement (La Barre 1964). To recover from the illness, the patient's social ties must be restored and reinforced. The family, and even the community, may participate in the healing process, thus reinforcing social bonds among everyone.[8]

In the community of Kaata, among the Qollahuaya of the Aymara nation in the Bolivian Andes, "people look to their own bodies for an understanding of the mountain. How they see themselves is how they see their mountain" (Bastien 1978:43). To the people of Kaata, "bodily illnesses are signs of disorders between the person and the land" or between communities. Sickness is like a landslide or an earthquake, and diviners cure

by gathering the members of the sick person's social group in ritual, and together feeding all the parts of Mount Kaata. The community and mountain are inextricably bound to the physical body, and disintegration in one is associated with disorder in the other. Sickness is usually linked with either a social disturbance or a land dispute. The diviner's role is to reveal this conflict and to redress it by ritual, which resolves the dispute and reorders the mountain. (Bastien 1978:129)

In many societies the body is understood as having an animating substance or entity for "the livingness of living bodies" to be explained (Sheets-Johnstone 1992c:135). In ancient Egypt, a cold was "an animate presence in the body, a presence having powers over the body, but a presence which could also be inveighed against and driven out" (1992c:135).

Healing traditions that clearly recognize both social and spiritual aspects of illness can be found in societies throughout the world,[9] and serious attention should be given to understanding the meaning of the body according to a worldview in which the spiritual dimension, not the biological one, is taken as primary. Spiritual conceptions of the body express power through relationships rather than material objects. Among Australian aborigines, the symbols of paint, blood, and feathers are used to mark and witness a nonmaterial power. The symbols, once created, are then set aside or destroyed, reminding all present that power resides in what is intangible.

Scholarly discussions of the body image reflect mainly the worldview of the observer. In the United States and Europe, much of the writing emphasizes the physical body as primary, to be overlaid with symbolic meaning expressed through ritual adornment and manipulation. These scholars often describe meaning as something assigned to symbolic objects, but this position is part of the Western emphasis on biology as the "real" material upon which everything else is built. This is only one particular view of reality, one that is projected onto other societies being studied. As some authors have argued, what Western culture regards as "the objective facts of anatomy" is yet one more symbolic rendering of human existence according to a worldview that is "scientific," based on a process of cultural selection and elaboration that reaffirms Euro-American body imagery. This scientific view of the body reflects the myths and rituals of Western society itself (Reynolds 1991). In this sense, Western anatomy is the projection of a particular culturally constructed somatic reality.

The Body Image in Cultural Context

Anthropology shows that people experience and understand their bodies according to a culturally defined body image. There is no objective physical body that is perceived in the same way by all cultures. Terms such as *fat, old, beautiful, strong, pregnant,* and *handsome* are defined within particular cultural contexts. Each different language encodes a set of culturally relative premises about body ideals.

A vivid example of the culturally specific dimension of beauty is provided by Estés (1992), who describes the mismeasuring of children according to a particular body ideal accepted in the United States. Her friend Opalanga was mocked for being too tall and thin, with a gap in her front teeth. Estés herself was criticized for being short and fat, which was interpreted as a sign of her inferiority and lack of self-control. But when each of these women traveled back to the land of her ancestors, each found many people who looked just like her, and who interpreted her body shape according to a different set of values. Opalanga journeyed to Gambia in West Africa, where many people are tall and slender like yew trees. They call the split between their front teeth *Sakaya Yallah*, or "opening of God," and interpret a space between the teeth as a sign of wisdom. When Estés traveled to the coast of Oaxaca, in southeastern Mexico, she met "giant women who were strong, flirtatious, and commanding in their size. They had patted me and plucked at me, boldly remarking that I was not quite fat enough. Did I eat enough? Had I been ill? I must try harder, they explained, for women are *La Tierra*, made round like the earth herself, for the earth holds so much" (Estés 1992:201–202).

It is impossible for humans to perceive or even describe our bodies without employing culturally loaded terminology. The language used to communicate influences the assumptions upon which the discussion is built. Using the English language biases the discussion in particular ways, for a concrete/abstract distinction is intrinsic to the semantics of English, as is the emphasis on the isolated existence of objects in space rather than relations between entities (Baugh and Cable 1978). By contrast, among the Wintu of the Sacramento River valley in California, language underscores "the immutability of essence and the transience of form . . . the fleeting significance of delimitation" (Lee 1959:123).

We need to be aware that the language used to discuss the body influences the direction of the discussion. Lee discovered this when asking about the Wintu word for "the body." She was given the term "the whole person," because the Wintu language emphasizes "the primacy of the whole." The Wintu concept of self is "as originally one, not a sum of limbs or members. . . . The Wintu does not say *my head aches;* he says *I head ache.* He does not say *my hands are hot;* he says *I hands am hot*" (Lee 1959:124). As Lee explains, "Wintu starts with an original oneness . . . a premise of continuity," which influences their perception of human relationships (1959:128). Whereas English speakers think of society as "an aggregate of individuals," for the Wintu "the unpartitioned whole" is paramount, and "it is society that is basic, not a plurality of individuals" (1959:139).

There is no concrete body that is decorated by culture. The body itself is a cultural creation. Although the human body has a physical existence, we can perceive it only in terms of a body image, for the act of perception is itself a culturally constructed process. Even when we focus on the physicality of the body as flesh and bone, we still perceive it in cultural terms. As Payer has shown in her cross-cultural study of medicine in the United States, West Germany, England, and France, each nation's physicians view their patients in accordance with that culture's particular concerns—whether they be viruses, heart pain, constipation, or liver crisis (Payer 1988). Wild points out that something thought to be so quintessentially objective as the "hard facts" of biochemistry is derived from chemical principles based on a body that is produced as an object of study. The biochemically constructed physical body does not represent an underlying truth above and beyond all others; it is but one body image among many (Helga Wild, 1991, personal communication). Reynolds shows that modern science and medicine are a ritual replication of a culturally constructed body image (1991).

Measurement itself is a cultural construction. Putatively universal systems of measurement are culturally determined and vary in terms of the actual measurement, be it pounds, kilos, stone, and so forth. We create cultural artifacts to measure, sometimes using the human body or other culturally significant reference points, but not all societies give the same weight to measurement.

Even something so apparently certain as the sex of an individual varies according to cultural definitions. Sexual categorization is constructed and "might well be constructed differently" (Butler 1990:-110). The external genitalia are not clear determinants of sex or gender roles cross-culturally. Genital anatomy may be ambiguous, but throughout the world gender roles are not assigned solely on the basis of anatomy. There are many ethnographic examples of societies that have three or four gender roles, assigned on the basis of behavior (Martin and Voorhies 1975; Medicine 1983; Nanda 1990; Whitehead 1981; Williams 1986).

As numerous feminist scholars have observed, in Europe and the United States, categories such as female/male and man/woman are used to define people in terms of gender. Although these gender terms are commonly regarded as both "neutral" or unbiased and "natural" or self-evident, they are actually negotiated and redefined through a process of social interaction. Depending on the context, gender terms are weighed more toward one sex than the other. For example, Jordanova views gender as asymmetrical because "the very idea of gender leads more directly to women than to men. . . . we have come to see

women as the problematic sex, indeed as *the* sex . . . relative to men
who become the central term, the norm, against which women, as the
deviations or variations, must be assessed" (Jordanova 1989:14). But- W.(
ler notes that " 'to be sexed' is always a way of becoming particular
and relative, and males within this system participate in the form of
the universal person" (Butler 1990:113).

When *body* is mentioned, this term implies male body, and only if
someone says *gendered body* are both male and female bodies included. This characterization of woman as deviation is demonstrated
by the majority of medical studies on illness and drug dosages, studies that use men as the standard and rarely consider that variations
might exist for women who have "different" bodies (Purvis 1990).[10]

To summarize, context is important for defining the femaleness or
maleness of a term in Euro-American culture. If *body* stands alone it
is male. When the context changes and *body* stands in opposition to
mind, then *body* becomes a female term in opposition to *mind*,
which is male. In the United States, white academics are especially
prone to using this body/mind division, which is reflected in their
clothing: "In academic circles, many professors say, clothing is perceived as 'material' (not intellectual) and, therefore, 'beneath con-
tempt.' There is a sharp division between 'the life of the mind and
that of the body'—and as a result (one professorial source quips)
academics tend to have 'bad bodies, and no one dresses well' " (Steele
1991:17).

Our understanding of the aging body is also influenced by cultural
context. In the United States, we don't think of children as having a self
that is separate from the body, and neither do the children themselves.
Body and self are one. But as they grow older, children are socialized to
accept a body/self dichotomy and to internalize it. This type of learning
occurs at an ever earlier age in the United States, with children becoming obsessed with dieting, weight, body shape, and plastic surgery, as
shown in current newspaper headings such as "Dieting Trend Risks
Kids' Health" and "Fear of Fatness Can Lead Children into Dangerous
Eating Disorders" (Scanlan 1993), or "School Breaks Have More Children Seeking Plastic Surgery" (Coady 1992), and "Growth Hormone
Research Resumes: Quest for Taller Kids Called Disturbing Hint of
Genetic Engineering" (Hotz 1993).

Gradually, as people grow older, they become defined as old, and
eventually they are characterized in terms of their bodily functions,
with the explanation that their bodies have broken down. The contrast

between body and self once differentiated in childhood gradually collapses when a person reaches a certain point in the life cycle, and the self is then reabsorbed into the body. The body is perceived as overwhelming the self, until the person once again becomes first and foremost a body.

The Body Image System

The term *body image* gained common usage in the early half of the twentieth century through the work of neurologists, surgeons, and psychoanalysts. In psychology, Fisher defined the body image in terms of the way people perceive their own bodies and included collective attitudes, feelings, and fantasies (Fisher 1968:113). In physiology Sherrington (cited in Sacks 1985:42) described *proprioception* as a sixth sense we have of our bodies, and subsequent researchers have recognized a variety of new senses, such as subcategories of touch and pain. In addition to vision and the organs that provide a sense of balance, a continuous unconscious sensory flow from the moveable parts of our bodies enables us to feel our bodies as our own (Sacks 1985:42).

Neurologists, psychiatrists, and psychologists all emphasize that the body image is fluid and interactive. From their research, Bender and Keeler conclude that there is "a universal tendency for the human organism to have fluid boundaries and an everchanging body image" (quoted in Tiemersma 1989:77). Critchley stresses that the body image is flexible—it is "projected into the external world and changes in love, in playful activities such as sport and dancing, and with the many normal physiological changes in the body" (quoted in Tiemersma 1989:123). African-American congregational singer, scholar, and activist Bernice Johnson Reagon explains: "song is a way to extend the territory you can affect. So people can walk *into* you way before they can get close to your body. And certainly the communal singing that people do together is a way of *announcing* that we are here, that this is *real*, and so anybody who comes into that space, as long as you're singing, they cannot change the air in that space, the song will maintain the air as your territory" (from an interview by Bill Moyers, "The Songs Are Free," 1991). According to Merleau-Ponty, whenever a new movement is learned, the body schema is restructured as the body incorporates the structure of movements and tools into the body schema. The boundary of one's body extends to include the end of whatever instrument is being used (such as a pen, keyboard, spoon, or car) (cited in Tiemersma 1989:228).

Schilder (1935) emphasizes that the surface of the body is of central importance, for clothing, paint, and tattoos—whatever comes in contact with the surface—are incorporated into the body image.[11] Clothes can take on symbolic significance just like parts of the body, and by imitating the clothes of others we take on their body image (Schilder 1935:204, cited in Tiemersma 1989:84–85). Advertisements for cosmetics and perfume build on this type of association by using the name and image of a famous person to sell the product. Material objects that have been in contact with the body become part of the body image, and when these are separated from the body they retain qualities of the body. This applies to blood, fingernails, hair, urine, feces, and even the space around the body (Schilder 1935:212, cited in Tiemersma 1989:85).[12] According to Schilder, body openings are the most conspicuous parts of the body image, for it is through our body openings that "we come in closest contact with the world and they are points of great erotic importance" (Tiemersma 1989:83).

The "plasticity" of body images makes it possible to identify with objects or animals, for we gain a sense of unity and connection with the world through identification (Tiemersma 1989:87). Communities that recognize a totemic kinship connection with animals, plants, or features of the landscape recognize at a deeper level a similarity of being that enables identification with forms that are very different from a person's body image (1989:88). Identification makes the pain and suffering of one the concern of others. This fluidity of body image is also connected with the human view of dreams, the soul, magic, and illness.[13]

These authors emphasize that the body image is dynamic. It changes each time we add or remove clothing and masks, perforate our bodies, or cut away parts of them (Schilder 1935:204). They also emphasize that the body image is interactive. According to Tiemersma,

> Even in an undisturbed situation, the body image shows a continuous dynamic process of destruction and construction in relation to other people. From the beginning there is a close connection between the body image of ourselves and that of others. We may identify parts of our own image with those of others. We may take parts of the bodies of others and incorporate them in

> our body image (appersonization) and we may force our own body
> images into others. It is a continuous interplay of parts and
> wholes. (Tiemersma 1989:86)

Tiemersma further explains that spatial and emotional distance also
affects the interrelation of body images. The closer the proximity of two
bodies, the stronger the possibility for a "melting" of body images or
"intercourse" between them (1989:86). This is especially true if people
are emotionally close, and it applies particularly to erotic body parts,
for these will seem "nearer" than other parts of the body (1989:86).

Although neuropsychology has long recognized that our body images interact with the world around us and change in response, anthropology shows that we interact and change in terms of a culturally
defined set of social relations. This book uses the anthropological
perspective to examine human interaction according to a body image
system in which body images are culturally defined by relationships
with other people, and every action upon our bodies is a symbolic act
that represents our social relationships. A person's social relationships and body image are reciprocally related and grow together, with
a change in one reflected by a change in the other. The body image is
not localized in the mind or the brain but is distributed throughout
the whole body, the whole person, and the person's social relationships. The body image system is dynamic, interactive, and so closely
integrated that neither body image nor social relations has priority or
precedence over the other.

We act upon ourselves and others in terms of a *perceived* versus
ideal body image as well as a perceived versus ideal set of social relations. Tension is created by the incongruence between perceived and
ideal images. In response, we attempt to bring the two into congruence
by altering our body image, our social relations, or both. What is most
important for us is how our body image is perceived by us and others,
and we continually try to make the perception fit the ideal.

The body image system involves both the *experience* of bodily
changes and their *social perception.* In the United States tattoos are
gaining popularity—not only those that are permanently incised on
the skin but also tattoo decals applied with water to stain the skin
temporarily. These painless decals create an impression of a tattoo,
but the experience of bodily change is quite different. Nevertheless,
both permanent tattoos and temporary decals create an image of
tattoos that affects both the wearer and the observer.

A similar situation occurs with the contrast between pierced versus clip-on earrings. If the former are visually indistinguishable from the latter, then the body image effect is the same for viewers. However, the two types of earrings correspond to physical differences in the ear lobes and the body image. When pierced earrings are made to emphasize the pierced hole in the ear lobe, as in ads for the "pierced look," this look conveys an additional set of meanings beyond the earrings themselves and the experience of ear piercing.

The premise of the body image system is that any act upon someone's body affects that person's body image and social relationships, as is dramatically conveyed in childbirth, tattooing, professional bodybuilding, and rape. This premise applies to how we perceive a corpse at a funeral and is reflected in such expressions as "part of me went with the deceased." Funerals help the community readjust to a social order from which a member has been lost or transformed into another existence, and everyone's body image is then readjusted, including that of the deceased. The reciprocal aspect of body image and social relations is also present every time we comb our hair, shave our faces or legs, apply makeup, put on clothing and jewelry, or decide what to eat. In all these details we are altering our body images and making a statement to ourselves and others.

Cross-Cultural Examples: The Essays

The central premise of this book is that a person's body image and social relations have a reciprocal influence on each other. This anthropological perspective is different from a psychological perspective that focuses on an individual's perception, and different from a biological perspective that focuses on the physical organism and assumes that biological processes are universal and that social relations and experience are generally irrelevant. People experience their lives in terms of a body image that expresses *both* cultural traditions and social relationships. If we are to understand fully the significance of the body image for human behavior, such as tattooing and bodybuilding, then we must consider both the cultural context of the behavior and the social relationships of the people involved.

The eleven chapters in this book explore social identities and relationships expressed through culturally defined body images. The book is organized into four sections, each dealing with a particular stance taken toward the body image by persons acting upon and reacting to themselves and others. The styles of the essays range from a personal account by Cathy Winkler to structural analysis by William Young. Most of the chapters draw on knowledge gained through participant observation and in-depth interviews conducted during extended periods of fieldwork.

Part I shows how people alter their bodies either temporarily or permanently to express a sense of themselves and their relationship to others. Part II presents a special kind of "body talk" through which people evaluate themselves and others in terms of ideal body types that are thin/fat or young/old. Part III examines the body/self division that occurs when personal conflict is translated into a struggle for control over the body. Part IV focuses on the constraints imposed by others to redefine a person's body image.

As different aspects of the body image are examined by each of the authors, certain cultural values become apparent. Particular words reappear throughout these essays—*control, power, boundary, separation, tension, flexibility, emotion,* and *healing.* These terms reflect the fact that in all of the cultures discussed, people struggle to define themselves in relation to others while living in social groups that simultaneously attempt to define them. The negotiation of self-definition and other-definition is a continuous, unending process that involves a tension between self and other. Control is the issue that predominates in all the discussions, whether the topic involves beauty, aging, food and dieting, eating disorders, birth and motherhood, exercise, violence and abuse, or self-esteem, but the meaning of control varies with cultural context.

NOTES

1   For example, in 1990 the main theme of the American Ethnological Association meetings was "The Body."

2   Todorov notes in *The Conquest of America* that when Columbus first mentioned the native peoples of the Americas in his diary, he said they "seem bestial and go naked." The fact that they did not cover their bodies in the same ways as Europeans meant that Columbus *saw* them as naked, and he took this to mean they lacked culture (Todorov 1984:34–35). As Columbus believed in the existence of cyclopses, mermaids, Amazons, men with tails, and men with dogs' heads, so his belief "therefore permits him to find them" (1984:15).

The equation of the body with the savage had a profound effect on both Native Americans and Jews. As Eilberg-Schwartz explains (1992:3–4): "From the eighteenth century onward, there was a consistent attempt to differentiate primitive and higher forms of religion, a pressing intellectual, moral and political problem given the discovery of and continuing European encounter with the peoples of the Americas." Enlightenment views of religion and ritual categorized Judaism as "primitive" because it was "deeply concerned with the body and bodily processes." In order to show that Judaism was "as reasonable as Christianity" and not a primitive religion, "Jews had to hide, jettison, or explain away the texts and practices that fell into those categories already defined as primitive." Eventually the "Jews internalized new aesthetic tastes that fundamentally changed not just their minds, but their whole persons, including what they experienced as disgusting and what kinds of matters evoked shame and embarrassment . . . the desire to spiritualize Judaism, to rid it of lower practices and texts, was an attempt to make Judaism palatable to Christian and rationalist tastes, which Jews had made their own."

3   This Cartesian view is now accepted as normal and universal, but it was not "common sense" to Europeans in the seventeenth century: "the rise of mechanism laid the foundation for a new synthesis of the cosmos, society, and the human being, construed as ordered systems of mechanical parts subject to governance by law and to predictability through deductive reasoning. A new concept of the self as a rational master of the passions housed in a machinelike body began to replace the concept of the self as an integral part of a close-knit harmony of organic parts united to the cosmos and society. Mechanism rendered nature effectively dead, inert, and manipulable from without" (Merchant 1980:214). The French scientist Julien Offray de la Mettrie called humans "perpendicularly crawling machines" (quoted in Kimbrell 1993:229).

Merchant notes that "the replacement of the older, 'natural' ways of thinking by a new and unnatural form of life . . . did not occur without struggle. The submergence of the organism by the machine engaged the best minds of the times during a period fraught with anxiety, confusion, and instability" (1980:193).

From this metaphor of the body as a machine came the idea of body "stress," and "an engineering mentality began to take root in medicine" (Kugelman 1992:109). People accepted that what is true for machines applies to the human body also (see Rothman 1989).

This view of the self as separate from the body did not hold sway during all of European history. The opposition between body and soul was a belief accepted by many ancient Greeks, but for much of Christian history the body and soul were viewed quite differently, as entertwined. As Bynum explains: "by the thirteenth century the prevalent concept of a person was of a psychosomatic unity, the orthodox position in eschatology required resurrection of body as well as soul at the end of time, and the philosophical, medical, and folk understandings of body saw men and women as variations on a single physiological structure. Compared to other periods of Christian history and other world religions, medieval spirituality—especially female spirituality—was peculiarly bodily; this was so not only because medieval assumptions associated female with flesh but also because theology and natural philosophy saw persons as, in some real sense, body as well as soul" (Bynum 1991:183). In the Christian tradition, "the body was given the ultimate sacramental value, as the early Church taught that the union of human beings and God was to be obtained through ingesting the 'body and blood' of Christ. And the body was to be exalted. The church promised those more worthy that their bodies, albeit 'glorified,' would be resurrected with them to heaven" (Kimbrell 1993:232). It was only later, during the Renaissance, that the hierarchy of soul (or mind or self) over body became widely accepted.

4   For example, when I describe gender roles in Mexico for colleagues who are not anthropologists, they frequently turn the discussion to the subject of Middle Eastern women's genital operations. Why do they connect these two distant geographic areas, and what does this tell us about their view of people in those countries, and women in particular? Why not consider the meaning of episiotomies in the United States, where this operation is "performed on over 90 percent of first-time mothers delivering in major U.S. hospitals," compared with eight percent in the Netherlands (Thacker and Banta, as cited in Davis-Floyd 1992:129).

5   According to Jordanova, for Julien Joseph Virey (1775–1847), who wrote an article in the dictionary of medical science (1820), if people do not use their faces in speech they cannot be interpreted: "nothing lies behind the veil of Eastern women, so that for a Western European man, they are blank" (Jordanova 1989:95). El Guindi's discussion of veiling (1983) considers its historical, political, and religious dimensions.

For an examination of the issues regarding genital operations see Gordon 1991, together with the commentary by Janice Boddy, Faye Ginsburg, Soheir Morsy, Carolyn Sargent, and Nancy Scheper-Hughes. Both Scheper-Hughes and Easlea (1981:133–136) point out that clitoridectomy was frequently practiced in Britain and the United States in the late nineteenth and early twentieth centuries.

6   Kroker and Kroker ask whether the "hysteria over clean body fluids . . . is a panic symptom of a more general anxiety about the silent infiltration of viral agents into the circulatory systems of the dead scene of the social: an invasion which succeeds in displacing fear about the threatening external situation into the inner subjective terrain of bodily fluids" (Kroker and Kroker 1987:10–11).

Miner provides a fascinating account of the ways the body is "managed" in Nacirema society, which is characterized by "a fundamental belief that the human body is ugly" and "a pervasive aversion to the natural body and its functions" (Miner 1956:507).

Vincent notes that even after "the harm of corsets had been recognized, the idiocy continued on moral grounds, for an unlaced woman had come to be regarded as licentious, a veritable vessal of sin" (Vincent 1979:13–14).

7   See Blier 1986; Easlea 1981; Keller 1986; Martin 1987; Merchant 1980; Reynolds 1991. Regarding American culture in the twentieth century, Reynolds observes that the body represents what is female, earthly, lower, and perishable; femaleness is defined as "incomplete, bloody, and contaminated," whereas the mind stands for male, celestial, superior, and enduring, for it is "pure, and fiery" (Reynolds 1991:95).

The equation of man with brain is demonstrated by the case of the mathematician in southern California who is engaged in a lawsuit to have his head surgically removed from his body (while he is still alive). He wants his head to be cryogenically frozen so that it can be preserved for a future time when science can cure his brain tumor and attach his head to another healthy body (*Orange County Register*, 1990, cited in Reynolds 1991). This man believes he *is* his brain, as though the body were just a container to hold the head with the brain (him) inside.

8   The connection between individual and community boundaries is also revealed in the way people perceive rape. Spencer describes an incident related to him by Matapaato Maasai in East Africa: "bitterness spread among the women after one of their daughters had been raped, then a groundswell of resentment, then a display of anger against the culprit expressed through a particular dance. Finally, when he foolishly attempted to defend his cattle from their onslaught, they seized him and maimed him for life. No sane man, it was claimed, would ever want

to cross the path of Maasai women performing this dance: their boundary had been violated and the response was a dance display that was transformed into an attack" (Spencer 1985:26).

9   Examples are found among the native peoples of the Americas, the early Christians, and many societies in Africa. See Jones 1972; Lambo 1978; Manning and Fabrega 1973; Wikan 1989; Sault 1990; and the special issue, *Social Science and Medicine* 27 (1988), no. 5, titled "Healing Words and Cultural Body Concepts," with articles by Pfleiderer, Taylor, Golomb, Kendall, Wikan, Reissland and Durghart, Mitchell, etc.

Huxley explains that in rituals and body symbolism, "images in fact seem to be connected with awareness of physical states which cannnot be verbally defined and ritual can be seen as a way of resolving the mind-body dichotomy by acting out the forces which the body proposes to the mind" (Huxley, as quoted in McDougall 1977:402). An example is presented in Levine 1992. Body memory plays an important role, for memory is not based on written practices alone. Images and knowledge "are conveyed and sustained by ritual performances," and that "performative memory is bodily" (Connerton 1989:70–71).

10   According to Purvis: "In June Congress's General Accounting Office released a report condemning the NIH for failing to promote studies that took adequate account of the differences between the sexes" (Purvis 1990:66). A congressional report "found that women routinely were excluded from groups studied in federal health research projects, despite NIH policy that they be represented," and women's groups are now demanding equal health research funding (Huckshorn 1991:7A).

11   Several studies focus on the importance of the skin for communicating meaning. In Mount Hagen, highland New Guinea, Strathern and Strathern (1971) found that face and body painting are important for marking personal characteristics and demonstrating the wealth and power of one's group, especially during ritual gatherings. Simons (1986) discusses variations in Maori facial tattoos which express gender, marriage, kinship, descent, occupation, rank, birth order, and tribal affiliation. Kanafani (1983) points out the importance in Arabian society of incense and perfuming not only in relation to beauty but in relation to cleanliness, health, religion, and demarcating social relations between guest and host.

12   Like the skin, body products can be used to show connection to others and integration into society as well as dissolution and disintegration. Milk, sexual fluids, and blood can symbolize and cement ties, but in other contexts blood or excreta are equally powerful symbols of witchcraft, death, or madness (Loudon 1977; Turner 1968; Wilson 1957). There is an abundant literature on ritual pollution connected with physiological states or body products like semen and menstrual blood (Sutherland 1977; Gottlieb 1988).

13   Tiemersma argues that the "fusion" of body images is never complete and that "they always retain a certain independence in the unconscious," for we experience two conflicting tendencies: "one to act personally toward the world as we see it, and, the other to unite the body image with the experienced objects or bodies in the world" (Tiemersma 1989:87).

REFERENCES

Arditti, Rita, Renate Duelli Klein, and Shelley Minden, eds. 1985. *Test-Tube Women*. Boston: Pandora.

Arms, Suzanne. 1975. *Immaculate Deception*. New York: Bantam.

Bastien, Joseph. 1978. *Mountain of the Condor: Metaphor and Ritual in an Andean Ayllu*. Prospect Heights, Ill.: Waveland Press.

Baugh, Albert C., and Thomas Cable. 1978. *A History of the English Language*. Englewood Cliffs, N.J.: Prentice-Hall. First published 1957.

Bleier, Ruth. 1986. "Lab Coat: Robe of Innocence or Klansman's Sheet?" In *Feminist Studies/Critical Studies*, ed. Teresa de Lauretis. Bloomington: Indiana University Press.

Bordo, Susan. 1990. "Reading the Slender Body." In *Body/Politics: Women and the Discourse of Science*, ed. Mary Jacobus, Evelyn Fox Keller, and Sally Shuttleworth. New York: Routledge.

Butler, Judith. 1990. *Gender Trouble*. New York: Routledge.

Bynum, Caroline Walker. 1991. *Fragmentation and Redemption: Essays on Gender and the Human Body in Medieval Religion*. New York: Zone Books.

Coady, Elizabeth. 1992. "School Breaks Have More Children Seeking Plastic Surgery." *The News* (Mexico City), July 30, pp. 1, 11.

Connerton, Paul. 1989. *How Societies Remember*. Cambridge: Cambridge University Press.

Corea, Gena. 1985. *The Mother Machine*. New York: Harper and Row.

Cowan, Jane. 1990. *Dance and the Body Politic in Northern Greece*. Princeton, N.J.: Princeton University Press.

Davis-Floyd, Robbie. 1992. *Birth as an American Rite of Passage*. Berkeley: University of California Press.

Desjarlais, Robert. 1992. *Body and Emotion: The Aesthetics of Illness and Healing in the Nepal Himalayas*. Philadelphia: University of Pennsylvania Press.

Douglas, Mary. 1966. *Purity and Danger*. London: Routledge and Kegan Paul.

———. 1970. *Natural Symbols*. New York: Vintage.

———. 1975. *Implicit Meanings*. London: Routledge and Kegan Paul.

Durkheim, Emile. 1954. *The Elementary Forms of the Religious Life*. New York: Free Press. First published 1915.

Easlea, Brian. 1981. *Science and Sexual Oppression*. London: Weidenfeld and Nicolson.

Ehrenreich, Barbara, and Deirdre English. 1978. *For Her Own Good*. Garden City, N.Y.: Doubleday.

Eilberg-Schwartz, Howard. 1992. *People of the Body: Jews and Judaism from an Embodied Perspective*. Albany, N.Y.: SUNY Press.

El Guindi, Fadwa. 1983. "Veiled Activism: Egyptian Women in the Contemporary Islamic Movement." In *Mediterranean Peoples*, nos. 22–23, pp. 79–90.

Ellen, Roy. 1977. "Anatomical Classification and the Semiotics of the Body." In *Anthropology of the Body*, ed. John Blacking. London: Academic Press.

Estés, Clarisa Pinkola. 1992. *Women Who Run with the Wolves*. New York: Ballantine.

Firth, Raymond. 1936. *We, the Tikopia*. London: George Allen and Unwin.

Fisher, S. 1968. "Body Image." In *International Encyclopedia of Social Sciences*, 2:113–116.

Geertz, Clifford. 1984. "From the Native's Point of View." In *Culture Theory*, ed. Richard Shweder and Robert LeVine. Cambridge: Cambridge University Press.

Gordon, Daniel. 1991. "Female Circumcision and Genital Operations in Egypt and the Sudan: A Dilemma for Medical Anthropology." *Medical Anthropology Quarterly* 5(1):3–14.

Gorman, Peter. 1991. "Trouble in Paradise." In *Annual Editions: Anthropology 91/ 92*, ed. Elvio Angelmi, pp. 213–215. Guilford, Conn.: Dushkin. Originally published in *Omni* magazine, August 1990.

Gottlieb, Alma. 1988. *Blood Magic: The Anthropology of Menstruation*. Berkeley: University of California Press.

Hotz, Robert Lee. 1993. "Growth Hormone Research Resumes." *San Jose Mercury*, June 29, p. 1A.

Huckshorn, Kristin. 1991. "Women Say They're Sick of Unequal Health Funds." *San Jose Mercury*, June 2, p. 1A.

Jones, David E. 1972. *Sanapia, Comanche Medicine Woman*. New York: Holt, Rinehart, and Winston.

Jordanova, Ludmilla. 1989. *Sexual Visions: Images of Gender in Science and Medicine*. Madison: University of Wisconsin Press.

Kaeppler, Adrienne. 1978. "Dance in Anthropological Perspective." *Annual Review of Anthropology* 7:31–49.

Kanafani, Aida. 1983. *Aesthetics and Ritual in the United Arab Emirate*. Syracuse, N.Y.: Syracuse University Press.

Katz, Richard. 1982. *Boiling Energy: Community Healing Among the !Kung*. Cambridge: Harvard University Press.

Keller, Evelyn Fox. 1986. "Making Gender Visible in the Pursuit of Nature's Secrets." In *Feminist Studies/Critical Studies*, ed. Teresa de Lauretis. Bloomington: Indiana University Press.

Kensinger, Kenneth M. 1991. "A Body of Knowledge, or, The Body Knows." *Expedition* 33(3):37–45.

Kerns, Virginia. 1980. "Aging and Mutual Support Relations among the Black Carib." In *Aging in Culture and Society*, ed. Christine Fry. Boston: J. F. Bergin.

Kimbrell, Andrew. 1992. "Body Wars." *Utne Reader*, May/June, p. 52.

———. 1993. *The Human Body Shop*. San Francisco: Harper.

Kivnick, Helen Q. 1990. *Where Is the Way: Song and Struggle in South Africa*. New York: Penguin.

Kleinman, Arthur. 1980. *Patients and Healers in the Context of Culture*. Berkeley: University of California Press.

Kroker, Arthur, and Marilouise Kroker. 1987. *Body Invaders: Panic Sex in America*. New York: St. Martin's Press.

Kugelman, Robert. 1992. "Life under Stress: From Management to Mourning." In *Giving the Body Its Due*, ed. Maxine Sheets-Johnstone. Albany, N.Y.: SUNY Press.

La Barre, Weston. 1964. "Confession as Cathartic Therapy in American Indian Tribes." In *Magic, Faith, and Healing*, ed. Ari Kiev. New York: Free Press.

Lambo, Thomas Adeoye. 1978. "Psychotherapy in Africa." *Human Nature*, March.

Lange, Roderyk. 1975. *The Nature of Dance*. New York: International Publications.

Leach, Edmund. 1969. *Genesis as Myth and Other Essays*. London: Jonathan Cape.

Lee, Dorothy. 1959. "Linguistic Reflection of Wintu Thought." In *Freedom and Culture*. Homewood, Ill.: Prentice-Hall.

Levine, Peter. 1992. "The Body as Healer: A Revisioning of Trauma and Anxiety." In *Giving the Body Its Due*, ed. Maxine Sheets-Johnstone. Albany, N.Y.: SUNY Press.

Lévi-Strauss, Claude. 1966. *The Savage Mind*. Chicago: University of Chicago Press.

Loudon, J. B. 1977. "On Body Products." In *The Anthropology of the Body*, ed. John Blacking. London: Academic Press.

McDougall, Lorna. 1977. "Symbols and Somatic Structures." In *the Anthropology of the Body*, ed. John Blacking. New York: Academic Press.

Manning, Peter K., and Horacio Fabrega, Jr. 1973. "The Experience of Self and Body: Health and Illness in the Chiapas Highlands." In *Phenomenological Sociology*, ed. George Psathas. New York: Wiley.

Marcus, George E., and Michael M. J. Fischer. 1986. *Anthropology as Cultural Critique*. Chicago: University of Chicago Press.

Martin, Emily. 1987. *The Woman in the Body: A Cultural Analysis of Reproduction*. Boston: Beacon.

Martin, Kay, and Barbara Voorhies. 1975. *Female of the Species*. New York: Columbia University Press.

Mauss, Marcel. 1973. "Techniques of the Body." *Economy and Society* 2(1)70–88. First published in 1935, in French.

Medicine, Beatrice. 1983. " 'Warrior Women': Sex Role Alternatives for Plains Indian Women." In *The Hidden Half: Studies of Plains Indian Women*, ed. Patricia Albers and Beatrice Medicine. New York: University Press of America.

Meigs, Anna. 1984. *Food, Sex, and Pollution: A New Guinea Religion*. New Brunswick, N.J.: Rutgers University Press.

Merchant, Carolyn. 1980. *The Death of Nature: Women, Ecology, and the Scientific Revolution*. New York: Harper and Row.

Miner, Horace. 1956. "Body Ritual among the Nacirema." *American Anthropologist* 58:503–507.

Nanda, Serena. 1990. *Neither Man nor Woman: The Hijaras of India*. Belmont, Calif.: Wadsworth.

Needham, Rodney. 1973. *Right and Left: Essays on Dual Symbolic Classification*. Chicago: University of Chicago Press.

Ness, Sally Ann. 1992. *Body, Movement, and Culture: Kinesthetic and Visual Symbolism in a Philippine Community*. Philadelphia: University of Pennsylvania Press.

Oakley, Ann. 1984. *The Captured Womb: A History of the Medical Care of Pregnant Women*. London: Basil Blackwell.

O'Neill, John. 1985. *Five Bodies: The Human Shape of Modern Society*. Ithaca, N.Y.: Cornell University Press.

Ong, Aihwa. 1990. "Medicalized Bodies, Disembodied Memories: Khmer Refugees in California." Paper presented at the American Ethnological Society meetings, Atlanta, Ga.

Payer, Lynn. 1988. *Medicine and Culture*. New York: Holt, Rinehart.

Polhemus, Ted. 1975. "Social Bodies." In *The Body as a Medium of Expression*, ed. Jonathan Benthall and Ted Polhemus. New York: Dutton.

Purvis, Andrew. 1990. "A Perilous Gap." *Time*, no. 19, pp. 66–67.

Reynolds, Peter C. 1991. *Stealing Fire: The Atomic Bomb as Symbolic Body*. Palo Alto, Calif.: Iconic Anthropology Press.

Romanyshyn, Robert. 1992. "The Human Body as Historical Matter and Cultural Symptom." In *Giving the Body Its Due*, ed. Maxine Sheets-Johnstone. Albany, N.Y.: SUNY Press.

Rosenberg, Kurt. 1991. "Musically Midwifing Death: Using Music to Ease the Way of the Dying." *Utne Reader*, September/October, p. 83.

Rothman, Barbara Katz. 1989. *Recreating Motherhood: Ideology and Technology in a Patriarchal Society*. New York: Norton.

Royce, Anya Peterson. 1977. *The Anthropology of Dance*. Bloomington: University of Indiana Press.

Sacks, Oliver. 1985. *The Man Who Mistook His Wife For a Hat*. New York: Summit Books. First published in 1970.

Said, Edward. 1979. *Orientalism*. New York: Random House.

Sault, Nicole. 1990. "The Evil Eye, Both Hot and Dry: Gender and Generation in a Zapotec Village of Mexico." *Journal of Latin American Lore* 16:69–89.

Scanlan, Christopher. 1993. "Dieting Trend Risks Kids' Health." *San Jose Mercury News*, June 1.

Scheper-Hughes, Nancy, and Margaret M. Lock. 1987. "The Mindful Body: A Prolegomenon to Future Work in Medical Anthropology. *Medical Anthropology Quarterly* 1(1):6–41.

Schilder, Paul. 1935. *The Image and Appearance of the Human Body*. New York: International Universities Press.

Sheets-Johnstone, Maxine. 1992a. "Charting the Interdisciplinary Course." In *Giving the Body Its Due*, ed. M. Sheets-Johnstone, pp. 1–15. Albany, N.Y.: SUNY Press.

———. 1992b. *Giving the Body Its Due*. Albany, N.Y.: SUNY Press.

———. 1992c. "The Materialization of the Body: A History of Western Medicine, A History in Process." In *Giving the Body Its Due*, ed. M. Sheets-Johnstone, pp. 132–158. Albany, N.Y.: SUNY Press.

Simmons, D. R. 1986. *Ta Moko: The Art of Maori Tattoo*. New Zealand: Reed Methuen.

Spallone, Patricia, and Deborah Lynn Steinberg. 1987. *Made to Order: The Myth of Reproductive and Genetic Progress*. Oxford: Pergamon.

Spencer, Paul. 1985. *Society and the Dance*. Cambridge: Cambridge University Press.

Steele, Valerie. 1991. "The f Word." *Lingua Franca*, April, pp. 17–20.

Strathern, Andrew. 1977. "Why Is Shame on the Skin?" In *The Anthropology of the Body*, ed. John Blacking. New York: Academic Press.

Strathern, Andrew, and Marilyn Strathern. 1971. *Self-Decoration in Mt. Hagen*. Toronto: University of Toronto Press.

Sutherland, Anne. 1977. "The Body as Social Symbol among the Rom." In *The Anthropology of the Body*, ed. John Blacking. London: Academic Press.

Taylor, Christopher. 1992. *Milk, Honey, and Money: Changing Concepts in Rwandan Healing*. Washington, D.C.: Smithsonian.

Tiemersma, Douwe. 1989. *Body Schema and Body Image: An Interdisciplinary and Philosophical Study*. Amsterdam: Swets and Zeitlinger.

Todorov, Tzvetan. 1984. *The Conquest of America: The Question of the Other*. New York: Harper.

Tsing, Anna Lowenhaupt. 1988. "Healing Boundaries in South Kalimantan." *Social Science and Medicine* 27(8):829–839.

Turner, Bryan S. 1984. *The Body and Society*. Oxford: Basil Blackwell.

Turner, Victor. 1968. *The Drums of Affliction*. Oxford: Clarendon.

Vincent, L. M. 1979. *Competing with the Sylph: Dance and the Pursuit of the Ideal Ballet Figure*. New York: Andrews and McMeel.

Vogt, Evon. 1969. *Zinacantan: A Mayan Community in the Highlands of Chiapas*. Cambridge: Harvard University Press.

Walker, Chip. 1993. "Retreat from the Battle of the Bulge." *San Francisco Chronicle/Examiner*, Sunday, February 14.

Webel, Charles P. 1983. "Self: An Overview." In *International Encyclopedia of Psychiatry*. New York: Aesculepius Press.

Whitehead, Harriet. 1981. "The Bow and the Burden Strap: A New Look at Institutionalized Homosexuality in Native North America." In *Sexual Meanings*, ed. Sherry Ortner and Harriet Whitehead. Cambridge: Cambridge University Press.

Wikan, Unni. 1989. "Managing the Heart to Brighten Face and Soul: Emotions in Balinese Morality and Health Care." *American Ethnologist* 16(2): 294–312.

Wilbert, Werner. 1987. "A Pneumatic Theory of Female Warao Herbalists." *Social Science and Medicine* 25(10): 1139–1146.

Williams, Walter. 1986. *Spirit and the Flesh: Sexual Diversity in American Indian Culture*. Boston: Beacon.

Wilson, Monica. 1954. "Nyakyusa Ritual and Symbolism." *American Anthropologist* 56: 228–241.

———. 1957. *Rituals of Kinship among the Nyakyusa*. London: Oxford University Press.

Zimmerman, Francis. 1988. *The Jungle and the Aroma of Meats: An Ecological Theme in Hindu Medicine*. Berkeley: University of California Press.

MARKING ONESELF

I n the following chapters, William Young, Natalie Beausoleil, and Alan Klein show how people use tattoos, cosmetics, and bodybuilding to define themselves within particular social groupings and to express their relationship to others. Among the Rashaayda Bedouin of Sudan, sometimes an unmarried girl has her thigh tattooed with a man's camel brand. Initially William Young interpreted this custom as reinforcing male control over women, but analysis of the clothing and tattoos of men and women shows that this first impression is misleading. Young learned that we must consider not only who is tattooed but who does the tattooing in order to get at the meaning inscribed on the skin.

The Rashaayda use tattoos to communicate meanings too powerful and condensed to express face to face in ordinary language. As with the telling of myths, tattooing the body is a dramatic method of expressing emotion, establishing identity, and acknowledging bonds with others. When adolescent Rashiidy girls gather together to be tattooed, they are making enduring statements about the power of their love for particular men and their friendship for each other. Young's insights help set the stage for appreciating the complexity of how human beings use their bodies to communicate. His chapter serves as a reminder that as long as our cultural assumptions remain unquestioned, our understanding of the body image system remains obscured.

Natalie Beausoleil also questions Western assumptions about the body image, but her research focuses on the use of cosmetics among women of different races and classes in the United States. A common assumption in this country is that women wear makeup to please men or to follow fashion. One common critique of makeup portrays its users as passive victims manipulated by the media and the political system. But Beausoleil finds that makeup users share a much more complicated set of motivations and that relationships among women themselves are key to understanding the faces they create when they choose to "make up" with certain cosmetics. Beausoleil also raises the issue of whether "being oneself" means wearing or not wearing makeup.

As in Young's essay, Beausoleil's work also discusses control through marking one's self to express identity and relationship to others. A woman may demonstrate control by using makeup to create a desired effect that influences others, conceal or dramatically express aspects of her identity, and to define a particular self that is presented. While makeup can be a resource in constructing an identity, it can also be a source of dissonance when others respond negatively to one's use of cosmetics. Both chapters provide dramatic examples of women altering their own body images, but in Young's work the alteration reflects a special social relationship that cannot be otherwise expressed, whereas in Beausoleil's, the motive is to realize an ideal of what the self should look like by following or confounding convention.

Alan Klein analyzes control among women bodybuilders who compete at the national level. Interviewing the top women competitors in a well-known gym, Klein found that the women repeatedly emphasized the need for self-mastery. These bodybuilders say they want to control their weight, improve their self-image, and feel complete. The women craft their bodies, reveling in a sense of strength and muscularity. As these bodybuilders lift and press heavy weights, they actively demonstrate their control to themselves and to others. They feel that they are resisting shapelessness and loss of control by creating a new shape with a new sense of self. They also believe that this new form enhances their social relationships, as their muscled bodies send out a positive message to others, making them more attractive and desirable.

Both men and women bodybuilders use control over weights and muscle sets to gain a sense of control in their lives. Klein examines what this means for women in a society where muscles and strength are seen as inherently masculine. His chapter raises interesting questions about body image, especially for the most heavily muscled women on steroids who continue to see themselves as feminine. In the process of gaining control over the self, what happens to that sense of self, and how do these women maintain their sense of femininity in the face of criticism by others? Do Americans see control as inherently masculine? Bodybuilding captures the attention of a broad range of people as it dramatizes key cultural values through the public display of one's body.

MAKEUP IN EVERYDAY LIFE

An Inquiry into the Practices of Urban American Women of Diverse Backgrounds

NATALIE BEAUSOLEIL

I studied art for about six years. And so when I would come in in the morning, I'd wash my face, look in the mirror, and I wanted to put makeup on. . . . In many ways even now, it's a way of sculpting, or doing art for myself. . . . I'd make it look the best that I could, that day.

—*Maureen Turner*

Makeup is a major concern for many women in American society. They spend money, time, effort, and energy in using makeup, and they experience a range of emotions with its use. Moreover, makeup and other daily appearance practices are a kind of invisible work women do. I refer here to Dorothy Smith's concept of work: the efforts, intent, time, skills, and competence involved in people's activities (Smith 1987).

Recent studies underscore that culture is inscribed on our bodies (Featherstone et al. 1991; Feher et al. 1989; Fisher and Davis 1993; Grosz 1992; Mascia-Lees and Sharpe 1992). Among everyday appearance practices in contemporary Western society, "visible" makeup clearly marks the production of "womanhood" and "femininity": overall, women are the ones who wear makeup, men do not. Makeup has become in the United States today an essential component and marker of female identity (Peiss 1990). Women's everyday makeup and appearance practices are indeed part of the social organization of gender, race, class, femininity, sexuality, and the social construction of self, among many phenomena. In other words, local makeup practices are points of entry into larger sets of social relations. Unfortunately, up to now few attempts have been made to study women's specific experiences with makeup.

There has been, however, some research on women's general concern with their looks. Much has been written by feminists on the political dimensions of women's beauty practices in American society. They explain that given the male/patriarchal domination of women's bodies, makeup and other appearance enhancements are actually oppressive to women. More specifically, feminists challenge the stereotypical and normalizing images of women in the media and, overall, the normalizing images of women in representations. They condemn the oppressive character of social pressures on women to attempt unattainable, narrow, and male-defined standards of beauty. They denounce women's participation, through consumption of beauty products and services, in the huge fitness, clothing, and cosmetic industries.

Feminist researchers locate the source of contemporary investment in appearance in the alliance of capitalism and patriarchy (Bartky 1982). Capitalism needs the commodification and commercialization of the body for profit (Hansen and Reed 1986; W. F. Haug 1987). Patriarchy is characterized by women's internalization of otherness (Beauvoir 1949) and the "male gaze," which leads to women's objectification (Berger 1972). The notion of the internalization by both men and women of the "male gaze" has been particularly important in feminist film theory. In their analysis, femininity is "false consciousness" (Gaines 1990:4).

These critiques have been fundamental to feminist thought. They denounce the exploitative images and myths of women's beauty. Yet their concern with media, images, and representations ignores how women actually engage with these ideals in their daily practices. Research on images and representations offers speculations about the psychological effects of ideal images on women; it does not account for women's lived relations to these images.

Moreover, the emphasis on the oppressive character of a male-defined beauty ideal limits our ability to understand women as other than manipulated and passive. The analysis of images and representations produces women as victims. Appearance, "beauty," and more generally "feminity" are seen as nothing more than forces imposed externally on women.

Recently, a few feminist scholars have questioned this unilateral characterization of appearance and beauty practices as oppressive; they point to women's need to attend to such phenomena as pleasure and creativity in fashion and body/appearance practices (Wilson 1990; Gaines 1990; Fisher and Davis 1993). Most important, they assert that "blaming 'manipulative' media has not helped our understanding of the way representation works ideologically" (Gaines 1990:5). As audience studies convincingly argue, people do not passively absorb cultural products and the images of popular culture; audience members actively make sense of and take up these images for specific purposes, in specific situations, and under specific conditions (Bobo 1988; Fiske 1989a, 1989b; Gaines 1990; McRobbie 1991). Women are not simply manipulated by images in the mass media.

The study of women's beauty and appearance needs to be refined to account for women's agency and their complex relations to ideal images. The analysis of representations is therefore necessary but not sufficient. It is not enough to theorize about ideal images; feminist research also needs to examine beauty and appearance practices empirically. We need to know about women's daily appearance practices because they are a point of entry into understanding the social organization of gender, race, class, and femininity.

Rather than speculate on the effects of ideal images, I suggest we ask the following: How do women deal with beauty standards? How do they invoke these normalizing images? How do women experience beauty and appearance in their daily lives? We need to examine "how things work," starting from women's lived experience. This chapter takes the stand that in order to eliminate oppressive beauty standards we first need a better understanding of how these standards enter into women's lives.

We are now at a different moment in feminism, Gaines (1990) aptly remarks. She notes that the strong moral stance that characterizes earlier feminist works on costume has recently been called into question and feminist researchers are now more open to this topic as a valid area of investigation. The same is true for other aspects of women's appearance which were previously unnoticed (in most cases) or recognized but rarely studied empirically (for rare and inspiring exceptions, see Chapkis 1986; F. Haug et al. 1987; Hudson 1984; McRobbie 1978). It is now possible to explore makeup as a valid area of study, whereas this was unthinkable ten or fifteen years ago.

In studying makeup practices, I do not assume that all women experience appearance, gender, femininity, and so forth in the same way. Black feminists, Latinas, and other women of Color within and outside academia have criticized white middle-class feminist conceptualizations of gender and the self (see Stack 1986; Hooks 1984, 1992; Collins 1990). Instead I interviewed Black women, white women, and Latinas of different social classes, precisely because women are located differently with regard to dominant white models of beauty. The study of makeup contributes to our understanding of what it is (or how it works) to be a Black woman, a white woman, a Latina, in specific circumstances and under specific conditions.

How can we appreciate women's agency in engaging with makeup and appearance practices? How do we reconcile the notion of women's alienation and oppression through "femininity" with a commitment to viewing women as competent agents, actively involved in all aspects of the production of social order?

Sociologist Dorothy Smith, in "Femininity as Discourse" (1990), views women's local appearance practices as part of the discourse of "femininity." More specifically, according to Smith, the femininity discourse encompasses the textual discourse of the media as well as women's local practices, which in turn intend and aim at the discourse. In other words, local makeup and appearance practices are understood by society's members in reference to the discourse of femininity, and specific practices are intelligible because there is such discourse. Smith's notion of discourse

> locates a 'field' in which relations and courses of actions are mediated by symbolic forms and modes of one kind of another. The practical activities of individuals aim at and accomplish primarily symbolic relations . . . in the area of femininity, the relation between the image in the fashion magazine and the production of a fashionable appearance on a particular woman's body. Such a conception of discourse does not contradict its uses as an analysis of meaning, but addresses it as social relations or social organization, as the organized actual activities of people. (Smith 1990:162)

Thus, according to Smith, femininity is "a complex of actual relations vested in texts." She emphasizes that "to explore femininity as discourse means a shift away from viewing it as a normative order, reproduced through socialization, to which somehow women are sub-ordinated" (Smith 1990:163).

Smith's work is fundamental in that she begins to tackle the issue of how representations work ideologically through a known-in-common interpretive frame, where women are active subjects. Her article stresses the necessity of understanding how women invoke ideal images. In her analysis, women are both subject-in-discourse ("deprived of agency") and subject-at-work ("active and skilled" who "enjoy the decoration of their bodies") (Smith 1990:206). This chapter starts from women's experience and begins to explore the ways in which women are this double subject.

For this study, which is part of a larger research project on women's makeup practices in contemporary U.S. society (see Beausoleil 1992), I interviewed over forty women. Most of the interviews were conducted during the spring and fall of 1989 and the beginning of 1990. To find the women I interviewed I proceeded in a snowball fashion, interviewing Black, white, and Latino women in Los Angeles. The respondents came from a range of socioeconomic backgrounds. I talked to women who wear makeup on a regular basis as well as women who do not. In these in-depth open-ended interviews, we explored each woman's history with makeup and appearance and her current practices and feelings about her body and her looks. To protect confidentiality, each woman chose a pseudonym for herself, and all the names used here are pseudonyms.

This chapter aims to show how women's makeup and appearance practices take part in the organization of daily life and how women use the practices meaningfully in elaborating who they are. This study confirms that while limited by structural forces of domination, women are actively "negotiating the body" (Fisher and Davis 1993).

Makeup as Part of Women's Daily Activities

Putting on makeup is often part of a whole routine of appearance or beauty care which women perform at specific moments throughout the day. Furthermore, women coordinate these makeup and appearance practices with other rounds of activity. Women who do not wear makeup nonetheless attend daily to their appearance; they also coordinate their appearance practices with other routines and activities.

The activity of putting on makeup and attending to one's appearance occurs typically at two sorts of moments in a woman's daily life; I have called them *morning routines* and *repairs* (or makeup maintenance throughout the day). In what follows, I discuss the morning routines of various women. I then briefly focus on repairs.

In contemporary American society, women's makeup routines are part of, and embedded in, a morning appearance-dressing-toilet. Women engage in these morning routines largely in the home. I asked Vanessa Morales, a woman who had to be at work at 7:30 A.M., about her routine and more specifically what she had done the morning of the day I interviewed her. Vanessa Morales is a twenty-one-year-old Latina who works as a receptionist in a physician's office in Santa Monica.

> I got up at six, took a shower. I live in the bathroom because I have to spend an hour and half every morning in there brushing my hair and drying it and everything. So I went to the bathroom and I have this big mirror with lights, so many lights. . . . I brushed my teeth. Then I brushed my hair and I put it up in a barrette. I always put it up in a barrette so it's out of my face in the morning. . . . And then I put on a little bit of foundation. Then I used the compact to smooth it over. . . . After that I use a blue liner and I line the inside of my eye and then the top. And then I put a little bit of blush and some lipstick and that's about it. . . . Then I iron my clothes and I get dressed and then I come in and fix my hair. I just blow dry it and tease it up a little bit and put some hair spray. When I come to work it's still kind of damp. . . . Then I go make my lunch and that takes me longer.

This segment illustrates how women engage in beauty and appearance care in a morning routine. The sequence seems familiar to many of us who engage in similar practices every day. Like Vanessa Morales, many women tie applying makeup to a range of other beauty and appearance activities performed sequentially, where each activity intends and calls for other, subsequent ones. Women thus coordinate and co-order their different tasks at hand in different steps: for instance, only when Vanessa's hair is "out of her face" does she apply makeup. On the other hand, many women who do not wear makeup engage in similarly ordered morning appearance routines.

Many women carry out their daily morning appearance practices in a private room in the home—the bathroom. Historians and various commentators, including feminist scholars, have noted the contemporary privacy (isolation) and near secrecy under which women in our society apply makeup in the house (Perrot 1984; Chapkis 1986). When women engage in makeup and appearance practices collectively in a less private place in the home, they usually do so with other women—girlfriends, a mother or daughter, sisters.

Most women I interviewed described their morning routines as oriented toward what they expected to do that day. They described specific appearance practices they engaged in if they intended to work for pay outside the home, for instance, and distinguished between day looks and night looks, basic looks and looks for special occasions, looks for weekdays and looks for weekends. Thus, through morning routines, women prepare for "going to work," "going out," "going to the store," "staying home," and so forth.

Moreover, women make distinctions within each type of activity. There might be striking differences as to what is acceptable for different jobs, for instance. DeeDee Lewin, a Black woman in her late thirties, works as an accountant for a corporation in downtown Los Angeles. She feels she always has to wear some makeup to work. She applies blush, eyeliner, and eye shadow, and she enjoys matching makeup colors (she particularly likes purple) with her outfits. She is a single mother who has to take her daughter to school before she goes to work, so everyday she applies everything in five minutes, "from putting on the [moisturizing] lotion to the eye shadow." Makeup is fun, gamelike for her. Lewin says she likes it to look nice, however, and therefore she wants to "not just slop it on there or something." In fact her makeup has to look nice because of the nature of her job. She contrasts her current job, and therefore makeup practices, with a previous, more casual one: "I went to work for a guy who owns pizza restaurants and it was totally cas. . . . It was very casual and I didn't really fool with the makeup that much. I didn't care about it really matching up. I'd just throw something on and go. Now I'm back in an office again and . . . well I have to look nice going to work, so you just do the whole thing. You just look nice from top to bottom and this kind of goes with it."

Inextricably tied with specific situations and occasions are the specific audiences women anticipate encountering. This approach to makeup and appearance more generally seems to confirm Goffman's dramaturgical approach in *The Presentation of Self in Everyday Life*

(1959) whereby individuals prepare their appearance for ("frontstage" or "on-stage") audiences, just as in theater.

One woman I interviewed clearly expressed her attentiveness to audiences and feels wearing makeup is warranted for nearly all audiences. Sydney Andrew, a white woman in her mid-forties, is a top executive, married, with two children. Andrew mentioned that she always wears makeup (makeup for her is part of being dressed). She said she is always ready for encountering all possible situations and audiences when she goes out in public: "I always think, well, you don't know who you're going to meet. And I'm always dressed for meeting someone, and even when I taught school, maybe because I was seeing my students at different places that was the reason, but I was always dressed. This isn't likely that you would catch me in a really—again unless I was coming from the pool, not dressed up."

On the other hand, some women do not view makeup as warranted for most of their daily life or for most people they encounter. For instance, Michelle Naylor , a Black woman of twenty, a student, and part-time office worker, rarely wears makeup. I asked her about her morning appearance routine: "I just wash my face, put my moisturizer on and go. . . . Now, if I have a date (laughs) and if it's with someone special, with an ex-boyfriend or whatever I just have to look cute, I would put a little foundation on and a little lipstick and eyeliner, cause eyeliner enhances my eyes, I don't know how but it does."

Michelle Naylor says she does something unusual with her appearance (such as wear makeup) when she goes out on a date. Note, however, that Naylor suggests she would only apply makeup lightly ("a little foundation on and a little lipstick and eyeliner"), which would not be such a major change from her usual look. For heterosexual women as well as lesbians, dates are often occasions for doing something special with one's appearance.

For women living with a partner, one dimension of engaging in appearance practices every day has to do with that partner's presence at home. Is a woman intimate enough with her partner (or date) to allow him or her "backstage" (where the preparation for "frontstage" occurs) or is s/he a main audience member? Where are the lines drawn between backstage and frontstage?

Some married women who always wear makeup, such as Sydney Andrew and Maureen Turner, emphasize explicitly that because they want to look good for their husbands, they do not see being home as "time out."

Maureen Turner, a white woman in her midthirties and the mother of a thirteen-year-old son, works at night as a nurse. She says she does not want to be like these women who do not wear makeup at home. She enjoys playing with makeup colors and stresses she always wants to look the best she can even in those situations that do not seem to warrant the use of makeup, such as staying at home with her husband and son, going down to the Jacuzzi, or going to the store. Turner mentions that she wants to look the best she can. I asked her what she usually does for makeup, more specifically what she did the day of the interview. Here is an excerpt from her detailed description:

> I put on a white base. I put it underneath my eyebrows, on my lids, smooth it over with my finger, so it's not cakey. Then I'll put on a deep brown, I will stay with my deep brown, and then over the deep brown I'll put a red, and then over that a blue. And then it creates a purplish kind of effect. . . . Oh I do my eyebrows first. . . . I used to not do my eyebrows at all, but now I do. It sort of frames everything I guess. I put, I just use brown, I'll use a little bit of liner sometimes and then a little brown powder and just kind of comb through it, my eyebrows. And then after the color I'll put on my eyeliner, and I put it on the top and the lower lid, but I don't put it on top of the lid, I put it on the inner lid. . . . I use light brown, or a dark brown eyeliner and then I use a dark brown mascara; I put my face makeup on first before I put anything on. And I use foundation on my lid. . . . I'll use foundation before I put the liner on. So it's a foundation and then the white and then the colors. And then the eyeliner. Then the mascara. And then some rouge. And lipstick. But some-times I'll put like a deep, it depends on what color eye shadow I wear as to what color my lipstick's gonna be. . . . I'll usually wear a basic pink kind of, deep pink lipstick and then because I use the purple, I'll put like an ultralucent purple over that. . . . That's sort of a rainbow color. Colors of all different—like a pearl with a purple kind of base.

Maureen Turner wears makeup when she is at home with her husband. She says at home she will "put on something a little bit different [so that] he does not see me looking the same way all the time." Turner's account shows that intimacy with a man may signifi-cantly affect one's appearance practices. Yet she says she always wears makeup; she hints further that makeup allows her to express herself (what she does with her makeup may vary with her mood).

Other married women talk about makeup quite differently. Nancy Brown, a white women in her midforties, is a housewife with a teenage son and daughter. She does not necessarily wear makeup when she is with her husband at home. Rather, she says, she wears a lot of makeup to go out and more specifically to go out to lunch with friends. ("I'm not into putting a lot of makeup on unless I know I'm gonna go out to lunch with somebody.") She emphasizes she used to wear more makeup when she was working (outside the home) and views a job as a major incentive to "get into" makeup.

What constitutes frontstage and backstage appearance therefore varies from one woman to another. When women orient their appearance practices to a partner or date as a main audience member, they engage in frontstage appearance. On the other hand, some women do not treat a partner or date as a main audience member, allowing him or her backstage.

Yet the distinction between frontstage and backstage may vary over time, or at times, in one particular relationship. Negotiations may occur between a woman and her partner or date, and as a result the line between frontstage and backstage may shift. For instance, some women mention that a partner or date asked them to wait a while before putting makeup on. Maureen Turner says: "I've always felt that I should look the best that I can, always. Sure I don't wear makeup to bed, but sometimes when I wake up, he'll tell me, 'Don't, don't put your makeup on yet. Just relax.' And I'll do that. But whenever we go out, even when we go down to the Jacuzzi, [I tell him:] I don't wanna go down there and not look the best I can for you." Many women say that men with whom they have been intimate have requested they wear less makeup, that they tone it down. Rowena Mitchell, a Black woman in her midthirties who holds two teaching jobs in South Central Los Angeles, says: "I told them all, you know, when you met me I wore makeup, but after they become more comfortable or familiar, they let you know, they tell you, they say, 'this is what I like, this is what I don't like.' " I asked Mitchell how she reacted to her boyfriend or husband's requests. She answered: "Sometimes I tone it down. And sometimes I become very rebellious. . . . I don't feel like I have anything to prove. But there are times when I want to wear more, then I do (pause). Cause it's my body, and it's my money (laughs). . . . I'll tell you with this relationship that I'm in now, I kind of compromise, you know. There are times when I tone it down . . . because I respect this other person's feelings and opinion, you know."

Women's makeup and appearance practices may be the object of negotiations with a partner or a date. Some women may change their practices, but not necessarily; women may also resist.

This discussion has described some of the distinctions women make about settings and audiences and how their appearance practices vary accordingly. Thus women approach makeup as a daily practice oriented to, and coordinated with, others and other activities.

Until now I have mainly described makeup and appearance practices women engage in the morning, in preparation for the day. Yet by it's very nature makeup does not last, and it is difficult to keep one's makeup looking fresh. Thus women who wear makeup often need to touch it up, to maintain it. Repairs call for another moment of daily makeup and appearance activities and routines. They occur amid outgoing activities and are oriented toward the activities. Freshening one's makeup is often done in public bathrooms of various settings and requires that one be prepared, including prior decisions to carry specific makeup items.

I asked women I interviewed whether they carry makeup products with them throughout their day. Some women, like Maureen Turner, carry all their makeup with them. Others bring only a few items: lipstick is often one of them. In some cases women initiated talking about repairs. For instance, while describing her makeup practices for work, Sydney Andrew said she does not want to take as much time as other women do to freshen her makeup during the day at work.

Aasha Cora-Jones, a Black woman in her midthirties, is an administrative assistant and an actress. She says she always puts on lipstick after she eats.

ACJ: I have gotten into the habit (laugh) of after I eat now, I put on my lipstick again (laugh). . . . I'm laughing because it's such a change. It's almost compulsive now. It's so funny, when I look at myself, I have to put my lipstick on (laugh). I don't feel dressed without my lipstick. . . . I feel like a different woman with my lipstick on. . . . Yes, that's so funny. And all it is, Natalie, is a habit. And I've always heard women say that, and I never believed them, but you get in the habit of putting on makeup, and the more you put it on, the more you get in the habit of having to have it on. . . . And I witness it in myself (laugh). Or I'll think, well one day I'll think, I'm not going to wear any lipstick today, and then maybe half-way through the day, I'll put it on or something. . . . I can tell you, this is a qualitative, documentable change in my life (laugh), me with this lipstick, this lipstick holder and myself. I always used to think that was such poor taste, people put on lipstick after they ate, at dinner tables, I thought, why don't they go to the restroom and do that? Now, I'm doing it. . . . Yea, that's the newest thing. . . . Before I used to feel self-conscious about it, now I don't feel self-conscious, you know, about doing it at the table.

INTERVIEWER: If you're with a date would you do it?

ACJ: It depends who the date is (laughing). (N laughs.) If it's a good friend, it doesn't matter, but if it's a someone else, a guy, I probably would go to the restroom.

In this excerpt Cora-Jones discusses both the novelty for her of wearing lipstick regularly and the change in her views with regard to (re)applying lipstick in public. She explains how putting makeup on in public may be considered in poor taste (she said she used to be self-conscious), and how her practices vary according to her audience. She and I, the interviewer, understand that the restroom or bathroom, as a more private room in a public place, is the most appropriate place in which to apply makeup. Yet we also understand that lipstick is the one item of makeup women may properly apply in public, for instance, at the table in a restaurant, especially in the presence of other women.

Some women do not engage in much repair, while others do freshen their makeup often on a daily basis. Yet at the other extreme of the decision continuum, some women opt for a radical solution that goes beyond their daily activities. For some women, keeping makeup in proper repair is experienced as so demanding that they seek such radical solutions as cosmetic surgery. Carol Lopez, a forty-one-year-old Latina, is a manicurist and beauty consultant. She describes why she would like a permanent eyeliner:

I have oily skin, and because my eyelids droop, which causes pressure right here cause I'm looking down all the time and causes all my eyeliner to kind of melt away and during the course of the day I have to go into the bathroom and take some tissue and wipe it away here otherwise, and I would like to be able to have a permanent eyeliner so that doesn't do that. And then all you have to do is you still put makeup over the eyeliner but you can take a little bit of powder or something with a brush and just go over the permanent eyeliner with powder, colored powder, and then it will stay all day, so that would be the reason I would want to do that also. So it's not strictly from a vanity point of view but from a practical point of view.

For women who wear makeup regularly, then, practicality is an important concern. Carol Lopez has assessed in detail what for her would be the advantages of permanent eyeliner. Part of her knowledge might stem from her work in the beauty industry; however, she shares with other women who are not occupational beauty experts a concern for the manageability of wearing makeup on a daily basis.

Women constantly assess what they can and cannot do throughout their everyday lives, with their specific daily constraints and possibilities. Thus women's appearance work is part of the organization of daily life.

Many women who wear makeup regularly establish patterns or routines based on distinctions they make about their lives under specific conditions. Establishing regular makeup practices is not a fixed endeavor. Rather the process fluctuates with assessments of what one can do and is willing to do about one's looks. In that process, of utmost importance are the situations, occasions, and audiences women anticipate encountering throughout their daily lives. While being very attentive and orienting to these situations, occasions, and audiences, many women experience joy at wearing makeup, and some see makeup as expressing their moods.

Women who usually do not wear makeup nonetheless engage in appearance practices and thus make distinctions about appearance for situations, occasions, and audiences occurring in their daily lives.

This section has begun to describe women's appearance practices, how makeup and appearance practices are part of various women's lives, and what these practices consist of. It seems that women's appearance practices are almost solely, or at least largely, determined by concerns with situations, occasions, and audiences, confirming Goffman's analysis in *The Presentation of Self.*

Yet women's experiences with makeup and appearance point to dimensions Goffman did not fully recognize: women may experience pleasure and creativity as well as satisfaction in wearing makeup and doing appearance work. Moreover, women develop competence and skills in daily makeup and appearance practices. Thus, simultaneous with attentiveness to situations, occasions, and audiences, more is going on in women's experiences. The accounts of the women I talked with suggest there is another level to women's appearance practices: women are not only oriented to others but they are active, competent, and creative subjects for their own enjoyment. Furthermore, as I suggest in the following sections, women express who they are through appearance; in other words, they use appearance in elaborating the self. In her brilliant "Femininity as Discourse," Smith (1990) addresses the issue of a double subject and the shortcoming of Goffman's analysis in these terms:

This investigation of femininity as discourse has disclosed a double subject, a subject-in-discourse who appears as passive, lacking agency, awaiting definition by a man, and a second layer of organization positioning an active and competent subject. While the subject-in-discourse is deprived of agency, the subject-at-work behind her is active and skilled. . . . Throughout the accounts we have used of women's work on their bodies we find the recurrent problem that Goffman has described as front and backstage, the problem of masquerade, of falsity, of deceit, of the high artifice in the construction of the natural, in the young man's insistence on a detailed conformity of appearance to text that denies presence to the imperfections of the actual body it conceals. Yet Goffman's account is made from only one viewpoint, that of on-stage and audience. Here we have given presence to an alternative site, generated in the multi-layered organization of discourse, backstage itself. From here indeed we find women at work as active, skilled subjects, enjoying the decoration of their bodies, and while some counterimages emerge from oppositional sites, some at least must emerge from the extrapolation of play, of expertise, of pleasure in the exercise of competence. An alternative discourse begins to emerge in which decorating one's body can be seen as an elaborated expression of who one is, who one might be, who one would like to try on for the evening. (Smith 1990:205–206)

Developing Makeup Expertise

Wearing makeup and more generally attending regularly to one's appearance require time, effort, and energy, in addition to financial resources. Wearing makeup becomes a competence for each woman who achieves doing her own makeup regularly: women develop knowledge and skills in learning, choosing, evaluating, and applying makeup. On the other hand, women who do not wear makeup also develop appearance skills and may recognize makeup work in other women.

In this section I examine some dimensions characterizing women's makeup and appearance expertise: the planning and organizing of makeup use; women's techniques and skills, and their creation of specific effects; and the ways in which women learn how to wear makeup.

One basic feature of makeup as skilled activity is the way women plan and organize their makeup use in coordination with other activities. Planning makeup use involves planning time to apply makeup; it also involves planning to have on hand the necessary makeup products. Going to stores and searching for and buying makeup must all be organized and fitted into one's schedule. Some women, like Maureen Turner, make sure they have ample makeup at home so they will not run out of a particular item: "Before I run out completely of makeup I'll stick it in the back of the closet and then I'll go out and buy more. So that, if I ever lose my purse or anything I'll still have a pretty good supply of makeup."

Other women replace makeup as it runs out. In describing their buying/consumption practices, some women I talked to assessed issues of quality of a particular product. Women therefore develop various strategies, in their specific situations and under specific conditions, to find the makeup they need.

Furthermore, and most importantly, women who wear makeup regularly develop knowledge that is both background to and constituted in strategies of buying or procuring makeup products: they develop knowledge about available makeup products, specific techniques and skills to use in applying makeup, makeup that works especially well for them, and makeup trends and fashion.

Applying makeup involves such skills as knowing which makeup to put where on the face and how much to apply. The women I talked with believe that another important facet of makeup skill is a good appraisal of one's features. In some cases women decide it is best not to accentuate a specific facial feature by using makeup. Simone Innes, for instance, feels that her lips are too small to wear lipstick.

Moreover, often women link technical skills in applying makeup with the competence to achieve specific styles and effects. Sydney Andrew says she spends a lot of time, energy, and money "constructing an appearance." More specifically, she aims for a professional look:

> You're trying to look good, is what it is. Attractive. Not in a sexual way, but in a kind of a positive way, that not only are you the smart woman, but you're a good-looking woman. . . . You would be wearing what was necessary to enhance your appearance, not attract or draw attention to yourself. . . . [You would avoid makeup that is] too dark, especially things like eye shadows. And again, it would be really the matter that it would not be, it would be distasteful, you know everything is a question of balance. So anything that would be in excess would be considered inappropriate.

Women talk about how they develop skills to avoid specific looks. Vanessa Morales, for instance, wears mascara every day. She says she wants to avoid the "Tammy Bakker look" or "thick look": she replaces her bottles of mascara frequently (because mascara thickens rapidly), and she carefully separates her eyelashes with a needle after applying the mascara.

Some women learn techniques and how to create specific effects from beauty experts in various settings. Aasha Cora-Jones, for example, said she learned how to apply makeup in acting school, using "the principles of shade and light." She says she knows which makeup to use and how to use it, depending on the kind of look she wants to create, whether "devastating" or "minimal." In the first case, her hair will be full and her makeup will include gold or purple eye shadow and blush; in the second case, for the minimal look, she will wear less eye shadow (not gold), will let her hair down, put a little bit of rouge on the front of her cheeks, enough to look "kind of healthy."

Among the women I interviewed, many have, at one time or another, consulted makeup experts at specialized makeup stores (such as Merle Norman) or have learned from makeup representatives in department stores. Some took special classes offered through cosmetic departments in large stores. But most women learn how to achieve specific effects with makeup without prolonged formal instruction. If they consult occupational beauty experts, these consultations seem to happen more on an ad hoc basis than in a continuing fashion. Most women indeed learn about makeup over time through a whole range of activities and interactions.

Certainly women learn about makeup and appearance practices from other women: girls and teenagers learn from sisters, mother, girlfriends, cousins, and so forth. Many women I interviewed remembered playing with makeup with girlfriends; some mentioned that they used to attempt to replicate specific makeup styles from magazines (such as *Seventeen*, a magazine marketed to teenagers).

Some adult women also mentioned they learned about makeup from magazines and television. Here, for instance, Nancy Brown replies to my question about whether she has different colors of eye shadow: "I have different tones of grays and blue-gray, and browns. I was told I was supposed to use grays and browns so that's basically what I have. . . . Well, you know, you read in magazines if you're fair skin, blue-eyed, not to use a blue mascara because it'll just—blue eye shadow will wash your eyes out. So to accent your blue eyes you use grays. . . . Well sometimes I read it in magazines, sometimes TV shows.

Women also learn by observing others. Recognizing what makeup other women are wearing is an important skill for women who wear makeup, as Sydney Andrew explains:

I study women so that when I see things that I like, that they're doing, then I try to copy them. I always attempt to read makeup. And watch what, the things that they're doing that looks very nice, things I might do. . . . I might even ask, I might say, "Gee, I really like what you do to your eyes." Um, and I ask to try their makeup, or I might ask them what they did exactly in terms of technique. . . . Take special note of what it is that I like, and go home and try it. Or stop on my way home and see if there was a particular thing I thought that they were using, and I might stop at the store and pick something up. It might inspire me. . . . So I would be watching very carefully, on that. Also, if I had a good friend who I thought was doing their makeup wrong, I would tell them.

Women who apply their own makeup regularly may become experts, and part of this expertise consists of recognizing the work that went into someone else's completed product. Thus, women can recognize other women's makeup as an accomplishment done ordinarily yet involving the mastery of technical skills. Moreover, these skills can be taught and shared with one another. Sydney Andrew's account shows how women develop many strategies for observing others' makeup, learning makeup tips, and replicating looks.

For Sydney Andrew, observing other women is one way to keep up to date with makeup trends. Knowing, recognizing, and reproducing what is fashionable are part of women's competence with makeup and appearance. Throughout the interview Sydney Andrew indicated that she is very fashion conscious. Here is another excerpt from her account:

> When the new makeup lines come out, I always study them for the new colors. And I always watch them re-do it to see what's in style, in terms of how you make up. I try to keep my makeup updated. So it doesn't look like it's, like it's out of date. So, for example, let's say I have no blue eyeliner. Blue is very outdated. The in thing is grays and browns, and much more natural. And you see pinks (showing me her eyes), I don't know if you can tell. . . . And it's matte colors. There's no iridescence. That's very out of style. And so I try to keep up on what is current in makeup. Cause it's actually about as unstylish as wearing a hemline that's incorrect. As I said, I really like makeup.

The knowledge of fashion—more specifically, recognizing the changes in fashion—becomes a specific competence and involves a specific kind of skill: the ongoing work of keeping up with what is current. Sydney Andrew clearly enjoys knowing about fashion trends. She also prefers particular cosmetic products (Lancome, Borghese, Chanel) more than others, of lesser quality.

Even some women who do not wear makeup closely observe what others are wearing: they "read" other women's makeup with reference to the discourse of femininity. Simone Innes, for example, who rarely uses makeup, says she is nonetheless "really critical" of others' use of it. When I asked Innes for an example of inappropriate makeup, she told me about a woman at work who "still wears Max Factor liquid eyeliner," the "wing tip eyeliner," who looks "so dated." Innes clearly indicated that the woman did not know what is current fashion in makeup.

Ultimately makeup is something to be learned for oneself through practice and trial and error. Many women say they have had to experiment with makeup in order to find out what they liked best on themselves and often their practices have changed over time.

My interviews show women as subjects, active and skilled in doing makeup and appearance work. Furthermore, the interviews suggest that in creating effects through makeup, and more generally in learning how to wear makeup and do appearance work, women emerge as active creators and elaborators of the self, or who they are. Women learn that not just any look is good but that they need to find the look that is good for them. That is, makeup and looks have to reflect the self. Women have come to recognize who they are through their looks. There is a discourse of makeup as expression of self which includes the "be yourself" of the cosmetic advertisers and media in general (Duflos-Priot 1987; Bordo 1990; Peiss 1990); women's practices are also part of that discourse.

Being Oneself with or without Makeup

While describing to me their makeup practices, the women I talked with reflected on who they are, or their conceptions of self. The interviews made clear that women create and invoke a self through their appearance practices (see LaBelle 1988). Makeup may become a central element of these practices.

Many women, for example, describe not feeling themselves without makeup. On the other hand, some women say they don't feel they are themselves when wearing makeup. Still others are unclear whether to wear it or not. It is useful to focus on the difficulties women encounter in deciding whether to wear makeup and, if so, what kind to wear. I propose that creating the self is a fundamental aspect of women's appearance work.

Many women who wear makeup regularly recognize "who they are" only when they wear it. Sydney Andrew mentions that even at home she never goes without makeup because without it she doesn't look like "who she is." She says: "I don't like the way I look if I don't have makeup on. . . . I don't look like me." Andrew insisted that I put that statement in my data, saying that it is very important to her.

Even women who do not wear extensive makeup may feel uncomfortable without any on. Deedee Lewin says she feels uncomfortable if she wears no makeup, especially to go to work; she says she always has to have a little something on, "like even just some blush or something you know, a little color."

Many women who say at least some makeup is essential express their feeling that wearing makeup is indeed as important part of being dressed. Sydney Andrew puts it succinctly: "my makeup is really a part of putting my clothes on." And while for her makeup is a basic, makeup can also mean more than just being dressed. For Aasha Cora-Jones it is dressier *and* provides a way to feel better: "I always feel like when I put lipstick on, I feel really different. . . . Dressed, dressier. If I'm feeling tired, I'm feeling haggard and washed out. You know I just want to give myself a lift, when I put on lipstick I look better." Like Aasha Cora-Jones who says she uses makeup to give herself a lift, many women say that when they look better they feel better.

Yet even women who enjoy wearing makeup find constraints in which products they can use to reflect who they are and how they feel. For instance, Cora-Jones says that looking like she has a white mask is terrible. It does not fit who she feels she is: "I guess one of the things I'm always looking for is in the right shade, buying makeup base, for example. . . . I just have to keep looking, which is time-consuming and costly. . . . You don't want it to just sit there on top of the face, like a white mask. . . . You're looking at the makeup instead of the person." Black women especially stress that they have less choice of products. Black women indeed have a very different relation to the cosmetic market than white women, for whom finding the right shade does not constitute a problem and is not talked about as something significant. Most cosmetics are made for white women or women with pale skin. Deedee Lewin, for example, says that brands such as Estee Lauder and Maybelline don't do anything for her; she needs darker blushes and eye shadows. She says she likes Fashion Fair "because they have more colors geared toward Blacks than Maybelline would." Lewin says she wants more than anything to avoid "looking like a clown." Finding the right color makeup becomes a crucial competence for Black women and Latinas. Failing to do so may bring on ridicule. Women of Color who enjoy wearing makeup want to avoid both ridicule and appearing to emulate "whiteness." They value their "blackness"/"brownness" and want to enhance their individual looks through their makeup practices.

Some women choose not to wear makeup on a regular basis.

Women like Simone Innes simply cannot recognize the person they see in the mirror—when they actually wear some makeup—as who they are: "You look in the mirror and you think, "God, I look like somebody else." Or like I'm dressing up but I don't like the way I look."

Other women who usually do not wear makeup feel that it is a "mask" behind which many women hide. These women often invoke notions of self-esteem and an inner sense of security. Rowena Mitchell sees a relation between needing to wear makeup and lacking self-esteem. She mentions that she wears less makeup than before: she does not need makeup as much as she used to since she now feels better about who she is.

While some women opt for wearing no makeup, others question whether to wear makeup regularly. Julie Atkinson, a white woman in her midthirties who is a graduate student, talked at length about her ambivalence toward makeup. For her a decision about makeup has to be made every day, when she sees her "drawer full of makeup." Atkinson enjoys colors, and she likes wearing makeup "to experiment or play or whatever." Yet most of the time she decides not to wear any. She says she does not "like the way it feels" on her skin and especially around her eyes, which she "rubs a lot" (then the makeup gets smeared, may go into her eyes, etc.). Atkinson further explains that the issue of looks and makeup is particularly sensitive in the context of her difficult relations with her sisters and mother and the message she got when growing up that her looks were not okay. Moreover, men's positive reactions to her when she wears makeup made her uncomfortable. Atkinson says she has not quite resolved whether to wear makeup on a regular basis.

For women who clearly do not like the way they look with makeup on, others' positive reactions may be disconcerting. Helen Morrison, a white woman in her early forties and a high school teacher, emphasizes: "If I wear a vivid [lipstick] color that makes *me* uncomfortable, I usually get a lot of compliments about how good I look." Morrison is confronted with the problem of being unable to reconcile others' reactions to her appearance and her own sense of feeling uncomfortable wearing vivid lipstick.

Makeup can become a domain in which women define the right look for self in explicit dialogue with others. When women become aware of others reactions and evaluations, they may in turn change, compromise, and resist changing makeup practices. Often explicit dialogues take place with other women. For instance, Julie Atkinson recalls how her roommate reacted to her when she wore more makeup than usual to go out dancing with some friends: "one of my room-mates, a female roommate, saw me with all the makeup on and later we were talking about makeup. And she told me that, well, yes it looked nice on me but it didn't seem like it was me, that it was too much for me, gee, whatever that means." Atkinson tried to elicit from her roommate what she meant exactly. She asked if she looks more like herself when she goes out wearing her usual makeup: "which is the other way I wear makeup which takes much less time. . . . I'll opt for not the whole effect . . . but the half of it or whatever. . . . Then I will only put the eyeliner under my eyes, put a little bit of mascara on, maybe a little blush, maybe not, with no powder, and lipstick, which gives me color, but leaves all this other tedious stuff out. . . . No eye shadow, it's very quick. And I asked her if that seemed more me, and she said yes, definitely (laughs)." Both Julie Atkinson and her room-mate (and all of us) interpret specific looks as related to specific activi-ties and specific sorts of persons. After their initial conversations, Atkinson and her roommate continued their discussions about makeup and clothing, during which Atkinson came to understand her roommate's perceptions of her. She recalled her roommate telling her she "dressed dowdy." When I asked Atkinson what *dowdy* meant, she answered: "it's just like the image of the little quiet librarian all dressed in gray with her hair skin tight back, away from her face, and big glasses and no makeup, and that's the kind of image that it conjures up. . . . That somehow fits into her perception of me and makeup."

Atkinson and her roommate were defining when and how Julie is "herself" in evoking a type of person others in the same society or milieu could recognize or imagine. Atkinson's account highlights how society's members make distinctions at the same time based on and constituting socially recognizable sorts or types of persons.

Thus, in evaluating how they look wearing makeup, women often define who they are and are not, who they want to be or not be. Women use makeup and appearance to create the self, to reflect on and elaborate who they are. Moreover, the interviews support the assertion by sociologist Murray Wax that the "typical" American woman "tends to view her body as a craftsman or artist views his [sic] raw material" (Wax 1957:591).

Many women I interviewed refered to what seemed to them an inherent sense of which makeup would be right or wrong for themselves. This sense of self seemed to transcend or operate independent of any particular situation and any other person. Yet, at the same time, these women were attentive to specific situations, occasions, and audiences. As I suggested earlier, Smith (1990) provides a framework for understanding this apparent contradiction.

Conclusion

This chapter has begun to analyze how makeup and appearance work are part of women's lives. Rather than speculating about the psychological impact of beauty ideals on women, this analysis concentrates on how various women actually engage with beauty ideals in their daily practices. Women's daily practices provide a point of entry into understanding the social organization of gender, race, class, and femininity.

Women coordinate their makeup and appearance practices with other ongoing activities. Moreover, in defining what makeup and appearance to put on, women distinguish between different situations, occasions, and audiences they encounter throughout the day. Yet women are actively involved in negotiating how and where the distinctions are to be made.

Furthermore, while being attentive to situations, occasions, and audiences, women emerge as active, creative, and skillful, experiencing pleasure and competence in elaborating the self. Women indeed use appearance to express who they are. Thus, the study of the meanings for women of everyday use of makeup offers insights into the social construction of self.

The analysis I offer shifts away from seeing and producing women as victims. Instead, it starts from women's perspectives in a serious attempt to understand what makeup and appearance work mean in contemporary U.S. society.

REFERENCES

Bartky, Sandra Lee. 1982. "Narcissism, Femininity and Alienation." *Social Theory and Practice* 8(2):127–144.

Beausoleil, Natalie. 1992. "Appearance Work: Women's Everyday Makeup Practices." Ph.D. diss., Department of Sociology, University of California, Los Angeles.

Beauvoir, Simone de. 1949. *Le deuxième sexe*. Paris: Gallimard.

Berger, John. 1972. *Ways of Seeing*. London: Penguin.

Bobo, Jacqueline. 1988. *"The Color Purple:* Black Women as Cultural Readers." In *Female Spectators Looking at Film and Television,* ed. Deidre Pribram, pp. 90–109. London: Verso.

Bordo, Susan R. 1990. " 'Material Girl': The Effacements of Postmodern Culture." *Michigan Quarterly Review* 29 (4):653–677.

Chapkis, Wendy. 1986. *Beauty Secrets: Women and the Politics of Appearance.* Boston: South End Press.

Collins, Patricia Hill. 1990. *Black Feminist Thought: Knowledge, Consciousness and the Politics of Empowerment.* Boston: Unwin Hyman.

Duflos-Priot, Marie-Therese. 1987. "Le maquillage, seduction protocolaire, et artifice normalise." *Communications* 46:245–253.

Featherstone, Mike, Mike Hepworth, and Bryan S. Turner, eds. 1991. *The Body: Social Process and Cultural Theory.* London: Sage.

Feher, Michel, Ramona Naddaff, and Nadia Tazi, eds. 1989. *Fragments for a History of the Human Body.* 3 vols. New York: Zone.

Fisher, Sue, and Kathy Davis, eds. 1993. *Negotiating at the Margins: The Gendered Discourses of Power and Resistance.* New Brunswick, N.J.: Rutgers University Press.

Fiske, John. 1989a. *Reading the Popular.* Boston: Unwin Hyman.

———. 1989b. *Understanding Popular Culture.* Boston: Unwin Hyman.

Gaines, Jane. 1990. "Introduction: Fabricating the Female Body." In *Fabrications: Costume and the Female Body,* ed. Jane Gaines and Charlotte Herzog. London: Routledge.

Goffman, Erving. 1959. *The Presentation of Self in Everyday Life.* New York: Doubleday.

Grosz, Elizabeth. 1992. "Le corps et les connaissances: Le feminisme et la crise de la raison." *Sociologie et Sociétés* 24(1):47–66.

Hansen, Joseph, and Evelyn Reed. 1986. *Cosmetics, Fashions and the Exploitation of Women.* New York: Pathfinder Press.

Haug, Frigga, et al. 1987. *Female Sexualization: A Collective Work of Memory.* Trans. Erica Carter. London: Verso. First published in German in 1983.

Haug, Wolfgang Fritz. 1986. *Critique of Commodity Aesthetics: Appearance, Sexuality and Advertising in Capitalist Society.* Minneapolis: University of Minnesota Press.

hooks, bell. 1984. *Feminist Theory: From Margin to the Center.* Boston: South End Press.

———. 1992. *Black Looks: Race and Representation.* Boston: South End Press.

Hudson, Barbara. 1984. "Femininity and Adolescence." In *Gender and Generation,* ed. Angela McRobbie and Mica Nava. London: Macmillan.

LaBelle, Jenijoy. 1988. *Herself Beheld: The Literature of the Looking Glass.* Ithaca, N.Y.: Cornell University Press.

McRobbie, Angela. 1991. *Feminism and Youth Culture.* Boston: Unwin Hyman.

———. 1978. "Working Class Girls and the Culture of Femininity." In *Women Take Issue: Aspects of Women's Subordination,* by Women's Studies Group, Centre for Contemporary Cultural Studies. London: Hutchinson.

Mascia-Less, Frances E., and Patricia Sharpe, eds. 1992. *Tattoo, Torture, Mutilation, and Adornment: The Denaturalization of the Body in Culture and Text* Albany: State University of New York Press.

Peiss, Kathy. 1990. "Making Faces: The Cosmetics Industry and the Cultural Construction of Gender, 1890–1930." *Genders,* no. 7 (March):143–169.

Perrot, Philippe. 1984. *Le travail des apparences.* Paris: Seuil.

Smith, Dorothy E. 1987. *The Everyday World as Problematic: A Feminist Sociology.* Boston: Northeastern University Press.

———. 1990. "Femininity as Discourse." In *Texts, Facts, and Femininity.* London: Routledge.

Stack, Carol. 1986. "The Culture of Gender." *Signs* 11 (2):321–324.

Wax, Murray. 1957. "Themes in Cosmetics and Grooming." *American Journal of Sociology* 62(2):588–593.

Wilson, Elizabeth. 1990. "All the Rage." in *Fabrications: Costume and the Female Body,* ed. Jane Gaines and Charlotte Herzog. London: Routledge.

THE BODY TAMED

Tying and Tattooing among the Rashaayda Bedouin

WILLIAM C. YOUNG

T he Rashaayda Bedouin of eastern Sudan impose their culture on human bodies as well as on the bodies of animals. They use tight saddle girths and painful nose rings to break their camels. Once the animals have been tamed they are branded. Rashiidy women also wear nose rings and bind their hair and face masks tightly with belts and straps.[1] They tattoo themselves, and some of their tattoos are shaped like camel brands. These tattoos are hidden by thickly embroidered pieces of cloth and heavy silver jewelry and are revealed only during sexual intercourse (which is likened to riding). Such practices are part of the social and semiotic reworking of the human body among the Rashaayda. The Rashaayda case represents one variant of the social construction of gender in the Arab societies of the Middle East.

The Semiotics of the Body in Middle Eastern Anthropology

Early anthropological interest in Middle Eastern models of the body was conditioned by orientalist assumptions and biases (Eickelman 1981:24, 30–33). Much of the writing on the subject was produced by amateur ethnographers who dealt more with costume, particularly women's costume (Prüfer 1933; Ulmer 1918), than with the body per se, although some research was carried out on tattooing. Perhaps the most voluminous record of tattoos was produced by J. Herber, a French physician working in Morocco during the first two decades of this century. He saw many thousands of tattoos, particularly those of Moroccan women, and concentrated on describing their shapes, placement on the body, links with specific localities or "tribes" in Morocco, and names (Herber 1922, 1948, 1949). He wondered, "what motivates women, who do not draw back from suffering in order to adorn themselves with this ornamentation? Could it be the desire to please their husbands? . . . Will they explain to us why, in certain districts, tattoos are spread out over the breasts like the decoration of Berber carpets, while in others tattoos are no wider than a piece of lace?" (Herber 1949:333). Unfortunately his answers to these questions—that tattoos can be (1) "manifestations of female coquetterie," (2) merely decorative, or (3) magical/medicinal (Herber 1922:40–43, 1949:333)—avoid the profound issues at stake. If these tattoos, the "manifestations of female coquetterie," are revealed to nonrelatives, how does this disclosure affect relations between husband and wife? If the most luxuriant flourishes appear only on parts of the body that are usually concealed, why is such elaboration valued? At what age are they applied, and for how long in her life does a woman continue to elaborate them?

At points, Herber's writing says more about French thinking than about Morocco. For example, although he titles one article, "Tattoos of the Neck, Breasts and Knees," he admits in a footnote that none of his examples were found on the knee but always were placed at least a few centimeters above the kneecap, on the thigh (Herber 1949:342). At the time this was written, of course, French women's skirts covered their knees, so for French men the knee was a focus of erotic attention. Clearly, Herber chose his title to arouse the interest of French readers, even though it misrepresented the significance tattoos had for Moroccans.

Current studies of the body in the Middle East are few, perhaps because the earlier studies placed such an emphasis on the superficial classification of body adornments (tattoos, ornaments, and clothing, all categorized according to region, shape, and name) that the subject no longer appeared interesting. Three notable exceptions are Kanafani's analysis of the aesthetics of food and clothing in the United Arab Emirates (Kanafani 1983), Rugh's survey of dress in Egypt (Rugh 1986), and Weir's study of Palestinian costume (Weir 1989). Kanafani's work disavows classification and presents a unified description of the ritualized serving of meals. She shows that the "range of complementary and contrasting tastes, textures, and colors" present during ritual hospitality constitutes a nonverbal communication system in which the colors and scents of the body are important elements (Kanafani 1983:106–107). Rugh's work documents the variety in Egyptian *baladi* (nonelite) dress in order to discover how dress "provides a code which can decipher the complexities of social structures and the values on which they are based." She gives examples of how Egyptians read clothing to accurately identify people as natives of the many historically distinct parts of Egypt and determine whether they are Muslims or Christians, poor or wealthy (Rugh 1986:vii–ix, 4–5). Weir's book contains detailed information about the social significance of clothing for both sexes, complete with a record of native terms for articles of dress and descriptions of their use in central Palestinian rituals (weddings and boys' circumcisions). Weir succeeds in treating costume "as a language" (Weir 1989:20) and in elucidating the structures and messages communicated by that language.

These works are important contributions to the semiotics of the body in the Middle East. They do not, however, trace the relationships in Arab societies between clothing and gender. In part this decision not to explore clothing and gender is a reaction to the monotonous and smug assertions by generations of anthropologists that veiled Muslim women have a uniformly low status. From this viewpoint, variation in the clothing of both sexes is unimportant, since Arab clothing, whatever its from, merely secludes and subjugates women. As Joseph has observed, such uninspired scholarship has "confined the consideration of Middle Eastern women to a limited discussion of veils, honor and shame, kinship, cousin right, polygyny, and Islam" (1983:3). Kanafani, Rugh, and Weir have broken away from these shopworn discussions to document important aspects of women's lives (their clothing and adornment) from new perspectives.

Two new ethnographies that specifically focus on the cultural modification of the body in the Middle East are also important departures from the earlier paradigms. The first, El Guindi's study (1990) of male circumcision, shows how Egyptians link male gender identity with the sexual division of space. The circumcisions are performed outside the home, with the boys' transformation into men celebrated in the streets, which are culturally identified as mens' space. Boddy's work (1989) analyzes genital operations in a northern Sudanese village. She notes that genital surgery "completes . . . a child's natural sexual identity" by removing the traits (the external genitalia in the case of females and the prepuce in the case of males) "deemed appropriate to his or her opposite." This "establishes the conditions of adult gender complementarity, and it is in the nature of this complementarity . . . that gender asymmetries arise" (Boddy 1989:58–59).

All of these works have influenced my analysis of tattooing among the Rashaayda. Like Kanafani, Rugh, and Weir, I have borrowed the analytical concept of code from linguistics (as well as the concepts of syntagmatic and paradigmatic relations).[2] El Guindi's and Boddy's work has inspired me to search for the impact of the cultural construction of the body on gender identity and conceptions of the self. In this chapter I build on their studies by searching for models of gender identity in the body adornments of some Middle Eastern women, the women of the Rashaayda Arabs.

Identity, Political Economy, and the Sexual Division of Labor among the Rashaayda

The Rashaayda Arabs are a "tribe" (*gabiila*) of about forty thousand people who live near Sudan's eastern border with Ethiopia. Prior to 1965, most Rashaayda were nomadic pastoralists, moving with their herds to desert pastures during the rainy seasons and forming large camps near wells during the dry seasons. Since then perhaps a quarter of the Rashaayda has abandoned pastoralism; there is no longer enough pastureland to support the entire nomadic population of eastern Sudan. Both public and private agricultural schemes have appropriated the best-watered pasture lands, and those areas which remain unfenced are overgrazed. Some Rashaayda have accepted tenancies in the government scheme of New Halfa, where they combine small-stock raising with commercial farming. Others have built houses on the outskirts of large towns and subsist on the wages earned by men, who work as tailors and merchants or go to Saudi Arabia for two- or three-year stints as unskilled laborers. In sedentary Rashiidy villages, women have become economically marginalized, since family members depend more on the cash earned by men than on the unpaid labor of women (Young 1984). Among still-nomadic Rashaayda, however, women's labor continues to be indispensable and highly valued. The sexual division of labor in nomadic communities is based on complementarity.

The complementary roles of Rashiidy men and women in pastoral production can be seen in their techniques for transforming natural raw materials into food, shelter, and tools. Their tents, for instance, are made of a framework of wooden poles (carved by men), ropes (made of fiber from palm fronds and twisted into shape by men), and cloth (woven by women using their own hand-spun yarn). Women make their yarn out of a mixture of cotton fiber and the hair of camels and goats. Men purchase the cotton fiber in the market and shear the hair from livestock periodically. Women set aside part of their yarn to make the bridles and cinches that men use to control their riding camels, and men carve the spindles that women use to spin it. Almost every other item in the subsistence sphere of their economy (including water skins, milk, meat, firewood, ointments, leather containers, and grain) is processed by both men and women before it is used or consumed.[3]

It is mainly in the sphere of commercial exchanges that nomadic women are at a clear disadvantage. People of both sexes own livestock (which is everywhere individual rather than collective property), but women speculate in livestock ventures much less than men. Partly this is because women spend much more time caring for children than men do, so they have fewer opportunities to visit urban markets. Another reason is that livestock markets in Sudanese towns are culturally defined as men's domains, so that women who enter markets feel uncomfortable. Thus women who buy and sell livestock must work through male intermediaries. Finally, Rashiidy women have less cash at their disposal than men because they have not generally entered the labor market.

Just as clearly defined sets of tasks are assigned to men and women, space is also divided between the sexes. Men and boys tend to sit near the simple bed of the household (on which the male household head sleeps), while women and girls sit near the hearth. At mealtimes males eat from a common bowl and females do likewise, each same-sex group being separated by a few feet. A married woman does not uncover her mouth while eating, however, unless no male (other than her husband) is in the tent; if her son or cousin is present she passes her food (which is eaten with the hands in any case) under her face mask. When guests arrive, the tent is physically divided into two sections; the section for resident and nonresident males is separated from the section of female residents and their guests by a hanging cloth.

The Rashaayda's Treatment of the Body

Tattoos

Rashiidy women tattoo themselves on three parts of the body: the forearms, the lower half of the face, and the upper portions of the legs and thighs. For the Rashaayda the tattoos on a woman's arms have little significance. They are simple decorative patterns that are frequently revealed when women push back their sleeves while working. What really matters are the tattoos that are usually hidden, that is, those on the face and legs, which only a woman's husband should see. I myself was never allowed to see these tattoos and so relied on the reports of Rashiidy informants.

Among the Rashaayda, women's facial tattoos are seldom seen because Rashiidy women wear masks over their mouths and noses. The tattoos on their legs are hidden, also, by their ankle-length skirts. Facial tattoos are of two kinds: either the simple black beauty mark or mole, which is tattooed on the cheek, or the green-colored *mishaaly*, which are tattooed near the mouth and on the chin and cheeks and which consist of short rows of parallel lines and other linear designs. In form, these green tattoos are similar to the linear designs women sew onto their clothing as decoration. The import of the tattoos, however, is not merely decorative; they have strong erotic associations.

No doubt the impact of facial tattoos is derived from their placement on a part of the woman's body that is never seen by a man except during sexual intercourse. These erotic associations were revealed to me by a man who had a reputation as a womanizer. When telling me about his sexual exploits with a number of married and divorced women, he sketched their uncovered faces on a scrap of paper. Each sketch consisted solely of the oval outlines of the woman's face, small circles for her eyes, thin lines to represent her mouth and nose, and heavier lines to indicate the *mishaaly* on her cheeks and chin. His insistence on secrecy and the speed with which he made the sketches all betrayed a mixture of fear and daring. He was apprehensive lest I judge him harshly (since the Rashaayda do not take extramarital affairs lightly) or, worse, discover who the women were.

The tattoos on women's legs have less to do with sexual passion and more to do with love. Not all women have them; only a woman who falls in love before she marries is likely to tattoo her leg. This kind of tattoo is not an arbitrary, decorative arrangement of lines and dots; rather, it is a duplicate of a man's camel brand. When a young girl falls in love with a boy, she tries to find out what his family's camel brand is and asks her girlfriends, in secret, to help her tattoo it on her thigh. The thigh is the same part of the body where the boy would burn his brand into a camel's hide.

This tattoo, the girl's declaration of love, is both silent and hidden; certainly her beloved never sees the tattoo unless he actually succeeds in marrying her. In fact, it would even be difficult for him to see the girl's completely covered figure, except from a distance, for young girls are strictly chaperoned. It is only when he marries her that she uncovers it for him, to prove she has loved him from the start.

It is not really surprising to find that the Rashaayda use nonverbal signs to express their deep feelings; most societies have love tokens of some kind. But why these signs in particular? These indelible marks are effective proof of unchanging devotion when they are seen by the right man. However, in this society, where a young girl's marriage is always arranged by her family, there is no guarantee that a girl will marry the boy she loves. If she marries someone else, her husband is confronted with the unwelcome evidence of her real affections on his wedding night. When he sees the tattoo, he realizes at once that his wife must have wanted someone else; but as long as she is a virgin he had no grounds for complaining to her family. Because it cannot be altered to suit changing circumstances, the girl's tattoo could be a troublesome source of tension between husband and wife. It certainly creates mistrust between the husband and his wife's beloved, who is so precisely identified by the property mark on her leg.

One might expect that a girl would choose some other, less risky way to declare her affection. Rashiidy boys certainly do not tattoo themselves in this way, and when they are in love they wear a very different token of it—a ring. When a boy wants to attract a girl's attention he sends her a message via a third party. This person is often a girl cousin or neighbor in his camp and with whom he can speak, as a neighbor, without arousing any suspicion of impropriety. If the girl wants to respond to his message she sends back a silver finger-ring, *zighra*. He wears this token for as long as his interest in the girl lasts, and if she happens to see him when he visits her camp she is silently reassured by its presence. For the two young people the ring certainly has meaning, but unlike the girl's tattoo it does not identify the object of the wearer's affections and does not commit the boy with such permanence. All it says to observers is that the boy has an unidentified admirer; perhaps he will try to marry her.

It would be equally possible, and less troublesome, for girls to wear boy's rings to express their feelings, but they do not. They prefer to "brand" themselves on their thighs, instead.

Jewelry and Clothing

To answer the question of why girls "brand" themselves, it is helpful to put women's tattoos in a wider context, viewing them as one aspect of the Rashaayda's treatment of women's bodies. This approach to tattooing requires more information about women's adornment in general and their jewelry and clothing in particular. Let us take the silver ring, mentioned earlier, as the point of departure for a broader exploration of Rashiidy designs on the body.

The silver zighra a girl sends to a boy is the only piece of jewelry that both males and females may wear. It is 'eyb, a "betrayal of gender identity," for a man even to try on any other kind of women's jewelry. The silver zighra itself stands in contrast to the gold zighra, the ring a groom gives a bride during their wedding. Like all gold objects, the gold zighra cannot be worn by men. If the groom who gives a gold zighra to a bride also happens to be the boy who inspired her love in the first place, this ring represents a return, with value added, of the silver ring she sent him as a love token. In any case, the gold zighra is one of four kinds of jewelry that a groom is required to provide. The others are a gold nose ring, silver ankle rings, and the cylindrical siilver *sa'af*, or wrist bands. Taken together, the rings of precious metal that either pierce a married woman's nostril or encircle her wrists, ankles, and finger are called *aS-Siigha*, "the precious metal stipulated by the wedding contract." As wedding prestations, these items all belong together.

The four kinds of metal jewelry are part of a larger set of objects which the Rashaayda call *awaany il-mara*, "the married woman's accoutrements." At least eighteen named articles of dress belong to this set, including the four rings or bands already discussed, eight other kinds of jewelry (plastic bracelets, earrings, bangled rings for the fingers, leather wrist bands, ivory arm bands, a tight silver neck-lace or choker, bead necklaces, and a silver chest plate), and six kinds of thickly embroidered cloths, belts, or straps. These latter include the *sirdaag* (an embroidered belt), the *burga'* (the married woman's ritual veil), the *ginaa*ʿ (married woman's mask), the *marbaTa* (married woman's hair binding), and other objects such as the married woman's head covering, and the strap for the married woman's ritual veil. A women may wear all of these articles at once on special occasions, for example, during weddings. They all have three features in common—weight, metallic shine, and tightness.

An effective way to highlight these common features is to compare three representative members of the set and examine them in detail. Let us begin with the *ginaa*ʿ, or "married woman's mask." The ginaaʿ is a tube of black cloth which is flared at the lower end, to cover the shoulders and torso, and is narrowed at the upper end, to fit snugly around the face. After slipping this tube over her head, the woman who wears it lays the posterior edge of its uppermost opening over the crown of her head. Then she pulls the opposite edge of this opening down across her face until it is almost taut against her chin. Some of the loose cloth can be pulled through the opening, resulting in a semicircle of cloth being stretched tightly across her nose and mouth. Once in place, the mask is so tight that the wearer cannot open her mouth widely. At the same time, the mask is covered by hundreds of tiny lead beads that are sewn around the opening as decoration. They perceptibly add to its mass, more than tripling the weight of the cloth.

The *sirdaag*, or belt, is also heavily encrusted with silvery lead beads, to the point where the black cloth of which it is made is almost covered over. It is tied securely to the woman's waist. The upper part of the belt, which fits her body closely, is seldom seen, because it is immodest for a Rashiidy woman to attract attention to the contours of her body. Hence the wearer of a *sirdaag* conceals the top part of it by pulling up the loose cloth of her dress and letting fall over the tight band around her waist. The belt has two large rectangular panels in front, however, that hang well below the waist and are designed to be seen.

The *marbaTa*, or "hair binding," is tied (*marbuuT*) to the two large rolls of hair a married woman gathers up close to her head, one roll behind each ear. Her marbaTa is a flat square of black cloth decorated with lead beads and laid atop her head. Its left and right edges are equipped with ribbons for tying up her hair, to keep it standing out from the contours of her temples. In this way her hair, although completely covered by the ginaaʿ, appears bulky, hence thick and plentiful.

All of these tight, heavy, and metallic articles contrast with the lightweight, loose components of a woman's costume which are made exclusively out of fabric. These latter are not parts of the *awaany* but make up a second named set of objects—*baalat il-mara*. The *baala* consists of a woman's loose, long dress (or *thawb*) and her long red underskirt (*tičča*). Her black *thawb* has long, wide sleeves and is brightly decorated with colored pieces of cloth. The red *tičča*, although never seen when worn because it is an undergarment, is decorated with black strips of cloth.

A Rashiidy woman's costume, then, is divided into the tight awaany and loose baala. The contrast between awaany and baala is especially marked when a woman dances, for instance at a wedding. As she turns quickly in the middle of the dancing ground, her face almost entirely covered, her long wide sleeves and brightly decorated black dress fan out gracefully around her. Her gleaming awaany, on the other hand, remain close to her body.

Syntagmatic Relations between Tattoos and Clothing

Women's articles of dress cover the two types of tattoo which are of greatest significance for the Rashaayda. The tight awaany and the loose baala constitute the immediate contexts for women's tattoos. Indeed, one kind of tattoo, the kind that duplicates a camel brand, is covered by a set of clothing—a woman's baala, her dress and her underskirt. The other kind of tattoo, the mishaaly of the face, is covered by the mask and other parts of the awaany. Thus there is a syntagmatic link between one kind of tattoo and a corresponding set of clothing:

facial tattoos/awaany :: camel brand tattoos/baala.[4]

Although we have identified the nature of the link between tattoos and clothing, we have not yet determined its meaning. Why divide the woman's costume into two sets, each corresponding to a type of tattoo? To discover the motivation behind this correspondence we must once again widen our field of inquiry. We have traced out all syntagmatic relations between tattoos and contiguous objects (both body parts and clothing), so nothing remains for us to do in this regard. Let us turn elsewhere, then, searching for connections between this entire assembly (tattoos, body parts, adornments) and other, still unexamined, objects and groups of objects in Rashiidy culture.

Paradigmatic Relations between Adornment and Taming

The most striking associations between the woman's costume and other, physically unconnected objects indicate a link between a woman's putting on jewelry and a man's taming of domesticated animals. These associations are found in the Rashaayda's vocabulary. For example, the terms for two pieces of women's jewelry, *zimaam* and *Hujuul*, have semantic links to either camels or horses. The term for a woman's nose ring, *zimaam*, also denotes the iron ring a man inserts into the septum of a young camel's nose when trying to break it to the saddle. He inflicts pain on the camel by pulling on the cord attached to this *zimaam*, forcing the animal to obey him. The word *Hujuul*, the term for the hollow silver rings women wear on their ankles, refers less directly to domestication. It is derived from a verb meaning "to skip, to hop on one foot" and brings to mind the gait of a person whose legs are shackled. A related adjective, *muHajjal*, means either "a woman wearing *Hujuul* on her ankles" or "a horse with white feet or ankles" (al-Jurr 1973:433; Qasim 1972:150; Spiro 1973:124; Wehr 1976:158). Other terms for jewelry or articles of dress, such as *ghawsha*, "bracelet," or *xirza*, "earring," do not have multiple references like the foregoing terms and so give us no clues to follow.[5]

Where to proceed from here? If the terms for other articles of dress provide no leads, perhaps the terms for categories of dress, awaany and baala, will direct us onward. As it turns out, the term *awaany* suggests another paradigmatic link between women's clothing and domestic animals—specifically, between a woman's awaany and the equipment tied to a male camel's back, also called "the male camel's accoutrements" (*awwany il-ba'iir*).

The male camel's awaany include the following objects, all of which are tied or fastened closely to the camel's body: the nose ring (*zimaam*), hobbling rope, saddle cinch, halter, muzzle (used when necessary to prevent the camel from grazing), man's riding saddle, the saddle pad for the underside of the saddle (used to protect the camel's back), the saddle cushion (for the rider), the leather cover for the camel's shoulder, and the leather strap that prevents the saddle from moving forward. We need not go into the technical uses for all of these objects; they are instruments for taming and managing the swift riding camels favored by men. What interests us here is the terminological equation between the "woman's accoutrements" and

the "male camel's accoutrements." The equation is not only terminological; it is tactile as well. Just as a woman's awaany are tightly
attached to her mouth, nose, crown of the head, and waist, so the
camel's awaany are attached to its mouth, nose, back, and mid-
section.

One might dismiss this apparent parallel between women's clothing and camel's equipment as illusory were it not for two more pieces
of evidence—the camel's *farwa* and *Tiyeyly*. The first is a wooly
sheepskin dyed red with a solution made from acacia bark.[6] The
farwa (pelt) is draped over a male camel's saddle, where it cushions
the rider from the hard shocks of travel. The second object, the
Tiyeyly (something rather long, *Tawiil*?), is made of two sheepskins
stitched together and dyed black. This item is also thrown over the
saddle and dangles down to the level of the camel's knees, flapping as
it moves.

In terms of their visisble characteristics, the farwa and Tiyeyly are
as opposed to each other as red is to black and as short is to long.
Such a relation is identical to the opposition in women's clothing
between two types of loose garments—the underskirt and dress. Recall that the woman's underskirt (tičča) is short and red, while her
dress (thawb) is longer and black. In other words,

farwa/Tiyeyly :: red/black :: short/long :: tičča/thawb.

Since the woman's tičča and thawb together make up her baala (loose
colored garments), one could also say that the camel's farwa and
Tiyeyly make up its own equivalent of the woman's baala. The Rashaayda do not say, however, that the farwa and Tiyeyly are "the camel's
baala"; the equation between women's loose clothing and a camel's
loose equipment is only made visually, not verbally.

In short, both a woman's garments and a male camel's objects
seem to be divided into two subsets: (1) woman's awaany + woman's
baala; and (2) male camel's awaany + (male camel's unnamed set: (a)
short, red; (b) long, black).

My claim, then, is that by naming, categorizing, and dying a
woman's clothing and a camel's equipment, the Rashaayda make
them seem equivalent.

This claim is supported by another set of ethnographic data which
can be summed up in one word—aS-Sagala. For the Rashaayda this
word names three things: (1) a succulent species of wild herb that
sprouts in the desert during the rainy season and is preferred as
forage for camels; (2) a prize awarded to the camels and riders who

take first, second, and third place in a camel race (each prize consists of a pile of paper currency that is tucked under the winning camel's halter, close to it's ear); and (3) a prize awarded to the women who are best dancers in a wedding (it consists of a pile of paper currency pinned onto the woman's ritual veil, *burga'*, close to her ear).

Clearly the latter two meanings are secondary and are derived metaphorically from the word's primary meaning. For the purposes of this analysis, however, the primary referent (herbs) is of less interest than the two artificial objects to which the name is applied—the racing camel's prize and the dancer's prize. Both of these prizes are attached to the same part of the winner's body by being fastened to the winner's awaany (the halter, in the case of the camel, and the burga', in the case of the dancer).

Interpretation

I pointed out the parallels between women's adornment and a camel's equipment to the Rashiidy men who were my friends: "According to you, a woman is like a male camel; you give her wild herbs and dress her in *awaany*." Most reacted with surprised delight. By themselves they would not have been so bold to suggest that women were like camels. After all, none of them would want to be likened to domestic animals. No matter how much sentimental attachment they might feel toward camels, the animals which bear their burdens, the Rashaayda by no means consider them the equals of human beings. Yet my observation briefly appealed to them because it suggested that, as men, they could be master of women, just as male riders were the masters of male camels.

Why were they surprised, however, when the evidence for some kind of equivalence between women's bodies and camels' bodies was so clear? One reason was that men are not encouraged to have much interest in or appreciation of women's clothing. It is *'eyb* (a betrayal of gender identity) for a man to show special interest or expertise in women's concerns, just as it is *'eyb* for a woman to concern herself with men's clothing or equipment. Socialization about gender identity inhibited speculation about these matters. There may well have been another reason, however: perhaps I did not express the equation correctly. It is not in fact the case that Rashiidy culture equates women with camels; the equation is more subtle.

If we scrutinize all of the examples I have given, including the "brands" on women's legs, the tight, restrictive clothing on their faces, and the heavy jewelry on their wrists and ankles, we find an implicit but clear distinction between agent and object in every case. The agent, who inscribes the tattoos, ties on the belts and veils, and drapes the loose baala over the body, is always a woman, not a man. Correspondingly, the agent who burns a property mark into a camel's hide, who breaks a male camel to the saddle with a nose ring and whip, and who hobbles the camel after riding it is always a man. Hence the correct equation between a woman's adornment and a camel's equipment centers on agent, instrument, and object:

male tamer $<$ awaany (nose ring, cinch, muzzle) $>$ male camel ::
woman dancer $<$ awaany (nose ring, belt, mask) $>$ female body ::
agent $<$ instrument $>$ object

Viewed in this way, women's tattoos and costume suggest that a woman's putting on adornments is like a man's taming a camel. The common element is control. It is as if the woman who puts on a mask is taming her own body.

This chain of thought brings us back to the love tokens girls tattoo on their legs. It seemed incredible, at first thought, that a girl would risk compromising her marriage by inscribing the brand of her beloved on her thigh. As it turns out, however, the risk is much slighter than we would expect, because the mark of the girl's love in no way indicates that she allows her passion to take control of her mind and body.

The Rashaayda speak quite frankly about the involuntary nature of love. They know that a single glimpse of an extraordinarily attractive person can capture the viewer's affections completely. The men also rank each other in terms of handsomeness and sex appeal with unflinching objectivity. No one expects the others to flatter him falsely, and if a man tries to insist that he is the equal of a better-looking man, he is regarded as temperamental and immature. Hence when a man learns that his new wife had fallen in love with another man, he does not conclude that she will look for ways to consummate her love with this man sexually. If he knows the man in question, he might admit that he would be attractive to any woman. The husband does not insist that his wife think of no one but him, for the Rashaayda do not imagine that human emotion is so shallow or easily uprooted. Why should he ask her to deny her feelings? To do so would be viewed as childish bad temper. He does expect, however, that his wife will retain her self-control and sense of honor and will not allow her feelings to lead her into disgrace. He has a right, moreover, to her sexual fidelity and is supported in this regard by every household in his camp and every aspect of the marriage contract.

In other words, the motivation behind the signs of equivalence between women's bodies and those of camels is the idea that women are in control of their bodies. In the case of women the struggle for mastery is internal, while for men it is external, a matter of a rider taming his mount.[7] For the Rashaayda women are not, as I first thought, like camels; they are like riders.

I suspect the Rashaayda knew that my first interpretation had missed the mark. But they said nothing. Either they could not find the words to make the actual metaphor clear to me—since they do not usually need to verbalize it—or they thought it was not worth the trouble to correct me.

Conclusion: The Body as Object

Now that we have understood what women's tattoos and clothing mean for the Rashaayda, we may ask what they mean for other human beings. How does the metaphor communicated by Rashiidy women's clothing (that is, male rider/male camel :: female dancer/female dancer's body) compare with the metaphors and images of the body represented in the other chapters of this work?

I suggest that this kind of metaphor establishes the basis for a positive and active sense of identity. In all societies, identity depends on self-knowledge, on self-objectification. To know who we are, we must be able to imagine how we appear to others. Identity consists of confirming some aspects of this outsider's view and rejecting other aspects (Boddy 1989:75; Fernandez 1974:122). In the Rashaayda case, a woman's self-objectification begins when she encounters a view of herself as a mindless body, not as a person. This view amounts to a male fantasy about women, according to which the woman's body responds automatically to the man's will, becoming a sexual object for him. But this image contradicts the woman's own experience, for whatever the extent of her attraction to a man, it can never absolutely eliminate her ego, her will. Self-objectification proceeds by displacing this male fantasy and reintegrating mind and body through expressive action—dancing, decoration, and tattooing. By achieving and demonstrating self-control, the woman makes her body the object of her will and becomes an acting subject in her own right.

NOTES

Funding for my research was provided by the Fulbright-Hayes Commission and the Social Science Research Council; I express my sincere thanks for their support. I am also grateful to Georges Sabagh, director of UCLA's Von Grunebaum Center for Near Eastern Studies and to the East-West Foundation for the grants they provided me while I was writing my doctoral dissertation. They gave me time to reflect on my material, some of which is included here. Above all, I thank Fadwa El Guindi and Dwight Read, my advisers and counselors while I was a graduate student, for their interest in my work and sustaining encouragement during the many years I have known them.

1   *Rashiidy* is the adjectival form of Rashaayda, which is itself a derived (plural) form of the name of the Rashaayda's eponymous ancestor, *rashiid*. Words in the Rashaayda's dialect of Arabic are set off in italic type when first used and transcribed according to the conventions adopted by Richard Antoun in *Arab Village* (1972).

2   Syntagmatic relations link dissimilar words to form a syntactically correct sentence, as in "The girl ran." When they are violated (e.g., "The ran girl"), the sentence makes no sense. Paradigmatic relations between two words exist when one word may replace another, similar word in the same structure or sentence, as in "The girl (or the boy, or the dog) ran." As we shall see, the syntax of Rashiidi women's costume combines tight head coverings with jewelry for the hands and arms, loose sleeves to cover the arms, and loose skirts. Their paradigm for jewelry permits a woman to replace a silver ring with a gold ring when she marries.

3   I do not wish to present an overly idealized portrait here. It could be that, although men are assigned the same number of productive tasks that are assumed by women, men work fewer hours per day than women. I have no numerical data that could adequately support or falsify such an hypothesis. An accurate time-allocation study among the Rashaayda would require a team effort, since men do much of their work in the open desert at some distance from their camps.

4   Note that the "brand" tattoo is covered by *two* elements of the baala—the underskirt and the dress. Facial tattoos are, on special occasions, likewise covered by *two* elements of the awaany—the "married woman's mask" and the "married woman's ritual veil," which is worn over the mask. Hence I am justified in claiming that the syntagmatic relationship is between a tattoo and a *set* of clothing, not just between a tattoo and a single article of clothing.

5   There is one exception. The term *sa'af,* "silver arm band," also means "the dried fronds of a date palm." Its dual reference suggests that the arm of a woman is like the branch of a palm tree, and the silver jewelry around it is like the fronds surrounding a branch. In short, the term suggests a comparison between a woman's body and a domesticated plant.

6   Note that acacia bark used to be the only red dye employed by the Rashaayda, at a time when they had little spare cash and utilized natural products to a greater extent than presently. In other words, it was the source of red coloring for both the camel's *farwa* and for the woman's red underskirt, *tičča*. The significance is discussed in the next few paragraphs.

7   Sanday 1981 documents parallel cases in preindustrial societies, where women's mastery of their bodies is explicitly likened to men's mastery in warfare.

REFERENCES

Antoun, Richard. 1972. *Arab Village*. Bloomington: Indiana University Press.

Boddy, Janice. 1989. *Wombs and Alien Spirits: Women, Men, and the Zar Cult in Northern Sudan*. Madison: University of Wisconsin Press.

Eickelman, Dale F. 1981. *The Middle East: An Anthropological Approach*. Englewood Cliffs, N.J.: Prentice-Hall.

El Guindi, Fadwa. 1990. "El Moulid: Egyptian Religious Festival" (an ethnographic film). El Nil Research, Los Angeles.

Fernandez, James. 1974. "The Mission of Metaphor in Expressive Culture." *Current Anthropology* 15:119–146.

Hale, Sondra. 1990. "The Politics of Gender in the Middle East." In *Gender and Anthropology*, ed. Sandra Morgen, pp. 246–267. Washington, D.C.: American Anthropological Association.

Herber, J. 1922. "Tatouages du pubis au Maroc" (Tattoos of the pubic area in Morocco). *Revue d'Ethnographie et des Traditions Populaires* 3(9):37–47.

———. 1948. "Onomastique des tatouages marocains" (An analysis of the names of Moroccan tattoos). *Hespéris* 35:31–56.

———. 1949. "Les tatouages de cou, de la poitrine et de genou chez la marocaine" (Tattoos of the neck, breasts and knees among Moroccan women.) *Hespéris* 36:333–345.

Joseph, Suad. 1983. "Working Class Women's Networks in a Sectarian State: A Political Paradox." *American Ethnologist* 10(1):1–22.

al-Jurr, Khalil. 1973. *Larus: Al-mu'jam al-'arabi al-hadith* (Larousse: The modern Arabic dictionary). Paris: Librarie Larousse.

Kanafani, Aida S. 1983. *Aesthetics and Ritual in the United Arab Emirates: The Anthropology of Food and Personal Adornment among Arabian Women*. Beirut and Syracuse, N.Y.: American University of Beirut and Syracuse University Press.

Prüfer, Curt. 1933. "Bemerkungen zur Jemenitischen Frauentracht" (Observations about Yemeni women's costume). In *Aus Fünf Jahrtausenden Morgenländischer Kultur; Festschrift Max Freiherr von Oppenheim zum 70 Geburtstag Gewidmet*, 1:87–88. Berlin: Archiv für Orientforschung.

Qasim, 'Awn al-Sharif. 1972. *Qamus al-lahja al-'ammiyya fi al-Sudan* (Dictionary of the colloquial dialect in Sudan). Khartoum: University of Khartoum.

Rugh, Andrea B. 1986. *Reveal and Conceal: Dress in Contemporary Egypt*. Syracuse, N.Y.: Syracuse University Press.

Sanday, Peggy Reeves. 1981. *Female Power and Male Dominance*. Cambridge: Cambridge University Press.

Spiro, Socrates. 1973. *An Arabic-English Dictionary of the Colloquial Arabic of Egypt*. Beirut: Librarie du Liban.

Ulmer, Friedrich. 1918. "Südpalästinensische Kopfbedeckungen" (Southern Palestinian head coverings). *Zeitschrift des Deutschen Palästina-Vereins* 41:35–53, 101–116.

Wehr, Hans. 1976. *A Dictionary of Modern Written Arabic.* Ithaca, N.Y.: Spoken Language Services, Inc.

Weir, Shelagh. 1989. *Palestinian Costume.* Austin: University of Texas Press.

Young, William C. 1984. "Cultural Change and Women's Work: The Sedentarization of the Rashaayda Bedouin in the Sudan." *Cultural Survival* 8(2):28–29.

THE CULTURAL ANATOMY OF COMPETITIVE WOMEN'S BODYBUILDING

ALAN M. KLEIN

O ver the last two decades, as women have begun to enter the field of bodybuilding, their presence has raised questions about why they (and others) become bodybuilders and what this interest says about their self-perceptions and body image. This chapter explores the meaning of these issues for women, although the work has implications for the larger relationship between the individual and culture.[1] Looking at bodybuilding, we can see how participants, especially female competitive bodybuilders, both reflect and obscure larger cultural interpretations of the body. This research shows that women's bodybuilding has created an equivocal presence, at once mirroring male definitions of bodybuilding and resisting male definitions of the sport subculture.

The Bodybuilding Community

This chapter is the result of my fieldwork at the Olympic Gym in California, one of the world's elite gyms among competitive male and female bodybuilders. I chose this particular gym in large part because I wished to avoid the problem associated with finding representative samples—that representativeness assumes comparative differences have been averaged out. Given the thousands of gyms and the millions who work out in them, I needed either to conduct an extensive investigation over a wide range of sites or to find one gym whose influence was central to all others. I chose the latter. Olympic Gym is perhaps the best-known gym in the world among competitors and noncompetitors alike. Its international recognition and profusion of world-class athe-letes makes it unlike any other gym, yet its influence trickles down to all other gyms. The bodybuilders at Olympic are unlike fitness devotees at gyms elsewhere. These men and women are among the most well-known bodybuilders in the world; they are all caught up in the quest for gaining as much muscle and related attributes as is humanly possible. Suppleness, fitness, toning, and sculpting of muscles are not valued in this setting as they are among more "normal" sectors of the population working out in gyms. The extremes to which the Olympic Gym bodybuilders take masculinity nevertheless become a standard of measurement that most others acknowledge and attempt to emulate in a modified form.

In discussing women bodybuilders a diachronic view is crucial since prior to 1980 women's bodybuilding did not exist. By 1985, however, women's participation in the sport had become widely recognized, had brought about changed views of women who participated, and was attracting different types of women. I was fortunate enough to document the initial entry of women into this male subculture (Klein 1985b) and as a result am able show that subsequent waves of women differ significantly from these early women. While social-psychological shifts have occurred in women's bodybuilding over the past dozen years, the fundamental issues have remained the same. The most significant work on women's bodybuilding since the late 1980s (Bolin 1992) reinforces many of the conclusions drawn in this chapter. I discuss efforts of the first female bodybuilders in an attempt to gain insight into the minds of women who took on such a hostile and male-dominated institution. I also look at the women's interpretation of what they do in comparison to the perceptions of outsiders, and at the changes that have come about in the subculture of women's bodybuilding that might reflect changing notions of the body.

Over the six years of this study I conducted a range of interviews (formal, field, informal) in every sector of the bodybuilder's world. I observed bodybuilders both in and outside of the gym and attended functions (parties and casuals meetings) with a core of over one hundred men and women in the subculture. When appropriate I conducted surveys, employed questionnaires, and had available to me various psychological tests conducted on members of this community.

The social structure of this sport/subculture consists of a few central gyms, with a handful of promoters and entrepreneurs at the top (Klein 1985a). As one moves down the hierarchy, one comes into contact with the many local representations of the subculture—the gyms, world-class bodybuilders, and contests at the regional levels. Olympic Gym is situated at or near the top of the structure. It runs its own contests, featured in all bodybuilding magazines, is internationally recognized, and franchises its operations with gyms and a complete line of sportswear. As the sport has become a cultural icon, the trio of owners who bought the gym for a few thousand dollars in the 1970s have grown wealthy and powerful within the subculture.

The gym itself comprises a tight-knit community of several hundred bodybuilders who make it the center of their lives. The number of members of the gym has grown over the years from the small, intensely private subculture of around one hundred in the mid-1970s to two thousand in 1988. Regardless of the overall growth in membership, however, the core of the community remains small and exclusive. It is to this core that I refer in this chapter. All of the bodybuilders' life functions are handled through the gym: jobs, living arrangements, competing, and the various prerequisites associated with contest preparation (e.g., tanning or photos). While this bodybuilding community is semi-closed, nevertheless it is fluid. Few people stay in the core over six or seven years.

Olympic Gym is staggered into a hierarchical pyramid (Klein 1985a, 1986). The *owners,* their lawyers, and specialists form the top echelon of the gym. They determine policy—who stays and who goes; who is promoted by the gym in upcoming contests (a lifeline for bodybuilders); who receives the special benefits of proximity to them (e.g., special keys allowing them to work out when they like). Immediately below the owners, numbering fifteen to thirty, are the *professional bodybuilders.* Olympic differs from other gyms by the sheer number of world-class competitors of which it can boast. Everyone seems to want to go there to fine tune before a big contest, but many work out there year round. These individuals (almost all of whom are men) hold the most status in the gym after the owners. Their status is reflected in the deference others give them in initiating conversations, allowing them first use of the weights, asking their advice, and so forth. *Amateur bodybuilders* come next. These are more numerous than professionals—typically more than forty—and do not earn cash prizes in contests. They also have high status in that they compete in national and international contests. Women are frequently found in this strata of the gym. Directly beneath amateurs is an even larger group of individuals (perhaps seventy to one hundred who look like bodybuilders but differ from the aforementioned because they do not compete. Typically referred to as *gym rats*, this group may include previous competitors or future competitors. Until they compete they retain their somewhat lessened status, for in this gym there is little real status until one takes the plunge into active competition. Here the core community of the gym ends, yet two further strata exist. The first is the *general membership*, made up of men and women who no longer look as large as bodybuilders; they are simply fit. In today's Olympic Gym they make up the vast majority of people, but a decade or so ago they were a much smaller group than the core community. This growth in membership is attributable to the gym's notoriety. The final group is unique in all of bodybuilding. *Pilgrims and onlookers* are devotees who revere the gym, coming to visit it almost like a holy shrine, and curiosity seekers who have heard about the gym and want to see it.

The women I worked with were primarily concentrated in the ranks of amateurs and gym rats. Over the past decade their numbers have grown from the trio that first came in 1980 to perhaps several hundred today. They typically represent 20 percent to 30 percent of the gym's ranks, with fewer in the professional rank.

It is worth reiterating that these men and women are not simply people who lift weights to keep fit, but world-class bodybuilders. Furthermore, they are affiliated with a gym and subculture that are intensely serious, competition-oriented, and full time. The exaggerated quality of the bodybuilding subculture can prove culturally valuable because it brings to light cultural properties obscured under more "normal" conditions. For example, in examining male bodybuilders one invariably encounters issues in relating to the American notion of masculinity, such as homophobia or hypermasculinity, which are more obscured by the larger society (Klein 1988, 1990).

Women Getting in the Front Door

Judging from the documentary film *Pumping Iron II*, and from the coverage now given women's bodybuilding events on ESPN and in various bodybuilding magazines, one would think that the sport readily took to women, but such was not the case. During the early years (1978–1981) almost no women seriously lifted weights, and those who did entered competitions still held more as beauty contests than bodybuilding events.[2] The male ideologues controlling bodybuilding did little to encourage women as bodybuilders.

However, the cultural currents in North America of the late 1970s increasingly heralded women's physical achievements. Women's athletic programs were fought for; female presence in such male-dominated sports as marathon racing was institutionalized; the Anapurna mountain expedition by an all-female team was successful—all were part of the attack on cultural myths about women. And foremost among these myths was the view that women were physically weak. At the same time, bodybuilding was rapidly rising in popularity as a result of Arnold Schwarzenegger's role in the documentary *Pumping Iron* as well as the emergence of various self-centered pastimes among members of the "me generation." Linked to issues of flight from aging and a generalized sense of cultural narcissism (Lasch 1979), the connection between bodybuilding and yuppy-like values served to catapult the sport-subculture to national prominence.

One of the most blatantly sexist and difficult barriers to women's increased presence in the physical world of the male were the elite gyms. Even large, well-muscled men were apprehensive about going into these gyms. Upon discovering that I had been doing research at Olympic Gym, bodybuilders would sheepishly ask whether I thought they were big enough to train there. What sort of obstacles would women attempting to work out there face? The range of men's reactions went from cold disdain and refusal to engage women, to taunts and curses which, combined with the size of the men hurling them, could be truly intimidating. One male bodybuilder proudly declared the gym as "anything but easy and ovary free." Another, only half in jest, bellowed at a television crew coming in to shoot a segment on the first women in the gym, "Hey, they [women] already got doctors, lawyers, cops, and now bodybuilders. Next thing you know they'll wanna be queer!"

At a shade under five feet tall, Pat was not physically intimidating and, because of her gregarious personality, had been a popular figure in her native Ohio. Yet back in 1979, the men at Olympic summarily dismissed her. Her odyssey into the weight world began in an effort to get her father rehabilitated after an injury. Pat had just finished high school where she was a cheerleader known throughout the school for her personality—"my smile," as she says, smiling. Her natural strength led her to hold two powerlifting records in her weight class. As an outgoing rookie powerlifter, she was ill prepared for her rebuff at Olympic when she initially arrived. The first day she walked around the gym overwhelmed by the array of equipment and the huge men who deftly manipulated the hundreds of thousands of pounds of weights. No one reciprocated her attempts at friendship. The second and third days were no better. On the fourth day, fed up with the rudeness, she stormed into the gym, loaded up an Olympic bar with three hundred pounds (three times her body weight), and proceeded to deadlift the entire thing three times (a deadlift is a required lift in powerlifting competitions). Pat let the weights crash to the floor to punctuate her anger and abruptly left the gym. When she returned the next day she was roundly greeted with, "Hey Pat! What's happening? You gonna squat [an exercise form] today?" By pound for pound outlifting the men, she had broken the barrier.

Pat (despite her Herculean efforts) and others were intially perceived by men at Olympic as toying with weights rather than actively pursuing an emerging field of bodybuilding and power training. Another competitor, Candy, remembers the condescension directed at her pioneering efforts and her humiliation: "I've gone through a lot of ridicule, I've been laughed at a lot, called 'grotesque,' been called a 'dyke' regularly, called names to my face, behind my back. 'What's a woman doin' here?' or 'Hey pussy!'—really disgusting things. At first I turned the rage inward, then I simply had to stand up to them. This was my proving ground, and I'd look them in the eye and say, 'Look jerk, I'm lifting twice my body weight on this set. Think you can do the same?' "

By mirroring male behavior (i.e., confrontational verbal challenges in response to insults) and by outperforming men, Candy, like Pat, gained grudging entrance into this male bastion. Although these women successfully broke into the macho world of the gym, they still had few outlets for their new sport. Women's contests were still more beauty pageants than sporting events, and it was one of Candy's complaints that she was regularly beaten in contests by women who had never lifted a weight. Within the year (1980), another pioneer, Linda, had organized and held a contest for serious women bodybuilders, women who trained hard and developed their bodies. Other offers from forward-looking promoters soon followed.

These pioneers and others fought their way into Olympic Gym as women, but the women there today need only test themselves as bodybuilders. The freedom from gender harassment, taken for granted by most of today's women at Olympic, is reflected in the kind of women who are now competitive bodybuilders. Looking at the most contemporary class of women bodybuilders, Candy reflects: "I think in the beginning you had a lot more women who were iconoclastic, more people who were in it for reasons other than sports. Now you get some real athletes and they aren't here for the super neurotic reasons or the 'feminist' reasons or to shake things up. In the beginning it was so new it was the kind of thing that attracted rebellious women. Today you got lots of women who look big as hell, but they're all followers, not leaders."

Bodybuilding as Psychosocial Construction of Gender

The cultural view of bodybuilding developed in my work stems in large part from the social-psychological assessments I have made over the years. In part, this view was prompted by bodybuilders' overwhelming preoccupation with the image and presentation of power and self-control. Since everything about this subculture so magnified power and self-assurance, I quickly began to wonder whether, in fact, the opposite (insecurity and weakness) might not be true. I gathered life histories and asked questions about motives, self-perception, and other issues. Pleck (1982) and Butts (1975), both psychologists, share my views and list bodybuilding as a sport primarily governed by a neurotic core. In fact, Butts's typology, which views all sports as revolving around one of three psychological cores—competence, aggression, or neurosis—lists bodybuilding as the sole example of a sport based on a neurotic impulse. There are a number of ways to evaluate this claim: (1) determine what brings people to the sport/subculture; (2) evaluate how they perceive the activity in the context of other aspects of their lives; and (3) look at the activities themselves to see what they compel the practitioner to do both in the short and long term.

Bodybuilding is a subculture that revolves around the individual's sense of insecurity and low self-esteem. Anthropologists shy away from using clinical terms for abnormality to describe (sub)cultural phenomena; however, I have concluded that in this instance it may be appropriate. If not actually neurotic, bodybuilding is a subculture whose practitioners suffer from large doses of insecurity, hence the self-presentation of power to the outside world. However, bodybuilding can also be seen as a form of compensatory behavior which, when engaged in by the individual, can be therapeutic (Klein 1987). As a subculture comprised of like-minded individuals, bodybuilding becomes vested in creating an ideology that obscures these fundamental insecurities. The split between the individual and the group (culture) is central to the following analysis because it contains the relationship of body image and self-presentation. Body image is the individual's self-view and reveals insecurities, while the cultural self-presentation (in this case the powerful body) is the mask which obscures perceived shortcomings. In looking at the individual's motives and self-view, we can assess the psychocultural core of the subculture/sport.

Motives

My core sample of 40 men and 35 women revealed several significant gender differences, but reasons for taking up the sport was not one of them. On this index the majority of both women and men gravitated to the sport because of self-perceived shortcomings. Most (34 of 40 men, and 20 of 36 women) came to the sport in large part to compensate for a variety of problems. All but 6 men of the core sample attributed their initial interest to a perceived shortcoming of a physical or psychological nature, for example, stuttering or shortness. The following quotes express typical motives of the men:

—I was picked on when I was a kid. There was no support from my parents. I was always wrong in my father's eyes.
—I got caught up in the sport just cuz I was thin and I wanted to put some body weight on, body size. I started setting specific goals and stuff, there I was all hooked in and I didn't wanna give it up.
—Outside if someone says something I'll go off [brag]. Inside, well, I think I'm good, but I don't really know cuz my parents they'd always go, "How come you lost [wrestling]?" So, now I'm super insecure, know what I mean?
—We had dyslexia growin up, so in school we didn't excel. But we excelled in physical things, we focused on that.

Women, too, tended to gravitate to the subculture from such pasts. Some were very open about their motives, which were similar to those of the men who focused on some past humiliation. The first quote is by Candy (who earlier cited iconoclasm as characteristic of her early entrance into bodybuilding); she directly expresses the neurotic motives behind her entering bodybuilding. The second quote describes a woman's humiliation of being "built like a boy" (parenthetically interesting and seemingly at odds with physical self-perceptions of young pubescent girls who strive for that look; see Nichter and Vuckovic in this volume). Others came to competitive bodybuilding in an attempt to control their perceived obesity:

—You have to have some neurosis in yourself which drives you to bodybuilding. If you don't have it you may wind up doing something else. Most women are just fine keeping fit and toned. Maybe they're very secure in other areas. Maybe they don't have to overcome a childhood like mine. I had to, so I became literally obsessed [with bodybuilding].

—God, I was extremely shy, introverted, almost no friends. . . . I was never dated, not even to the senior prom. I had such bad acne, and people used to laugh at my chest, my legs. When I'd wear a bikini, they'd call me chicken legs. Back then I had no shapeliness. I was built like a boy. People used to really laugh at me.

Peta came to Olympic Gym in the mid-1980s as a serious competitor. Like Candy, she was seen as one of the "overly muscular" women. Her past as an exotic dancer in New Mexico, through which she partially overcame her poor body-image, served as her entrance into bodybuilding: "I'm fat in my mind. I got into bodybuilding to control my weight." She quickly realized her potential to make muscular gains relatively easily and so, after competing in several local contests, came to Olympic to train for serious competition. Her oral history reveals a nondescript teenager who was regularly passed over for dates: "The only time a boy would call me is when he needed his homework done. Then suddenly they'd be nice to me. God, I didn't care. It was just nice to have someone seem like they liked you."

Maria represents that segment of the female population in the gym that has more recently come to the subculture. Most of these women have come as competent and secure athletes, and not so much to compensate for perceived shortcomings: "Hey, I'm in it for the sport. I ran track in college, played three sports in high school. After that accident a few years back I had to stop marathon racing. Weight training was part of my rehabilitation, and since I made good gains [muscular] so easy, I began getting serious about this [bodybuilding]."

Whereas Candy and Peta realized their discipline and determination once they were in bodybuilding, Maria had inculcated it throughout her life: "Hey hon, my dad taught us all to work our asses off. You'll never see me slack off in there [the gym]. Right now, I guess I'm at a point where I'm too selfish with myself as far as time and energy goes to be interested in anybody. I'm enjoying what I'm doing. Probably later I'll regret it, but I'm not interested in ten years from now. Hell, I could be dead by then."

Keeping in mind the woman who argued that "You have to have some neurosis in yourself that drives you to bodybuilding—If you don't have it you may wind up doing something else," one can still ask whether there is something particular about the sport that makes it attractive to that pool of insecure and potential recruits. The reasons bodybuilders choose this particular subculture over others are revealing. The individual nature of the activity is frequently mentioned by the men in the study:

> —I liked football and all, but there was too much sharing. I just didn't wanna depend on anyone. I wanted to do something totally by myself.
> —I was always turned off by team sports. . . . I just didn't like being part of a team and the back-slapping and gropey sweating and all that shit. I would rather spend the time by myself in the basement pumping iron. . . . I didn't like sharing the glory or the defeat.

The theme of selfishness with a hint of antisociability is noted in the unwillingness to share and the preference for being on one's own. Bodybuilders would often describe themselves as loners and would demean social relationships both inside and outside of the gym as untrustworthy and unreliable. One cannot escape seeing the defensiveness in such responses:

> —I'm not a secure person. I'm not a good mixer. I don't go to bars and don't like to go to parties unless I know everyone there.

—For some reason I don't like social obligations. I don't like the phone to ring. I don't know if it's laziness or what.

—You'll never see me running around, goin out with a body-builder. Nope, friends I don't have. I don't believe in 'em. I'm a loner and in bodybuilding you have to be. And I don't believe in training partners either because depending on 'em is no good.

One cannot escape the conclusion that male bodybuilders have a relatively low opinion of social relations, are somewhat distrustful of others, and view themselves as loners, all of which dovetails nicely with the individualistic style of bodybuilding. Women, we shall see, have a different outlook on these matters.

Compensation for Low Self-Esteem

Male bodybuilders' low level of sociability and disdain for dependence on others are compatible with one of our culture's values—individualism. Coupled with many bodybuilders' low sense of self-esteem, their statements concerning autonomy and self-reliance ring a bit hollow, suggesting instead a psychological defensiveness.

Personal defensiveness is less evident when the individual functions in the gym, however. At Olympic Gym, like many others I have studied, there exists a strong sense of social cohesion, and members rely on each other to fill a variety of needs (friendship, jobs, living arrangements, training). Bodybuilders in the core group develop strong ties among themselves and project to the outside world an exclusive, haughty community. Here the individual's insecurities are fused into a social structure that projects the opposite—security and exclusivity.

At the center of all of these deliberations is the body. Bodybuilders craft *themselves,* going beyond anything the ordinary fitness devotee might attempt. Their notion of using the body to remold both their physical self and psychological sense of self, and doing so in a way considered so extreme, begs for interpretation. Working with weights, developing a nutritional standard and diet designed to add bulk and reduce fat, and using steroids, all in a seemingly endless array of combinations, the bodybuilder doesn't fashion the body, but rather builds it. For the bodybuilder, maximizing muscularity (not suppleness or fitness) is the goal. Explicit in all of this repudiation of normal bodily dimensions (referred to in such pejorative terms as "wimp", "pencil neck," "polio" legs or arms, etc.).[3]

Recalling the Charles Atlas ads prevalent in comic books and pulp magazines of the 1950s which called for building the body to compensate for physical weakness (low esteem), the imposing physique is both a defense against a world perceived as intimidating and a means of overcoming that intimidation, that is, of feeling more attractive, more accomplished, and more in control.

Expressing Control

Control is a theme that runs through this volume, and the search for control over one's life and environment is a central cultural theme in bodybuilding as well (Klein 1987). In this instance, control is synonymous with mastery over one's body. A strict regimen in which the contest competitor seeks to do the exact same thing each day enables him or her to sense that life (the body) can be controlled. Getting up each morning at a predetermined time, eating only so much of carefully selected items in a regular cycle, waiting a required time for the food to digest, and heading off to the gym for a precisely calculated workout has an institutionalized, compulsive quality. One informant boasted to me that he had his routine down so well he did not need an alarm clock; instead he rose each morning at precisely 7:00 A.M. to the urge to evacuate his bowels. This was his view of self-mastery.

Not only do the life patterns of the bodybuilder reflect preoccupation with control but so does the body itself. As one informant stated: "With us [bodybuilders] we can sculpt ourselves however we want. I can add a little deltoid here, thicken my back, reduce my obliques, whatever I want. That's what we do and do it better than anyone."

William Young, in his work on women and tattoos in this volume, discusses a useful psychological component to this sense of mastery. Women bodybuilders also reveal this dimension of controlled self, whether it be in muscularity or delaying the aging process:

—My thing is to get as big as possible, to revel in my own strength and muscularity. Just make sure it's real hard earned and not artificially inflated. My thing is not to be afraid that I'm going to lose my femininity. I wanna establish myself as the role model for those women who wanna be big and muscular.

—I feel control over my physical being, far more than most women. I feel that most women let things happen [to them]. They have babies, get out of shape. Things happen. By the time they're thirty they feel washed up. I was determined not to feel that way. . . . I'm going to challenge the degenerative process, I'm going to take control of aging.

Self-mastery via building one's body, making it do what one wants it to, is seen as a means of accomplishing this metamorphosis. Women bodybuilders, in their emphasis on power and self-mastery, are reminiscent of the informants in Bordo's work on eating-disordered women and their struggle to repudiate the status quo notions of what women ought to be: " 'It was about power,' says Kim Morgan, speaking of her obsession with slenderness, 'that was the big thing . . . something I could throw in people's faces, and they would look at me and I'd only weigh this much, but I was strong and in control, and hey you're sloppy' " (Bordo 1990:105).

To many outside bodybuilding, such statements appear boastful, presumptuous, and narcissistic, but in bodybuilding subculture these elements play a therapeutic role (Klein 1987). Because low self-esteem is so widespread in bodybuilding, the narcissism found in mirroring and grandiose displays of self actually elevate self-esteem to a point where the bodybuilder can harness it in the development of a more secure sense of self: "I began to realize that it's okay to be a woman. I've come all the way back around, and it's okay. And, I don't feel like a jock. I don't feel like I have to prove myself anymore. I feel very feminine, yet very strong. In the beginning I felt like its not okay to be a woman. That you connect motherhood with womanhood, and womanhood with slavery and reduced options, and so you say, 'not for me.' I saw my mother being depressed and drinking, and I saw motherhood as a big rat fuck. But I think a lot of women I deal with here have come back around."

While this woman felt that bodybuilding had enabled her to overcome some of her ambivalence concerning women's issues (motherhood, femininity, athleticism, for example), other women encountered at the gym did not agree. Some viewed pregnancy as inopportune and intrusive to their competitive careers. Since quite a few of the women who competed menstruated infrequently (some not at all), their claims that competition hindered the possibility of having children were underscored physiologically. These women had so cut down their subcutaneous body fat content, and so dieted and trained, that they had temporarily compromised their reproductive capacities. This extreme behavior is not only further testimony to control over the body, but is rationalized in nongender terms as part of the price an athlete has to pay.

A strong sense of security and control achieved by adhering to the monastic, somewhat obsessive regimen of contest preparation (i.e., workouts, dieting) and social bonding of like-minded questers. What was striking about the bodybuilders' lifestyle was the degree to which they could psychologically circle their wagons, that is, create an insular world, small enough in scale to allow their control of it. In all likelihood there is an inverse relationship between controlling key areas of one's life (e.g., relationships or work) and seeking to master one's body. As one bodybuilder said to me, pointing around the gym, "They can't get me in here!"

Muscularity and Gender-Identity Conflict

The foremost issue in women's bodybuilding is just how muscular women can become and remain within the bodybuilding mainstream. This issue raises a series of others, the most important being the often-overlooked fact that masculinity means different things to women than it does to men.

The documentary film *Pumping Iron II* centers on a contest featuring a range of women bodybuilders competing for a prestigious title. Two types of women in particular are the focus of attention; one is a conventionally slender woman, the other heavily muscled.[4] The slender competitor, Rachel Macliesh, has won often. She approximates male society's ideal of an attractive woman—model pretty, demure in movement, and finely striated through not overly developed muscles. The other competitor, Bev Francis, is heavily muscled, not as conventionally pretty of face, and moves awkwardly. Her poses more resemble the poses men use in contests. Macliesh has learned to pose as women "ought" to, more or less along the lines of fashion models.

A heavily muscled competitor such as Bev Francis is chronically depicted as man-ish, and lesbianism is commonly implied. Her dense and pronounce musculature makes her better developed than most men, as a result of which she is set up to deal with a certain amount of gender-role conflict (Coakley 1989: 177–202). Such sanctions as not winning and explicit ideology regarding women who violate society's gender norms set up tight perimeters around women's behavior. Hence, women who persist in developing themselves beyond the acceptable limits are often viewed by adherents of male-imposed convention as women who resist. Feminists, too, are quick to pick up on the implied resistance in such women: "A number of oppositional discourses and practices have appeared in recent years. An increasing number of women are 'pumping iron,' a few with little concern for the limits of body development imposed by current canons of femininity" (Bartky 1988:83).

This statement is not, strictly speaking, accurate. Although women have pushed for greater size, a distinction must be made between what these women want to do with their bodies (get big), what it means within the contexts of their careers in bodybuilding, and how outsiders interpret their bodies. Clearly, Bartky and others find the refusal to capitulate to bodybuilding's male ideologues on this issue to constitute serious cultural-gender resistance—a position receiving some support in the following willingness to risk condemnation:

> —I get flak all the time from the people at the AAU [Amateur Athletic Union] and contest promoters. They don't think women should be developed. They say, "Sure, you can come down here and compete, but I don't wanna see too much muscle. I don't wanna see biceps." S. is a lot more concerned about her femininity. She's a lot less secure. People tell her, "Oh, oh. Your arms are getting big," and she worries over it. I don't get too concerned. I know I'm a woman.
>
> —I was really devastated when B. got eighth place, cuz she was huge. B. is my role model, she's the epitome of what I'm going for—big. It pissed me off that all these people are bitchin' about her, but I knew they would hold it against her.

This heavily muscled group of women has been willing to proceed with their view of what a woman's body ought to look like. Nevertheless, it is critical to see how these issues are framed within gender perspectives. The push to raise the ceiling on what is acceptable in women's bodybuilding has been successful. Since the late 1970s women have been getting bigger and winning. Women who in the early 1980s were being drummed out of competition as too large and muscular, now are seen as too small by their peers: "Now I'm a peanut. They're so big! Some are thirty pounds heavier than I am. These girls are monsters. I'm really small [now], and I aways was, that's the joke. It's just that people weren't used to me [as muscular] in those days. It's all so relative."

What these physical gains mean is less explicit. Again, there is a dualistic character to interpreting this new form, a binary view of convention and iconoclasm. The notion of "symbolic male" is discussed in a later chapter in this volume by Robbie Davis-Floyd, who looks at professional women who deny pregnancy and motherhood. It is certainly tempting to interpret these heavily muscled women in the same way. Their interrupted reproductive cycles and periodic use of steroids for heavier musculature suggests this. At the same time, statements by these women indicate the opposite as well—capitulation to male institutions by adopting male practices without challenge. Rather than set up their own organizations, women have pushed for only the mildest gains in the most conciliatory tones. They have wanted acceptance on male terms.

The large women I interviewed were still as preoccupied with pleasing men by being attractive to them as were other more traditional women. Bev Francis was just as preoccupied with being feminine and "getting her man" as was Rachel Macliesh, but Francis has a very large build, and such musculature is deciphered as male, making her conventional desire to be attractive to males confusing to the outsider. Another of the very large women also cast her potentially intimidating physique in a traditional way: "One of the things I enjoyed most about bodybuilding was going from flat-chested and being razzed about it, to people all of a sudden noticing my body. I had this nondescript body. Now men say, 'Wow, check out the bod!' "

After getting large, this is what another woman had to say. Note the shift in frame of reference and identification from small to large men: "It was scary up there [Montana]: the guys were big and loud and rowdy. And they'd grab you. The lifestyle was so different and the men were also. I was used to faggy-type guys, and I started to feel my assertiveness up there and change; and when Daryl came up, I saw through his whiny little ways. I kicked him out, and found Kurt who was more like me, assertive and imposing."

At times, even women who had themselves been labeled as unfeminine, rather than side with their "sisters in arms," would deride the new "overly muscled" women. Said one, "What I see now is exactly what I fought so hard to remove from the minds of bodybuilding skeptics three years ago. I see a bunch of men parading in women's bikinis, and that's gross. . . . I am very disappointed by the current direction of women's bodybuilding."

The picture of muscular women unilaterally rejecting traditional perceptions of femininity is only half correct. These women are bodybuilders, and bodybuilders are supposed to push their form to the limits. The problem lies in the fact that women bodybuilders are acting on the basic precept of a sport/subculture designed for men, and that precept is size. While women have pushed on in this regard, they have not done so on other hotly contested issues (e.g., union formation, the notion of competition, and steroids). When, for instance, they are given the option of selecting an all-female orientation, women bodybuilders persist in selecting male training partners and managers. When arguing for muscularity, they do so with an eye toward being accepted by the ideologues: "Why should I be made to pay the price, to limit myself by what Joe Weider [the most powerful figure in the sport] says is the largest a woman can be, when Mike over here [another bodybuilder] is rewarded for being as big as a Clydesdale [horse]?"

Increased Use of Steroids by Women

The increased use of steroids by women is further testimony to women's uncritical acceptance of a male standard for the body, advanced at great risk to one's health. Use of this synthetic male hormone has the effect of making one larger (how much depends on the dose, the kind of steroid, and the person using it), harder, and somewhat stronger. While not as many women as men use steroids, their use in the gym has increased significantly. Some of the women I interviewed admitted readily to taking them:

> —Sometimes [I use steroids] for contests, sometimes for experimental purposes. It does give a little bit more striation, vascularity, and hardness. It takes me a little too far for most people though. I don't tell other women I take it.
> —The stuff really works! You get harder, you get stronger. When you're dieting, you hold your strength, and your skin is tight, like a pump, and I'd stay that way all day long. I'd be lying if I said I didn't like it. I did.

Drug testing has just been introduced into contests but is haphazardly implemented. Most bodybuilders are usually one step ahead of the authorities doing the testing and can find ways of avoiding detection. One can only assume that women taking steroids—estimates in the gym ranged from 25 percent to 60 percent—are doing so for the same reasons as men. Contest preparation is the most often-cited reason, but one female competitor's comments reveal that many who are not competing take them to achieve the look of a bodybuilder as well as to belong to the subculture:

> I'm training with this guy. He doesn't compete, and he's got a new girlfriend who hangs around with him. And she wants to be a bodybuilder cuz he is, so she's training with us. One day he's sick and she shows up. So I'm paying attention to her and I'm going, "My god, you're using the same weights I use at a heavier body weight." And she goes, "You know, that stuff really works!" I say, "What stuff?" She goes, "Methyltestosterone." My mouth just hung open. And she looks at me, she's only been training for three months. So, she goes, "Oh my god, is that the wrong stuff? What are you using?"

Even the undesirable and potentially harmful side effects of steroid use for women, ranging from growth of facial hair and deepening of the voice to enlargement of the clitoris and liver damage, did not seem to deter those using them. Like the men, they would invoke such gym-bred myths as the reversibility of effects and altered dosages to rationalize continued steroid use.

Women in quest of maximum muscularity who wind up accepting the more questionable forms of male behavior hardly constitute oppositional discourses. In simply reading the form (the body), one risks entirely missing the intent, the essence. Many of the women at Olympic were indiscriminately replicating male excesses; there was no critique of masculinity in their actions or motivations.

Distinctive Features of Women's Bodybuilding

Immersed in a male subculture and not yet possessed of their own style of bodybuilding, women differ from men in several significant ways. These features mirror elements of women's values in the larger society, values that could form the base of a uniquely female approach to the sport as well as a critique of the masculine core within it.

Class-Gender Differences

On a social structural level, one striking difference between the men and women in Olympic Gym was class. Of my core sample of 40 male bodybuilders, 32 (77 percent) came from traditional blue-collar families. Women, on the other hand, tended to come from more afflu-ent backgrounds. A sample of 35 women revealed that 24 (68 percent) came from professional or semiprofessional homes (engineers, teach-ers).

The women's educational backgrounds underscored their socioeco-nomic roots as well: 28 (80 percent) had attended college or university, 14 (40 percent) had graduated, and 3 (8 percent) had gone on to gradu-ate school. By comparison, only 22 (55 percent) men had attended college, while 4 (17 percent) had graduated, and none had attended graduate school. One of the women felt these differences resulted "be-cause women have only recently gotten into bodybuilding. We've had to do other things in the past, like go to school." The lower educational levels of men in the core community were reflected in their occupa-tions. At the time of the interviews, 23 (58 percent) worked at jobs classified as semiskilled. The women at Olympic tended to have jobs in keeping with their higher educational accomplishments: 21 (60 per-cent) held white-collar professional or administrative jobs (e.g., tea-cher, entrepreneur, editor) or worked in the arts (artist, dancer). The gym was divided in such a manner that gender and class were fused: women tended to come from more affluent backgrounds, were better educated, and held better jobs than the men. In short, women were of a higher social and economic class than men.

The Social Meaning of Bodybuilding

The women bodybuilders differed from the men in their responses to questions designed to see how complete was their immersion in the world of competitive bodybuilding. The men questioned overwhelm-ingly viewed bodybuilding as an end in itself, that is, they wanted to remain in bodybuilding and saw building the body as the goal, the end result. Men's motives for entering the sport were identical to their goals.

Women, on the other hand, treated bodybuilding as a means to an end. While their motives for going into bodybuilding were often the same as men's—poor body-image and insecurity—they meant something different:

> —Bodybuilding is the right thing to be doing now, but it's going to lead to other things in time. . . . It's not enough for me by itself. I've worked in gyms for years and I find them deadening. It's just not stimulating by itself.
> —To me, right now, bodybuilding's just a stepping stone. This "Beast" thing [the logo chosen by this woman for her mail order ads in bodybuilding magazines] is going to take me places. I can see that the IFBB [International Federation of Body Building] and AAU [Amateur Athletic Union] is not the ultimate goal.

Like men, women often commented on their strength and power as benefits derived from bodybuilding, but these benefits meant different things to each sex. For women, gaining strength and building their bodies was integral to testing new definitions of womanhood: "I wanna lift more than any woman ever did and set records that no one can touch." For men, on the other hand, building one's body was nothing more than validating old notions of masculinity: "Bodybuilding is about size. We wanna see size, thickness. These guys [pointing around the gym] are drawn to bodybuilding for some reason—insecurities or whatever. That's why they pump their lats [latisimus dorsi] out and walk around like that." Hence, for women, bodybuilding symbolizes something new and potentially challenging of gender convention, while for men it props up gender conventions.

Social Relations

The most significant difference between men and women was evident in the area of sociability. Women at Olympic were, overall, more social—more affable, outgoing, less defensive and, most important, less competitive and backbiting (Klein 1993).

This difference was most evident in contest behavior. These events are notorious for the quality of ruthlessness between men. Once a bodybuilder decides to compete, his view of those around him alters rapidly from ally to nemesis. He is apt to stop at nothing to show off his build at his rivals' expense as well as destroy his competitors' chances. Prior to walking on stage men are often silent, brooding, asking for and giving nothing. Women, by contrast, tend to aid one another, toning down the more ruthless elements of competition:

—Women are tighter. They're real friendly. I've seen girls swap clothing, posing suits at contests. And they helped me with my hair and makeup when my hairdresser didn't show up on time. At the Best in the West contest these two girls were getting dressed and the one says, "Hey, that suit doesn't look right on you." The other one says, "I know, it's too baggy." The first one says, "Here, try mine." And she gave her the most flattering one she had.
—Somebody else needed oil, and I lent them mine. People help each other and that's what I like about the [women's] competitions. I enjoy being able to help my competitors like that or talk to them without saying, "Well I'll see you out there chump."
—They [men] are off. They don't know the experience is about being together, that it's not a one-man show. This is a group experience, and the other parties [competitors] allow you to do it. Male bodybuilders are really thick. They really think that the trophy is important. What happens sometimes is you get in with them and you start being influenced [by them] and you get a little screwed up.

In these statements we see the degree of social bonding that exists among women and what one competitor pinpointed as the major difference between men and women: men are more goal-oriented, while women focus on relationships. At least one well-placed insider has claimed that as women become more ensconced in the world of competitive bodybuilding, they lose their ability to subordinate the negative behavior in competition. I once thought I glimpsed this at a contest. Backstage the women were more tense than I had seen; they were pacing, talking to themselves, or looking intently at the wall. A few husbands, male partners, and trainers were seen whispering to them in hushed tones, admonitions like, "Watch out for her, she's gonna screw you in the pose-down." There was no doubt that the presence of men in these settings was contaminating the competition women normally set up for themselves.

It is in social bonding and in the ability to limit the effects of intense male competition, while promoting sharing, that women can develop their own style of bodybuilding. It is also in women's sense of sociability and interpersonal relations that they can mediate the insecurities that may have prompted their entrance into bodybuilding. As discussed earlier, men have a less well developed sense of sociability, so let their insecurities play out: their poor sense of self is amplified by their sense of being loners, which in turn results in contest behavior that is extremely competitive and individualistic. It is in this crucial difference (from men) that women can offer an alternative to status quo male bodybuilding and mediate the perceived shortcomings that led them to this subculture in the first place.

Culture, Class, and Women's Bodybuilding

Based on the preceding observations, bodybuilding seems to represent different things, depending on gender, and even class. For a certain segment of men, found disproportionately among blue-collar workers rather than professionals, a large body has been a form of masculine identity as well as a source of compensation for poor self-esteem.[5] Until recently, bodybuilding was a component of hypermasculine behavior which has always been associated with a blue-collar class/cultural style (contemporary notions of muscularity as culturally approved for upwardly mobile and/or professional men don't predate the past decade). For women, on the other hand, class barriers never prevented their entrance into bodybuilding; rather for them the prohibition was gender. It is noteworthy that historically it was middle class, more affluent women, rather than their male counterparts, who made the major inroads into this hypermasculine, blue-collar world. The world of the gym was certainly hostile to women, but it was equally hostile to men who could not measure up physically (i.e., middle- and upper-class men). For middle-class women to break the barriers to the gym before men of similar background or lower-class women is significant. Certainly the increased socioeconomic opportunity of more affluent women is one factor in explaining why they entered the gym before lower-class women, but it does not explain why they did so before higher-status men. Other class-related factors that might play a role include the following: (a) better-educated women are more likely conscious of and able to articulate discontent and thus construct alternatives; (b) these women possess a requisite degree of confidence to move into an intimidating and hostile environment; and (c) while Olympic posed a hostile environment for women, for middle-class women it was more of an unknown setting (compared to working-class women), hence more easily approached. Relative to blue-collar women, middle-class women were not as likely to be inundated with images and information about this world, hence less anxious and intimidated before the fact. This ironic twist in which middle-class women led the way for middle-class men to enter the formidable and intimidating world of bodybuilding is too tempting to ignore.

Body and Culture

There can be little doubt that the advances made by the women's movement were significant for women's bodybuilding. Without claiming to be feminists, these women bodybuilders had, as a result of the dramatic gains made by women of the time, sufficient cultural-ideological reserves to draw on. The numerous cultural and social barriers against seeing women as athletes were falling in the late 1970s, ranging from passage of Title IX to promote equity between women's and men's intercollegiate athletics, to Billie Jean King's widely televised symbolic victory over an avowed male chauvinist, to the entry of girls into the Little Leagues and Pop Warner football. In this regard, women's bodybuilding was part of the overall resistance to male physical and cultural hegemony. Also significant for the emergence of women's bodybuilding was the relatively more tolerant cultural climate of California.

In the last fifteen years, women's body presentation and body image have been intensely interpreted. The brunt of analysis has come from those looking at the cultural preoccupation with slender women (e.g., Orbach 1982; Chernin 1981; Bartky 1988). Putting the struggle for slenderness in a more dialectical light, Bordo (1988, 1990), following Crawford (1985), argues that slenderness in women mirrors a tension between the need to repress desires for instant gratification and the tendency to indulge impulse (Bordo 1988:96). In this light, diets invoke the tension between gluttony and self-mastery. Hunger (that which we seek to suppress) as a metaphor for women's sexuality and diet as the means to control it are likewise interpreted by Bordo as a cultural tension. Exercise also becomes emblematic of these opposing forces by simultaneously calling forth what we hope to look like against the invidiousness of our present condition. In this light, slenderness and fitness (or masculinity) becomes codes for both the denial of our sexuality (read "reproductive capacities") and the enhancement of that sexuality in copying societal notions of fitness. More important for the purposes of this study is the connection between the "tyranny of slenderness" (Chernin 1981) and the drive for muscularity that comes out of Bordo's work. Both slenderness and muscularity have at their core two traits—resistance and control.

This in-depth look at women in bodybuilding shows their sport/subculture as a contested terrain. There is ample support for the view that female bodybuilders form cultural resistance to male cultural domination as well as evidence to show their capitulation to male (sub)cultural convention. The key is to look at the level of analysis. Viewed from within their subculture, including their self-perceptions, women bodybuilders are, at critical junctures, seen to embrace sexist conventions. This dualistic view mirrors Bordo's work on slenderness as repudiation and capitulation to societal dictates. On the cultural level, however, women's bodybuilding contains within it the possibility of generating a style that is both distinct from male bodybuilding and a critique of masculinity.

Cultural Hegemony and Women's Bodybuilding

Without really ever having given the subculture a thought, Foucault, in *Discipline and Punish* (1979), drives to the heart of bodybuilding as a cultural entity. In critiquing modern culture by talking of its rise out of traditional forms, Foucault writes:

> What was then being formed was a policy of coercions that act upon the body, a calculated manipulation of its elements, its gestures, its behavior. The human body was entering a machinery of power that explores it, breaks it down and rearranges it. A "political anatomy," which was also a "mechanics of power," was being born; it defined how one may have a hold over others' bodies, not only so that they may do what one wishes, but so that they may operate as one wishes, with the techniques, the speed and efficiency that one determines. Thus, discipline produces subjected and practiced bodies, "docile" bodies. (Foucault 1979:138)

This assessment of the commodification, specialization, and alien-ation of the contemporary mind to body can easily be extended to include the subculture of bodybuilding, in part because in its linkage of body to both mastery and the lack of mastery, Foucault has pro-vided us with an extremely valuable insight. However, as Bartky (1988:64) astutely points out, Foucault failed to engender his view of the body. Instead, he assumes that men and women experience cul-ture identically. Obviously they do not, and to that degree, Foucault's otherwise valuable insights need to be recast. Here is where hard bodies become expressions of denial of female conventions at the same time as they promote Foucault's "docile body." How?

Massive muscularity has the appearance of iconoclasm—a com-plete disregard for convention fused with an extreme body construc-tion. Because the body is massive (rather than lean) it is perceived as robust and powerful, and culturally viewed as epitomizing individual, rather than societal control. However, borrowing a page from Herbert Marcuse, this alleged individual control is little more than an example of repressive tolerance in which the appearance of autonomy and freedom of expression is overlayed by societal and cultural constraint. Insofar as bodybuilding is, as a more recent expression of the body industry, so rapidly growing in our culture, we can interpret it to mean nothing more than the individual need being derailed into a consumer base. The cultural fears that so many Americans have of aging are at once fueled and quelled by consuming one or another form of cultural elixirs, be it dieting, dressing, running, weight train-ing, and so forth. Hence, appearance and reality are illusory and one (Klein 1993). By looking at female and male bodybuilders, we can see that the form may be revolutionary, but the essence often bespeaks of tradition. The means of forging a body that symbolizes "the great refusal" belies a mindset that is much more traditional and a method of attaining size that smack of all Foucault's docility.

If bodybuilding has historically occupied a less than high-status position in our society, it nevertheless feeds our current cultural view of the body as partible and bounded (see the chapter by Sault, this volume). The bodybuilder's perception of the body as made up of parts (chest, abs, back, arms, legs) and subdivided (traps or trapezius, front, rear delts or deltoids) fits this partible notion perfectly. This view even extends into the psychoperceptual realm in that bodybuilders objectify each body part (Klein 1993). The bodybuilder's body is bounded in a series of subcultural perceptions and practices that have to do with absolute control of diet and physical regimen, and viewing the body as a system that has to be mastered.

In the sense that it mirrors perfectly, if in exaggerated form, the alienation, objectification, and specialization so characteristic of our society, bodybuilding lends itself to the view of the body as docile rather than revolutionary. Women's bodybuilding may not be as completely implicated in this docility as is men's, but there is little doubt that the underlying premise of the subculture/sport (rooted in a body image of personal insecurity) threatens women in the subculture who remain uncritical of their handiwork.

In regard to "reading" women bodybuilders, I have distinguished between a number of levels. At the individual level we see these women as desirous of developing physically imposing bodies that strongly suggest repudiation of convention. They are willing to face societal sanctions against doing so. These women are also interesting in that they show little gender-role conflict, that is, difficulty reconciling femininity and musculature. In this instance, the difficulty is generated by men's interpretation of their behavior. However one sees it, these women possess conventional self-perceptions, and personal desires and goals of being attractive to men, while ready to risk that approval. They get around this dilemma by being part of the subculture of bodybuilding, in which they find men who are attracted by their cultural choices.

At a subcultural level we have seen how women struggled to gain acceptance against intimidating odds, how they had to perform as men, to break down existing barriers against women. With acceptance, the original iconoclastic women gave way to mainstream female bodybuilders and fitness advocates, so that not only is Olympic Gym more mainstream, but the potential for feminist consciousness has been reduced. I have shown that women in the subculture increasingly seem to imitate men indiscriminately by using steroids and allowing male forms of competition to invade their more humane form.

On the grand cultural level, both men's and women's bodybuilding is emblematic of having gone beyond the pale, that is, achieving a musculature to which most outsiders have negative reactions (Klein 1993). While female bodybuilders distance themselves from the societal norms for women's bodies, they do not seek to repudiate the traditional notion that it is desirable for women to be sex objects. They do not repudiate wanting to be desirable to men: posing is a turn on; there is as much talk of makeup and hair as training regimen. There is nothing unequivocal about women's bodybuilding. It is neither feminist nor compromised, but rather contested.

Beyond women's bodybuilding is the issue of just what bodybuilding as a whole represents. We must remember that bodybuilding is a complex of behavior historically premised on a male need for increased size, partially to compensate for feelings of inadequacy. There are many ways in which one can attempt to compensate for low self-esteem. Bodybuilding is only one way, but has always been perceived as a low-level—hence, less successful—form of compensation. The implication is that it is practiced by men who are not particularly capable (class bias). If bodybuilding is a suspect activity or subculture as practiced by men, then for women to take on the quest for maximum size is to replicate the least psychologically adaptive form of compensatory behavior. But bodybuilding means different things to men and women. For a man, increasing his muscularity is his individual attempt to validate his atavistic sense of masculinity (to avoid being stigmatized for lack of it). For women, on the other hand, size is wrapped up with more recently constructed gender issues. There is no history to women's bodybuilding, reflecting the cultural stereotype of women as nonmuscular.

The subculture of bodybuilding is a male-derived, male-dominated world which women have only entered in the past decade or so. The conditions under which the women entered, and continue to enter, the subculture of California's competitive bodybuilding, their self-perceptions and views of their bodies, and what bodybuilding means to women and men have been explored in this chapter. While the study focuses on women's bodybuilding, the implications of the study are about the larger relationship between the individual and culture. This examination of the body distinguishes between body image and body presentation: the former pertains to one's self-perception, while the latter is communicated to another person. While these two may reflect each other, they need not. In the subculture of competitive bodybuilding, we saw that body image is often built on a low sense of self-esteem. Body presentation is a compensatory collective cultural construct that bodybuilding (as a subculture) generates and then projects to the outside world. In looking at bodybuilding, we glimpse the ways in which individuals (particularly female bodybuilders) both reflect and obscure larger cultural interpretations of themselves.

It is critical to remember that while this study is about women, the sport/subculture of bodybuilding is grounded on male insecurities. Thus, for women entering the subculture, the agenda rooted in insecure masculinity can obscure women's issues as well as the meanings women assign to their bodies. To deal with these complex and contradictory layers, gender has been discussed in the context of three levels of body-meaning: (1) the individual, (2) the subculture, and (3) the wider cultural milieu. The individual's motives for taking up bodybuilding and then for entering the subculture were explored. The bodybuilder's position in the subculture was also examined. At the subcultural level I looked at the social and psychological premises of bodybuilding as well as the way the subculture is organized. As regards women, I examined how their entrance into a male bastion exerts an even greater pressure on them than on men. This is assured in the small size and elite makeup of the subculture described here. A remarkable degree of uniformity is achieved within this setting, hence opposition to the powers that control competitive bodybuilding is not tolerated. It is within this setting that women's bodybuilding forged an *equivocal* presence, at various times differing from and reflecting male bodybuilding. At the cultural level I examined the meaning of masculinity for women and men. Gender differences as mediated by the sociocultural relations they bring to the subculture were shown to differ. It is in this area that serious challenges to the male-centered world of bodybuilding can take place.

NOTES

1   Earlier versions of this chapter appeared as "Pumping Iron," *Society* 23 (1985), and in *Little Big Men: Bodybuilding Subculture and Gender Construction* (Albany: State University of New York Press, 1993). The fieldwork was carried out between 1979 and 1986. All names used in this study are fictitious.

2   Because they view themselves as serious athletes, bodybuilders frown on outsiders who suggest that bodybuilding competitions are like beauty contests (although they insist that the competition is artistic).

3   While there is no such thing as too much muscle in male bodybuilding, there is a concern with bodily proportion and symmetry (e.g., making one's chest in proportion to one's arms and waist).

4   The film's duel between Francis and Macliesh was somewhat artificial in that Francis did not actually place high enough on her own to warrant coming out for the final pose-down. Francis gained entry, after the filmmakers convinced the judges to allow her to pose down for the benefit of the film drama of large and small women.

5   One should distinguish between bodybuilding and building one's body. Bodybuilding is a subculture, a complete and internally consistent social world

which can articulate its member's needs and behavior to the larger culture of which it is a part. Building one's body is an individual act, only partially capable of being rationalized to the outside on positive terms by the subculture.

REFERENCES

Bartky, S. L. 1988. "Foucault, Femininity, and Modernization of Patriarchal Power." In *Feminism and Foucault: Reflections on Resistance,* ed. Irene Diamond and Lee Quinby. Boston: Northeastern University Press.

Bolin, A. 1992. "Vandalized Vanity." In *Tattoo, Torture, Adornment, and Disfigurement: The Denaturalization of the Body in Culture and Text,* ed. F. Mascia-Lees. Albany: State University of New York Press.

Bordo, S. 1988. "Anorexia Nervosa: Psychopathology as the Crystalization of Culture." In *Feminism and Foucault; Reflections On Resistance,* ed. Irene Diamond and Lee Quinby. Boston: Northeastern University Press.

———. 1990. "Reading the Slender Body." In *Body/Politics: Women and the Discourses of Science,* ed. M. Jacobus, Evelyn Fox Keller, and S. Shuttleworth. New York: Routledge.

Butts, D. 1975. *The Psychology of Sport.* New York: Van Nostrand.

Chernin, K. 1981. *The Obsession: Reflections on the Tyranny of Slimness.* New York: Harper and Row.

Coakley, J. 1989. *Sport in Society.* 4th ed. St. Louis: Moseby.

Crawford, R. 1985. "A Cultural Account of 'Health': Self-Control, Release, and the Social Body." In *Issues in the Political Economy of Health Care,* ed. J. McKinlay. New York: Methuen.

Foucault, M. 1979. *Discipline and Punish: The Birth of the Prison.* New York: Vintage.

Klein, A. M. 1985a. "Muscle Manor: The Use of Social Metaphor and History in Sport Sociology." *Journal of Sport and Social Issues* 9:4–19.

———. 1985b. "Pumping Iron." *Society* 22:68–74.

———. 1986. "Pumping Irony: Crisis and Contradiction in Bodybuilding." *Sport Sociology Journal* 3:112–133.

———. 1987. "Fear and Self-Loathing in Venice: Narcissism and Fascism in Bodybuilding." *Journal of Psychoanalytic Anthropology* 10:117–138.

———. 1988. "Juggling 'Deviance': Hustling and Gender Narcissism in Bodybuilding." *Deviant Behavior* 10:11–27.

———. 1990. "Little Big Men: Hustling and Gender Narcissism." In *Sport, Men, and the Gender Order,* ed. Don Sabo and Michael Messner. Champaign-Urbana, Ill.: Herman Kinetics Press.

———. 1993. *Little Big Men: Bodybuilding Subculture and Gender Construction.* Albany: State University of New York Press.

Lasch, C. 1979. *The Culture of Narcissism.* New York: Norton.

Orbach, S. 1982. *Fat Is a Feminist Issue.* New York: Berkley.

Pleck, J. 1982. *Myth of Masculinity.* Cambridge, Mass.: MIT Press.

NEGOTIATING MEANING

he three chapters that comprise Part II describe a special kind of "body talk" in which people evaluate themselves and each other with reference to a culturally defined ideal body that is thin/fat or young/old. As social beings we are always reassessing and renegotiating the body images of ourselves and others; the following three chapters emphasize the dynamic and interactive aspects of the body image as it is constantly redefined in accordance with changing circumstances.

In their research on adolescent girls in Arizona, Mimi Nichter and Nancy Vuckovic found that weight and body size are key reference points for teenagers to express how they feel about themselves and others. The authors show that "fat talk" is not idle talk but rather a linguistic measure of an adolescent girl's concern for self-control. According to this worldview, no girl should be satisfied with her own body. To be attractive and popular, a girl must work toward achieving the ideal of thinness. By talking about fatness and dieting, she demonstrates that she is concerned and thus above reproach. Actual dieting is not necessary and runs the risk of failure, whereas diet talk almost guarantees success. Talking about dieting shows that you do not feel superior to other girls, that you share their concerns about working on getting thin, and that you are one of the group.

The concern with thinness has also redefined moral behavior. A girl should never appear to be too hungry (piggish) or eat too much in front of a boy. For past generations the key feature for defining a girl's morality was her sexual behavior, demonstrating self-control by maintaining a virginal ideal. But here the emphasis is on demonstrating self-control through dieting to attain the cultural ideal of thinnesss.

The "fat talk" described by Nichter and Vuckovic is richly multi-vocal—a ritualized form of speech that serves to communicate mood and feelings, define status and role, call for support, or affirm group membership. The social context for each statement shapes its meaning. An adolescent girl can use fat talk to redefine her own body image, to test how others perceive her, or to affect the perception of others. Controlling one's body is a means for enhancing social relations, but it is control of the body image that is crucial. A girl's "body image talk" reflects the status of her social relationships, so her sense of group membership and popularity are shown in how she feels about her body. The following two chapters by Valerie Fennell and Elisa Sobo, as well as a later one in part 3 by Dixie King, also show connections among eating, body shape, and sexuality.

Multivocal meaning, as Fennell points out, is important to definitions of the aging body. In the small Southern town she studied, Fennell frequently heard men and women disparage aging, which they characterized in terms of slowing down, graying, and wrinkling. During her work with people of different ages, races, and class backgrounds, she found that the town residents had a set of characteristics they associated with old people based on a negative stereotype of body changes associated with aging; these characteristics contrasted with a positive image associated with young people and their youthful bodies. But when Fennell asked the townspeople to describe themselves and their friends, they resisted applying the stereotypes, emphasizing that they were still active and not yet "old." The more intimate their knowledge of a person, the less abstract age categories mattered. Instead the person's individual characteristics became important, and town residents defined each other in terms of who they were and what they did.

When townspeople did use age-based categories, these varied according to the context. The same person could be referred to as old on one day and young the next. People described themselves this way too. In judging a person, health and activity became more important than chronological age. One individual could be seen as old in some respects but youthful in others—the ideal being a combination of "mature" and "young" characteristics. Here we see a marked contrast between an abstract fixed-age category based on a number of years, and a flexible classification of individuals based on knowledge of personal behavior, capacities, and self-image. Fennell's analysis shows that the definition of body image is context- specific and that people use this flexibility to express a particular mood, refer to an event, or suggest a temporary appraisal of the person being discussed.

Sobo, in the last chapter in Part II, focuses on another kind of "body talk" in Jamaica, where fat rather than thin is the ideal for the healthy, attractive body. These people are compared to fruit that becomes plump as it ripens, full of juicy vitality. In Jamaica plumpness is a sign of reproductive ability and healthy kinship ties. A thin person is dry, without energy, weak, and unable to bear children. A thin person also fails to nurture others by fattening them with food. Terms denoting thinness label a person as stingy and antisocial, someone who hoards material goods rather than fulfilling kinship obligations to share and exchange with others. Just as people who love each other feed each other and grow fat, so a thin body bears witness to the unsociable character of the person.

This fat/thin contrast is used to evaluate the behavior of others and ascertain their character. A person labeled thin is on bad terms with others, either for refusing to share with kin or from worry about a disruption of kin ties. Like the other chapters, Sobo's essay confirms that the body image is linked to social relationships, though here the emphasis is on sociability through sharing food by eating together. Concern for a person is expressed as worrying about their body shape and size. The ideal is to be fat, so a person who is losing weight becomes a focus for concern that problems with kin have upset the person and caused him or her to wane in size. On the other hand, those who are thin and get rich and rise above others are viewed as antisocial, having used their resources for personal material gain rather than sharing to keep everyone fattened. People with strong, active kin networks should be fat, because their kin always provide, while a person who neglects kin networks in order to grow rich will become thin. Here *thin* is a pejorative term for a self-absorbed person. A thin body is interpreted as a sign of economic wealth based on money, whereas a fat body is a sign of social wealth based on people.

Sobo shows how body image is negotiated using a fat/thin model that is applied to both behavior and intent. People use "body talk" to evaluate others, manipulate them, and implicate their social relationships. The seemingly simple exclamation—"How thin you are getting!"—conveys very different meanings for people in Jamaica and the United States.

FAT TALK

Body Image among Adolescent Girls

MIMI NICHTER
and NANCY VUCKOVIC

Routinized forms of indirect speech are an important component of social exchange in many cultures. In a region of South India where one author worked, a common greeting was "Are your meals finished?" If the person responded "yes," the next question would be "What did you have?" (Nichter 1978). As her stay in the field area continued, it became clear that the greeting was not really about food at all. The meal was only a reference point; what was being indexed were events in an individual's home, life, or emotional feeling state. If a large meal with several dishes was described, it would indicate that something special had happened in the speaker's house that day; a small meal would indicate that it was an ordinary day. Discourse utilizing the idiom of food indirectly provided a great deal of information about one's family situation. It also gave permission for a playful interchange of small talk. Although the people involved were quite poor and there was little variety in their diets, responses to the question were varied, involving humor, exaggeration, and deception. Each response was an invitation for further talk.

In the United States, where food is abundant and diverse, weight is a reference point for conventionalized statements about the way people feel about themselves and events in their lives. Such statements may not reflect actual behavior, but rather index important personal and cultural concerns. The issue of weight also promotes ritual exchanges which serve multiple purposes in conversation.

One statement often heard in the United States, particularly among white, middle-class adolescent females, is "I'm so fat." During ethnographic interviews with adolescent girls about body image and dieting, we were struck with the commonality of the statement, particularly as it emerged in focus group discussions. In this chapter, cultural meanings of talk about weight, which we term *fat talk,* are discussed. Of particular note is the role fat talk plays in the negotiation of self and peer group interaction among adolescent females.

The present chapter represents a departure from many of the existing studies on adolescent weight control behavior. While literature on eating-disordered females has relied on case studies (e.g., Millman 1980; Orbach 1987), research on weight control among normal adolescent females has largely been behaviorally based, focusing on such issues as present dieting status, methods adopted to lose weight, and extent of bodily dissatisfaction (Casper and Offer 1990; Desmond et al. 1986; Greenfield et al. 1987; Rosen and Gross 1987). Despite reports of a "dieting epidemic" among adolescent females (Berg 1992), researchers have not given voice to those afflicted. Specifically, the meaning of weight control to adolescent females has not been explored from the perspective of their lived experience. Instead, girls have been asked to self-report their behavior into researcher-specified variables. An ethnographic approach allowed the researchers to explore the meaning of weight-related behaviors among this cohort rather than imposing meaning through survey questions. This chapter attempts to broaden the scope of weight-related studies by examining how adolescents' preoccupation with weight manifests itself in discourse.

Sample

This chapter reports on data collected by the Teen Lifestyle Project, a longitudinal project on body image, dieting, and smoking among adolescent females.[1] Ethnographic interviews were conducted with informants once during each school year. The pilot study population consisted of 60 girls in the eighth, tenth, and twelfth grades at two urban schools in the southwestern United States. The longitudinal study began in the fall of 1989 with a cohort of 300 girls in the eighth and ninth grades at four urban middle and high schools. Over the three years the cohort was followed, 47 girls left the study because they moved out of town, were unreachable, or declined participation because of increasing time commitments at school. The total number of girls who remained in the study at the end of the third year was 253. Attrition of the subjects, approximately 15 percent, was lower than anticipated.

Informants came from a range of lower- to upper-middle-class families. Seventy-three percent of the girls were Caucasian, 16 percent Hispanic, with the remaining 11 percent of the girls of Asian and African-American ethnicity. The majority of these girls were within normal height and weight ranges. The mean height and weight for the eighth grade cohort was 120 pounds, five feet, three inches, while the mean for the ninth grade cohort was 125 pounds, five feet, four inches.

Research Method

The project utilized anthropological research methods. Ethnographic interviews were generally conducted one on one, with a student spending approximately one hour talking with an interviewer. The format of the discussion was a structured, open-ended interview. In addition to individual interviews, some girls ($N = 74$) took part in focus-group interviews formed by the girls themselves and consisting of one or two interviewers and three to five informants.[2] The format of these interviews was likewise structured but open-ended. While individual interviews focused on perceived body image, dieting, and smoking behavior, focus-group interviews elicited generalized attitudes about these issues as well as about perceived group behaviors. Focus-group interviews proved an extremely important methodology for obtaining occurrences of interactional speech between informants (Labov 1972), including how weight control issues emerged in discourse among friends.

We first became aware of the prevalence of talk about feeling fat in response to a general question raised in focus-group interviews: "Do you think that a lot of girls your age are concerned about their weight?" Girls generally responded with head nods and laughs, which led us to ask, "How do you know that?" Girls then described how their friends complained about being fat and began to act out common conversations using the expression "I'm so fat." In order to investigate the commonality of fat talk more closely, we asked each informant during an individual interview, "Do you hear many girls saying 'I'm so fat'? What do you think it means when they say that?" The vast majority of girls acknowledged that they heard this expression used frequently.

In addition to ethnographic interviews, one survey, developed by project researchers, was administered each year to quantify subjects' report of dieting and smoking behaviors. The same instrument, with minor modifications, was administered during each year of the longitudinal phase.

Fat Talk: An Overview

The following excerpt from a focus-group discussion typifies the kind of exchange which occurs among adolescent females. The conversation took place between two fourteen-year-old girls in response to a question about the reasons for weight control.

JESSICA: I'm so fat.
TONI: Shut up, Jessica. You're not fat—you know how it makes you really mad when Brenda says she's fat?
JESSICA: Yeah.
TONI: It makes me really mad when you say that cuz it's not true.
JESSICA: Yeah, it is.
TONI: Don't say that you're fat. Don't you think we'd have said something to Brenda by now, if she, all the time said, "I'm so fat. I'm so fat." Don't you think we'd have said something by now. "Brenda, Brenda, I don't think you're overweight, I think you're chunky or whatever."
JESSICA: You wouldn't say that!
TONI: Well, we're best friends, Jessica, and I mean, she would rely on me to tell her something that was like, you know how people, like something's wrong with someone. You don't want to tell them but you do because you want to, you want . . . them . . . to help them, you know.

Females, and to a lesser degree males, engage in ritualized talk about their weight (Hope 1980). According to our informants, the dialogue above—the "I'm so fat" discourse—is frequently repeated during the course of a day. By the time a white middle-class female reaches adolescence, she has probably become a competent user of the discourse, whether or not she actually practices weight control.

Fat talk is multivocal. At times, the statement "I'm so fat" can be used as an idiom of distress (Nichter 1981; Swartz 1987), allowing a person to allude to widely diffuse feelings. Fat talk constitutes a final common pathway (Carr 1978) describing a wide range of feelings about uncontrol. The speaker does not have to be specific. Sometimes, when feeling bad, rather than saying "I'm so sad," a person may say "I'm so fat" to index that she is depressed. One informant remarked that among her family and friends, the saying "I'm having a fat day" indicated that things in general were not going well.

When examining the "I'm so fat" interchange, we find disparity between the message's inherent properties or meanings and its effects (Austin 1962). The statement "I'm so fat" is not just an observation about one's weight. It is a call for support from one's peers, for affirmation that one is in fact *not* fat. It can also act as an apology or excuse for behavior, or as an invitation to listeners to reaffirm group solidarity. The hearer uses contextual cues provided by the speaker and the situation to interpret the message so that it is understood in the manner in which it was intended by the speaker (Grice 1975). When "I'm so fat" is said in the girls' locker room, the impetus for the statement may come from the vulnerability of exposing one's body to the sight of others. Understanding this cultural cue, it is then appropriate for the listener to respond in a way that mitigates the speaker's discomfort. When the statement comes before eating, it provides an apology or excuse by the speaker for the indulgence at hand (in effect, a secular "grace" before eating).

A Call for Positive Strokes

During adolescence, there is an increased concern with emotional self-understanding and negotiation of status among one's peers. Not uncommonly, discussion among friends—"girl talk"—centers around the identification and negotiation of group norms (Eckert 1990). These discussions provide an opportunity for girls to influence or change group norms through disclosure of personal opinions or experience. At the same time, girl talk serves as a mechanism of social control by encouraging girls to measure themselves against the standards set by the group.

Another main goal of conversation during this developmental period becomes understanding the self in relation to others, with vulnerability in self-disclosure as one mechanism for achieving this goal (Gottman and Mettetal 1986). Saying "I'm so fat" performs the function of disclosing vulnerability and may give other girls the impression that one is "withholding nothing." Through the sharing of thoughts and feelings, friends increase each other's self-esteem, provide feedback, and help support one another (Sullivan 1953). Research on female adolescent development reports that girls are socialized to rely heavily on external acceptance and feedback to inform their identity (Steiner-Adair 1990).

Not uncommonly, a speaker says "I'm so fat" to a friend to evoke a positive response such as "Oh, no you're not." This response tells the initiator that her fears of fat are ungrounded, as the following comment illustrates: "People say 'Oh, I'm fat,' you know, and you're supposed to tell them 'Oh no, you're not.' It's just like something that people say." Our fourteen-year-old informants were well aware that this was an appropriate response:

> INTERVIEWER: What usually happens when someone says [I'm so fat]?
> JAMIE: About six or seven girls go "No you're not!" Probably it's just because, you know, you like to hear that people don't think you're fat. And it's mostly like in gym, cuz when you change into your gym clothes those are so bunchy anyway they make you look fat. And, uh, but I'd say, I'd say not very many of them mean that, mean it when they say it. They just want to hear "Oh no you're not."

It was generally agreed upon by our informants that girls who say "I'm so fat" are not significantly overweight and are not usually the girls who attempt to change their weight for sustained periods of time. Rather, for many girls, the motivation in saying "I'm so fat" is to gauge what other people think about them. As one informant noted, it makes you feel good about yourself when people say "No, you're not fat": "They're always like 'I'm so fat,' like that. Then I'm like, 'No, you're not.' 'Yes, I am.' Some people I know that say that are really skinny and they just wanna be, they just want people to say that they're skinny so that they'll feel better about themselves. I go 'No you're not,' but they keep on saying that so they can hear you saying that they're not fat." In response to one girl's discussion of feeling fat, an interviewer asked: "Do you tell your friends that you feel fat?" She replied: "Yeah, and they sit there going 'No you're not,' but I don't know really if they're telling me the truth. I really would like to know. Even if I say 'Tell me the honest to God truth,' they'll probably say 'No, you're not.' And they're probably saying 'Yes, you are,' but I don't really know that but I would like to."

Some of our informants noted that girls who were significantly overweight would not say "I'm so fat" as that would call attention to their problem. It is also inappropriate for another to call attention to their fatness. Similarly, in a discussion of survey results collected from junior high school students, Ogaitis et al. (1988) note that given the option of "talking with a friend about eating concerns," only a few of those students who actually were over- or underweight expressed interest in doing so. Girls who felt they were overweight (but were normal weight) were more likely to want to talk about such concerns than girls who actually were overweight.

There seem to be tacit cultural sanctions at play which prevent females from commenting on another's overweight or recent weight gain. Although we find discourse about weight loss and thinness, we do not find corresponding discussion among women about another's weight gain or overweight. The presence and conspicuous absence of certain phrases in everyday conversation provide examples of how these sanctions operate. A statement such as "Gee you look great. Have you lost weight?" is generally welcomed as a compliment. Yet few women would approach another female—even a close friend—with the comment "You look like you've gained some weight."

Absolving Oneself of Guilt

Another time "I'm so fat" is said is at the beginning of a meal, particularly before eating calorie-laden food or enjoying a buffet-style meal where an individual is faced with making public food choices. Stating that *you know* you are already fat is an admission that you know you shouldn't be eating, that you know you should be on a diet. It is a public presentation of responsibility and concern for one's appearance (Hope 1980). The admission of a little guilt forestalls further scrutiny (Barthes 1973) and frees the speaker to do as she pleases. This statement also puts her in control of the situation. She has announced that she knows the true state of her body and has therefore precluded anyone else from telling her.

Marker of Group Affiliation

"I'm so fat" is sometimes used as a marker of group affiliation. As one girl noted, "Sometimes I think girls just say it to fit in with the group. One person will start saying it [I'm so fat] and everyone will say 'God, I am too!' " Several researchers have noted the importance of crowd or group affiliation across adolescence (Brown et al. 1986; Dunphy 1972). Group identification is a central developmental task of early adolescence, with a more autonomous sense of identity achieved in late adolescence.

Group fat talk offers the opportunity for all group members to obtain affirmation that they look good. It becomes a way for group members to share positive strokes as well as to build group solidarity. For example, one girl noted, "I don't know, like somebody will make a comment in the like girls' locker room or something and everybody like adds 'Oh my god, look at these legs of mine' or something, you know. 'You think you're fat! Look at me!' It's fun though. I mean, it's not really fun, but . . . You get input on what everybody else thinks.

One informant explained that even though she didn't really think she was too fat, she felt she had to say it when she was with her friends. In fact, she was fed up with fat talk and diet talk but knew that if she did not acknowledge that she shared those feelings, she would separate herself from the group by implying that she was perfect. In other words, saying that she didn't diet would be an admission that she didn't need to work on herself—that she was satisfied. To be satisfied with one's appearance displaces the goal of working toward the perfect future. As she explained, "I was talking to my friends, and they wanted to lose weight even though they weren't really fat. They just wanted to be the perfect weight."

With a high degree of agreement, our informants described the perfect girl as between one hundred and one hundred ten pounds with a height of five feet, seven inches.[3] Ethnographic interviews revealed that among many of our teen informants, the right weight was perceived as a ticket to the perfect life. Words such as *perfect* have the power to evoke an entire framed scenario (Fillmore 1977; Quinn 1982). Thus, the girl with the perfect body who can "eat and eat and eat and not gain anything" is described as being "perfect in every way." By extension, the girl with the perfect body has a perfect life: she gets the boy of every girl's dreams. One informant stated: "Most girls buy *Seventeen* magazine and see all the models and they're really, really skinny, and they see all these girls in real life that look like that. They have the cutest guy in the school and they seem to have life so perfect." The perfect girl provokes jealousy, sometimes to the point that girls feel their own efforts are futile: "You just see all these older girls, like when you go to the mall, and there's like, it's like, 'why was I born?' because they're so perfect."

Despite the desire to be perfect, a female who is extremely attractive may find herself shunned by her female peers. Some informants noted that when they saw a beautiful girl at school, in the mall, or even on television, they would label her a bitch. Since the perfect girl's flaw is not visible, it is assumed to exist in her personality. One girl remarked: "If a girl is really pretty, then I want to see her flaw. All of it—all of it. I want to know every single part of her flaw (laughs)." Not uncommonly, girls would decide that they hated this girl, despite the fact that they didn't know her. Some girls remarked, "I want to hurt her" or "I feel like killing her." Spiteful comments afford the speaker a feeling of superiority at a time when she may be experiencing the opposite emotion.

While the statements above describe interactions among strangers, some slender adolescents in our study spoke of similar though less malicious experiences involving acquaintances. These girls described how their friends practically "accused" them of being thin, "as if it were my fault or something." One ninth grader thought that girls reacted to her in this way due to jealousy. Other girls felt that comments about their thinness implied that they had an eating disorder.

> VANESSA: Brandy and I were talking one day about when you say "Oh, you're so skinny." How do you think that makes someone feel? Good or bad?
> ERIN: I think it would make me feel totally happy.
> VANESSA: It makes me feel bad. "Oh you're so skinny." What is that supposed to mean, you know? Do I have a problem? I don't know, it just makes me feel uncomfortable.

The ambiguity of the message "you're so thin" caused some girls to complain that they didn't like to hear it. Even when it was meant as a compliment, it was difficult to accept as that, for to do so would be to indicate satisfaction with one's self. Denial becomes the appropriate counter to the compliment.

From a clinical standpoint, if so many girls are talking about being fat, what is the potential impact on girls who are at risk for eating disorders? Girls who are anorexic and bulimic also participate in this discourse but may mean it literally. When friends respond "No you're not" to their complaints of being fat, these responses may not be believed. For distressed girls, the impact of fat talk may not be transient. Indeed, this discourse pattern may serve to normalize and legitimize a position that is potentially dangerous.

Misuse of Fat Talk

While one needs to be involved with the "I'm so fat" discourse in order to maintain group affiliation, a majority of informants emphasized that it is important not to overuse it. To continually complain about body dissatisfaction is to provoke the anger of your friends. Several informants described girlfriends whose constant body complaints led them to respond that they indeed were too fat. They noted, "When she says 'I'm so fat' we just say 'yeah, you are' to shut her up." Another informant described her strategy for dealing with what she perceived to be an annoying situation: "I think they just say it so they can hear other girls say 'Oh no you're not, you're skinny.' It kind of makes me mad. My friend in eighth grade said that every day, so when she'd say it I'd just say 'Oh.' She'd get mad and say, 'Well aren't you going to say something?' She stopped doing it. She just wanted attention. Now I just look at people when they say it." Other girls noted:

> Even the thin people, they'll walk around saying "I'm so fat." I just want to hit them on the head. Maybe their idea of gaining weight is like one or two pounds and they like weigh one hundred. I just want to say "Shut up, you don't even know what being fat is."

> It annoys me. Because a lot of them are like totally skinny. They're like perfect. And they're like, "Oh, look at my butt. It's like cheese." And that's really annoying because they know they're not fat. They just want to get the attention. They want to hear they're not fat. Like from other people. So that annoys me really.

Teens: A Homogenous Group?

We have been discussing adolescent girls as if they belong to a singular, homogenous group, but from observational and interview data we learned that girls tend to cluster into particular social groups. Group membership is particularly salient during adolescence due to its perceived ability to facilitate friendships and social interaction as well as provide emotional support (Brown 1990). We wanted to assess to what extent social-group affiliation influenced girls' desire to be thin and their use of fat talk. Specifically, did those girls who considered themselves "stoners" or "mods" adopt similar discourse patterns to girls who were "preps"?[4] Through their dress, stoner and mod girls seemed to adopt counterculture values. Did these girls also reject mainstream notions of preferred body size, resulting in less fat talk?

Through ethnographic interviews with girls from a variety of social groups, we found that among white middle-class adolescents, desire for thinness crosscut social groups. One self-identified stoner informant was asked whether she thought there was pressure among girls in her group to be thin. She noted:

STACY: There's pressure to be thin in all groups. I think with stoners it's not as bad, but it's still there.
INTERVIEWER: Stoners seem to be against other things—like adopting dress that preps are wearing. So why do you think the importance of being thin still holds?
STACY: Everyone loves to be thin (laughs). Every girl wants to be thin. Well, the guys are still after thin girls.

Another girl, who considered herself a mod, commented: "The mod chicks and the punker girls that I know, they all, I think it's the same with every girl. Cuz all my friends, no matter how skinny they are think they are fat. And no matter what they are, they think they're fat, even if they're not. I think everyone wants to be attractive."

Who Are They Doing It For?

Why is fat talk such a salient discourse strategy among adolescent females? In this section we ask for whom they are doing it and suggest that fat talk and dissatisfaction with weight are a result of several factors, including social comparison with other girls, a desire to be popular with boys, and media and family influences.

Teenage girls exist in a highly interactional environment in which comparison to other girls is commonplace. Early adolescent thinking has been characterized as excessively concerned with physical appearance, bodily changes, and personal behavior. Cognitive developmentalists such as Elkind (1967) have described how an adolescent believes that *others* are even more preoccupied with his or her appearance and behavior than he or she is. Elkind notes: "The adolescent takes the other person's point of view to an extreme degree. He is so concerned with the point of view of others and how they regard him that he often loses sight of his own point of view" (1967:153). From Elkind's perspective the adolescent, especially in early adolescence, is always on stage, viewing himself or herself as the main actor, with peers as an imaginary audience. This concept of adolescent egocentrism may help explain the importance of peers during adolescence. Research findings reported by Pesce and Harding (1986) reveal that such perceptions are more common among girls than boys.

Researchers have noted that in contrast to males, for whom identity development is the outcome of increasing experience of separation and autonomy, the female personality develops through attachment and relation to others (Chodorow 1978; Gilligan 1982). While feminists have argued that gender differences are socially constructed, research has found that girls are more social in their orientation than boys (Berndt 1982; Blyth et al. 1982; Fischer and Naurus 1981). In a series of time studies (Richards and Larson 1989), girls were found to be more social than boys before adolescence and became even more social with adolescence. Girls spend more time talking than boys, more time grooming in front of friends (Duckett et al. 1989), and more time doing homework in the company of friends (Leone and Richards 1989).

Intimacy, emotional closeness, and trust are more characteristic of girls' rather than boys' relationships at all ages (Youniss 1980). Through interactions with friends, social skills such as the ability to empathize with and understand the point of view of others are learned and practiced (Rubin 1980). This social orientation is also reflected in girls' greater concern for physical appearance. Girls are taught from an early age that attractiveness is an intrinsic part of pleasing and serving others and, in turn, of securing love (Brownmiller 1984; Striegel-Moore et al. 1986). Exploring the impact of cultural standards on adolescent girls and boys, Wooley and Wooley (1984) found that girls are more influenced by and therefore more vulnerable to mandated cultural standards of the ideal body.

Clearly, social comparison with regard to body size is important for females. Streigel-Moore et al. found that college-age informants engaged in frequent comparisons between their own bodies and those of other women, "as if they needed to check where they stood" (1986:945). One adolescent informant in our study stated, "People just compare themselves to popular people who are really skinny. You just look at other girls and wish you were like them."

To assess how important girls considered thinness with regard to friendship with other girls, we asked informants to agree or disagree with the statement "A girl has to be thin to be popular with other girls." Survey responses among eighth and ninth graders indicate that for the large majority of girls (85 percent, $N = 241$), thinness is not considered a prerequisite for friendships with other girls. In a focus-group interview, however, two girls described how being thin was an important factor for membership in the highly desirable "popular group":

> I think that for people that are socially active, that go to a lot of parties and see a lot of other people from other schools, you know, it is important. I don't think that a lot of, like really overweight people feel comfortable at a party, you know, because of first impressions. People *do* look at your weight. They do notice that. I guess if you're more socially active, you'd feel more comfortable being, being at a decent weight.

Boys' Influence on Girls' Discourse

In interviews, we asked girls why they thought talk about being fat emerged so commonly in discussions with their friends. One obvious reason adolescent girls believe it is important to be thin is to attract boys. To assess the perceived importance of thinness in relation to boys, we asked our eighth- and ninth-grade informants to respond on the survey to the following statement: "A girl has to be thin to be popular with boys." Almost half of our informants (44 percent) believed that boys preferred girls who were thin and that a girl would have difficulty being popular with boys unless she were thin. The remaining 56 percent disagreed that thinness was a requirement for popularity with boys.

Some informants overtly complained about how fat they were in front of boys to obtain a contradictory response from them. One girl explained this behavior: "Sometimes you need a guy to tell you, like, it sounds better when a guy tells you you're skinny than when a girl does, you know what I mean? Cuz you're not trying to look skinny for girls. You're doing it for yourself and for guys."

The desire to be thin to please boys sometimes resulted in changes in food consumption patterns in the presence of boys. While such patterns have been documented among adult women, our findings show that these patterns are socialized early in adolescence. Eighth-grade girls in our study described how they would eat "just a few fries or a bite from a salad" if they were with boys, so as not to appear "piggish." They explained that boys didn't like to see girls eat a lot of food, that it was somehow unfeminine for girls to do so. Boys, on the other hand, were described as "inhaling" food whenever possible (Nichter and Nichter 1991).

Influence of the Media

Another powerful influence on girls' perception of self is the media and the role models presented therein (Nichter and Nichter 1991). Television programs present slender women as the dominant image of popularity, success, and happiness (Aldebaran 1975; Collins 1988; Garner et al. 1980; Horvath 1979, 1981). Other sources of this image are the approximately four hundred to six hundred advertisements we are exposed to daily. Downs and Harrison (1985) estimate that one in every eleven commercials includes a direct message about beauty. These messages are almost exclusively directed toward women. Similar messages are disseminated to adolescent girls in the guise of self-improvement features found in "teenzines." Both articles and advertisements in these publications convey the message that "the road to happiness is attracting males . . . by way of physical beautification" (Evans et al. 1991:110). We asked girls if they thought the media affected their self-image. One girl responded with regard to magazines: "On the front cover they always say 'How to lose weight, how to look skinnier.' I think that's good because they give you tips on how you can manage your weight and lose it. But it's also bad because then it's like 'Am I fat?' And then I start saying, 'Hmm, maybe I can lose weight.' "

Mothers and Daughters

In addition to pressures from sources outside the home, ethnographic data indicate that girls are significantly influenced by familial dieting behavior, particularly that of the mother. Over 30 percent of the girls questioned in the Teen Lifestyle Project survey reported that they had been told by their mothers that they needed to lose weight, although less than 5 percent of those girls were clinically overweight. It is likely that a mother's advice reflects her own concern about weight control. While 59 percent of our informants described their mothers' weight as "just about right," 68 percent reported that their mothers were commonly dieting. Some girls noted that when their mothers began a diet, they would also have to diet. An eighth-grade girl explained, "Well, me and my mom are like, both built the same way, so if she gets fat that means I have to go on a diet." With regard to fat talk, some girls reported that they said "I'm so fat" to their mothers and that their mothers also used the phrase.

Weight Watching: Myth or Reality?

Through ethnographic research, we have found that discourse and action about dieting are as multivocal as those about feeling fat. Saying you are on a diet indexes an intention of gaining control over your environment. Among our adolescent informants, the need for control or the ability to control is often short-lived. We have found that the same girls who "talk fat" often do not engage in sustained weight-reducing action:

> Well, I mean, everybody thinks they're fat. Well not everybody, but, you know, most people, I guess, well, I mean, I don't know. If you see people your age that look skinny but weigh more than you, you know, it feels good, right? But sometimes I'll think I, I'm fat or something. After usually I get weighed. You know, but, I never really do anything about it. I just say "I'm going on a diet" you know?

Despite some girls' statements that diets are more a matter of intention than action, national survey results continue to show high rates of dieting behavior among adolescent girls. As part of the Teen Lifestyle Project annual survey, girls were asked, "Are you trying to change your weight now?" Responses indicate that on the day of the survey, 44 percent of the girls were trying to lose weight while 51 percent were *not* trying. The remaining 5 percent were trying to gain weight.

While our survey results seemed to substantiate the commonality of dieting among adolescents and the similarity of our sample to a much larger national sample ('Body-Weight Perceptions' 1991), we emphasize that survey data taken alone can be misleading. Three important questions need to be clarified: What do teenagers mean when they say they are dieting? What behaviors and practices are associated with dieting? What is the duration of a teenager's diet? These kinds of questions are generally not included in self-report surveys (Nichter et al. 1993).

In interviews, we asked girls to define what it meant to go on a diet. Responses ranged from "eating right" (i.e., eating "good" food as opposed to "junk" foods) to "just eating salads" or "cutting down on what you eat" to "Jane Fonda every day." As one eighth grader noted: "Dieting—well it's like eating the right foods or like not eating anything—like between those two." As these responses indicate, concepts of dieting are varied and loosely defined.

An important finding which emerged from interviews was that diets among teenagers were extremely short-lived. Some girls said a diet just lasted a few hours—from breakfast until lunch, when temptation in the cafeteria or boredom would compel them to have something to eat:

> INTERVIEWER: Do you ever diet with your friends?
> SANDY: Yeah, but it didn't work. I was dieting with my friend Sheila, and like, I'd say I wouldn't but then like a few hours later I'd eat like a candy bar or something.

To others, dieting meant eating a candy bar with a diet Coke and then skipping meals. Still others talked about dieting as a social ritual, an almost amusing pastime to engage in with friends: "Well, we both thought we were fat, so we thought we would go on a diet together. And we kept saying, 'Oh, we'll do it tomorrow,' and the next day, 'Oh, we'll do it tomorrow.' And it kept going on and finally we did but then we just ate whatever we wanted." Others drew on the resources available to them from mothers and older sisters:

> MELANIE: We like, we like would be over at her house and we went, we went through *all* the diet books and um all of the magazine articles and everything, and we like planned out what we would eat a day. What we would eat every day, and how many calories they had and what, what exercises we'd do. And everything. That didn't last for too long (laughs). That lasted about a week.
> INTERVIEWER: Is that because you got bored with it or just
> MELANIE: We just, Amy started. Amy went off it at lunch, and so I'd be like, "ok, well she's off then I will," and I ate this huge old dinner.

A few girls who had more serious weight problems spoke of counting calories or joining weight loss programs with the support of their parents.

Some girls said they never actually went on a diet but controlled their weight by watching what they ate each day (Nichter et al. 1993). As one girl explained, "If you consider it a diet, then you're in trouble because then you'll *have to* lose weight. If you don't lose weight, then, you know, you realize you've failed." For this informant and for many others who shared her thinking, to define or label how she was going to eat was to establish expectations and be faced with potential failure. Furthermore, if she didn't say she was dieting, a little cheating would be no big thing.

Survey questions on dieting behavior among teenagers which ask girls to self-report their behavior into researcher-specified categories may lead to misreporting. To date, data on adolescent dieting behavior have been obtained from cross-sectional surveys in which behaviors are assessed generally without attention to issues of intensity and duration. Among adolescents, labels may misrepresent habitual behavior. Being a dieter may represent a range of behaviors, and thus cross-sectional surveys may mask the variety of behaviors which can occur under the same label.[5]

Questionnaires not grounded in preliminary ethnographic research may impose categories not culturally appropriate for a teenage population. Taking into account the variety of meanings and durational differences noted among respondents, what do survey data reveal? When adolescent girls say they are dieting, do they mean they start a diet in the morning that lasts until noon? Do they overreport dieting because they feel they *should* be on a diet? Do they underreport because they don't call their restrictive eating a diet for fear of failure?

Attention to the details of language may facilitate the creation of survey questions. For example, after identifying the category of "watching what one ate" as distinct from "dieting to lose weight," we included several survey questions to quantify this phenomenon and the behaviors associated with it. Results revealed that a significant number of girls classified themselves as "watchers" as opposed to "dieters" (Nichter et al. 1993). Further study of the relationship betweeen data and ethnographic records is important to the validation of both methodologies. Sociolinguistic and semantic theories may provide useful tools in studying the meanings that can be derived from either method of culture study.

What is important to consider with regard to survey data is not merely the number of girls purporting to be dieting, but what is indexed by talk of dieting. As we have demonstrated, for many girls, talking about body dissatisfaction and the need to lose weight is a strategy for improving one's social position. It provides a plan of action toward a more perfect life. From one girl's perspective, "If I was thin, I'd be totally happy."

Discussion

Our society encourages engagement in body work—directed effort to improve the body in an attempt to achieve perfection. Improving one's body no longer means simply losing weight. Adolescent girls discussed their desire to develop a toned physique with a hint of muscle definition. The imperative to maintain a thin, toned body is not merely a matter of aesthetics. Bound into the image are expectations and hopes for acceptance and a deeply embodied cultural model which reflects a "taken-for-granted social world" in which events and relations take place in a simplified, prototypic manner (D'Andrade 1987; Holland and Skinner 1987; Quinn and Holland 1987). Within this world, thin females are popular, desirable, and successful. Conversely, overweight females are ostracized and expected to have less satisfying personal lives than their thinner counterparts (Dion et al. 1972; Seid 1988). Previous research (Vuckovic-Moore 1990) has revealed that a cultural model exists which equates weight control with morality. Within this model, "good" behavior leads to thinness, while "bad" behavior results in overweight.

It is apparent that adolescent girls and women are "worshipping at the shrine of slimness" (Brumberg 1988:257). The discourse we are hearing among teenage girls shows evidence of ritual talk about weight and a rhetoric indicative of a cultural mandate for weight control. Under such a mandate, even if a girl is not actually working on herself, she must at least talk about it. Talking about weight control in itself constitutes action as it serves to create and project an image of self. By engaging in fat talk, females present themselves to others as responsible beings concerned about their appearance. As noted by Rodin et al. (1985), our culture promotes an extremely thin female beauty ideal and thus creates a normative discontent with weight. The woman who experiences herself as dissatisfied with her weight resembles rather than deviates from her peers.

Our examination has stressed the need to look not only at reports of weight-related behavior (as previous research has done), but at the speech which accompanies or replaces such behavior. Discourse about weight may be particularly prevalent during adolescence, when concern about appearance is high, but appetite, social settings, and parental presence may preclude other actions. The litany of weight-related discourse and its importance in peer-group social activity indicate that adolescent girls are greatly concerned about body size. Irrespective of what action girls are taking to achieve their body goals, they are attempting to reproduce the cultural ideal through their discourse.

NOTES

1   Research for this chapter was conducted within a larger study of adolescent behavior, Food Intake, Smoking, and Diet among Adolescent Girls, funded by the National Institute of Child Health and Human Development, grant number HD24737.

2   Focus-group interviewing is a methodology that involves talking to several people at a time about a particular topic. Through experience we learned that focus groups which disregarded social networks did not function effectively because girls were reluctant to express their opinions in front of others they did not consider their friends. To assure more open discussions, we asked girls to form a

group of friends with whom they would feel comfortable discussing issues about body image and dieting. During the focus-group interviews these topics were discussed generally and not specifically in regard to individual behaviors.

3   The ideal girl was also described as having a good figure, long blonde hair, and big blue eyes. To many girls the ideal girl is a living manifestation of the Barbie doll. According to Susan Brownmiller, the ideal girl exhibits the characteristics of fairy princess: "Who can imagine a fairy princess with hair that is anything but long and blonde, with eyes that are anything but blue. . . . The fairy princess remains one of the most powerful visual symbols of femininity the Western world has ever devised, and falling short of her role model, women are all feminine failures to some degree" (1984:67).

4   Preps are characterized as very involved in school activities and often come from wealthier families. Their style of dress, hair, and makeup follows the latest mainstream fashion dictates. Jocks are the more athletically oriented preps. Stoners are characterized as indifferent toward school and as smokers and users of drugs. Their wardrobe revolves around jeans and t-shirts advertising heavy metal rock bands. Mods are another fringe group, often students involved in the arts. Their style tends to be an amalgam of fashion from previous eras.

5   The fact that the same label can identify a variety of behaviors came to our attention when analyzing smoking behavior. Girls who smoked as few as two or three cigarettes a week sometimes referred to themselves as smokers, whereas some girls who smoked more frequently thought of themselves as nonsmokers.

REFERENCES

Alderbaran, V. 1975. "Uptight and Hungry: The Contradiction in Psychology of Fat." *Journal of Radical Therapy* 5:5–6.

Austin, J. 1962. *How to Do Things with Words.* Cambridge: Harvard University Press.

Barthes, R. 1973. *Mythologies.* Trans. A. Davis. London: Paladin.

Berg, F. 1992. "Harmful Weight Loss Practices Are Widespread among Adolescents." *Obesity and Health,* July/August, pp. 69–72.

Berndt, T. 1982. "The Features and Effects of Friendship in Early Adolescence." *Child Development* 53:1447–1460.

Blyth, D., J. Hill, and K. Thiel. 1982. "Early Adolescents' Significant Others: Grade and Gender Differences in Perceived Relationships with Familial and Non-Familial Adults and Young People." *Journal of Youth and Adolescence* 11:425–450.

"Body-Weight Perceptions and Selected Weight-Management Goals and Practices of High School Students—United States, 1990." 1991. *Mortality and Morbidity Weekly Report* 40:741–750.

Brown, B. B. 1990. "Peer Groups and Peer Cultures." In *At the Threshold: The Developing Adolescent,* ed. S. S. Feldman and Glen R. Elliot, pp. 171–196. Cambridge: Harvard University Press.

Brown, B. B., S. A. Eicher, and S. Petrie. 1986. "The Importance of Peer Group ('Crowd') Affiliation in Adolescence." *Journal of Adolescence* 9:73–96.

Brownmiller, S. 1984. *Femininity.* New York: Linden Press/Simon and Schuster.

Brumberg, J. J. 1988. *Fasting Girls.* Cambridge: Harvard University Press.

Carr, J. E. 1978. "Ethno-Behaviorism and the Culture-Bound Syndromes: The Case of Amok." *Culture, Medicine and Psychiatry* 2:269–293.

Casper, R., and D. Offer. 1990. "Weight and Dieting Concerns in Adolescents: Fashion or Symptom?" *Pediatrics*, September, pp. 384–390.

Chodorow, N. 1978. *The Reproduction of Mothering.* Berkeley: University of California Press.

Collins, M. E. 1988. "Education for Healthy Body Weight: Helping Adolescents Balance the Cultural Pressure for Thinness." *Journal of School Health* 58(6):227–231.

D'Andrade, R. G. 1987. "A Folk Model of the Mind." In *Cultural Models in Language and Thought*, ed. D. Holland and N. Quinn, pp. 112–148. New York: Cambridge University Press.

Desmond, S., J. Price, N. Gray, and J. O'Connell. 1986. "The Etiology of Adolescents' Perceptions of Their Weight." *Journal of Youth and Adolescence* 15(6):461–474.

Dion, K., E. Berscheid, and E. Walster. 1972. "What Is Beautiful Is Good." *Journal of Personality and Social Psychology* 24:285–290.

Downs, C., and S. Harrison. 1985. "Embarrassing Age Spots or Just Plain Ugly? Physical Attractiveness Stereotyping as an Instrument of Sexism on American Television Commercials." *Sex Roles* 13:9–19.

Duckett, E., M. Raffaelli, and M. Richards. 1989. " 'Taking Care': Maintaining the Self and the Home in Early Adolescence." *Journal of Youth and Adolescence* 18(6):549–564.

Dunphy, D. C. 1972. "Peer Group Socialization." In *Socialization in Australia*, ed. F. J. Hunt. Sydney: Angus and Robertson.

Eckert, Penelope. 1990. "Cooperative Competition in Adolescent 'Girl Talk.' " *Discourse Processes* 13:91–122.

Elkind, D. 1967. "Egocentrism in Adolescents." *Child Development* 38:1025–1034.

Evans, E. D., J. Rutber, C. Sather, and C. Turner. 1991. "Content Analysis of Contemporary Teen Magazines for Adolescent Females." *Youth and Society* 23(1):99–120.

Fillmore, Charles. 1977. "Frame Semantics and the Nature of Language." In *Origin and Evolution of Language and Speech*, ed. S. Harnad, H. Stecklis, and J. Lancaster. New York: New York Academy of Science.

Fischer, J., and L. Narus. 1981. "Sex Roles and Intimacy in Relationships." *Psychology of Women Quarterly* 5:164–169.

Garner, D., P. Garfinkel, D. Schwartz, and M. Thompson. 1980. "Cultural Expectations of Thinness in Women." *Psychological Reports* 47:483–491.

Gilligan, Carol. 1982. *In a Different Voice: Psychological Theory and Women's Development.* Cambridge: Harvard University Press.

Gottman, J., and G. Mettetal. 1986. "Speculations about Social and Affective Development: Friendship and Acquaintanceship through Adolescence." In *Conversations of Friends*, ed. J. Gottman and J. Parker, pp. 192–240. Cambridge: Cambridge University Press.

Greenfield, D., D. M. Quinlan, P. Harding, E. Glass, and A. Bliss. 1987. "Eating Behavior in an Adolescent Population." *International Journal of Eating Disorders* 6(1):99–111.

Grice, H. 1975. "Logic and Conversation." In *Syntax and Semantics 3: Speech Acts*, ed. P. Cole and J. Morgan, pp. 41–58. London: Academic Press.

Holland, Dorothy, and Deborah Skinner. 1987. "Prestige and Intimacy: The Cultural Models Behind Americans' Talk about Gender Types." In *Cultural Models in Language and Thought*, ed. D. Holland and N. Quinn, pp. 78–111. New York: Cambridge University Press.

Hope, C. 1980. "American Beauty Rituals." In *Rituals and Ceremonies in Popular Culture*, ed. R. B. Browne, pp. 226–237. Bowling Green, Ohio: Bowling Green University Press.

Horvath, T. 1979. "Correlates of Physical Beauty in Men and Women." *Social Behavior and Personality* 7:145–151.

Labov, W. 1972. *Language in the Inner City*. Philadelphia: University of Pennsylvania Press.

Leone, C. M., and M. H. Richards. 1989. "Classwork and Homework in Early Adolescence: The Ecology of Achievement." *Journal of Youth and Adolescence* 18(6):531–548.

Millman, Marcia. 1980. *Such a Pretty Face*. New York: W. W. Norton.

Nichter, Mark. 1981. "Idioms of Distress: Alternatives in the Expression of Psychosocial Distress: A Case Study from South India." *Culture, Medicine and Psychiatry* 5:379–408.

Nichter, Mark, and Mimi Nichter. 1991. "Hype and Weight." *Medical Anthropology* 13:249–284.

Nichter, Mimi. 1978. Anthropological fieldwork. South Kanara District, Karnataka, India.

Nichter, Mimi, Cheryl Ritenbaugh, Mark Nichter, Nancy Vuckovic, and Mikel Aickin. 1993. "Weight Control Behavior among Adolescent Females: Report of a Multimethod Study." Typescript.

Ogaitis, S., T. T. Chen, and G. P. Cernada. 1988. "Eating Attitudes, Dieting and Bulimia among Junior High School Students." *International Quarterly of Community Health Education* 9(1):51–61.

Orbach, Susie. 1987 "Anorexia and Adolescence." In *Fed Up and Hungry*, ed. Marilyn Lawrence, pp. 74–85. New York: Peter Bedrick Books.

Pesce, R., and C. Harding. 1986. "Imaginary Audience Behavior and Its Relationship to Operational Thought and Social Experience." *Journal of Early Adolescence* 6:83–94.

Quinn, Naomi. 1982. " 'Commitment' in American Marriage: A Cultural Analysis." *American Ethnologist* 3:775–798.

Quinn, Naomi, and Dorothy Holland. 1987. "Culture and Cognition." In *Cognitive Models in Language and Thought*, ed. D. Holland and N. Quinn, pp. 3–40. New York: Cambridge University Press.

Richards, M. H., and R. Larson. 1989. "The Life Space and Socialization of the Self: Sex Differences in the Young Adolescent." *Journal of Youth and Adolescence* 18(6):617–626.

Rodin, J., L. Silberstein, and R. Striegel-Moore. 1885. "Women and Weight: A Normative Discontent." In *Psychology and Gender: Nebraska Symposium on Motivation, 1984, ed.* T. B. Sonderegger. Lincoln: University of Nebraska Press.

Rosen, J., and J. Gross. 1987. "The Prevalence of Weight Reducing and Weight Gaining in Adolescent Boys and Girls." *Health Psychology* 6:131–147.

Rubin, Z. 1980. *Children's Friendships*. Cambridge: Harvard University Press.

Seid, R. P. 1988. *Never Too Thin: Why Women Are at War with Their Bodies*. New York: Prentice-Hall.

Steiner-Adair, Catherine. 1990. "The Body Politic: Normal Female Adolescent Development and the Development of Eating Disorders." In *Making Connections: The Relational Worlds of Adolescent Girls at Emma Willard School*, ed. Carol Gilligan, Nona P. Lyons, and Trudy J. Hanmer, pp. 162–182. Cambridge: Harvard University Press.

Striegel-Moore, R., L. Silberstein, and J. Rodin. 1986. "Toward an Understanding of Risk Factors for Bulimia." *American Psychologist* 41:246–263.

Sullivan, H. 1953. *The Interpersonal Theory of Psychiatry.* New York: W. W. Norton.

Swartz, Leslie 1987. "Illness Negotiation: The Case of Eating Disorders." *Social Science and Medicine* 24(7):613–618.

Vuckovic-Moore, Nancy. 1990. "Things That Are Good and Things That Are Chocolate: A Cultural Model of Weight Control as Morality." M.A. thesis, University of Arizona.

Wooley, W., and S. Wooley. 1984. "Feeling Fat in a Thin Society: Women Tell How They Feel about Their Bodies." *Glamour Magazine*, February, pp. 198–252.

Youniss, J. 1980. *Parents and Peers in Social Development.* Chicago: University of Chicago Press.

Youth Risk Behavior Survey, Center for Disease Control. 1991. *Journal of the American Medical Association*, November 27, pp. 2811–2812.

THE SWEETNESS OF FAT

Health, Procreation, and Sociability in Rural Jamaica

ELISA J. SOBO

I n the United States there is a well-known saying that you can't be too rich or too thin, but in rural Jamaica, amassing wealth and keeping slim have antisocial connotations. Ideally, relatives provide for each other, sharing money and food. Because kin share wealth, no one gets rich; because kin feed each other, no one becomes thin. Cultural logic has it that people firmly tied into a network of kin are always plump and never wealthy.

Especially when not well liked, thin individuals who are neither sick nor poor are seen by their fellow villagers as antisocial and *mean* or stingy.[1] These individuals do not create and maintain relationships through gift-giving and exchange. They hoard rather than share their resources. Their slender bodies bespeak their socially subversive natures: thinness indicates a lack of nurturant characteristics and of moist, procreative vitality—things on which a community's reproduction depends.

Rural Jamaicans' negative ideas about thinness are linked with their ideas about health. As Sheets-Johnstone points out, "The concept of the body in any culture and at any time is shaped by medical beliefs and practices" (1992:133). Notions concerning health can profoundly influence the interactive and symbolic communications made through our bodies. These notions greatly influence the ideal standards set for bodies and affect the ways we experience, care for, and shape (or try to shape) our bodies and those of others (Browner 1985; Ehrenreich and English 1979; Nichter and Nichter 1987; Payer 1988).

Importantly, notions about health are—in a very tangible way— notions about body ideals, and they have social meaning. Health traditions do not exist in isolation from other realms of culture, such as gender relations and economy (Farmer 1988; Jordanova 1980; Martin 1987), nor are they isolated from extracultural influences, such as ecology and global political conditions (Farmer 1992; Vaughan 1991). Often, ideas about the body and its health are put forward as rationalizations or ideological supports for conditions, such as class and gender inequalities or personal maladjustments (e.g., Kleinman 1980; Laws et al. 1985; Lock 1989; Scheper-Hughes 1992). In this chapter, I describe the traditional health beliefs that inform understandings of body shape in rural Jamaica, and I trace the connections between these ideas and Jamaican understandings about sociability (see also Sobo 1993b).

For rural Jamaicans, the ideal body is plump with vital fluids, and maintaining the flow of substances through the body is essential for good health. Taylor (1992) argues that an emphasis on maintaining a continuous, unimpeded flow through the body is common among those who value reciprocity and emphasize the obligation kin have to share with each other, which Jamaicans do. Sickness occurs when the flow is blocked or otherwise "anomic" (Taylor's term, 1988); individual pathologies are homologous with social pathologies, caused by disturbances in the flow of mutual support and aid.

Taylor shows that health-related symbolism "establishes implicit connections between the bodily microcosm and the social macrocosm" (1988:1343). "Liquids are especially privileged vehicles of this symbolism," he says, "because they possess the capacity to flow, and thus to mediate between distinct realms of being . . . attenuating the opposition between self and other" (1988: 1344). In rural Jamaica, people are physically linked by bodily liquids—fluids like semen and the blood that flows from mother to fetus during gestation. They also are linked through food that is shared. Both vital bodily fluids and foods fatten the body, making plumpness an index of the quality and extent of one's social relations as well as an index of good physical health (see Cassidy 1991).

The concept of the body-in-relation may seem foreign to U.S. or Western European readers who tend to view the body like they view the self—as autonomous, individual, and independent. Their bodies serve primarily as vehicles for the expression of the individual self, and so of self-directed denial, control, and mastery (Becker 1990: 1–10). Jamaicans, however, recognize the body's shape as an index of aspects of the social network in which a person is (or is not) enmeshed and of those individual character traits that affect that person's social connectedness, such as the ability and willingness to give (see Cassidy 1991).

Influenced by British interests, much of the anthropological literature on Jamaica deals with kinship and social structure (e.g., Blake 1961; Clarke 1957; Douglass 1992; Smith, 1988). Some studies examine the cultural construction of kinship, but none examine the ethnophysiology of blood ties and most overlook the body as such, despite its necessary role in procreation. Some works concerned with Jamaican family planning include descriptions of the reproductive body (e.g., Brody 1981; MacCormack 1985), but the health-related significance of blood and the physical intricacies of consanguineal and other consubstantial kin ties (and of their behavioral ramifications) are left unexplored. Pan-Caribbean ethnomedical notions about blood are discussed by Laguerre (1987), but the social and cultural meanings of body morphology and of bodily components (and the sharing thereof) have received little attention.[2]

Methods and Setting

Research for this chapter was carried out in a coastal village of about eight hundred people in the parish of Portland, where I lived for a year in 1988 and 1989 (see Sobo 1993b for a full account of the research). Data were collected through participant-observation and interviews that took place in community settings and in private yards. I also solicited drawings of the body's inner workings from participants.

Like most Jamaicans, the majority of the villagers were impoverished descendants of enslaved West Africans.[3] Many engaged in small-scale gardening, yet few could manage on this alone. To supplement their meager incomes, people also took in wash, hired themselves out for odd jobs, engaged in part-time petty trade like selling oranges, and relied on relatives for help.

Jamaican villages typically consist of people brought together by ancestry, or by proximity to a shop or postal agency. In some cases, they are organized around an estate where village members sell their labor. Households are often matrifocal (see Sargent and Harris 1992: 523; Smith 1988: 7–8), and nonlegal conjugal unions and visiting relationships (in which partners reside separately) are common. Houses are generally made of wood planks and zinc sheeting; often they lack plumbing and electricity. People build their houses as far apart as possible, but they are usually still within yelling distance of a neighbor.

Body Basics

Jamaicans value large size, and they *build* the body by eating. Different foods turn into different bodily components as needed, either for growth or to replenish substances lost through work and other activities. Comestibles that do not so much build the body but serve to make people feel full are called *food*. In common Jamaican usage, *food* means only tubers—belly-filling starches not seen as otherwise nutritious.

Blood is the most vital and the most meaning-invested bodily component. It comes in several types. When unqualified by adjective or context, the word *blood* means the red kind, built from thick, dark liquid items such as soup, stout, and porridge and from reddish edibles such as tomatoes. Red wine, also referred to as tonic wine, can be used to build blood, and blood is sometimes called wine. Some think that the blood of *meat-kind*, such as pork or beef, is directly incorporated into human blood; others say that meat's juices build blood. Wild hog meat, redder than regular pork, is supernutritious and vitality boosting because wild hogs feed mainly on red-colored roots, said to be beneficial blood-builders. People point out that meat-kind left sitting out or from which all vital fluid has drained (as when cooked for a long time in soup) loses its nutritive value and serves only as *food* to *fill belly*.

Sinews, another type of blood, comes from okra, fish eyes, and other pale slimy foods, such as egg white or the gelatinous portions of boiled cow skin or hoof. *Sinews* refers to, among other substances, the joint lubricant that biomedical specialists call synovial fluid, which resembles egg white. Sinews is essential for smooth joint movements and steady nerves. The functioning of the eyes depends on sinews too: the eyes are filled with it and glide left and right and open and shut with its aid. Sinews, also associated with procreation, is found in sexual effluvia and breast milk. Many call sinews *white blood*, as opposed to red.

People have less elaborate ideas about what edibles other bodily components are made of. Vitamins, contained in the strengthening tablets and tonics that are popular and easily available, build and fatten. Some Jamaicans argue that meat-kind builds muscles. Most agree that corn meal builds flesh. A few suggest that milk builds bones, at least in children but not necessarily in adults whose bones have already developed.

The most important part of the inner body is the *belly*, where blood is made. This big cavity or bag extends from just below the breast to the pelvis. The belly is full of bags and tubes, such as the *baby bag* and the *urine tube*. A main conduit leads from the top of the body through the belly to the bottom, with tributary bags and tubes along its length. Sometimes, tube and bag connections are not tightly coupled. A substance improperly propelled can meander off course, slide into an unsuitable tube or bag, lodge, and cause problems.

Food Sharing and Social Relations

In reviewing the social significance and health benefits of big size cross-culturally, Cassidy (1991) found that socially dominant individuals who are enmeshed in sound relationships are usually large. Bigness tends to ensure reproductive success and survival in times of scarcity, and plumpness is generally considered attractive. According to Brink (1989), such is the case in many of the West African societies from which people were taken to Jamaica as slaves. In these societies, those who can afford to do so seclude their adolescent girls in special "fattening rooms" and, after a period of ritual education and heavy eating, the girls emerge fat, attractive, and nubile.

In Jamaica, where a respected adult is called a *big man* or a *big woman*, good relations involve food sharing, and people on good terms with others are large. Weight loss signals social neglect. A Jamaican seeing someone grow thin wonders about the sorts of life stresses that have caused the weight loss (rather than offering congratulations for it and attributing it to a "good" diet, as many middle- and upper-class people in the United States do).

In the ideal Jamaican world, mothers feed their children, kin feed kin, and lovers feed each other. Men involved with women put on pounds from the meals their women serve them. Likewise, women display the status of their relations with their measurements; the breadth of the *backside* is particularly symbolic. Villagers noticed when a woman named Meg began to *mauger down* (get thin, grow meager) and lose her once-broad bottom; they knew—and they broadcast—that her affair with a rich old man had ended as she apparently no longer received food or resources from him.

Food sharing is a part of good social relations, and it, as well as other kinds of sharing, ends when people fall out. People with *something between them* (i.e., strife) both cease to give gifts and refuse to receive them. For instance, they refuse food from each other (often because they fear being poisoned; Sobo 1992). A disruption in the flow of goods and services signals the disintegration of a relationship.[4] Sister Penny knew that her relationship with Mister Edward was in trouble on the day he refused and sent back the dinner that she regularly prepared and had her daughter carry down the road to him at his mother's house, where he lived.

Good relationships and good eating go hand in hand, but plumpness depends on more than mere food—it depends on pleasant household conditions. Living in a household where *the conditions* (that is, the group dynamics) are harmonious and agreeable ensures both physical and mental vitality. No matter what they eat, unhappy people who live where *the conditions* are unpleasant lack energy, and they *draw down* (get thin) as fat *melts off.*

When a young woman named Amy lost weight and grew lackadaisical, villagers knew that she and her live-in boyfriend were having problems. Indeed, Amy's young man had taken up with his sister's boyfriend's sister. Amy's declining physical state and lethargy indicated this change in the conditions. Even with plenty to eat, a person in her position would lack energy and pull down mauger because, as one woman commenting on the situation explained, "people with worries can't fat."

Sweetness, Ripeness, and Decay

Fatness at its best is associated with moistness, fertility, and *kindness* (a sociable and giving nature) as well as with happiness, vitality, and bodily health in general. People know that drinks and warm, moist, cooked food can fatten them, while cold rice, *overnight food* (leftovers), and *dryers* such as store-bought crackers usually cannot. Fatness connotes fullness and juicy ripeness, like that of ripe fruit *well sweet* and soon to burst. Young boys fill out when they approach adulthood; young girls plump up in late adolescence as a prelude to childbearing. Men often call pubescent girls *soon ripe*, and they allude to sex with *ripe* girls through talk of harvesting.

Jamaicans call pleasing things *sweet*. When someone unexpectedly laughs or smiles, they are commonly asked, "Is what sweet you so?" People associate sweet goodness with fatness too. Men often describe plump women whom they find attractive as sweet. Good food also is sweet. Something sweet is ready to eat or ripe for enjoyment. As it approaches maturity, fruit swells and sweetens. A dream of fruit at its fullest, sweetest stage of development means that the time is ripe for whatever project the dreamer had in mind. Ripeness connotes urgent readiness (as for sexual relations). It can also mean ill-mannered precociousness, just as *green* (unripe, unprocessed) can describe naiveté. Unruly, disrespectful children are put down: "You too ripe!"

Overripe fruit rots and its sweetness sours. After it swells and ripens it declines, coming to resemble feces—soft, dark, fetid, and sometimes maggot infested. Overripe fruit is never eaten. By picking fruit just as it *turns* (from green), Jamaicans avoid the possibility of contamination with rot.

Ideas about decay give expletives power. The curse *rhatid* expresses, as a homonym, the connection between rotted matter and problems worthy of wrath, pronounced "rhat" or "rhot" (see Cassidy 1982:175). The negative connotations of rot and decay make *bumbo clot, rhas clot,* and *blood clot* among the most insulting epithets available, for these phrases describe the cloth (*clot*) diapers used to sop up dangerous waste that seeps out from the bowels of the body. *Bumbo clot* loosely refers to the diapers once used to catch the fecal and other matter that oozes from corpses when they are moved (morticians generally take care of this now), while *blood clots* serve as menstrual rags. *Rhas clots* do either.

Ideas about decay also fuel subversive banter. While playing bingo in the back room of a shop on the main road, which only more rebellious characters do as it brings disapproval, one rowdy woman named Pet denounced another boisterous player, Glory, for not having bathed. Glory, who had bathed, retorted: "You stink like ripe banana" (in other words, "you stink like feces"; picture overripe banana flesh). Pet playfully drew power from this complaint, warning Glory that most of the bellyful of ripe fruit that she had lately eaten was ready for gaseous rectal expulsion.

All that gets taken into the body, whether to build or fill belly, must get used or expelled because unincorporated excess begins to swell and decay. This knowledge leads people to associate superfluous or unutilized food, fat, health, and such with filth and the inevitable process of decomposition that accompanies death. Some Jamaicans speak of "good" fat and "bad" fat, the good being firm like a fit mango and the bad being spongy, soft, hanging slack, and denoting declining fitness as if a person was an overripe fruit, beginning to break down or rot.

Waste and Washout

Not all that gets ingested is transformed into specific components like sinews or blood, and some things are not utilized in the body's structure at all. Extra liquids become urine, and solid food turns to *didi* or feces, which move out from the belly cavity through the *tripe* (digestive tubing) and are expelled. People who do not use the toilet often enough literally fill up with waste. Trisha once asked her five-year-old daughter why the white missionaries always had such soft and overfat bellies. The little girl explained that "the tripe them fulla didi." Delighted, Trisha reiterated, "they fulla shit!"

A body that does not efficiently rid itself of excess and rotting waste turns septic inside because too much decomposition then takes place internally (most of waste's decomposition should take place outside of the body). A number of things can cause digestive inefficiency. Too much of a rich, strength-giving food such as cheese or cream can *clide* or clog the inner works, causing sluggish digestion and a backup of food in the belly. So can gluttony, which also reduces the amount of food available to others. Things like coffee grinds or undigested *hard food*—tough edibles such as bones or coco (a very hard tuber)—can also cause problems by settling in the *belly-bottom* and blocking the exit tubes. Held too long, food rots in place, festers, and sickens. The belly might even burst from buildup.

The most popular cure-all, the *washout* or laxative purge, eliminates blockages and harmful waste from the system. A washout once a month—a schedule modeled gynocentrically on the menstrual cycle (Sobo 1993a)—is advised. The importance of keeping clean inside explains one woman's choice of survival essentials (made as she fled her house during the 1988 hurricane), which included only "the ingredients for a washout" plus a blanket and some biscuits. It makes clear why every household medicinal supply includes, if nothing more, a purgative such as Epsom salts, cathartic herbs, or castor oil. And it explains why so many people understand the life-support devices seen in hospitals, such as the nasogastric tube, to be mechanically effecting washout cures.

The importance of keeping clean inside so that proper, balanced flow can be maintained parallels the importance of keeping goods and services flowing through networks of kin and corresponds in a number of ways to the idea that hoarding is bad. An overbundance of perishable resources not passed on will rot. Even money uncirculated is associated with decay, as the traditional association between feces and money (Chevannes 1990) reveals. Hoarding means neglecting one's social network, possibly allowing others to experience avoidable hardship, which can lessen the network's cohesiveness.

Thinness

Like cleanliness and balance, plumpness is important for good health. Few rural Jamaicans want to reduce. Diet foods and beverages are only seen in bigger towns. People generally assume that they are meant for diabetics, because no one should wish to be thin. Thinness is associated with ideas antithetical to those that "good" fat connotes. Thinness and fatness are to each other as the lean, dry, white meat of a chicken is to its fatty, moist, dark parts—the parts that most eaters prefer. Ideas about infertility and unkindness are linked with the notion of thinness. People taunt others by saying they will dry up and grow thin from antisocial *meanness.* Their observations of the elite and those in power who are light-skinned and whom they see as thin reinforce this belief.

Thin people are understood to lack the vitality associated with moist and juicy "good" fat. Like an erect penis or breasts plumped with milk, like a fat juicy mango, the body seems more vital when full of fluid and large in size. While too much blood or food overburdens the body and can rot and cause sickness, as noted above, *dry* bodies have no vital nature at all (low levels of bodily fluids and fat can lead women to have trouble conceiving). A slim person, especially a slim woman, is called *mauger*—meager and powerless—as if not alive at all and, like a mummy or an empty husk, far beyond that powerfully dangerous state of decay. A thin, dry body reveals a person's non-nurturant nature and his or her lack of social commitment.

Being Skinny, Being Mean

Kindness involves altruistic, kinlike sharing. Kind people give what is asked for and also offer things. They treat others as if family. A mean person, like a stranger (not kin), never shares and always refuses requests. Everyone hates a person who is *near* or *exact*, such as someone who never cooks extra dinner—someone stingy with food and so with their sociability. People concerned with their reputations are free with what money they have, buying drinks and putting on a show of kindness so that others cannot call them *mean.*

Mean people use very little salt in their cooking. Salt costs money, and it is associated with (among other things) imported foods, healing, good spiritual forces, and heaviness. It affects food's flavor, and most Jamaicans declare that they simply will not eat *fresh* (unsalted) food because it tastes bad. Like their cooking styles, their bodies give mean people away. Those who are *near* have a *cubbitch hole* or dent of covetousness at the *neck-back;* in other words, they are thin. Jamaicans say that mean people's bodies "dry down," "dry out," and "come skin and bone."

Vy and her brother, both in their early twenties, laughed about the mean old woman with whom their mother sent them to live fifteen years ago when she had no money and could not *keep* (support) or care for them herself. The old woman's thin body and flat cooking betrayed her nearness. Some stingy people draw down mauger or slim because, on top of not feeding others, they starve themselves, Vy explained.

When the woman did share food, it was *fresh* (unsalted) and otherwise ill prepared. She doled out small portions not big enough to *fill belly* but only, Vy said, to "nasty up me teeth" (to dirty the mouth without satisfying hunger). The woman would boil soup from the same piece of dried fish every day for a week, removing the piece each evening to use the following day. The soup carried nothing of substance and lost its salted taste by day three. It served as a sign of this woman's lack of a will to nurture, as did her thin, husklike form. A body with more vital juices inside would have housed a more social and giving person.

Store-bought snack food is also associated with thinness. The procurement and ingestion of packaged ready-to-eat foods (e.g., cookies, cheese puffs, sweet buns) do not involve the regular division of labor and tradition of sharing. Money is instrumentally exchanged for packaged food so that no reciprocity expectations ensue. Not having been prepared by a loving and morally obligated other and especially when ingested alone and away from home, store-bought foods—not coincidentally called *dryers*—represent the antisocial. Accordingly, those who eat dryers in lieu of home-cooked meals will be thin.

Kinship and Sociability

Jamaican kinship ideally involves a sense of interdependence and obligation, which ensues from shared bodily substance. Thin people have little bodily substance to spare. But sharing one's substance and having children generally are required to attain full adulthood because they affirm one's link to a social network.[5]

Through procreation, a person puts the parental gift of lifeblood from which his or her body was built back into social circulation, confirming and tightening his or her bonds to kin and community. Those who do not reproduce their social networks through procreative relationships physically subvert the social and moral order, as do those who act selfishly, hoarding resources or keeping to themselves so that others cannot ask for favors and so entangle them socially. The bodies of those elite individuals who are thinner than the poor reveal (to the poor) how they came to enjoy their *uplift:* through stingy meanness and by divorcing themselves from a social network of kin.

Jamaicans ascertain kinship through blood ties, in which both kinds of blood figure. Male and female sexual fluids are parallel types of white blood, and mingling white blood is key to conception. Pregnancy occurs when male semen meets a *ripe* female egg (sometimes equitably referred to as a sperm) or the female equivalent of semen—female white blood—in a woman's reproductive tract. Eggs mature and are discharged either monthly or upon sexual excitation. They burst when overripe and no longer fertilizable (as if decaying fruit), and they are excreted through the *tube* (the vagina).

During gestation, parents feed and so build and *grow* the fetus with their bodily substances. At first the fetus develops through simple accretion. After a few months, the *babymother's* (red) blood and food that she has ingested get eaten by the fetus and are then transformed into its bodily components. The fetus also eats semen ejaculated into its mother during its gestation. If a woman has many lovers, whosoever has invested the most sperm should receive credit for paternity.

The white blood that lovers share in nonreproductive sex only mixes temporarily. But in reproductive sex, blood mingles permanently in an offspring, creating an indirect link between parents. Siblings are related by virtue of having incorporated blood from the same source (or sources, when both parents are shared); other kin links, such as those between cousins, are similarly traced to a consanguineal origin.

The creation of kinship is not always seen as fixed or finished at birth. Older, more traditional Jamaicans say that babies continue the consubstantiation process that creates kin even after birth by drinking their mothers' milk, which is a kind of white blood. Accordingly, kinship ties can be created between a baby and an otherwise unrelated wet nurse. While biological motherhood is central in establishing maternity rights, traditional Jamaicans subscribe to an attenuated form of what Watson (cited in Meigs 1987: 120) refers to as "nurture kinship"—kinship that can be altered after birth by what Meigs calls "postnatal acts."

A child not related by virtue of received blood can become as if related to someone by virtue of that person's caretaking efforts. Feeding children is important outside of the womb as in it; food sharing can be a source of, as well as an index of, relatedness. A woman who feeds a child after it is born can claim motherhood: she *grows* it, as the genetic mother did when she fed it in her womb. Likewise, a man who spends his money on food for a child can claim fatherhood. Following the ethnophysiological model of parenthood, kinship can be established and claimed by a caretaker who puts great amounts of effort into raising, growing, feeding, and so building a child. Food from a caretaker that is taken into and made part of a child's body works like incorporated blood to create and maintain kin ties.

A big family provides, ideally at least, a big network of unselfconscious, altruistic support. People are physically driven to lend this support simply because they originate from or share *one blood* and are thus of *one accord*, sharing *one heart* and *one love*. Kin terms express and add an enduring, unconditional quality to relationships, and so cloak instrumental dealings that would otherwise seem self-centered, competitive, antisocial, and thus distasteful, given the ideology of sociable reciprocity.

Fecundity represents reciprocation—blood for blood. This reciprocity is practical, tangible, and homologous with the idealized reciprocal exchange of resources between kin. A daughter often sends one of her own children to live with and help her mother, giving a life (in the form of her young child) in return for having been given her own life. My neighbor Estelle could hardly wait for her grandson to *come up* in age so that she could send for him to come live with her and help with those tasks she could not manage.

Procreation confirms male and female virility and fecundity, demonstrating that one has life inside to give and that one's vital essence or life blood will persist. Thin people have little nurturant, willingly sociable capacity, while plump ones—including those with pregnant bellies—are full with it. Those who do not reproduce only serve to work. Their blood disappears from the social circles that individuals, joining together in the culturally recommended fashion, create and re-create.

The Infertile Mule

Mules do not reproduce. Mules just work. Like mules, women are known for their carrying capabilities; women carry wood, water, and so on, and mules serve as pack animals. Donkeys and old women are traditionally associated (Chevannes 1990). One saying about women holds that God made two kinds of donkeys, but one kind cannot talk (Hurston 1990: 76). Nonfecund women are called mules: unlike fertile women and donkeys (the more common beast of burden), mules do not breed.

Mules (and so nonfecund women) are traditionally associated with prostitutes (Chevannes 1990). In addition to defying female role expectations and posing an antisocial challenge (whether intended or not), nonmonogamous and nonfecund women fulfill the culturally informed sexual but not the procreative needs of men (nor do they fulfill their own culturally constructed childbearing needs). Although as sexual and subsistence workers nonfecund women, like prostitutes and mules, are useful, those who do not provide society with children are said to "have no use" in the end. This phrase implies that the ultimate purpose of the individual—and of sex, which ideally ends in *discharge* (the release of sperm and eggs)—is to re-create society.

Mules do not reproduce and so cannot establish any enduring form of community. They do not share their blood with other mules—they do not establish relationships confirmed by offspring. They are stubborn and uncooperative. Mules represent particularly antisocial and selfish beings uninterested in growing up to establish new bonds and unable to return the gift of life by fulfilling the social obligation of creation.

The dependence of those with no outside ties or offspring remains like children's dependence on parents. Nonfecund women can never really achieve social adulthood because they, like mules, do not overtly signal childhood's end by having babies and establishing bonds—blood bonds—with the larger society outside their immediate family circles (infertile men can, of course, claim to have fathered children not really their own).

Those who do not have children are generally not well articulated into a social network. They have no *blood ties* to any *babyfathers'* households (so no paternal grandmothers, aunts, or uncles are bound to help them with the children). Furthermore, without children to *response* for, their claims on the resources of their own natal networks are weak. (Such a situation does not always entail suffering. Those with small networks and no offspring are minimally obligated to others.)

Having children expresses a readiness to fulfill obligations to society and one's relatives. It demonstrates a willingness to share resources and also one's body's substance in order to maintain and regenerate the social environment into which one was born. People who do not create and maintain network ties tacitly release themselves from their social group's hold.

Plumpness and Sexual Fluids

The thin body lacks vital fluids, which can cause embarrassment and shame because this means a person can be cast as infertile and antisocial. That is why it *cut* Dara when a girl who hated her asserted that Dara had to wear two *suits* or layers of clothing to look presentable—to pad her mauger frame. Dara was slim, but Jamaicans denigrated for thinness were never extraordinarily slender in my culturally conditioned opinion. Even the women pictured in a British hardware company's Jamaican give-away calendar would be judged fat by mainstream U.S. standards. But two teenaged male participants in this research laughed at their pictures, calling them *mauger dogs.*

People are sensitive to such insults. Some prepubescent girls buy special so-called *anorexa* pills to help them put on weight. Pharmacists sold the Anorexal brand until it was withdrawn from the market; now most carry a brand of anorexa pill called Peritol. The pill, an antihistamine (cyproheptadine) that enhances the appetite, can be bought with no questions asked.

As a child matures and begins to develop a healthy libido or *nature,* the body swells with sexual fluids. A good shape is a matter of firmness and proportion. Men should be muscular, never flabby. Women's bottoms should be broad (my fictive brother boasted that Jamaican women have the broadest bottoms in the world) and breasts should *stand up* high. A sagging or diminutive bosom indicates a lack of plumping juices. Thin, tomboyish girls with short hair and girls whose hair stays short because it is dry and brittle and breaks off are insultingly called *dry-head pickney,* which alludes to their immaturity (*pickney* means child or children) and, moreover, to their lack of vital moistness and so to their potential roles as infertile subversives.

Sexual fluid, like fatness itself, is good, but here again too much can be harmful and balance must be maintained. Orgasm releases body-swelling sexual fluids. Celibate women or those with poor lovers may become sick through the retention of too much *sweet water.* (Wet dreams help keep males well.) A young woman, Jean, once pointed to her friend Titia's crotch, calling "punani fat, eee?" Jean's joke about the size of Titia's *punani* or pubic area implied its disuse. If Titia did not have sex soon, Jean suggested, a buildup of overripe sexual juice would cause bodily harm.

A buildup of unreleased semen or sweet water can cause *teenager bumps* or pimples as excess sexual fluid tries to work its way out through the pores. The association between pimples and unused sexual discharge is a logical extension of the notion that a good thing like money or vital fat can go bad if not properly dispersed, and of the idea that overfull, overripe fruit bursts and sours. Some say teenager bumps are more common among youths whose caretakers can afford to provide them with expensive rich foods but who also insist that they remain celibate, in keeping with the behavioral expectations for those of high station (regarding the maintenance of respect, see Wilson 1973).

Discharge and Decay

Bodily equilibrium is essential, so sexual fluids must be discharged now and again. Women receive men's discharge during intercourse. Like their own sexual fluids, sperm taken in fattens women, making them sexually appealing and attractive. A teenaged girl's increasing plumpness is as much a perceived result of her becoming sexually active as it is a positive result of her own growing moistness and fertility. Some people, to support their claim for the health-enhancing value of sperm, say that prostitutes and other women who perform oral sex get fat.

But prostitution and oral sex are not condoned (Sobo 1993a). The reasons for prostitution's poor standing have to do with its instrumental nature and the popular belief that prostitutes seek to avoid pregnancy. Conception does not have to happen during sex, but the possibility of conceiving should exist; the interpersonal flow of sexual fluids, like resources, should not be blocked. With oral sex, conception cannot occur; furthermore, the mouth is meant for food, not sexual fluids. So in situations where the morality of oral sex and prostitution are called into question, people will say that the toxicity of discharge improperly or excessively taken in makes women who have oral sex or who prostitute themselves *pull down* or lose weight.

Semen can cause problems even for women who participate only in socially sanctioned sex acts. When conception does not happen, discharge can lodge in inaccessible spaces. It rots quickly, growing toxic and polluting. Menstruation serves as a purifying *washout* for the female reproductive system (Sobo 1992).[6]

Dry Spine

Men also need to be careful about semen, albeit for different reasons. Men emphasize the importance of intercourse and ejaculation for *clearing the line.* If this is not done, excess amounts of undischarged semen and sinews harden up in the spine, causing back pain and sexual problems. Drinking beer helps promote the flow of fluids through the penis. It is assumed that men will find partners and so need never masturbate to clear the line. Women who stay celibate too long may get *nerves* problems, as the *nerves* system contains sinews.

Discharging cleanses the body, promoting as well as signaling good health. People—mostly men—use this knowledge to justify frequent sex and to coerce others into partnership. Asymmetric gender power relations find support in traditional health beliefs.

Jamaicans believe that men, as opposed to women, always want sex and cannot easily control their urges. Male sexual behavior is justified as an inherent part of their biology. However, sex taxes the male constitution. Men lose much more sinews when discharging than do women. Like any resource, semen must be shared. But people with too many demands on their energy or resources inevitably end up feeling *sucked out, eaten out,* or even *dried out.* A man who runs out of sinews comes down with *dry spine,* a condition involving ejaculatory dysfunction.

Dry spine can occur if a man invovles himself with an abnormally libidinous or *white liver* woman—a woman who *works* her men far too hard, that is, bone-dry as well as to the bone. The livers of sexually hungry women may be described as white because they are full of sinews, because of the symbolic link between egoism and lightness, or because such women conform to the stereotyped view of sexually ravenous white female tourists. White liver women are feared by men insecure about their power to satisfy women sexually. Such men experience performance anxiety, and impotent men or those who simply *can't do the work* of sex are vindictively called soft, which harms their reputations.

Men with dry spine will *draw down* thin as their stores of vital juice are dried out and depleted. They grow infertile (like mules) and are sexually *useless.* Some have trouble urinating: not a drop of sinews remains to help ease urine's passage through the genital tube. Squatting like women helps. Ma Bovie, telling me about a man so damaged by an overenthusiastic partner that he could hardly walk, offered a story about a cock with light, dry, stringy meat. Rooster meat should be dark, moist, fatty, and rich. Hindsight told her that this cock must have suffered a terrible case of dry spine: she remembered that his hen wives demanded "plenty" sex.

Dry spine can reverse itself over time, but recovery demands total sexual abstinence so that the body can renew its store of sinews. Sufferers can take lime juice because, as it draws out heat, it dissipates the libido or *nature.* One woman surmised that the pope must drink lots of lime juice, for having nature is only natural and health requires expurgating it rather than simply repressing and not spending it. But anyone who has gone too far in expressing his nature and has dried his sinews or juice stores must add plenty of slimy okra, gelatinous cow foot, and other sinews-building foods to his diet. Drinks made from condensed milk and soursop (*Annona muricate*) juice or from the seaweed Irish moss (*Gracilaria spp.*), which resemble semen, and coconut *jelly* (the white, gel-like meat of young coconuts) are especially helpful to *put it back.*

A healthy libido or nature, which demonstrates one's physical and social vitality, depends on healthy blood. *Roots* tonic, made mainly from plant roots gathered during the full moon (when they are supposedly plumpest and most powerful), energizes the body by building, cleansing, and mobilizing the blood. A man with dry spine takes roots tonic once every morning and night to replenish and enrich his blood stores. After a year of this treatment, his spine and his sex life should be fine. His body will have grown moist and full with vital fluid. Many men whose spines are fine take the roots regularly anyhow, swearing by its effects on potency. Women take it too, for general health enhancement.

Bad Shape

Fluid loss in women is most noticeable in the bosom, which, after a woman has had children or after a miscarriage or abortion, sags flat and low. A sagging bosom indicates a declining physical condition—a *used up*, postreproductive body. Too soft, with no babies in her belly and no life-giving milk to make firm her breasts, a woman with a "bad" shape is, like an overripe fruit, on her way to decay.

Cow's milk and other foods that build sinews increase a woman's store of breast milk and so plump the bosom. Sperm also increases the amount of white blood women carry. A nursing woman should only have intercourse with lovers whose sperm helped grow the nursing child. Otherwise, the child will get sick from drinking breast milk that contains foreign sperm and from contact with or the ingestion of any foreign sweat that remains on the mother's breast after sex with the nonfather. The baby will fail to thrive.

A woman with a small, slow child risks being accused of having an *outside man.* People may surmise that economic instability forced the woman into the liaison. This will shame her, and it will shame her *babyfather* by indicating that he failed to provide for his child.

Through early weaning, women with new lovers can avoid harming their babies, their reputations, or their conjugal relationships. Early weaning also helps women maintain figures that are attractive to men, as prolonged nursing *tires* their bodies.

Bosoms sag with use and age, but they also fall after abortions or miscarriages, or when a body is overworked and so depleted of its stores of blood. Women not blessed with firm breasts risk being accused of taking purgatives to *wash away baby* (abortion is not condoned; Sobo 1995). They risk being labeled prostitutes, who overwork their bodies with sexual labor exchanged directly for instrumental gain and which is therefore antisocial labor. The body shape associated with a separation between sex and reproduction, and with aging and death, is thin and flaccid, not firmly plump like the sociable one.

Sociable Plumpness

Meanings attributed to personal appearances are context-specific, and circumstances such as personal vendettas affect which meanings get linked with whose bodies. The good as well as the bad can be highlighted. For example, a thin individual can escape ridicule if his or her svelte shape is caused by working long and hard for the benefit of others. As a general rule, however, and especially when a slender person's behavior gives others cause to disparage him or her, the thin person is cast in a bad light as lacking the willingness and the capability for giving life. The individual is branded selfish and mean, and people point to his or her body's dry, husklike nature as a confirmation of these antisocial, nonprocreative leanings. Like the person too rich, the person too thin—whether through circumstance or choice—is seen to shirk his or her social duties to share with and nurture kin. The thin individual is seen to contribute little to society, and the shape of his or her body is used to bear witness to this.

The condition of a person's relationships is inferred by others when they observe and comment on the state of his or her body. In turn, people try to mold the shapes of their bodies in order to affect the inferences other people make. Bordo (1990) explores mainstream U.S. dieting and body sculpting through exercise with this notion (and typical U.S. ideas about self-control) in mind. While mainstream Americans prefer regimes that lead to thinness, Jamaicans attempt to fatten their bodies (and those of others whom they *care* or *re-*

sponse for). Both types of manipulations are efforts to construct and promote oneself as a sociable, desirable individual within a given cultural context.

A fuller understanding of the interactive dimension of body sculpting and the reading of bodily shape opens one avenue to the study of the cultural aspects of ideas about nutrition and the standards for physical beauty and health. The study of traditional health beliefs and social and moral ideals exposes much of the logic behind body shapes and the regimes people attempt to adhere to in order to affect them.

The life-affirming, prosocial associations of the plump body in Jamaica are expressed in the traditional saying that "What don't fat, kill; what don't kill, fat." Foods or events either fatten or bring death. People try to stay fat because the plump body is healthily dilated with vital lifeblood and because it suggests to others that one is kind, sociable, and happy to fulfill obligations to kin and community. Thinness is ultimately linked with death, but the fat person's body is richly fertile, and the fat person is judged a nurturant and constructive member of a thriving network of interdependent kin.

ACKNOWLEDGMENTS

This chapter is part of a larger study of Jamaican health traditions and their uses; ideas and information presented in this chapter are discussed more fully in my book, *One Blood* (Sobo 1993b) and in various articles (1993a, 1992, 1995). The research and much of the writing were carried out with the guidance of F. G. Bailey. Tom Csordas, Mark Nichter, Nicole Sault, William Wedenoja, and Drexel Woodson provided thoughtful comments and suggestions.

NOTES

1   Many of the institutional and structural barriers to class mobility remain invisible to most of the people that they hinder, and blame for impoverishment is frequently placed on fellow villagers (Austin 1984).

2   Works dealing with "racial" body characteristics are exceptions (e.g., Henriques 1958; Hoetink 1985; Phillips 1973). Features such as hair texture and skin color are used to determine one's ancestral heritage. Features considered more "Black" or more African are denigrated. Some people bleach their skin and straighten their hair to affect a "whiter" appearance. Color consciousness is greatest among the middle class because of their realistic concern over social mobility. The ways people manipulate the "racial" features of their bodies may be shifting as pride in the African portion of Caribbean heritage increases.

3   For this reason, and because many urban dwellers were born rurally (see

Brody 1981: 101) or have rural mind-sets (Brody 1981: 69), and also because many elite, modernized Jamaicans retain traditional beliefs, I often refer to the participants simply as Jamaicans.

4   Drexel Woodson notes that people who have had a falling out—people with *something between them* (strife)—do, in fact, continue to give and receive *something*—ire, enmity, or spleen. The flow of enmity between individuals marks a shift in the relationship's character (D. Woodson, personal communication).

5   Just bearing children does not confer social adulthood; as I argue elsewhere (Sobo 1995, 1993b), responsible parenting and accepting responsibility for the well-being of others are essential for gaining and maintaining adult status. Nonfecund women who establish a name for themselves as excellent foster mothers or those who demonstrate a high level of social commitment through good works or through a service-oriented career, such as that of a doctor, healer, or pastor, can sometimes gain adult standing in the community (but they are not guaranteed it).

6   The menstrual period is often called an *unclean* time, and menstruating women are often denigrated as *unclean*, yet menstruation purifies the body. The association with uncleanness has to do with the *dirt* (unused, rotting semen) that the menstrual flow washes out. Moreover, it has to do with the power women have to carry out *unclean business* (magical manipulations) with their menstrual blood. Women can secretly add the blood of menstruation to others' food. Once ingested and incorporated into the body, menstrual blood obligates victims just as *blood ties* obligate kin. (For a detailed analysis see Sobo 1992.)

REFERENCES

Austin, D. 1984. *Urban Life in Kingston, Jamaica: The Culture and Class Ideology of Two Neighborhoods.* New York: Gordon and Breach Science Publishers.

Bailey, F. G. 1971. *Gifts and Poison.* New York: Schocken Books.

Becker, A. 1990. "Body Image in Fiji: The Self in the Body and in the Community." Ph.D. diss., Harvard University.

Blake, J. 1961. *Family Structure in Jamaica.* New York: Free Press.

Bordo, S. 1990. "Reading the Slender Body." In *Body/Politics*, ed. M. Jacobus, E. F. Keller, and S. Shuttleworth, pp. 83–112. New York: Routledge.

Brink, P. J. 1989. "The Fattening Room among the Annang of Nigeria." *Medical Anthropology* 12:131–143.

Brody, E. 1981. *Sex, Contraception, and Motherhood in Jamaica.* Cambridge: Harvard University Press.

Browner, C. H. 1985. "Traditional Techniques for Diagnosis, Treatment, and Control of Pregnancy in Cali, Colombia." In *Women's Medicine: A Cross-Cultural Study of Indigenous Fertility Regulations*, ed. L. F. Newman, pp. 99–123. New Brunswick, N.J.: Rutgers University Press.

Cassidy, C. M. 1991. "The Good Body: When Bigger Is Better." *Medical Anthropology* 13:181–213.

Cassidy, F. G. 1982. *Jamaica Talk: Three Hundred Years of the English Language in Jamaica.* London: Macmillan Education. First published in 1961.

Chevannes, B. 1990. "Drop-pan and Folk Consciousness." *Jamaica Journal* 22(2):45–50.

Clarke, E. 1957. *My Mother Who Fathered Me: A Study of the Family in Three Selected Communities in Jamaica*. Boston: George Allen and Unwin.

Douglass, L. 1992. *The Power of Sentiment: Love, Hierarchy, and the Jamaican Family Elite*. Boulder, Colo.: Westview Press.

Ehrenreich, B., and D. English. 1979. *For Her Own Good: 150 Years of the Experts' Advice to Women*. London: Pluto Press.

Farmer, P. 1988. "Bad Blood, Spoiled Milk: Bodily Fluids as Moral Barometers in Rural Haiti." *American Ethnologist* 15(1):62–83.

––––––. 1992. *AIDS and Accusation: Haiti and the Geography of Blame*. Berkeley: University of California Press.

Henriques, F. 1958. *Family and Colour in Jamaica*. London: Macgibbon and Kee.

Hoetink, H. 1985. " 'Race' and Color in the Caribbean." In *Caribbean Contours*, ed. S. Mintz and S. Price, pp. 55–84. Baltimore: Johns Hopkins University Press.

Hurston, Z. N. 1990. *Tell My Horse: Voodoo and Life in Haiti and Jamaica*. With a new forward. San Francisco: Harper and Row. First published in 1938.

Jordanova, L. J. 1980. "Natural Facts: A Historical Perspective on Science and Sexuality." In *Nature, Culture, and Gender*, ed. C. P. MacCormack and M. Strathern pp. 42–69. New York: Cambridge University Press.

Kitzinger, S. 1982. "The Social Context of Birth: Some Comparisons between Childbirth in Jamaica and Britain." In *Ethnography of Fertility and Birth*, ed. C. P. MacCormack, pp. 181–204. San Diego: Academic Press.

Kleinman, A. 1980. *Patients and Healers in the Context of Culture: An Exploration of the Borderland between Anthropology, Medicine, and Psychiatry*. Berkeley: University of California Press.

Laguerre, M. 1987. *Afro-Caribbean Folk Medicine*. South Hadley, Mass.: Bergin and Garvey Publishers.

Laws, S., V. Hay, and A. Eagan. 1985. *Seeing Red: The Politics of Premenstrual Tension*. London: Hutchinson.

Lock, M. 1989. "Words of Fear, Words of Power: Nerves and the Awakening of Political Consciousness." *Medical Anthropology* 11:79–90.

MacCormack, C. P. 1985. "Lay Concepts Affecting Utilization of Family Planning Services in Jamaica." *Journal of Tropical Medicine and Hygiene* 88:281–285.

MacCormack, C. P., and A. Draper. 1987. "Social and Cognitive Aspects of Female Sexuality in Jamaica." In *The Cultural Construction of Sexuality*, ed. P. Caplan, pp. 143–161. New York: Tavistock Publications.

Martin, E. 1987. *The Woman in the Body: A Cultural Analysis of Reproduction*. Boston: Beacon Press.

Mauss, M. 1967. *The Gift*. New York: W. W. Norton.

Meigs, A. S. 1987. "Blood Kin and Food Kin." In *Conformity and Conflict: Readings in Cultural Anthropology*, ed. J. P. Spradley and D. W. McCurdy, pp. 117–124. Boston: Little, Brown.

Nichter, M., and M. Nichter. 1987. "Cultural Notions of Fertility in South Asia and Their Impact on Sri Lankan Family Planning Practices." *Human Organization* 46(1):18–27.

Payer, L. 1988. *Medicine and Culture: Varieties of Treatment in the United States, England, West Germany, and France*. New York: Henry Holt.

Phillips, A. S. 1973. *Adolescence in Jamaica*. Kingston: Jamaica Publishing House.

Sargent, C., and M. Harris. 1992. "Gender Ideology, Child Rearing, and Child Health in Jamaica." *American Ethnologist* 19:523–537.

Scheper-Hughes, N. 1992. *Death without Weeping: The Violence of Everyday Life in Brazil*. Los Angeles: University of California Press.

Sheets-Johnstone, M. 1992. "The Materialization of the Body: A History of Western Medicine, A History in Process." In *Giving the Body Its Due*, ed. M. Sheets-Johnstone, pp. 132–158. Albany: State University of New York Press.

Smith, R. T. 1988. *Kinship and Class in the West Indies: A Genealogical Study of Jamaica and Guyana*. New York: Cambridge University Press.

Sobo, E. J. 1992. " 'Unclean Deeds': Menstrual Taboos and Binding 'Ties' in Rural Jamaica." In *Anthropological Approaches to the Study of Ethnomedicine*, ed. M. Nichter, pp. 101–126. New York: Gordon and Breach.

———. 1993a. "Bodies, Kin, and Flow: Family Planning in Rural Jamaica." *Medical Anthropology Quarterly* 7(1):50–73.

———. 1993b. *One Blood: The Jamaican Body*. Albany: State University of New York Press.

———. 1995. "Abortion Traditions in Rural Jamaica." *Social Science and Medicine*.

STATIN (Statistical Institute of Jamaica). 1982. Census. Unpublished Portland information, in author's files.

Taylor, C. C. 1988. "The Concept of Flow in Rwandan Popular Medicine." *Social Science and Medicine* 27(12):1343–1348.

———. 1992. "The Harp That Plays by Itself." In *Anthropological Approaches to the Study of Ethnomedicine*, ed. M. Nichter, pp. 127–147. New York: Gordon and Breach.

Vaughan, M. 1991. *Curing Their Ills: Colonial Power and African Illness*. Stanford: Stanford University Press.

Wilson, P. J. 1973. *Crab Antics*. New Haven: University Press.

MEANINGS OF AGING
IN A SOUTHERN TOWN

VALERIE FENNELL

Many excellent ethnographic descriptions of the lives of elders have been published since the early 1970s (see Brown and Kerns 1985; Myerhoff and Simic 1978; Sokolovsky 1987), but few attempt to show how individuals of varying ages grapple with utilizing cultural stereotypes about the aging process in their everyday worlds. Nor do they discuss the human body as symbolic of the aging process. They usually do not consider the different bodily features as symbols that have meanings. As Csordas (1990) put it, they study the body as an object in relation to culture. In this description of how local people talked about their aging bodies (and those of others), I present people's responses within cultural context, in the hope that the processes creating cultural symbols of aging will become clearer.

The people of Curlew Point (all names are fictional), while constantly making judgments of one another's age, obviously did not see aging merely as a biological process of the body. Mood, personality, fashion, awareness of community, and national (occasionally international) events all played important parts in the social and cultural construction of the aging process. Just as fascinating was the use of aging as a metaphor (e.g., characterizing sick youth or very serious youths as "old" or labeling energetic and mischievous elders as "adolescent"). The interplay of the physical, social, cultural, and psychological in their ideas about aging became apparent. The aging body was not solely a physical object to them; it was also a field of cultural symbols.

Curlew Pointers' complex and diverse approach to bodily symbols of aging made it possible for persons to be simultaneously positive and negative in their evaluations of various cultural categories of age. Negatively valued categories (such as *middle age* or *old*) could be maintained, while persons placed in these categories could also have other important features that belied the category, casting more positive evaluations on the individuals.

In a small town, rich social contexts encompass individuals. They have multiple social identities, and such knowledge certainly exists among the closely bonded. In my research, I asked persons to apply cultural labels both to those who were close and to strangers. Raybeck (1988) found people reluctant to "label" deviants in smaller-scale societies where everyone is known to one another. Perhaps this is true for other negative labels as well. Certainly Curlew Pointers struggled with the negativity of the cultural categories of aging more than most of the gerontological literature overtly suggests. Subtly, though, rich and complex cultural contexts for elders are delineated in many ethnographic descriptions where aging per se is not valued, but familiar elders are (see Kerns's 1980 work with the Garifuna).

The Setting

In a small town I call Curlew Point, many people allowed me to do participant-observation in various settings and gave me innumerable opportunities (at church, festivals, voting centers, club meetings, parties, in their homes, etc.) to ask them about aging and age relations. My fieldwork continued from October 13, 1972, until that day one year later. I also spent many hours talking with people while surveying households and workplaces, and while conducting formal in-depth interviews. All these interactions focused on aging and age relations.

Curlew Point, a small southern U.S. town located on an estuary of a river, included 2,492 persons within the city limits and about 1,400 in the surrounding areas (Fennell 1977). The economy of the town grew out of its governmental functions, excellent fishing, and support of tourism. My field year occurred during a boom time arising from the construction of a nuclear power plant near the community.

Major sources of the data for this discussion are in-depth interviews with 35 persons. I selected them from a larger population (458) whose names were gathered during a survey of households on streets oriented from east to west in the town. The eldest person was eighty-five; the youngest was four. Talking with children gave me different types of information less comparable to data gathered from my talks with adults. Other data sources are my field notes describing my participant-observational activities. These are filled with anecdotes about aging perceptions, daily interactions, and events I attended.

Labeling People

An important aspect of symbolizing aging rests in how people categorize and label one another as members of age groups. Labeling persons attributes certain qualities to them as well as the values and rights in their roles. How this labeling occurs determines how people may interact in relationships and as group members. Labeling has enormous significance in human communities. Some age categories are more highly valued than others.

Many persons in conversation with me have noted the peculiar irony of an elder person's disdain of another elder's appearance or behavior.[1] Perhaps in the case of aging, people are generally less aware of the political bases of disparagement, and they imagine their own aging will not bring them similar treatment. Women and other political minorities behave similarly in many instances as well.[2] Consultants who talked with me during my fieldwork in this small southern town faced similar dilemmas as I asked them about age and age groups.[3] Some quickly realized a discomfort at categorizing themselves and others by age. Others simply reported as best they could what they typically did, without considering the impact on anyone's (including their own) sensibilities.

For example, some consultants indicated that they were uncomfortable assigning chronological age definitions to words like *middle-aged* and *old*. These age categories are not as highly valued in the youth-oriented culture of the United States (Clark and Anderson 1967). Several consultants adjusted age ranges (i.e., defining an age group) when they consciously recalled a friend or kinsperson who fit within the initial range but who, they felt, did not belong in these categories.

Responding to in-depth questions, Janet, a shy young woman (European-American, working class, fifteen years old), seemed almost apologetic as she offered the age range of 32–45 years as a definition of *middle-aged*. She noted that she had friends in this age group: "Well, I have some friends [that age] . . . , but I don't consider them *that* way." A sensitive high-schooler just discovering the delight of group acceptance among her age-peers, she realized that the cultural meaning of *middle-aged* was negative, particularly among younger persons.

In his riverside house (a renovated old structure), Marty, an outgoing new father (a European-American middle-class person, thirty one years old), answered my interview questions, including one requiring him to define *old*. To him, *old* intellectually included persons sixty and over. Then, slowly, ill ease showed on his face as he recalled outloud that his parents were over sixty. He commented that he didn't think of them as old.

Other consultants also reminded me frequently that there were always individuals who were exceptions to the descriptions they gave me of age groups. It was particularly difficult for consultants to define what they felt were negative age categories in such a way that persons close to them were included and thus were implicitly insulted. Maureen, from a construction-worker family, was partly Cherokee and twenty eight years old. She redefined *young adult* from ages 21–29 to 21–33 in order include her eldest brother of thirty three. Family were crucial to her, despite much geographical mobility and the associated disruption of kin ties. This way she avoided labeling her older brother as middle-aged, the next logical age group.

Perhaps the greater the intimacy, the less relevant chronological age and cultural age categories seemed. People's avoidance of using negative age categories is similar to Raybeck's (1988) comments, mentioned earlier, about people's reluctance to label as deviant those close or well known to them. People interviewed knew kin, neighbors, and friends of many different ages and did not hold solely negative feelings for the elders or solely positive feelings for the youthful, despite popular stereotypes.

Physical Appearance

Physical appearance plays an important part in how people categorize one another into age groups. The most frequently mentioned words describing "old" people were (1) *slow*, (2) *gray*, and (3) *wrinkled*. All, of course, refer to bodily features. For example, a troubled and rebellious young European-American man named Rodney conformed with the majority of consultants when he recalled that an old person "looks tired and acts slow." *Gray* (one person said *white*) referred to hair color and is simply accepted as an objective bodily indicator of aging.

A jovial elder woman (European-American), Greta, thoughtful in the interview, recalled her kinsman whose hair had become gray around the age of thirty. Everyone, she said, had always thought of him as old, even though she now noted that this catagory must have been inappropriate for some of his lifetime. He and other men of her family were riverboat pilots, a highly respected occupation reserved only for white men of elite families at that time (around the turn of the century). Perhaps the prestige of family and job made youth less relevant, as he wore the hair of an elder, consistent with his other prestigious roles.

Melissa, a twenty-four-year-old mother from an old Curlew Point family, was African-American and working class. she adamantly recounted many social situations in which people behaved in age-inconsistent ways. She warned me that graying was not a dependable indicator because some people began graying in their twenties. She attended to the exceptions to the cultural assumptions about aging and graying. A twenty-nine-year-old, European-American woman recalled the wrinkles she noted on elders: "They're getting their wrinkles; they have their wrinkles; they are wrinkled." Her compact review of verbs denoting older people's relationships with wrinkles is fascinating. She moved from process ("getting") to finished trait now possessed ("have their wrinkles"). The first two verbs seem to examine aging from the perspective of a person experiencing the process. The last verb, "are wrinkled," implies detachment, an outsider's perspective. This woman also spoke about her young son's fear of elders. She worried that he lacked opportunities to have positive experiences with elders because his grandparents lived so far away.

Other physical characteristics mentioned were noted by only one or two consultants but are culturally familiar bodily indicators of aging in the United States. These features include overweight, rounded shoulders, sunken chest, dark circles around the eyes, tiring easily, poorer hearing, weakness, prominent veins, and thin hair.

Most of these descriptions of the physical appearances of agedness were offered because I directly asked people to tell me what old ones looked like to them. In ordinary discourse, however, people did not talk about how they recognized oldness. Some consultants found it difficult to describe their ideas of oldness. Part of the difficulty may have arisen from my question, which asked them to isolate bodily features from other unconscious, equally important considerations. Bodily features are but one dimension of aging, and in many contexts not the most important dimension. Yet people could not consciously state what all the dimensions were. That sort of analysis seemed artificial to them. I think, however, that bodily features of aging are interwoven with the other less conscious dimensions and are clearly associated with them. I summarize these dimensions below.

Traits and Attitudes

Personality traits, attitudes, and lifestyle were mentioned as indicators of oldness by some. These descriptions move away from bodily features but are often associated with the physical symbols of aging mentioned above.

Commenting on old people, Frank (European-American, middle-aged, forty-five) explained that they had critical attitudes arising from lack of work. We talked in his office where he oversaw the operations of a small boat harbor: "It's from a lack of anything else to direct their complaints about. When they were working they could complain about the work, the hours, or the people, employers. But when they get to that age, they don't have that, and they just complain about everything in general, I think." Not working, he felt, could be interpreted as an element of lifestyle which influences attitudes in old people. Younger persons have a common focus that older people lack—work. Frank believed that old people were *more* critical or complaining as they generalized their discontent, but he also seemed to feel that all persons were inclined to complain.

Others noted that elders were often nervous and grumpy. Margaret, an athletic sixteen-year-old from an old Curlew Point family (European-American, middle class, and including many brothers), characterized elders as unable to "take too much of any one thing . . . [they] get tired or it gets on their nerves . . . [they've] got bad nerves." Another consultant, Billie (aged thirty two), saw the lives of old people as having a repetitiveness: "They stay in the same rut, the same course of events all the time." This European-American, middle-class, native Curlew Pointer of old family lines enjoyed his exciting and occasionally dangerous occupation in law enforcement. In his own life, he chose work with more excitement than aging allowed.

Some consultants with quite different opinions saw old people as helpful and tolerant. Some children said their grandparents were nicer to them than their parents, an observation confirmed in the cross-cultural descriptions of age relations (Foner 1984). Jimmy, a fourteen-year-old from the European-American middle class, characterized old people as "easy-going, easy to get along with, always seeming to help somebody." He seemed to think of his own grandfather as he talked. Jimmy was puzzled that his grandfather didn't require his favorite football team be winners. He supported them no matter how they played, and this attitude lacked the masculine values that emphasized dominance and winning in competition.

"More experience" and "innocence" were also associated with agedness, though these qualities are often considered antithetical. Porter, a twenty-four-year-old mother to an infant son, and daughter to an old Curlew Point family (European-American, middle class), told me that "Every old person has a lot of different experiences and knows life." She talked with her husband's grandmother "like a friend." Dorothy, another European-American consultant, also twenty-four, noted that "An old person is innocent; maybe they've done wrong like in the past, but they're at the stage now that they've lived and been forgiven." Innocence was not lack of experience, as it may be in children. It was living long enough to be forgiven.

Some consultants were aware that old people enjoyed life, but they seemed somewhat baffled at what pleased elders. Steven, a thirty-two-year-old European-American from the middle class, saw them as "just taking advantage . . . of the years they have left." Others noted that elders frankly enjoyed talking about the past. Mary, a fourteen-year-old high school girl from an upwardly mobile working-class African-American family, noted that aged persons (from senior generations including her parents) were old-fashioned. A working-class, fifteen-year-old European-American girl named Nettie said, "they feel things should be the same as when they were young." Grayson Little, son of an elite European-American family from another part of the state, was a successful professional man of sixty-two. Commenting on those he considered his peers, he noted that old people were "not current generally with the affairs of the day." All implicitly commented that such focused interest in the past and the present might be considered inappropriate or a less desirable characteristic.

Finally, consultants saw old people as enjoying giving advice and having a good sense of humor. Johnson, from an old Curlew Point family of the African-American working classes, characterized elders' behavior as "someone giving you advice." He was twenty-three. Della, an attentive young mother (European-American and middle class) who had a fine relationship with her elder in-laws, emphasized, "Most of them have a good sense of humor that I know." Advice-giving and good-humored exchanges were a part of life for these persons' families, as was sharing problems (Fennell 1981).

Puzzlement at the pleasures of elders suggests that people consciously agree that growing old must be largely negative. When they sense that it isn't all negative, the puzzlement ensues. The social psychological literature (working, it would appear, largely from survey questioning of large populations) supports the idea that the very negative view of aging in the culture is more in the eye of the "younger beholder," as Fisher notes:

> There is no question that advanced age bears with it body infirmity and a decline in attractiveness as conventionally defined. At the same time, the available scientific data do not indicate a corresponding decline in self-appraisal or body satisfaction. It is also impressive that there is no increase in conscious death anxiety attributable to aging. (1986: 230)

While the rewards of aging in the United States are not clear to the young, and elders typically do not consciously specify what these rewards are, nevertheless there are enough rewards to belie the cultural assumptions. These youthful and incorrect cultural assumptions— that self-appraisal and body satisfaction decline, and that death anxiety increases with age—are also implicit in Sankar's (1987) analysis of the cultural construction of elder age groups in the United States (that old age is associated with disease and decline, which entails dependency on others). These assumptions, Sandar notes, led to the creation of an additional category of agedness. Agedness is revealed to be quite a different state when its rewards are seen from the perspective of elders.

Gender Influences on Perceptions of Aging

While both women and men were concerned with physical and behavioral changes in themselves as they aged, they tended to emphasize different characteristics. These differences in perspective are consistent with the ideals of femininity and masculinity in U.S. culture. Curlew Point women learned to think of their bodies as attracting the sexual interests of men and the admiration of other women, whereas men tended to see their bodies as energetic, competitive sources of control over others, both men and women. Hence, men's concerns were often connected to authority issues.

Women generally were concerned with hairstyling, clothes, health, and sexual attractiveness. Over the year of fieldwork, women in conversation with me spoke frequently of feminine beauty, theirs and others'. Discussions of strategies for appearing more youthful in hairstyle, fashion, and behavior suggested that youth is the stage of life when physical appearance is most consistent with U.S. cultural ideals of beauty. In her own shop, in the presence of several middle-aged and aging European-American women, Millie, a hairdresser, discussed women's hairstyling habits with me. The older women added comments as they wished, occasionally offering anecdotes.

Young adolescent women, Millie noted, didn't get their hair styled in the beauty shop. They did their own or one another's hair except when they planned to attend a special, formal event. Women began frequenting the hairdresser after they married and were older.[4] Around age forty-five or fifty, a woman tended to settle on a particular hairdo, which she continued to prefer for some time, unless a hairdresser or a younger family member or a more fashionable friend talked her into trying a new style. Millie added that even then, "They don't want people to think they are trying to be too young."

Other women in the beauty shop that day added that their husbands often wanted them to grow their hair longer (this was the fashion for younger women at the time) and to use more colorful hair ornaments. The husbands did not like for them to change their hair color, however, even if it was graying. Middle-aged to older women reported that they felt foolish wearing the same hairstyles as younger women, and they thought their husbands strange not to realize that they would surely appear foolish to others. Connie, in her early fifties, was a younger wife to a retired man. She commented with some wonder that her husband seemed to be unaware that she had grown older.

Being told that they looked younger than they actually were usually pleased elder women (and men as well). Many complimented older persons by noting that they appeared more youthful. An African-American retired schoolteacher named Katherine recalled with delight her visit to her own teacher-daughter's classroom. There the students protested she couldn't possibly be their teacher's mother because she had no wrinkles on her face.

When Greta (seventy-two years old, European-American, middle class) modeled a currently fashionable and sporty sweater for her grandniece, she said she feared it was too youthful-looking for her. When her grandniece, Alice, responded that the sweater helped her look younger, Greta appeared very pleased. She said she would wear it "the rest of my life." Greta's statement of her fear may well be what Mimi Nichter and Nancy Vuckovic, in another chapter in this book, see as a "call for positive strokes" (or supportiveness). When a girl says, "I'm so fat," others should quickly deny it. Here Greta doesn't say she's old but instead focuses on the sweater as too youthful. Alice quickly denies this, giving the supportive comment Greta sought.

Marriage, or seeking to be married, was much discussed among younger to middle-aged women. Typically, they assumed publicly that everyone was heterosexual and that younger women would seek respectable expression for that orientation in marriage.[5] However, elder women who usually had already been married, and were often widowed, rarely expressed much concern over marital status. Though they discussed husbands, these conversations were far less focused. The women were much more likely to discuss their adult children. Prestige by association probably was greater in old age for a woman who spoke about her adult children. Doing so also announced that she had done her reproductive and maternal duty in rearing children. Sometimes, elder women stated this more directly, saying, "I've done my duty."

Humorous references to sexuality and sexual liaisons, however, were frequent among the elder women and seemed much less frequent among the younger ones. At a bridge club gathering, a friend of Greta's teased her about having lived with three men, all younger. Greta teased back delightedly, "only two; now you exaggerated." She clearly enjoyed being presented (safely among friends) to the anthropologist as having been sexually disreputable with younger men.

In fact, Greta had rented a room in her house to these young men serially, not all at once; there had been a severe housing shortage in the community that year resulting from a hugh construction project just outside town. Greta, in other contexts, revealed a desire to be seen as uninterested in sexuality. She worried that her aging son (in his fifties) would be embarrassed by her if she had any romantic associations at all, even with age-appropriate men.

Some women were concerned about their privileges as elders in work competition with junior age groups. They spoke of their greater sense of responsibility, their more predictable performance of roles, their greater flexibility, and their rights to assert authority. Both adolescent and elder women acted as baby-sitters for young families. In this context Greta recalled a time when a young couple was away for a full weekend and she shared childcare responsibilities with a teenager. The couple had allotted a set sum for their pay. When the teenager asked for more than expected, they assumed Greta would be satisfied with less than they promised. She recalled that she felt "belittled" by their assumption.

Elder women decried their waning energies at times, and then they emphasized the need for "younger blood" to take official responsibilities. A Methodist church in town went several months without leadership of the women's umbrella organization (there were several church women's groups) because elder women who had held leadership for twenty years refused reelection. They declaimed "younger blood" should now take over. However, no younger women were willing; they had to be pressured for several months before agreeing to run for office.

Elder women discussed their physical problems and ill health a great deal. Informal talk before club meetings was usually full of news about their health and that of those they knew. They discussed the details of these illnesses with familiarity, a little sadness, and kindly solicitude for one another. Their group behavior also showed this solicitude and awareness of diminished abilities. They quietly reminded each other to clean faces or clothes of food that had been unmindfully dropped. They helped each other to walk and have what they needed.

Men spoke about aging differently, reflecting their concern with keeping authority and remaining competitive sexually and economically. In contrast to women, men focused more on their own sexuality and sexual opportunities in relation to that of younger men. Agreeing in the privacy of a woman's space, older European-American women in the hairdresser's shop collectiveely commented that they felt men worried more about growing old than they did. One woman added that they worried in particular about their "sexual potency."

Younger men often assumed older men would not be sexually interested in younger women and often were surprised to discover this was not the case. Younger men also felt compelled to show embarrassment (and sometimes resentment) when older women expressed sexual interest in them.

Elder men joked about younger men's reputations for extensive sexual activities. They sometimes linked these with premature aging. The first joke I heard during my fieldwork year made this point and was told me by Stockton, a European-American realtor-manager who rented me one of the only available apartments in town. Stockton, in his fifties, told this joke:

> An elderly, decrepit man walked with a cane barely getting along. Another man stopped him to ask him what he attributed his long life to. He replied that when he was hungry, he ate. When he was sleepy, he slept. When he wanted to make love, he just made all kinds of love, as much as he wanted. When the younger man asked him how old he would be on his next birthday, he said, "if I make it—twenty six."

Disapproving comments made about relationships between elder men and younger women, or elder women and younger men, implied that exploitation must be occurring (Fennell 1981; Hess 1972). Either the elder inappropriately enjoyed youthful sexuality, an exploitation, or the junior inappropriately enjoyed an elder's wealth, an exploitation. These assumptions suggest there is a hierarchical dimension to age relations in human communities (Fennell 1974; Foner 1984). But in the United States, sexual relationships should be between those of the same generation rather than allowing elder males privileged access to junior-generation females, as is common in many other cultures (Foner 1984).

One intergenerational marriage was described sympathetically by Billy, a European-American consultant aged thirty. Billy's father was in his sixties and had married a woman forty years his junior and lower class as well. Sensing that others made negative comments, Billy defended his father's marriage by saying, "It's good for her and it's good for him." The reciprocity he felt was there belied the disapproval of others. However, people generally don't support such matings and marriages, and those who do are pressured to justify that support.

Men of different generations do not feel the same about sexual competition. Junior men don't want it, and elder men do, as implied in their diverse protests. Elder men felt pressured not to be sexually competitive with junior men, and they protested this even as wives reported that men their age feared losing sexual potency. The social loss and the fear of physical loss may well be linked. Cultural ideals practiced in Curlew Point, however, did not always negatively label physical signs of aging in men. Gray hair on men was often said to be distinguished, an attractive symbol of social strength and maturity.

Elder women talked a great deal about maintaining their fashionableness, but they avoided any implication of competition with younger women, though frequently they mentioned humorous sexual interest in younger men. Younger women even joined in reassuring elder women of their attractiveness, but there seemed to be the assumption that these women would not seek younger men's attentions. Community cultural ideals also assured this by labeling the physical signs of aging in women as sexually undesirable to men.

Men spoke about job competition and their fears about performing well in work settings. Junior men feared that others would reject their assertions of authority. Teachers at the middle school described a young male teacher (in his twenties, European-American) known for his severe spankings of male students at the school (grades six through eight). Female teachers whispered their disapproval. They guessed that he felt insecure in his authority. No one really tried to stop his behavior. An elder male teacher (in his sixties, European-American) was openly ridiculed by students in his classroom, showing that people do flaunt men's authority. Thus elder men's fears of losing authority are based on how others respond to them.

Having their authority unchallenged on the job was not a sure thing for younger men. A hiring pattern I didn't expect also showed up in my business surveys examining age relations. Men in the position to hire others consistently hired younger persons, even when they themselves were in their early twenties. At a downtown street celebration, Kenny (a construction worker, twenty-three and European-American) talked with me for some time about his work. He dreaded having older men work under him on the four-worker team he supervised. He said trying to assert authority over an older man made him uncomfortable. The senior men gave him a hard time as well because they resented having a younger man as a boss. He expressed the problem that stood behind the patterned hiring practices.

Junior men also discussed the adequacy of elder workers, often finding them lacking. For example, David (European-American, in his early thirties) and Luke (European-American, almost seventy) were both fishing boat captains, but David thought Luke depended on him to find the good fishing areas and to get him and his boat home safely in threatening storms. Yet David was never quite sure because Luke never admitted his dependence, and David never felt it appropriate to confront him.

Considering these issues from an older man's view, Robeson, who was African-American and about fifty-five, talked about his executive responsibilities. In a long workplace interview, he revealed contradictory attitudes. First, he preferred to hire younger persons, he said, because they seemed more receptive to newer methods and work techniques. Elders, by implication, were less receptive to newer methods. Second, he recalled that he had felt in the past that he would retire earlier because he felt aging diminished a person's capacities. However, he noted that he was far better organized as an older man than when he was younger. He had come more recently to believe that elders offered good preparation and efficient organizing skills that were lacking in junior people. He saw one set of features in older subordinates (resistance to new techniques) and another in himself as an aging person (organization skills). Despite this irony, he continued to prefer younger workers, perhaps because they accepted his authority and direction with less resistence.

Women and men shared concerns with their attractiveness, but while it was a focus for women, men were covert about their wishes to remain youthfully attractive. For example, while repairing my car, Bob (European-American, probably in his forties) talked briefly about his responses to aging. He admitted that as his hair grew longer, he noticed his gray hairs were less apparent, so he deliberately let his hair grow for this reason.

Men also worried about their loss of physical agility and vigor generally. David, the younger fisher mentioned earlier, recalled that in his younger days he could sort fish for twenty-four hours straight while sitting on a soft drink crate. Now, in his early thirties, he had acquired back problems. He let younger boat workers help a lot more.

Perhaps losing their vigor stimulates men's fears that others may admire them less. A phrase used in a number of different settings in Curlew Point suggested local admiration of masculine energy—"sap's rising." It was used as a wry comment on male responses and humorously to explain the vigorous excesses of adolescent males, either in rowdiness or sexuality. The same phrase was also used to acknowledge an old man's unusual sexual interests in young women. Greta

(European-American, aged seventy-two) told of an old man in the nursing home who wanted to return home for the spring to put in one more garden. It was then, too, that she smiled and said, "Sap's rising." The phrase is an acknowledgment of powerful response to nature and season and reproductive urges. A metaphor that likens men to trees is also a humorously exaggerated phallic reference. Curlew Pointers laugh but also admire the energy. Perhaps it is the loss of this admiration that especially stimulates men's dread of losing their vigor.

Women and men, then, were attentive to different aspects of the aging experience. Women's concepts of femininity urged them to concentrate on fashion and the beauty of their bodies, faces, and hair. Their bodies as symbols of beauty were intended to please and attract others. Elder women tended to deemphasize an implied competition with junior women, though they enjoyed humorous references to their sexual interests in younger men.

On the other hand, men's concepts of masculinity urged them to speak about their bodies as energetic and competitive sources of control. Nicole Sault, in another chapter in this volume, notes the remarkable cultural concern in the United States with assisting men to maintain their "body boundaries" and control their bodies. This control is linked to ideals of achievement and self-sufficiency. The data from Curlew Point support this interpretation. Elder men assert their right to compete with younger men for sexual opportunities and authority, thereby showing achievement and self-sufficiency through their vigor and sexual capacity.

Women acknowledge their concern over loss of vigor more in discussing illnesses frankly and with sympathy. Men deemphasize illness most of the time and talk instead of losses in authority and sexual capacity.

Implicit Dimensions of Aging

It is apparent that people in Curlew Point implied several important dimensions which they used to judge age and to comment on the aging process. Individuals ranged from young to old on any of these dimensions: (1) physical development, (2) psychological maturity, (3) healthfulness, (4) modernness, and (5) chronological age. Underlying people's discussions was the assumption that a person can be young on one or two dimensions and old on others. While *old* is usually associated with less-valued characteristics, someone who is physically old may have youthful interests or dress (modernness) or be more physically fit than chronological peers. A teenager (ages 13–19) may be admired for her or his maturity of judgment.

Physical development as a dimension of aging usually revealed itself in discussions of the relative sizes of persons at various stages of life. This approach was utilized by consultants of all ages in the in-depth interviews I conducted late in the field year. Younger consultants spoke of older persons being "bigger." Big Mamma was an affectionate term for grandmother. But the pinnacle of desireable development was adulthood; oldness characteristics, as already noted, were seen as negative.

Agedness also seemed persistently associated not with normal aging, but with lack of healthfulness. Murphy (European-American, middle class, forty-five) felt old people were "more feeble because of diseases and sicknesses that came with age." Richie (European-American, sixty, middle class) pointed out that he would have called himself a young retiree except for his ill health, which made him feel more like an old man. Polunin (1977:95) notes the tendency for "health to be associated with higher status and disease with lower status" in the world's cultures.

Being up to date or current with the larger society's interests, tastes, and fashions was often mentioned as positively characterizing younger age groups. Elders were frequently disparaged as old-fashioned by younger people and their peers. An elder could be deemed more youthful by sharing youthful interests and fashions. Symbols of youth were compelling even when they were associated with elders. Interestingly, Schilder notes that "Since clothes are a part of the body schema, they gain the same significance as parts of the body and can have the same symbolic significance of parts of the body" (1950:203).

Chronological age was important for classifying one another, but once an individual clearly became adult, there was a tendency to disregard publicly exact chronological age.[6] In Curlew Point, adults may wait some time before inquiring about one another's ages. A birthday brings the issue up easily and inquiries are expected then. Yet consultants persistently reminded me that absolute chronological age was less important than the way a person behaved in showing symbols of age.

Once the various dimensions of age are kept in mind, the qualities of adultness and youth together combine the best of age positions to yield the greatest prestige. An adult has indisputable physical development and psychological maturity while youth is associated with healthfulness and modernness. Consultants described themselves as both adult and young whenever they could.

Consultants also revealed that they occasionally used the terms denoting age categories to describe their moods and the way they felt. Schilder points out the importance of multiple identifications for humans: "everybody builds his [her] own body image in contact with others. There is . . . a constant giving and taking so that it is true that many parts of body-images are common to persons who see each other, meet each other, and are in an emotional relation to each other" (1950:273). Richie (sixty, European-American, mentioned earlier) felt like an old man because of the ill health he often saw in men who were much older. Referring to the difficult day she had had before our interview, Lisa (European-American, twenty nine) responded facetiously to my question about how she would describe her own age. She said, "Yesterday I would have said 'elderly.' " She imagined what she felt was akin to being physically old. Richie also described the foolishness of his own peers by answering humorouusly that "sixty-five and beyond" chronologically defined the term *adolescence*.[7]

Preadult and older categories in these usages had negative connotations. *Old* was associated with ill health and feeling sad or disappointed; *adolescence* was associated with robust immaturity and playfulness. Symbols of age, then, can be metaphors to describe moods that are transient or personality traits that endure, or to describe social roles that emerge with cultural situations.

Conclusions

Discussions with Southern consultants in this small city showed much puzzling over United States cultural stereotypes for age groups. The symbols of aging were associated not only with chronological aging, but with physical development, psychological maturity, healthfulness, and modernness. Women concentrated on their physical appearance, whereas men showed concerns with their bodies as energetic and competitive sources of control. People's views on the aging process were influenced by these diverse concerns. Any one individual could be characterized as old or young on any of the five dimensions. Thus, anyone could be both young and old when all dimensions were considered. This complex view of aging allowed much flexibility in how people could characterize the aging processes and how they labeled one another. It also suggested that no person need be solely negative about the age-group membership of another. Curlew Pointers could praise or disparage one another on the basis of age as needed in whatever socio-cultural situations arose.

ACKNOWLEDGMENT

Funding for this research was provided by the Center for Studies of Metropolitan Problems, National Institute of Mental Health, grant number 1RO1 MH21550-01.

NOTES

1   I use the term *elder* as either an adjective or noun to describe or label an old person. Local people called the fragile old ones *elderly*, and in a comparison, *elder* simply means senior to another. These old ones are not fragile and may never be, but they are senior to most others in the community. I also like the cross-cultural connotations of *elder* (coming from ethnographies of smaller-scale societies), the implication that these people have judical authority and/or wisdom. I do feel that local elders showed more clear-sighted wisdom than their juniors.

2   Age and gender ranking systems are taught and practiced throughout the life cycle within the familial setting. Insults are part of the social control system that perpetuates age and gender stratification. As a result, people build up extensive psychological defenses against these disparagements. The primary defense mechanism used is denial of awareness of these disparagements.

3   Anthropologists traditionally use the term *informant*, which has always seemed to me too similar to *informer*, a word which not only implies higher authority to the one informed but also demeans the moral stance of the one offering information. Today anthropologists often speak of the expert knowledge of people about their own cultures. In the working world of United States culture, an expert is a consultant to the less educated. So I speak of the people who have helped educate me as consultants. They certainly gave expert information and opinion to this professional on the job. I do not wish to imply I have higher authority of interpretation either. *Informant* has this lingering connotation. Thus, I refer to people who helped me learn with the term *consultant*.

4   In another setting during an in-depth interview with a white, nineteen-year-old working-class man, he reported that he could recognize middle-aged women from the formal hairstyles they received at the beauty shops.

5   That some women and men were homoerotic was well known but only spoken about in private with close friends of the same generation. Public discourse denied the existence of homosexuality, pointing up the extreme importance in the community of maintaining enculturated sexual orientations for heterosexuality in people.

6   Chronological age is, however, far more important to scientists attempting "objectively" to track the indicators of human development along the dimension of age.

7   This merely suggests that peer-friendship behavior is similar in all stages of life, but the adolescent state is most recognized for this peer-friendship behavior, which often involves some deviant behaviors, a type of risk-taking to enhance group solidarity. We usually see this behavior as exuberance or playfulness.

REFERENCES

Blacking, John, ed. 1977. *The Anthropology of the Body*. London: Academic Press.

Brown, Judith K., and Virginia Kerns. 1985. *In Her Prime: A New View of Middle-Aged Women*. S. Hadley, Mass.: Bergin and Garvey.

Clark, Margaret, and Betty Anderson. 1967. *Culture and Aging: An Anthropological Study of Older Americans*. Springfield, Ill.: Charles C. Thomas.

Csordas, Thomas J. 1990. "Embodiment as a Paradigm for Anthropology." *Ethos* 18(1):5–47.

Fennell, Valerie. 1974. "Hierarchical Aspects of Age Relations." Ph.D. diss., University of North Carolina, Chapel Hill.

———. 1977. "Age Relations and Rapid Change in a Small Town." *Gerontologist* 17:405–411.

———. 1981. "Friendship and Kinship in Older Women's Organizations: Curlew Point, 1973." In *Dimensions: Aging, Culture, and Health*, ed. Christine L. Fry and Contributors. Brooklyn, N.Y.: J. F. Bergin.

Fisher, Seymour. 1986. *Development and Structure of the Body Image*, vols. 1 and 2. Hillsdale, N.J.: Lawrence Erlbaum Associates.

Foner, Nancy. 1984. *Ages in Conflict: A Cross-Cultural Perspective on Inequality between Old and Young*. New York: Columbia University Press.

Haddon, Genia Pauli. 1988. *Body Metaphors*. New York: Crossroad Publishing.

Hess, Beth. 1972. "Friendship." In *Aging and Society: Sociology of Age Stratification*, vol. 3, ed. M. Riley, M. Johnson, and A. Foner. New York: Russell Sage Foundation.

Jaggar, Alison M., and Susan R. Bordo, eds. 1989. *Gender/Body/Knowledge: Feminist Reconstructions of Being and Knowing*. New Brunswick, N.J.: Rutgers University Press.

Kerns, Virginia. 1980. "Aging and Mutual Support Relations among the Black Carib." In *Aging in Culture and Society*, ed. Christine L. Fry and Contributors. Brooklyn, N.Y.: J. F. Bergin.

Moore, Henrietta L. 1988. *Feminism and Anthropology*. Minneapolis: University of Minnesota Press.

Moore, Sally Falk. 1978. "Old Age in a Life-Term Social Arena." In *Life's Career—Aging: Cultural Variations on Growing Old*, ed. B. Myerhoff and A. Simic. Beverly Hills, Calif.: Sage.

Myerhoff, Barbara, and Andrei Simic, eds. 1978. *Life's Career—Aging: Cultural Variations on Growing Old*. Beverly Hills, Calif.: Sage.

Polunin, Ivan. 1977. "The Body as an Indicator of Health and Disease." In *The Anthropology of the Body*, ed. John Blacking. London: Academic Press.

Raybeck, Douglas. 1988. "Anthropology and Labeling Theory: A Constructive Critique." *Ethos* 16(4):371–397.

Sankar, Andrea. 1987. "The Living Dead: Cultural Constructions of the Oldest Old." In *The Elderly as Modern Pioneers*, ed. Philip Silverman. Bloomington: Indiana University Press.

Scheper-Hughes, Nancy, and Margaret M. Lock. 1987. "The Mindful Body: A Prolegomenon to Future Work in Medical Anthropology." *Medical Anthropology Quarterly* 1(1):6–41.

Schilder, Paul. 1950. *The Image and Appearance of the Human Body: Studies in the Constructive Energies of the Psyche.* New York: International Universities Press.

Sokolovsky, Jay, ed. 1987. *Growing Old in Different Societies: Cross-Cultural Perspectives.* Acton, Mass.: Copley.

SPLITTING THE SELF

I n the following chapters, Dixie L. King and Robbie E. Davis-Floyd show how personal conflict is expressed through a divided body image in which the self is defined as mind and separated off from the body. A woman's lack of control in her relations with others is translated into a sense of powerlessness regarding her own body. Whether consciously or not, she sees her body as a separate entity against which she must struggle for control. Her body becomes a source of embarrassment and shame, a symbol of weakness and disorder.

King's research was conducted in a residential recovery house whose program is based in Overeaters' Anonymous, a Twelve-Step Program for persons with eating disorders. Significantly, most of the residents were women, and King's discussion addresses their experiences in particular. The residents were incapacitated by food and body obsessions, but not particularly anorexia or bulimia (bingeing and purging). They shared the feeling that their bodies had betrayed them and were out of control. The residents spoke about their bodies in the third person, betraying their perception of the body as separate and distinct from the self. Individuals openly talked about the hatred they felt toward their bodies, feeling ashamed of their bodies and their sexuality. To survive emotionally, they projected these negative feelings onto the body as a way of distancing the self from pain.

At many points during the recovery program, the staff and residents recognized the interconnections between body alterations and social relationships. In narrating their life histories, the residents described early childhood traumas, abuse, and disrupted social ties—events commonly linked to the onset of eating disorders. For these residents, social upheaval was expressed through personal fragmentation into body versus self.

Residents tended to stay in the program because they believed it was the only way to succeed and they could continue to live with their families. Although twelve-step programs on the outside offer guidelines, these groups do not provide a place to live; also, because these programs do not enforce their rules, the risk of failure is greater. For persons with eating disorders, no alternative reference group offers the same ongoing sense of identity and belonging as does the residential program King examined. The staff of the program teach a resident that if she follows the guidelines, her body will change, she will become attractive, and her social relationships will improve.

The recovery program members are also taught that their problem is not located in the body, for they suffer from a spiritual distress physically manifested in the body as loss of control. According to the staff, this spiritual problem requires a spiritual solution—a spiritual recovery achieved through surrender to the will of God, using a twelve-step program derived from Alcoholics Anonymous. Yet in this program, spiritual success is demonstrated through control of the body measured by losing weight and becoming thin, for the ideal woman is a thin woman. The staff imply that it is better to be thin because a thin woman is sexy, whereas a fat woman is not a sexual being. They believe that a woman's sexuality is important because she can use her body to control others instead of being controlled. Recovery is measured by the ability to stay thin. The contrast between the emphasis on a spiritual source for the problem and the physical measure of recovery creates a tension in the program that neither staff nor residents recognize.

King's research shares certain elements with the work of Mimi Nichter and Nancy Vuckovic, such as the discussion of body weight and size, the emphasis on the control of eating behavior, and the social ideal of the thin woman, but the contrasts between the two studies are marked. In the chapter by Nichter and Vuckovic, the adolescent girls feel the need to talk about being fat and dieting, but they do not actually diet extensively in order to lose weight. The emphasis is on verbally showing a concern for self-control as a demonstration of shared values and group identity as defined by their peers. They use "fat talk" to become popular, maintain group relationships, and mark their participation in a particular peer group. However, the women

King describes are expected to work the twelve-step program seriously and measurably lose weight, as judged by the staff who are the authority figures in the program.

The chapter by Davis-Floyd examines another mind-body split, one that occurs in the self-image of professional women as they experience pregnancy, childbirth, breast-feeding, and motherhood. In conducting interviews with this group of women, Davis-Floyd found that they see their lives as divided into two separate worlds with two separate selves, namely, the personal and the professional. According to this worldview, the professional self has priority, for it represents the true self. These women feel that the personal world of home and family conflicts with the professional world of work. They struggle to keep the personal out of their professional world, although they accept that the professional continually intrudes upon the personal world.

The contrast between professional and personal worlds is reflected in a parallel contrast between the self as mind and the body as other. The mind represents the professional world of work, while the body represents the personal world of home and family. Here control over the personal is interpreted as control over the body—which keeps the body from intruding upon the mind, while enabling the mind to act upon the body. For these professional women, pregnancy is an obvious violation of the boundaries separating these two worlds. When the personal intrudes upon the professional, it undermines the carefully constructed image a woman hopes to present of herself as a "business kind of guy." Professional women want power and control, and like the bodybuilders described by Alan Klein, these women want to make things happen, rather than letting things happen to them. Both the women bodybuilders and the women professionals see pregnancy as intrusive. They want their minds to control their bodies and the larger world, rather than the other way around. The women professionals experience pregnancy as a loss of control and feel awkward, alienated, overwhelmed, and sometimes terrified. Later, their experience of childbirth heightens this sense of powerlessness, for they cannot control the contractions and the pain in their bodies, much less control others.

In this situation, disassociation from the body enables these women to achieve a sense of distance from unpleasant bodily experiences and to regain some semblance of control through the mind which is defined as self. Anesthesia and cesarean section offer an opportunity for the women to be present at the birth of their children, but only intellectually, for they have chosen not to be present "physi-cally." They use technology to translate conflict and pain into a hierar-chy of mind over body—creating a safe distance between the self and the problematic body and replicating the hierarchy of the profes-sional over the personal. As we saw in King's research on eating disorders, once again the body image of a divided self expresses the discord present in the larger context of social relations.

FOOD, SEX, AND SALVATION

The Role of Discourse in a Recovery Program for Eating Disorders

DIXIE L. KING

athy, a popular cartoon character created by Cathy Guisewite, is the American "any woman." Cathy is perennially obsessed with her makeup, her hair, her clothes, her boyfriend—and her body. In one 1989 strip, Cathy muses about what is happening to her body unbeknown to herself. "I tortured myself with diets for nine months," she proclaims, "and I gained fourteen pounds. I forgot all about dieting for three weeks, and I lost six pounds." After silently contemplating her body for a moment, she adds ruefully, "Even when I'm totally by myself, everyone in the room is doing something I don't know about."

Cathy's plight is something we laugh about, something to which almost any American woman can relate—the sense that somehow, without our conscious knowledge or consent, our bodies are living lives of their own, fluctuating, ebbing and flowing, sometimes larger, sometimes smaller, often out of our conscious control. For a growing number of American women, the body's ultimate betrayal takes the form of a culturally constructed, socially validated, medically diagnosable eating disorder.

Eating disorders have reached epidemic proportions in the United States in recent years, as in other Western, industrialized countries (Garner et al. 1980:484). The medical and psychiatric communities traditionally have recognized both anorexia (self-imposed starvation) and bulemia (binge-purging) as legitimate disorders, and a growing treatment market offers a variety of medical solutions for each. In addition, a number of prominent self-help organizations have sprung up over the last twenty-five years to offer support and services to self-diagnosed sufferers of eating disorders.

Interestingly, however, a substantial number of the members of these organizations are not and have never been anorexic or bulemic—and often, in fact, do not have a "weight problem," even by the svelte standards of American society. Describing themselves as compulsive overeaters, these members are almost exclusively women. The two things they have in common with the anorexic and bulemic are (1) an obsessive preoccupation with food and/or body weight and size, and (2) the increasing inability to function normally in society because of that preoccupation.[1] In addition, they share a range of symptoms that includes severe body-image distortion, often expressed in the separation of body and self. "When I'm fat," explains one female participant in Marion Woodman's 1980 study of eating disorders, "I'm not good friends with my body. When I'm thin I am. When I can talk to it, I'm nine-tenths out of the depression." Another claims, "My car is more important to me than my body, more a part of me. When I think of myself, I think of my mind." "I have a good relationship with my body," insists a third, "but I don't like being tied to a dying animal" (Woodman 1980:25–26).

That eating disorders, by whatever definition, appear to be a culture-bound syndrome, that the number of people affected have grown almost exponentially, and that the vast majority of sufferers are women have concomitantly increased the interest of the social science community in the topic. Since 1973, when psychiatrist Hilda Bruch published the findings of her forty years of clinical work with eating disorder patients, anorexia, bulimia, and obesity have been the subject of historical research (e.g., Bell 1985; Brumberg 1988), clinical research (Szekely 1988; Woodman 1980), social science research (Spitzack 1990), and impassioned social crusades (e.g., Orbach 1978, 1982; Schoenfielder and Wieser, 1983). Whether using a family systems model to explain the inexplicable and posit a treatment hypothesis (e.g., Minuchin et al. 1978), or a feminist perspective to move the argument to a societal level with perhaps even less individually attainable solutions (e.g., Boskind-Lodahl 1976; Chernin 1981; Spitzack 1990), there appears a general acceptance that the study of eating disorders has much to reveal about the experience of North American women, individually and collectively.

In a society still bound by the rules and power configurations of patriarchy, our questions remain linked to the psychosocial and sociopolitical: Why does the problem affect so many more women than men? Can obsessive behavior around food and body be a kind of psychological outlet for anger, frustration, or impotence (whether personal, familial, or social)? Can it be a conscious or subconscious behavioral "choice" among many deviant-behavior options? If so, what is the social and/or cultural significance of that particular "choice"? Can eating disorders be a cultural metaphor for the experience of powerlessness? And perhaps the most important question of all: If, indeed, obsessive eating behavior is a symptom of social malaise which resides in the female body, is any treatment resulting in a return to so-called normative behavior possible or even desirable?

Despite the attention eating disorders have gained, however, and the clear relevance of political and social phenomena to both their existence and their treatment, little grounded research and no long-term ethnographic research have been published to date that link either the psychosocial or the sociopolitical context of women's lives to women's experience of treatment and recovery.[2] Yet research that examines treatment choices, notions of what constitutes recovery, and women's long-term experience of the recovery process have perhaps more explanative value than our studies of eating disorders themselves. It is in the context of treatment and recovery that definitions of normative behavior become fixed, that realization of and challenges to cultural norms may occur, and, through the response of institutions, that the social order is reified.

The ethnographic and life-history research I conducted over a sixteen-month period at Meridian House, a residential recovery house for persons with eating disorders, was an attempt to begin to address this gap in the literature. Because it was a residential facility, and because its program was based on that of the most popular self-help group in the United States today (Alcoholics Anonymous, adapted for Overeaters Anonymous), Meridian offered the ideal opportunity to conduct a long-term study on a popular, nonmedical concept of "recovery," and to see how recovery was defined for and manifested in the lives of program participants.

In the remainder of this chapter, I describe the recovery program at Meridian House and the residents' response to it. I demonstrate how the use of what I term "recovery discourse" simultaneously served to resocialize women into a particular concept of recovery and provided the criteria for evaluating residents' commitment to the recovery process. I also show that while discourse was the primary indicator of residents' level of commitment, body size remained the primary indicator of success in recovery for both staff and residents. Finally, I describe how conflicting ideologies of what constitutes recovery reflect a cultural construct of femininity within our society, which implicitly and explicitly devalues, controls, and exploits the female body.

Meridian House

A four-bedroom house located in the residential district of a small desert community, Meridian House offered its residents a recovery program based on the Twelve-Step Program of Alcoholics Anonymous. Meridian's facilities accommodated approximately eight residents at any given time, with two staff people in residence. The initial time commitment required upon entry into the house was three months; average length of stay was approximately four. The cost of a stay at Meridian was nominal, about $800 per month.

There were no resident physicians, psychotherapists, psychiatrists, or other medical personnel on staff at Meridian. Staff defined themselves as recovering alcoholics and compulsive overeaters. The house offered no diet or food program, for diets were seen as the antithesis of recovery in this program. Residents ate three moderate meals a day, served family style. Twice daily the residents were taken through a guided meditation, the focus of which was establishing contact with the damaged "inner child," toward whom much of the recovery process was directed. Residents wrote down and shared with either staff or volunteer mentors (sponsors) feelings experienced during the course of their day. Finally, and most importantly, they "worked the twelve steps" of Alcoholics Anonymous.[3]

"Working the steps" included writing a detailed "moral inventory" that was a combined life history and critical assessment of personal faults and failings, particularly as these were manifested in one's relationships with others. Residents attended meetings of Alcoholics Anonymous, Overeaters Anonymous, and Adult Children of Alcoholics, and some participated in outside experiential therapy workshops. Additionally they were expected to participate in house raps, where residents shared publicly their feelings about their own progress and received feedback from staff. They attended daily "book studies," conducted by staff, which included reading from and interpreting the text of the Big Book of Alcoholics Anonymous.[4] In short, residents were totally immersed in a resocialization process explicitly designed to bring about a change in consciousness, termed by staff a "spiritual awakening."

The Residents

Between January 1988 and March 1989, I spent approximately three days a week living at Meridian House. I combined participant observation with intensive one-on-one interviews of both residents and staff. Initial interviews were totally unstructured; I asked each resident to tell me his or her life story. These interviews ran from two to thirty hours in length, averaging about six hours. Several residents provided me with excerpts from their journals. I taped a number of house raps and observed one of the experiential therapy workshops in which two residents participated. In addition, I conducted follow-up interviews periodically with five residents in the year following their departure from the house. The result of this aggressive schedule was over three hundred hours of taped interviews and house meetings, and the opportunity to work intensively with fourteen residents and four staff people over the sixteen months of the study and the follow-up period.

Residents initially appeared to share few characteristics, apart from their self-identified obsession with food and weight. Not all were overweight, not all were bulimic. Upon entry into the house, their weights varied from normal or slightly below normal to morbidly obese (defined as one hundred pounds or more above recommended body weight). Of twenty-two people who lived in-house, however briefly, during the sixteen months of the study, only three were male. Residents came from every social class and ranged from a high school dropout to an electrical engineer.[5] They ranged in age from eighteen to fifty-five. Some identified themselves as alcoholics or drug addicts as well as compulsive overeaters. Roughly half had had previous exposure to Twelve-Step programs.

Life-history work with residents, however, disclosed that there were indeed common underlying themes in the lives of many. All but two had experienced either physical or sexual abuse as children. (In this context, I define physical abuse as frequent and/or intensive beatings or beatings with belts, brushes, sticks or other instruments; kicking, punching or throwing; and other forms of extreme physical violence.)[6]

One resident claimed she did not know if she had ever suffered abuse; at eighteen years of age and three hundred pounds, she had no memories of her life preceding her mother's death when she was ten years old. Most residents came from divorced families; two-thirds had at least one alcoholic or drug-addicted parent. More than half were incest survivors. Half considered themselves alcoholics or drug addicts. Six came into the house on some form of prescribed tranquilizer or antidepressant. (They were weaned of medication within a few days to a month of their arrival.) One woman entered as a cocaine addict, and one a heroin addict. All but one of the nineteen women entering the house during the period of the study defined themselves as heterosexual, although a few had experimented with same-sex partners. One of the three men identified himself as gay.

There were definite gender distinctions in the behavior and attitudes of the women and men. None of the men came into the program voluntarily; two came out of medical necessity and the third to save his job. Raymond, entering at five hundred pounds, had been referred to Meridian by a medical practitioner in another state who had heard about Meridian from a graduate of the program. Now in his early fifties, Raymond had suffered a series of strokes, had spent several months in the hospital, and, upon arriving at Meridian, was barely able to walk or care for his most basic needs. He left within a week, unable to tolerate the structure of the program. The second, Ben, at thirty-six years of age and 475 pounds, had spent the last ten years of his life confined to a hospital bed in a hotel room, from which he sold drugs to support his food habit. Busted for selling drugs and physically incapacitated by both his weight and cystic ulcers that had destroyed the circulation in his legs, he served time in the medical unit of a county jail. His brother, a recovering addict, made arrangements for him to come to Meridian after his release. During the first three months of his year-long residence at the house, Ben adamantly maintained his right to "be who he was, at the weight he was" and participated grudgingly in the program; in the early days, he often used his bulk when angry to physically intimidate staff and other residents. The third man (who self-identified as gay), a drug and alcohol counselor at a neighboring facility, was approximately forty pounds overweight. He was told by his supervisor that he would associate himself with Meridian as closely as possible (while still maintaining his duties) and deal with his eating problem or lose his job; consequently, he lived in-house a few days a week for about sixty days.

The story was considerably different for the women. With the exception of Jessica, an eighteen-year-old (whose widowed father informed her that he had "enrolled" her without her knowledge the day before she entered the house), all the female residents entered voluntarily. For several, this was one in a series of treatment attempts that had included repeated stays in eating disorder and psychiatric units in hospital recovery programs. With the exception, again, of Jessica and one other eighteen-year-old, all the women interviewed perceived themselves as powerless to control their reactions to life events and as socially dysfunctional. They identified their isolation, their inability to maintain personal relationships, and the demoralization brought about by their dysfunctional eating behavior, more than any desire (or need) to lose or gain weight, as what brought them to Meridian.

Everything residents were to learn from staff about the consequences of "living in the disease" (continuing to eat compulsively) had been confirmed by these women's past experience. As long as they were fat, or saw themselves as fat, they could not function socially. Their weight had affected their primary relationships; it kept them from entering into sexual relationships. It affected their ability to obtain and retain good jobs. It made them the overt object of ridicule, a social judgment which reflected their intense internal shame. This shame was not exclusive to their physical condition; their bodies were for them the symbol of deep feelings of personal unworthiness, inadequacy, and self-hatred.

None of the male residents, including the man who was gay, had ever experienced having their masculinity called into question *because of their weight,* probably because appearance is not the primary criterion used to define or judge masculinity in American society. Female residents, on the other hand, accepted and even embellished the messages given them by the media and society: fatness is the antithesis of femininity. Fat equals lazy, slothful, stupid, and sexually unattractive. It also equals dirty, sinful, and shameful, an outward reflection of the state of the inner self.

Several of the women came to Meridian within fifteen to twenty pounds of ideal body weight, but every one of them beleived, and expressed with compelling certainty, that she internally fit the criteria of fat; it just hadn't yet physically manifested. These women told of their increasing inability to make their "insides" match their "outsides." They *looked* functional, and in many cases maintained good, often high-paying jobs; in short they "looked good." But they were increasingly obsessed with their bodies—how thin, how fat, how sexually attractive—and spent most of their waking hours attempting to control their food intake and weight. They lost all perspective on the actual size of their bodies. Residents understood and accepted that, fat or thin, as long as they remained obsessed with body size or food itself, they did not need to—in fact, had no time to—attempt to resolve the confusion between familial protestations of love and the reality of past physical abuse, between life as they thought it should be and life as it was. They could not make sense of chaotic family and life situations, they claimed, so they had retreated from life. They could not deal with their own sexuality, and so they had become asexual. They wondered, sometimes with anger, sometimes with resignation, what it was about themselves that made them the objects of the abuse they knew they must deserve.

Abstinence and Recovery

The proclaimed goal of the Meridian recovery program was not to make residents feel better about themselves or even to make them thin. Rather, staff attempted to bring about a cognitive change in residents' self-perceptions, in short, to help them realize a valid and independent selfhood.

Despite the fact that they explicitly defined compulsive overeating as a disease, the staff stressed that this disease is not located in the body; the body is merely manifesting the physical symptoms of what the staff defined as a disease of the soul—a spiritual problem requiring a spiritual solution.

A compulsive overeater cannot abstain from compulsive eating behavior of her own accord; if she were capable of making this choice and carrying it out, she would have done so long before arriving at Meridian. She suffers from a disease that, like diabetes, can never be cured; it can only be brought into a state of remission. Residents were taught that they are incapable of controlling the body, that loss of control over the body is merely the symptom of a sickness that goes much deeper. By practicing the first three steps of the Twelve-Step Program, that is, by (1) admitting her powerlessness over the disease of compulsive overeating, (2) coming to believe that God has the power to "restore her to sanity," and (3) "turning her will and her life over to the care of God," a resident could gain the power to abstain from compulsive eating behavior. This would allow her spiritual recovery to begin, which in turn would be manifested in the recovery of her body. She would, in essence, achieve a spiritual awakening. This awakening was seen as the cornerstone of the recovery process, the single essential element without which a resident would be doomed to repeat the behavioral patterns that would eventually lead her to the brink of insanity and death.

A recovering resident would in time come to realize that her social dysfunction was not her fault. She was not stupid, unworthy, dirty, sinful, or evil. She would learn to place the blame for the onset of her condition on the messages she was given in childhood. Through written inventory work, attendance at Adult Children of Alcoholics meetings, and constant encouragement to explore her own feelings, a resident would come into touch with the forces in her past which were responsible for her dysfunctional behavior.

The recovery process would not stop with the resident learning to blame something or someone outside herself for her condition, however. Meridian staff sought to provide residents with a new infrastructure for dealing with relationships and the problems of daily living. Residents learned to invoke a higher power on their own behalf—a God, an ultimate authority that outranks even their parents and sexual partners. Staff taught residents that while they might have been victims as children, they were not victims as adults, unless they chose to be. Residents were told that, as adults, their selfishness and self-obsession had created most of the problems they faced. Their self-obsession and their food obsession may have saved them from a psychotic break or death as children; as adults in recovery their task was to unlearn the past. Through abstinence and the steps, residents would be resocialized into functional adult living.[7]

Residents demonstrated their commitment to the recovery process in a number of ways beyond maintaining their abstinence from compulsive eating behavior—for example, by adhering without question to staff orders, participating without reluctance in house chores and activities, and using the language of recovery. A resident's use of "recovery talk," that is, language that demonstrates understanding and acceptance of such program principles as powerlessness and surrender, was a key indicator in the staff's assessment of a resident's degree of recovery. Staff were aware that some residents were quite capable of "talking the talk" without "walking the walk," that is, using appropriate language but failing to demonstrate through their actions their willingness to surrender self-will. Consequently, staff constantly assessed both language and behavior to determine residents' sincerity and commitment to the recovery process. It is this complex interplay of language and behavior that I came to call *recovery discourse*, and that I use to analyze the relationship of the recovery concept to the broader context of American social norms and standards.

Recovery Discourse and the Process of Socialization

Recovery discourse performs three functions at Meridian. First, it establishes a cosmological framework (the Twelve-Step Program) within which residents are taught to examine and reinterpret past experience, including those behaviors related to obsessive patterns of eating. This process begins with the first writing assignment: "Tell your life story, beginning with 'Once upon a time there was a little girl . . .' " Residents "uncover" the events in their past that contributed to the onset of their disease, "discover" the relationship of those events to dysfunctional patterns of behavior in the present, and "discard" those behaviors by "turning them over to God." This process establishes the spiritual nature of the malady and the need for a spiritual solution.

Second, recovery discourse establishes causality by relocating the locus of control with the individual. That is, while compulsive eating behavior is defined in recovery as a disease requiring a spiritual solution, responsibility for recovery is placed squarely on the individual. She demonstrates her desire for recovery through obedience.

A successful resident must continually demonstrate a willingness to cede control over every aspect of her daily experience in the house to the staff. Staff determine when she gets up, what she eats, when she eats, what chores she will perform, even, occasionally, what clothes she will wear. A willingness to discard self-will in obedience to staff is seen, in essence, as a willingness to turn control of her life over to God. By the same token, refusal to obey, reluctance to participate in every aspect of the program, being late for meditation or other activities, and otherwise slothing off, were seen by staff as indicators of willfulness and could put a resident's tenure in the house in jeopardy.

Finally, recovery discourse reinforces the standard American social/ medical paradigm of women's health and illness by defining the imperfect body as diseased and equating spiritual health (recovery) with normative standards for physical attractiveness. The woman who fails to lose or gain weight as appropriate is judged as "not working her program," "not interested in recovery," and "spiritually lazy." In essence, then, the message of recovery is much the same as the message received from American society at large, but here it is couched in spiritual terms and raised to a new level of cosmic authority. The woman who cannot recover, as recovery is defined here, is truly damned.

The Use of Recovery Discourse in Reframing the Past

During a lengthy life-history interview, eighteen-year-old Kelly explained to me how she came to see herself as fat.

> When I was in sixth grade I was maybe about thirty-five, forty pounds overweight. . . . I had a boyfriend and had a whole bunch of friends and it was just like I didn't see my problem. I saw that I wasn't as thin as her, but she was really thin, so—you know. I was never fat in my eyes. So it was like no big deal in my life. And then . . . my boyfriend and his friends wanted to go jetskiing and they wanted to get a couple of my friends together. Well, I have not one overweight friend, okay? They are all either too thin or [have] just great bodies. So we decided to go. And it was the first day that I realized for one that I was the biggest one there, and that I was the only one in a one-piece bathing suit. I was real uncomfortable, and to get that feeling away [I got] loaded. That is when it finally hit me that this is why these girls are that thin, because they do drugs and they don't go home and eat like I do. And I'm just going to have to start this because they're looking really good. So I started [doing drugs], and it was for my weight.

Kelly originally learned that her overweight body was not acceptable through comparing herself with her friends as well as through a host of other social messages. Drugs became for her both a way to restructure her physical self, so that she might enter into full membership in her friends' social world, and a strategy for surviving the pain of failure.

To describe the process of recovery as practiced at Meridian as a resocialization process is not euphemistic. At Meridian, the attempt was made to resocialize Kelly, through the language of recovery, into seeing herself as an emotionally damaged child in the fat physical body of an addicted, dysfunctional adult—in short, diseased. However, neither of the two overweight eighteen-year-olds entering the house saw themselves as particularly dysfunctional. If their body images were distorted, it was not to the negative. They would have to learn their dysfunctionality and, following Step One, admit it, before recovery could begin. The lessons were sometimes brutal.

Carolyn, the founder of the recovery house and chairman of the board, took Kelly publicly to task one day for her lack of willingness to grow spiritually, that is, her failure to admit she was a compulsive overeater. "Don't you know how grotesque you look?" she concluded. Kelly was devastated. She told me,

> There's people here that are at a good weight and they feel like they are fat inside and [that] was never my problem. If I was thin, I knew I was thin and I knew I looked good and there was no problem with that. . . . the clothes I used to wear, half-shorts and little skirts, I felt real comfortable with. I look in the mirror now and I say, "You are so fat and I hate you."

Kelly's experience is one that documents the progress of assuming the gaze of the other and incorporating it such that it begins to define one's sense of self. This process began with Kelly's (negative) comparison of her body with those of her friends and was confirmed through her experience at Meridian. However, through her writing assignments as well as her participation in book studies and house raps (where she would hear others processing similar experience), Kelly would learn to reframe her physical noncomformity and growing disgust with her body as a disease requiring the outside intervention not of diet experts, but of God. She would enter into the discourse of recovery.

For women, the disease of compulsive overeating need not manifest itself physically to be present. A woman need not be fat or bulimic to be diseased, although these states indicate the presence of disease. She need only be obsessed.

For example, Mia, a twenty-nine-year-old electrical engineer, was escaping the demands of a controlling father who pushed her far beyond her desires or capabilities academically—and whom she adored. Calling her the son he'd never had, he insisted that she enter the pre-med program at Stanford. As her grades slipped and she began to fail her classes, Mia began to eat.

> I just did whatever I could to reward myself, to give myself the ability to stick with whatever I was doing. I almost dropped out of school many times, emotionally just was a mess most of the time I was there. Yet I always knew if I dropped out I'd never go back. I would fall apart and end up in a mental institution. Four padded walls. So I see today that eating really was how I survived. How I kept myself going. I was angry that I had gotten myself into these situations where I felt compelled to stick with it. I didn't want to be a quitter, but I didn't want to be doing what I was doing, either.

Mia knew, she said, that there was something wrong, something "sick" about her eating.

> I was a freshman and we'd have pizza parties in somebody's room late at night. And I remember I'd go to the cafeteria for the meals and starting to say to myself, "What will they think if I take seconds on dessert?" Or, "Do I have too much? Does this look too out of bounds?" Then, with pizza, "How many slices can I get before it looks bad?" Just constantly worrying about how it looked. And weight-wise I was normal. Absolutely normal.

Mia's body had not yet betrayed her by manifesting her diseased state. She was not overweight, but she had already learned to scrutinize her food intake; she had learned that overeating carries the taint of moral depravity. She was terrified that someone might judge her food intake as excessive. At Meridian, through taking moral inventory, she would learn that it was self-will, wanting to do things her own way, that caused her obsession with food. She would continually practice Step Three, consciously "turning her will and her life over to the care of God," so that she might experience freedom from her obsession. I asked her how she had come to realize this as the solution. Her response was revealing: "I have been humiliated at the group level into being willing to be more honest about my shit."

Christine, a thirty-six-year-old college administrator, would explicitly elevate the battle against self-will to a cosmological plane. She told me, "Recovery is all based on surrender and the knowledge that I can't do it, but God can and will if He's sought. All these vices that we have things that we're missing in our moral fiber [sic]. Parts of us, you know, lust and gluttony and greed, the seven deadly sins. It [recovery] is real spiritual, because it is a way of life, a manner of living." In the Twelve-Step Program, as it was interpreted at Meridian, the individual must concede her diseased state and her powerlessness to combat her disease; she must confess her moral transgressions through the process of moral inventory and public self-disclosure. In so doing, if she follows this course of action thoroughly, with complete honesty, and she maintains the willingness to forgo her personal, "selfish," willful desires, she paradoxically achieves power—the power to abstain, the power to attain physical health, the power to conform to the standards society has set for her as a woman.

Recovery Discourse and Locus of Control: The Responsibility for Recovery

Because compulsive overeating is couched in the terminology of moral malaise, because the solution, or cure, is seen as a spiritual one, responsibility for recovery is placed firmly back on the individual. All a woman needs is the *willingness* to recover and her recovery is assured; God will do the rest. Through recovery discourse, the battle with defects of character is reinterpreted within a theological framework: since "God is everything or He is nothing," if a woman truly turns "her will and her life over to the care of God," she cannot fail to recover. Failure to commit to recovery is indicative of spiritual laziness.

"So," I asked Linda, an unemployed single parent, "what does surrender look like? What does it mean to surrender?"

Oh man! It means to die, is what it means. It really means to die. That's what it feels like. It just feels like you just fuckin' are dying, real slow death. . . . Surrender feels like peace. It feels like serenity. It feels like a good, long sigh. You know, real deep. What it means to surrender literally is that I got to die, because I fight. And I kick and I scratch and I claw and I scream and I yell and I holler and I shout and I bleed and I fight. . . . And then I just, slowly, die. . . . Usually what happens is I end up literally curled in a ball in a fetal position on the floor or on my bed sobbing. And thinking that I am dying . . . and then I walk around in an altered state, where I just can't cope. It's like, breathe in, breathe out . . . drive the car, go to work, breathe in, breathe out. And then [in] a few days it breaks, and I realize it's been surrendered. Then next time the situation comes up, I don't get crazy—I do that sigh, then I feel that feeling.

The woman who surrenders need not eat. The woman who surrenders attains spiritual well-being. In short, the woman who surrenders attains salvation.

The physical plane being a reflection of the spiritual plane, a resident at Meridian must demonstrate her willingness to recover through her speech and her actions. The demand for obedience and submission to staff is interpreted as the outward demonstration of spiritual surrender to God; a woman committed to recovery, therefore, is willing to cede control over not only her food, but also the everyday decisions of her life to staff and/or her sponsor. Consequently, residents learned that their most personal decisions were subject to staff approval, and more than once staff members ordered residents to change clothing, put on makeup or change their makeup, wear a bathing suit on an outing, and so forth.

As might be expected in a setting of constant surveillance requiring unremitting demonstration of commitment through words and actions, covert power struggles over the issue of control and self-will versus surrender and recovery broke out continuously between staff and residents. Staff saw winning these struggles as necessary to the residents' recovery. While residents rarely rebelled openly against staff orders, most experienced and reported (to me) periods of intense resentment and anger against what appeared to be arbitrary commands and injunctions. For example:

- Residents were told that they were to give up trying to control their food intake, but must restrict their meals to three times a day.
- Residents were told that they were responsible for their own abstinence, but content of meals (see note 7) and helping size were monitored, and putting anything into one's mouth without staff approval, including a breath mint or chewing gum, was grounds for immediate expulsion from the program.

- Residents were told that most of their issues stemmed from codependency (that is, from excessive dependence on other people's behavior, opinions, or attitudes toward themselves) and that their recovery was dependent upon learning to stand up for themselves, becoming secure, developing self-esteem, but staff frequently used public humiliation as a tool of correction, and if residents questioned staff decisions they were told they could choose to leave the house.

Most contradictory of all, however, was the attitude toward body size and weight. Residents were not allowed to weigh themselves and were told that they were to "abstain from compulsive eating behavior and leave the results to God." "Your body size," residents were told over and over again, "is none of your business." If one abstains, one is working the program. One's body is sacrosanct, perfect as it is, and it is inappropriate to express discontent or to dwell obsessively on one's looks. Nevertheless, the primary means by which staff judged the long-term success of residents, graduates, and themselves remained weight loss or gain. Neither staff nor residents questioned the implicit belief that to be fat is to be dysfunctional and is indicative of "living in the disease." An alcoholic is judged by what he does; a recovering alcoholic who takes a drink is no longer sober. A compulsive overeater, on the other hand, is judged by how she looks; if she is not thin—a state defined by the media-based norms and standards of American society—she has "broken her abstinence." (It is no accident that the majority of those claiming membership in Alcoholics Anonymous traditionally have been male, but that in Overeaters Anonymous, women outnumber men ten to one or more.)

The implicit connection between physical recovery, sexuality, and locus of control was drawn constantly. The recovered—thin—woman was seen first and foremost as a sexual woman, and a sexual woman controls rather than is controlled. This attitude was often expressed by staff overtly, as when the director discussed her wardrobe with the residents, describing a particular article as "my come-fuck-me dress." Or when a staff person said to one woman about another whose recovery was seen as faltering, "She needs to get up off her butt and get herself laid." Or when a "friend of the house" who had gained twenty pounds expressed her dismay over her husband's request for a divorce, and a staff person whispered to a resident, "Would you want to come home to that ass?"

Staff, all female themselves, were genuinely unaware of the contradiction between the model they espoused—ceding control over body weight and size—and the methods by which they assessed and categorized women's behavior and bodies—achieving and maintaining a particular body weight and size. Simply put, staff and residents shared a cultural bias regarding the appropriate way females should look, speak, and behave. This bias reflects explicit media images of women and implicit constructs regarding the ways in which sexuality can be used to achieve control within the framework of a social hierarchy that devalues or limits the expression of femaleness. Consequently, in this setting, recovery is seen as resulting in female sexual potency, and sexuality becomes both an expression of physical recovery and the only legitimate means of owning power.

Recovery Discourse and the Reinforcement of Social Norms

In her book *Confessing Excess* (1990), Carol Spitzack analyzes what she calls anti-diet discourse—an appeal to women to reject dieting, defined as patriarchal and oppressive, in favor of taking control of one's own life on one's own terms. The appeal is to transcend patriarchal values, achieve freedom from the need to diet, and move toward a higher and acceptably enlightened goal—health. Paradoxically, Spitzack points out, health for women in American society is defined through physical appearance—thin, young, and beautiful—and thus conforms to those self-same social norms from which the anti-diet supposedly offers escape (1990: 12–20). In other words, by whatever road a woman chooses, the diet or the anti-diet, individual self-realization is normatively defined for her in terms of her body. Her freedom of choice is illusory; it is confined to which path she will tread toward the same end.

As Spitzack notes, anti-diet discourse has an ominous aspect to it. In exhorting women toward health, it defines women's bodies as diseased. The chronically underweight, obese, or bulemic body may metaphorically represent, as authors and research subjects alike have contended, the repression of rage, an act of social defiance, or the memory of physical, sexual, or emotional abuse; it may represent only genetic predisposition. But when the label "disease" is applied to the imperfect body, control is taken away from the individual woman and ceded to the socially recognized "experts"—whether they be diet clubs, health spas, or medical professionals—who will effect her cure.

The appeal—and, from the perspective of social control, the danger—of Twelve-Step recovery discourse is that it depends not on any fallible human authority, but on the limitless authority of a higher power. Like anti-diet discourse, recovery discourse is framed in the imagery of paradox: a "disease" caused by self-will, freedom through dependence, physical recovery through spiritual surrender, gaining control by ceding control.

This imagery is not whimsical but rooted within the dominant cultural paradigm; it is hardly coincidental that God, in this context, is perceived to have the same normative standards for women's behavior and appearance as American society as a whole. Here "freedom from the disease of compulsive overeating" offers a vision of control, power, and independence which is totally illusory. *The woman who achieves the power to conform has achieved nothing at all. She remains psychologically bound by cultural idiom. She remains socially controlled and controllable.* By first incorporating the gaze of the other, then by making it her own, she becomes her own jailer. No energy is required by the state or any outside entity to keep her imprisoned; she takes on that task herself. As one resident noted:

This is where I'm supposed to be. I feel like I've come to brink sometimes of blowing my abstinence, even if it was just by licking off the butter knife . . . but I don't want to get into that shit. Because I know, and I think this is what has kept me here, there is no place else to go. Absolutely no place for me, where I can go and feel okay about myself, if I screw up here. So it's just not an option. Therefore, doing whatever it takes to stay here is the only choice. And it feels good. It feels real good.

Borrowing from Foucault (1979), Spitzack points out, "In contemporary culture . . . power in the form of surveillance makes a demand on the individual to monitor the actions of the self, subjecting behavior to ever-greater examination, making visible each transgression, and punishing oneself for wrongdoing" (1990:43–44). Like Mia, Christine welcomed the staff's reinforcement of the lessons she was learning about her own "denial." In the passage below, she describes the conversation with Carolyn (the founder of the recovery house) after Carolyn's first meeting with Christine's boyfriend:

Carolyn met Johnny and liked him, and that meant a lot to me. She came up and hit me on the ass afterwards and said to me, "You lose this fat ass of yours for him—and for you." And then I went up to her that night and said, "I really appreciate your telling me that." And Carolyn said, "Really? I was really hard on you." I said, "It's what I needed to hear."

Nearly three months later, during a visit in her home, Christine explained to me the need for constant self-assessment, constant self-surveillance:

There is a danger that you forget. I think that's the biggest danger, and perhaps the biggest reason that it's good to go to meetings and have a sponsor, is that danger of forgetting. Just like Nazi Germany, you know. And anything might cause us to forget what it was like [to be in a state of disease], and what could happen. I think that's a real legitimate danger. It's a danger for me.

When Christine left Meridian only to find that she was still unable to achieve the body weight she desired (recovery), she searched to discover additional areas of transgression. Her search led her to Debtors Anonymous, where she began to relate her obsessive eating behavior to obsessive spending; and later, to Sexual Addicts Anonymous, as she reframed her addiction in terms of her "selfish and rapacious desire for sexual repletion" *with her husband.* "As the staff always tell us," Christine told me, "if you want a healthy relationship, you have to learn to 'Give, bitch, give.' "

Hence Christine came full circle. What masquerades as an avenue of self-knowledge becomes a self-perpetuating system of transgression-acknowledgment-surrender-restitution in hopes that the right combination will be found so that she may achieve freedom from her disease. And in the end, she begins to see her ultimate transgression as her sexuality.

Culture, Family, and Society: Some Conjectures about the Nature of Recovery

Culture, to the extent that anthropologists dare define it at all, is an implicit set of assumptions that actors share about the nature of the world and their own place in it, assumptions that are communicated between individuals and groups. Culture is not static; these assumptions are in a constant state of transformation. As we interact with others, we are continuously redefining our boundaries, the limits of our beliefs and understanding, to accommodate information received. As we seek to communicate with others, our reality—our view of the world and our place in it—constantly shifts and evolves as it meets the reality of those with whom we attempt to communicate. In effect, we negotiate a third, composite reality in order to carry out the act of communication successfully. It is implicit in our understanding of culture, however, that that composite reality makes sense to the participants—or at least that it does not outrage the intellect.

The act of communication is both impersonal and the deepest expression of self. Whether our interactions with others are simple or complex, our background, experiences, and beliefs color the way we pattern our speech, even the tone and expression we use. Our body language (or, more appropriately, our body's language) expresses these as well. On occasion, we communicate a mixed message—we say or do something that directly contradicts either what we have explicitly indicated are our beliefs or what our body's language is communicating. But over all—assuming, of course, that our experience of our mind and body is integrated—my body's language conforms to other, outward forms of communication. What happens, then, when early experience does not give us an integrated sense of self? What happens when survival depends on a *division* of self?

We learn our patterns of communication as children, of course, as part of the culture package. When a child grows up in a dysfunctional home, her sense of reality is skewed. Often parents maintain one version of reality through speech, but another through actions. For example, a child may be punished for telling lies, yet a sober parent, by word and act, may deny the drinking and dysfunctional behavior of an alcoholic parent.

A patriarchal society that denies its own patriarchy—that offers women the opportunity to "be all they can be," but makes no allowances for any woman who is not young, white, middle class, thin, and willing to use her sexuality to attain her "proper sphere of influence"—has the same characteristics as the dysfunctional family. For the woman who is old, black, working class, fat, or unwilling to buy the illusion of power with sex, the message of social acceptance (like that of

the familial message of love to the abused child) is a message of contradiction. Most women, like most children who grow up in dysfunctional
homes, choose to doubt themselves rather than the message; we may
be aware of the contradiction, but more often we choose to sublimate
our confusion. As we seek to cope with mutually exclusive images of
reality, we begin to mistrust ourselves and our perceptions. Our
woman's body becomes the repository of confusion, fear, anger, pain.
We divorce ourselves from it to survive. If we are given no opportunity
to resolve that confusion, it may begin to communicate itself through
psychological malaise, physical addiction, or both—or we may come to
wear our shame in the form of an eating disorder. We become as we
have always seen ourselves—social misfits.

Every woman who voluntarily walked through the door of Meridian
House perceived herself as socially dysfunctional—unable to carry on
in the real world. She felt that way primarily because her obsessive
behavior impeded her ability to cope with people, places, and things
in socially appropriate ways; and secondly because the past and present social messages underlying her compulsion made it increasingly
difficult for her to function at all.

By making residents aware of their own impotence, the Meridian
program strips away the illusion of control. It then offers them access
to a benevolent power greater than themselves, which will save them
from themselves. But it also translates "their" problem into politically
acceptable language—language that reifies the structure and dysfunction of the society that created and made it theirs in the first place.

The translation goes something like this: "I am a substance abuser
who can no longer control my addiction, an obsessive personality
unable to control my compulsions. I need a God [substitute: a program, a group, a shrink, a religious or social organization] that will
allow me to see my powerlessness [but not the sociopolitical structure
that produces, encourages, and maintains it] and that will offer me
hope for dealing with it in a manner that may make it possible for me
to survive."

The equation of femininity and sexuality and the issues of sexual
shame, body alienation, and loss of control are certainly not exclusive
to American women with eating disorders. Admitting powerlessness
over one's body is, for women in this society, a redundancy. However,
eating disorders—as broadly defined as they are in this context—are
intimately bound to cultural beliefs about gender and sexuality in a
way that alcoholism and drug addiction are not, which makes a

Twelve-Step "solution" all the more open to question. This analysis does not assume an inherent weakness in the Twelve-Step Program model itself, but only in its application to what is certainly a women's social issue but not necessarily (outside the context of a patriarchal society) a women's disease. The experience of women at Meridian points to the incompatibility of two very different worldviews—one based on complete and total acceptance of oneself and one's weaknesses as a human being, the other based on a particular construct of the way that women—and their bodies—should be.

Addendum

Linda was the only resident at Meridian during the time I spent at the house who came to question the staff's view of recovery. In our last follow-up interview, she offered a very different concept of recovery, one based on the Twelve-Step Program philosophy but which challenged in many ways the dominant American paradigm:

> To me what recovery looks like is freedom from the obsession to do it perfect. Freedom from the obsession to have the perfect body, the perfect meal, to eat the perfect amount; freedom from having to eat the "right" kinds of foods. Freedom from having to act the "right" way. Freedom from "have to." You don't have to do those things any more. If you choose, on your own, to do them, that's okay, and if you choose to stop, that's okay, too. I think livin' in recovery is a daily choice of freedom.

Within a month of leaving Meridian, Linda was told she was no longer welcome to visit the house. She was forbidden to speak to residents, forbidden to interact with women who were "serious about their recovery." Linda was seen as being in denial, as interested in excuses for doing what she wanted to do, not in recovering from compulsive eating. She refused to recognize the staff's authority over her personal decisions. She refused to surrender her will to the staff. In her actions, she was seen as refusing to surrender her will to God.

Hurt and bitter, Linda stopped all contact with Meridian. But she has clung, stubbornly, tenaciously, to her own views, views she does not see as inconsistent with Twelve-Step recovery.

There is no right or wrong way to recover. No right or wrong abstinence. Or any of that stuff. Just like what dress looks good on you is going to look like shit on me, and vice versa. Not because the dress is pretty or not pretty, and not because your skin is lighter or mine's darker. Just because. It just does. If more of us, being compulsive overeaters, bulemics, anorexics, could give up that shit [about there being a right way], we could recover. But we can't. We gotta do it right. And we go from hospital to hospital, to recovery house to hospital to recovery house to meetings to this to that to find the right . . . formula to make me look like Cheryl Tiegs. I'm never going to look like Cheryl Tiegs. I don't have blue eyes, I don't have blond hair. . . . I'm never going to look like that. I've had two children. I have a freckle right here that she doesn't have. And I just wish there were more people out there who knew that. Because when I fall apart I don't have anybody to remind me, "Oh, Linda, it's not about being a size five."

NOTES

1   In the wake of swelling organizational membership rolls, many hospitals are now revising their definition of bulemia to include "compulsive eating behavior" or "food or body obsession." Under the expanded definition, many sufferers who would otherwise be unable to afford treatment may qualify for insurance benefits. A six-week visit in the eating disorder unit of one popular southern California hospital, for example, costs the patient from $16,000 to $35,000.

2   I do not mean to suggest that the research published in the last decade and a half has been exclusively theoretical, or that none of the work has considered the issue of treatment and recovery. Several authors have published the results of extensive *clinical* research with patients and clients (see, in particular, the works of Chernin 1985; Szekely 1990; Woodman 1980); Spitzack (1990) based her analysis of anti-diet discourse on the results of fifty interviews with women. To my knowledge, however, no one to date has published the results of ethnographic research with women in treatment and recovery.

3   The Twelve-Steps of Alcoholics Anonymous, as adapted for Overeaters Anonymous, read as follows:
  1. We admitted we were powerless over food, that our lives had become unmanageable.
  2. Came to believe that a Power greater than ourselves could restore us to sanity.
  3. Made a decision to turn our will and our lives over to the care of God, as we understood Him.
  4. Made a searching and fearless moral inventory of ourselves.
  5. Admitted to God, to ourselves, and to another human being the exact nature of our wrongs.

6. Were entirely willing to have God remove all these defects of character.
7. Humbly asked Him to remove our shortcomings.
8. Made a list of all persons we had harmed, and became willing to make amends to them all.
9. Made direct amends to such people whenever possible, except when to do so would injure them or others.
10. Continued to take personal inventory, and when we were wrong, promptly admitted it.
11. Sought through prayer and meditation to improve our conscious contact with God as we understood Him, praying only for knowledge of His will for us and the power to carry it out.
12. Having had a spiritual awakening as the result of these steps, we tried to carry this message to compulsive overeaters, and to practice these principles in all our affairs. (Alcoholics Anonymous 1976: 59–60)

4   Written primarily by Bill Wilson, co-founder of Alcoholics Anonymous, in the late 1930s, the Big Book is the basic recovery text of all Twelve-Step programs.

5   To protect the anonymity of participants, occupations and some details of life histories have been changed. Changes made in occupation accurately reflect the socioeconomic status and class of participants. No changes to life histories were made which compromise the real life experience of participants; rather, changes were restricted to place names and so forth.

6   I do not attempt to specifically relate the onset of eating disorders to the experience of physical or sexual abuse; as the director of the eating disorder unit at a prominent research hospital told me, "The prevalence of physical and sexual abuse, particularly of women, in this society is so great that even a national survey could probably not establish a significant correlation between abuse and eating disorders."

7   What constitutes abstinence, according to the Overeaters Anonymous program, is self-determined. For some, it is three moderate meals a day with nothing in between (as at Meridian). For others, it is abstinence from refined sugar and flour. For still others, it is a combination of the two. At Meridian, anything approximating a diet, in terms of eschewing particular foods, was considered an attempt to "control food"—something that a surrendered person need not do. A woman who has truly turned her will and her life over to the care of God is empowered to abstain from compulsive eating behavior and is able to maintain adherence to a structure of three meals a day. Residents were expected to demonstrate that they were not dieting by eating a range of the foods put before them, including desserts. Breaking abstinence by eating between meals, however, was grounds for immediate dismissal from the program, without recourse. Only once during the sixteen months was someone allowed to stay having broken her abstinence; others had their bags packed and were dropped off at the local bus station within an hour of having admitted their infringement.

REFERENCES

Alcoholics Anonymous. 1976. *Alcoholics Anonymous.* 3d ed. New York: Alcoholics Anonymous World Services. First published in 1939.
Bell, R. M. 1985. *Holy Anorexia.* Chicago: University of Chicago Press.
Boskind-Lodahl, M. 1976. "Cinderella's Stepsisters Revisited: A Feminist Perspective on Anorexia Nervosa and Bulimia." *Signs* 2:342–356.

Bruch, H. 1973. *Eating Disorders: Obesity, Anorexia Nervosa, and the Person Within.* New York: Basic Books.

Brumberg, J. J. 1988. *Fasting Girls: The Emergence of Anorexia Nervosa as a Modern Disease.* Cambridge: Harvard University Press.

Chernin, K. 1981. *The Obsession: Reflections on the Tyranny of Slenderness.* New York: Harper and Row.

Foucault, M. 1979. *Discipline and Punish: The Birth of Prisons.* Trans. Alan Sheridan. New York: Vintage Books.

Garner, D., P. Garfinkel, D. Schwartz, and M. Thompson. 1980. "Cultural Expectations of Thinness among Women." *Psychological Reports* 47:483–491.

Minuchin, S., B. Rosman, and L. Gailer, eds. 1978. *Psychosomatic Families: Anorexia Nervosa in Context.* Cambridge: Harvard University Press.

Orbach, S. 1978. *Fat Is a Feminist Issue.* London: Berkeley Publishing.

______. 1982. *Fat Is a Feminist Issue II.* London: Berkeley Publishing.

Schoenfielder, L., and B. Wieser, eds. 1983. *Shadow on a Tightrope: Writings by Women on Fat Oppression.* San Francisco: Aunt Lute Book Co.

Spitzack, Carole. 1990. *Confessing Excess: Women and the Politics of Body Reduction.* Albany, N.Y.: SUNY Press.

Szekely, E. 1988. *Never Too Thin.* Toronto: Women's Press.

Woodman, M. 1980. *The Owl Was a Baker's Daughter: Obesity, Anorexia Nervosa and the Repressed Feminine.* Toronto: Inner City Books.

MIND OVER BODY

The Pregnant Professional

ROBBIE E. DAVIS-FLOYD

The fundamental assumption of this book is that social relationships are mirrored in body image. Because the human body is a focal point for so many issues that confront our society, including sexuality and reproduction, physical changes become heavily imbued with symbolic social significance. This premise parallels my own long-standing research interest in how our technocratic society symbolically transforms the natural processes of pregnancy and birth, and in how that transformation affects women's own perceptions and experiences of these biological events.

I suggest that body image not only mirrors social relationships but also worldview. Here I examine that suggestion through the body images, social relationships, and worldviews of thirty-one professional, career-oriented women, especially as they deal with the physical changes of pregnancy and the symbolic aspects of motherhood in relation to their professional conceptions of self.[1]

These thirty-one professionals hold a wide range of occupations. Three are midlevel managers for banks and two for insurance companies, two head up fund-raising for political campaigns, one is a museum curator, two are realtors, two physicians, three college professors, two regional sales managers, six managers or directors of large government agencies, one is a CPA, one a high-level manager for a major airline, and five own their own companies. Most of them make as much or more money than their husbands.

The Professional/ Personal Split

During the interviews, it quickly became apparent that these women live their lives in terms of a fundamental and clearcut distinction between the personal and professional realms. How these women primarily define themselves in relation to society at any given moment is usually a function of the realm they are in. In the professional realm they *are* their role—professor, division manager, CEO. Secure in their professional identities, many of these women in the personal realm seem amused to define themselves as John's wife or Suzie's mother, almost as if such a role were a game they sometimes played. Some perspective on this security of identity was provided by an older woman I spoke with recently who had been Mrs. James Bowen since she was twenty, and hated it. She said, "I have always been defined by who my husband was. Now that he is dead, I am forced to confront the fact that I am sixty five years old and have no identity of my own." In dramatic contrast stands Lina's explanation of why she defines herself so strongly in terms of her career, while many of her friends do not:

I find that some of my friends that I was in college or graduate school with have given up too much. . . . They have compromised their careers in really significant fashion. Either they don't work or they will work part time, and they just haven't really made a go of it professionally but . . . have put their energies into the relationship and into the family. [That] is very dangerous.
[Q. Why?]
Men leave. Men leave. . . . They are relying on their husbands to such a degree that if they leave they are really in trouble. They have totally compromised their careers. They have great potential and they let it go. . . . They didn't balance it. They in essence capitulated to the family.

Presence in either the personal or professional realm is expressed through bodily adornment—suits and tailored dresses at work, shorts or jogging suits at home. Leah explained:

I see [the body] as a way to have people respond to you. The way you present yourself draws an equal reaction from the bodies that respond to you. . . . I definitely see that in the professional environment. The way I dress reflects the level of professionalism that I have and the type of response I get from other people. I don't dress in flounces and frills, I dress very tailored and that is reflected even in the glasses I wear. They are pretty much

straightforward and businesslike. . . . I like to give a straightforward presentation so that people can deal with me straight.

I found it noteworthy that when I interviewed these women in their
homes, they almost invariably would glance down at their casual
sweats and tennis shoes and laughingly comment, "You are seeing
my other self, my home self," but when I went to their offices they
never said, "You are seeing my professional self." For most, the professional self was the primary self.

In general, any overlap between the personal and professional
realms went one way: personal aspects, like children, relationships,
and emotional display, did not belong at work, while professional
aspects, like paperwork, faxing, and phone calling, often were taken
home. (The specific and notable exceptions to this rule are discussed
later.) Enforcing the boundaries of this one-way street did not present
much of a problem for most of these women at first; even those who
dated or married male colleagues were usually able to keep these
relationships separate from their everyday professional activities.

Pregnancy as a Violation of the Professional/ Personal Split

Pregnancy perforce entails a violation of the conceptual boundary separating these personal and professional realms of life. Sexuality and
children are plainly part of the personal domain; they do not belong at
work. But pregnant women visibly and obviously not only take their
children into the workplace, but also to even the most important meetings! Predictably, many of these women worried about how this boundary violation would affect their work relationships with their colleagues and superiors. I asked one woman if she were worried how her
colleagues might react to her pregnancy. She responded:

Yes, that's an unqualified yes. . . . they look at me as the president, and I . . . was worried that they might start thinking
about me not as much as a professional, but as a woman, and
that shouldn't necessarily be bad, but I was worried that it
might affect the respect level. . . . it's kind of more obvious that
you're a woman, I think, if you're pregnant, I mean it's just

constantly reminding people of that rather than just thinking of you as a professional. It gave them another thing to think about, and it wasn't something I wanted them to think about, because I wanted them to think about me as a business kind of guy.

However, in contrast to what I had originally expected to find, very few of these women found their fears justified. Only three reported that they suffered any sort of job discrimination as a result of their pregnancy, while most others reported the joyful discovery of unexpected benefits from their physical blurring of the personal/professional distinction:

> When I was pregnant for the first time, I was working in a large corporation, and always it was to dress for success, and you were very much on guard as a woman. And as soon as I revealed I was pregnant, people who were not friends of mine, executives many levels up on the corporate ladder, just opened up their personal lives. They identified so strongly with being a father or having a wife who was pregnant. I mean, they would go into ten- or fifteen-minute conversations. I was stunned at how open and personal everything became when they were around a woman who was bearing a child.

As it evolved for most of these women, the conflict between work and pregnancy was not between their pregnant bodies and their male colleagues, as most had expected, but between their own expectations for their work performance and the biological realities of those pregnant bodies. Catherine said:

> I hated it that people were always wanting to have personal conversations with me about how I was feeling. I was not interested in that at all, and so I made it very plain right at the start that I didn't want to deal with any of that stuff. When I'm at work I am strictly business. I think the reason I didn't have any problems with how I was treated when I was pregnant was that I made it so clear that there was no difference. [Q. Did pregnancy pose any problems at all for you at work?] I would sometimes get so tired that I would tell my secretary to hold my calls, and put my head down on my desk and just sleep for an hour. But I never let anyone know about it, and I made sure that I always got just

as much work done anyway, even if that meant I had to stay there longer.

The Centrality of Control

This tension between the professional and personal domains is often heightened by the woman's own perception of herself in relation to her body. Just as with the middle-class women in Martin's study (1990), an overriding concern of these professional women is control. They hold the strong belief that life is controllable, and that to be strong and powerful in the world, one must be in control. As long as these women feel in control, they are "happy," "everything is fine." They achieve control over their *lives* through careful planning and organization of their time and activities. (I asked all of them what they thought about the notion of applying corporate management techniques to family life, such as scheduling family summit meetings, etc. A few thought the notion detracted from the unstructured flow, which they saw as the essence of the personal, as opposed to the professional domain, but most heartily approved of the idea.) Control over their *bodies* is achieved through regularly scheduled exercise—most were very athletic in school (see Alan Klein's chapter in this volume for a discussion of the kinds of control sought by women bodybuilders). They achieve control over their own *destinies* through reaching positions of independence and importance in the wider society. Interestingly, those who admitted to wanting and enjoying power insisted that it was not power over others that appealed to them, but power to make things happen in the world. Lina said: "I didn't want to be like my mother. . . . I didn't want to be picked on by my husband all the time, and be powerless. You know, she was powerless." When asked what she did to be powerful, Lina replied, "I got a Ph.D. and a job."

The Self/ Body Split: Pregnancy and Birth as Out of Control

These professional women seem to judge every situation by the degree of control they feel they can maintain over it. Even their pregnancies were usually carefully controlled, planned to occur at just the chosen time in their careers. But those processes, once set into motion, became uncontrollable, and thus presented these women with a division within their most treasured notions of self, between the cultural, professional parts within their control and the personal, biological processes outside of it. Lina experienced this division so intensely that she could hardly believe it when she became pregnant:

> Deep down inside of me I believed that I had desexed myself by being the successful professional and I would have to pay for that. . . . I thought I would have a hard time getting pregnant because I thought I would have to pay for what I had gotten away with. . . . I have succeeded at a man's game. . . . A couple of my male faculty colleagues, when they would see me on the campus with the baby, would constantly say, "I can't believe you are a mother, I can't believe you are such a good mother—you are like my mother. I can't believe it." What they were really saying to me is, "I thought you were a guy."

This separation of self from biology is clearly reflected in the body concepts held by many of these women. I asked each one, "How do you think about your body? What is your body?" Most, instead of giving me a definition, immediately began to talk about how they judged their bodies—as too fat, not in good enough shape, or healthy, in good shape. Such statements reflect their shared belief that the body is imperfect:

> I think it's pretty functional [but] . . . it's fat around the middle, and my boobs are too small. (Lou)

> I used to always hate my body. I always had this joke that I got my mother's eyes and my father's chest. I used to think I was flat, you know, I wanted new boobs and liposuction. In the last five or six years, I like it better. It's mine. That's a really loaded question, because you know—women, unless we've had it greatly enhanced by plastic surgery, I don't think we like it. I don't know anybody who *likes* their body. But I've gotten OK about it, and my husband thinks it's the cutest thing he's ever seen. (Louise)

The words of most of those who did provide definitions expressed the additional and equally fundamental belief that the body is separate from the self:

> You know, I think there is me and then there is what I'm like physically which can be changed or modified—clothes, makeup, exercise, hairstyles, food. (Georgia)

> My body is mine. It's only mine. I think it was something that was given to me for a reason, you know, to get around in this particular life, because I think it's a place for my soul to be. (Lou)

> A vehicle. Something that moves me from place to place. A repository for thought, for creation, for beliefs, philosophies. (Leah)

> My body is a vehicle that allows me to move around, a tool for my success in the world. (Joanne)

> My body is the recipient of the abuse from the lifestyle that I choose. . . . It's my weakest link—it's like you have to pay the price somewhere—I'm out of shape, overweight, and not eating right—my body to me is what has paid the price for this career. [Q. Can you describe your relationship with your body?] Abusive. (Beth)

Predictably, then, the physical state of pregnancy was problematic at best for some of these women. For intrinsic to the notion of the body as a vehicle, a tool for the self, are the corollary ideas that the body is worth less than the self it houses, which, being worth more, should control the body, should be "in charge." Concomitantly, most of these women experienced the bodily condition of pregnancy as unpleasant because it is beyond the control of the self, or, as they put it, "out of control." Here is how they expressed that feeling. Linda said:

> I think there are a lot of women who love being pregnant and they would say that. My sister, the Earth Mother, did. Especially before I got pregnant, I thought, "Maybe I'll get into it." But I didn't get into it. I felt bad and large and awkward and nause-

ated. And oh, I love having the baby, but I wish there were an easier way.

To the question "How did you feel about your body while you were pregnant?" Lina responded:

I didn't like it. It just overwhelmed me, the kinds and the variety of sensations, and the things that happen to your body because of the pregnancy. I didn't like it at all. I felt totally alienated from my body.

Even Leah's positive experience of pregnancy is expressed in terms of separation and a feeling of lack of control:

I really did feel very healthy. It was different being so focused in my body. That's what was so curious. I was watching all this happening. It was something taking control all over me and it was all good. To a certain extent I try to live outside my body so it doesn't control me. Only in this case it was very much control-ling me. And that's ok—it was guiding me.

Joanne added:

I was real apprehensive about going into labor. It kind of terri-fied me, mostly because I like to be in control . . . and you don't have any control when that happens. I used to have nightmares about standing in front of the president and making a presenta-tion and having my water break.

And here is how Beth experienced birth:

I mean, it's like a demon to me. There's another being in your body that has to get out and it's looking for a way to get out. And all of a sudden, it's like my center of control left my brain and went to this, this thing in my body. And I had no control. I'm very much an in-control person. I like to think that I'm in con-trol of what's going on here, that I can control whatever hap-pens. It was like the control center moved from me to this other being. And you know, all I was doing was lying there—I had to do whatever this other being said was going to happen. And it was my body that it was happening to. That was the thing I liked the least.

As they viewed the body as a vehicle for the mind or soul, so these women tended to see the pregnant body as a vessel, a container for the fetus (who is a being separate from the mother) and to interpret its growth and birth as occurring through a mechanical process in which the mother is not actively involved. (Sarah flatly stated, "You're just a vessel. That's all you are, just this vessel.") These beliefs were behaviorally expressed in myriad ways during pregnancy. For example, the evidence these women relied on for proof of the baby's health and growth was objective, coming primarily from ultrasound photographs and electronic amplification of the fetal heart rate. They understood the importance of nutrition and knew that they had to eat well so the baby would be well nourished. They tended to see this in terms of a simple, mechanical cause-effect relationship. If they ingested good foods, the necessary nourishment would travel to the baby through the placenta, enhancing overall development and especially brain growth. Excessive ingestion of alchohol or junk food, however, might result in a child with less-than-optimal brain capacity. Thus, eating well was a mother's duty to her unborn child and one of the most important things, along with ultrasound and amniocentesis, that she could do to ensure optimal growth conditions. Although most of these women experienced giving up alchohol and junk food as something of a burden, to them it was also a logical necessity, something they did as a matter of course. But it did not, conceptually speaking, entail their active participation in growing the child. It merely made them into the best possible "vessels."

In keeping with these attitudes, most of these women did not view the processes of labor and birth as intrinsic to their feminine natures. Said Linda, "If my husband could do it the next time instead of me, that would be just fine." Added Joanne:

Even though I'm a woman, I'm unsuited for delivering . . . and I couldn't nurse. . . . I've told my mother—I just look like a woman, but none of the other parts function like a mother. I don't have the need or the desire to be biological. . . . I've never really been able to understand women who want to watch the birthing process in a mirror—just you know, I'm not, that's not—I'd rather see the finished product than the manufacturing process.

The Mind/ Body Split: Mind over Biology

Emergent in Joanne's words we see the technocratic notions that birth is a mechanical process and that there is no intrinsic value in giving birth "naturally," because technology is better than nature anyway. Thus we can understand when Joanne says that she enjoyed her cesarean birth because her anesthesiologist explained what was happening step by step, and because, since she felt no pain, she was able to be so *intellectually* present to the birth that she could watch the clock to see which of her many friends who had placed bets on the time of the birth would win the eighteen dollars in the pot. She stated:

> [I liked that because] I didn't feel like I had dropped into a biological being. . . . I'm not real fond of things that remind me I'm a biological creature—I prefer to think and be an intellectual emotional person, so you know, it was sort of my giving in to biology to go through all this.

Here Joanne expresses a view held by most of the women in this group: The ideal, whole woman is intellectual and emotional, but not necessarily biological.

Like Joanne, Katie preferred the sense of control provided by a cesarean; in no way did she see the procedure as a disempowering loss but only as an empowering gain because it was something *she* had caused to happen. When her baby was two weeks overdue and labor had not begun, she told her doctor, who was urging restraint, "I am really getting sick of this. Please schedule [the cesarean]." In response to the question "How did you feel about yourself after the birth?" she responded, "I felt pretty special. Proud . . . I felt as if I had accomplished quite a bit."

Kathy, who also described her cesarean as personally empowering, said:

> I don't feel like I missed out on anything. With my first two I was put to sleep. With my third, Bryan, I was given an epidural. Heaven! I would never do it any other way. A cesarean with an epidural. I was awake, everything. Ah, it was just wonderful. . . . I would have to say, hey, I participated in it. I was awake and I felt the pulling and the tugging. I did not push or anything. But I was definitely a part of what was going on.

Elaine summarized:

> Well they induced labor and I wasn't very good at my relaxation
> techniques and my breathing and after about four hours of la-
> bor I decided I would prefer to have a cesarean and so that's
> what we did. . . . I know some women get all uptight about that,
> that it wasn't a normal delivery, but I didn't feel the least bit
> cheated and I feel my birth experience was just as happy as it
> would have been. I was very happy when I heard them cry, and it
> was a very pleasant experience.

In their words we hear again the value these women place on
control, and the belief they strongly hold that the mind is more
important than the body, that as long as their minds are aware, they
are active participants in the birth process. We hear this expressed
even in Clara's recounting of her rapid and unmedicated vaginal
delivery:

> Travis came in a little over an hour and that was just not enough
> time to get mentally prepared. I felt . . . my body was pushing
> me into having this baby. My mind was not there to work with it.
> I needed more time to be able to get on top of it and be there.

As a corollary of the idea that technology is better than nature,
most of the hospital birthers in this study felt strongly that labor is
naturally painful, that pain is bad, and that not to have to feel pain
during labor is good and is their intrinsic right as modern women. To
the question "What did you want out of the birth experience?" Joanne
responded:

> Out of the birth experience itself I wanted no pain. I wanted it to
> be as simple and easy and uncomplicated as most everything
> else has been for me.

Said Leah, "I made the decision—I had two hits of Demerol in the IV. I
controlled the pain through that." Beth, who "had planned for but did
not end up with natural childbirth," was nevertheless very pleased to
feel that she also was in control of the decisions that were made. She
had expected a long labor with little pain. When the pain became
severe, she asked for relief, "and you know, even though I hadn't

planned on an epidural, they were very responsive when I said I wanted one." The next time around, Beth planned for an epidural:

> When I got there, I was probably about five centimeters, and they said, "Uh, I'm not sure we have time," and I said, "I want the epidural. We must go ahead and do it right now!" So, we had an epidural.

And Elaine stressed:

> Ultimately the decision to have a cesarean while I was in labor was mine. I told my doctor I'd had enough of this labor business and I'd like to have a cesarean and get it over with. So he whisked me off to the delivery room and we did it.

In keeping with this high value on making their own decisions, the major discontents these women expressed with the medical handling of their labors and deliveries resulted not from the administration of anesthesia, but from the witholding of it. Kay reported:

> I [asked] for an epidural at one point, but they said they didn't have time to do it. [Q. Was that okay with you?] Not really! I was awfully uncomfortable and I had remembered how wonderful it was [with my first birth] and that I had instantly felt terrific. . . . I was mad that I was in so much pain, and then they would tell me something like "we don't have time," you know—that just drove me wild. I didn't like that at all—I wanted to have it when *I* wanted to have it.

Another woman expressed outrage that a friend of hers in advanced labor had been denied anesthesia for the same reason as Kay, saying earnestly, "No one has the right to tell you that you have to go through that kind of pain." Although a good bit of evidence exists on the depressive effects of analgesia and anesthesia on the baby during labor and birth, most of these women felt strongly that they had an absolute right to the mind/body separation offered by such drugs, especially the epidural.[2] Lina spoke for the majority when she said,

> I read all this stuff that told me I would be a complete asshole to have an epidural and I revolted. [The books were saying that]

I would be able to see that it's much better for the baby and it's a natural experience, and there's just all this pressure. . . . I quit smoking, ate meat, drank milk for months and months—I had been such a good girl. A couple of hours of whatever an epidural was going to do to me, tough. You can put up with it, kid.

Mediation and Integration through Nurturance

Hand in hand with their intense desire for control, for not "dropping into biology," goes, at least for some of these women, a lack of interest in breast-feeding for any extended length of time. To breast-feed is to be out of control—the milk comes unbidden and runs down your blouse; you must drop what you are doing and attend to the child's hunger. Bottle-feeding, on the other hand, enables someone else to do it for you and frees you from enslavement to biology as surely as does an epidural. With good reason, a woman in a novel of the 1930s tells her daughter, "The bottle was the war cry of my generation!" (Mc-Carthy 1954:247). That cry is echoed in 1990:

I really thought I wanted to breast-feed, but I didn't. I wanted my body back. (Lina)

Yes, it's good for the baby, but if you're uncomfortable with it, for any reason, don't do it. It just isn't worth the trauma. This time I'm not going to do it at all, uh-uh. Part of it goes back to not having the need or the desire to be biological. The other is the confinement of nursing. You know, I wanted to be able to get up and go, and let somebody else feed the baby, and the idea of expressing just nauseated me. (Joanne)

Linda, who did want to nurse, ran into problems with the distinction between the personal and professional realms:

I don't have my own office, so I've been trying to think where I'm going to pump when I'm at the hospital. The best I've come up with is the examining room, you know, because that has a lock on the door and I hope it'll work out, because it's not optimal, its not optimal at all.

Yet, in spite of the difficulties, she was willing to find a way because, as she expresses it,

> a lot of my friends who have worked and have nursed say they feel a little better about working if they're nursing. You know, you still have that connection—I was talking to one of my friends yesterday and she said, "That's one thing the babysitter can't do, you know—that's mine." And I sort of feel that way too. That makes it a little better, a little easier about going back to work. Plus the immunological aspect about putting him in day care—I feel a little better about that, giving him a little better chance of fighting all the germs out there.

Nursing for Linda, as well as for several others, provided a much-valued mediation/integration of the personal and professional realms. Another seeker of integration was Kay, president of her own company, who kept both her babies in her office until they were a year old. (When I went there to interview her, her two-month-old was sleeping on a chair.) Carol, head of the governor's office of energy conservation, does not hesitate to bring her children to the office and bed them down in a corner if they are sick, and Tara often works at home to be more available to her children. Lillian, a family practice physician, strives for such integration but must make careful choices about when to take her three-year-old along. She explains,

> If I am going to the nursing home, and only to see one or two patients, then I will take him. And very rarely I may take him to the hospital with me. But I really have to watch that—my reputation would suffer if I did that too much.

Joanne says,

> I think there is that split, and that's one of the toughest transitions that professional women have to deal with, and that is, I want to be the soft mommy, and then I have to strip my gears and get back into being the tough businesswoman. And I think that's a tough transition to make.

She goes on to describe two women who serve as role models for her who are "very tough businesswomen," yet who will bring their children to the office, and will even get down on the floor in full corporate attire in the middle of a busy day to play with someone else's children. She continues:

> It's very encouraging to see people break out of the corporate mold because the corporate personality is so hard and cold and really kind of distasteful. . . . I think having families makes people kinder. . . . If people would just step back from corporate greed and get back into relating to people in terms of their interdependence and their affection for each other, it would be a better world.

Louise, when asked what she thought about applying corporate strategies to family life, replied that for her, it was more a question of applying family strategies to the business world:

> I treat my clients as if they were as important to me as my family, and it pays off. They really respond, and I have turned this business around from losing to making money in less than a year because of it.

As is evident in Louise's statement, these women place high value on their emotional and nurturing abilities—abilities which they feel spill over from the personal to the benefit of the professional realm. For example, when Janis was head of the electric customer service office, she often worked intensively, one on one, with delinquent bill payers to help them develop an overall economic plan that would work for them. She said,

> And I still get visits from people who tell me that I turned their lives around for good, because instead of being their adversary, I nurtured them, and I'm proud of that. I think being a mommy makes me a better professional.

Likewise, Kay specifically designs her presidential style to be "participative" and "democratic," "understanding" and "kind." Thus her caring for her children in her office can be viewed as an extension of her presidential self rather than a contradiction to it; their presence in her office simply represents further integration of the personal and professional spheres which she as president has tried to bring to-gether from the beginning of her company.

These women in general, even as they devalued feminine biological processes, consistently placed high value on what they saw as the feminine qualities of nurturance and emotionality, and sought to bring these qualities into the workplace in a very conscious effort to "humanize" the office environment. Their efforts toward such integra-tion included both more personalized relationships with clients and employees (such as implementing client education programs, flex-time, etc.), and creating friendlier environments—wherever these women had enough control, they redecorated sterile office buildings with softer colors, warmer lighting, conversational areas, art work, and potted plants, finding that such efforts repeatedly paid off in enhanced intraoffice relationships and increased productivity.

The Parent/Child Split: Quality Time as Mediation

Kay's example notwithstanding, most of these women were unable to extend their value on nurturance to incorporating their children into the workplace. About leaving her six-week-old baby at a day care cen-ter, Linda, the pediatrician, had this to say:

> [Q. Do you feel that it would be better for your baby to be with you?]
> Possibly. On the other hand, I also feel like I probably wouldn't be very happy. I'd probably start climbing the walls, and in a way that would be a bad thing to do to him, to say well, all right, I'm going to throw away twenty years of education to stay home with you so that you can be the perfect child.

Thus we arrive at a central question for most of these women: Where are they going to put their bodies, carriers of their selves, in relation to their children? The answer in general is, at some distance. The major-ity of these women work ten-hour days, usually from eight in the morn-ing until six at night, and so see their children for a maximum of one and a half to two hours per day. To get at how they think about this parent-child separation, I asked them all to rank on a scale from one to ten (where ten is total commitment and involvement) their professional lives, their parenting, health, relationship with husband, leisure/play, religion, and homemaking/housekeeping/cooking. Most ranked their commitment both to work and to parenting at a nine or ten, and to their health and their relationship with their husband at an eight. (Clearly something had to give—religion, leisure/play, and homemaking usually got two or three at best.) To rationalize the time differential between parenting and work, most hung their hats on the popular notion of quality time. Those with older children who came home from school to a caretaker or an empty house relied heavily on the telephone, communicating with their children in a form of "disembodied parenting" (Nicole Sault, personal communication) that deserves further investigation.

In his recent essay "Politics and Reproduction," W. Penn Handwerker (1990) notes that in earlier times in England, women saw marriage and child rearing as investment activities because they could expect to be provided for by their husbands and cared for in their old age by their children. But for men, marriage and child rearing were consumption activities that could reduce their material welfare. The same might well be said for today's professional women, many of whom indeed choose not to have children for much the same reasons. So it seemed logical to ask the professional women in my study why they chose to have children in the first place. Interestingly, none could really give any "good reasons," at least not the same sort of reasons they all could give for almost every career decision they had made. When agonizing over whether to have a child, Joanne tried to make a decision chart which was supposed to list all the pros on one side and all the cons on the other. But she gave up, saying:

You can write down all the negatives you can dream up, but nobody can tell you what the positives are until you've had a child. My obstetrician said, "Why are you trying to make a logical decision about allowing yourself to have a family? Why don't you allow yourself an emotional decision once in a while?" And I never do that—you know, the last emotional decision I made was to marry Mark.

Clara said:

I feel that as a woman there is that need to have something else besides your spouse. I don't know. I couldn't imagine my life without them.

In the same vein, Lisa answered, "I think it is a very tangible acting out of bringing two people together." Kari responded:

We wanted a family. It was just a feeling that we both had deep within, and I do not know if words can describe it and I know that sounds stupid. It's hard. We did not want them for any other reason except that.

In contrast to the emotional and personal diffuseness of most of the answers to this question, Beth framed her thinking about whether to have children in the same terms as her career. She said, "When David and I were engaged and talking about measures of success in life, having children was a part of those measures of success."

In an effort to gain more insight into this issue, I interviewed one professional woman in her late thirties who has so far chosen *not* to have children:

[Q. Given that you are so happy without children, why do you think so much about whether or not to have a child?]
I don't really know—I know that part of it is because it's in my face every month—you know. There is this constant biological reminder that it is still possible. And I am thirty nine. Every time "it" comes, I can hear that biological clock ticking.

Her response indicates that her body is the prime motivator here, mirroring the possibility to her regularly, "in her face" through the monthly appearance of menstruation.

In "Society and Sex Roles," Ernestine Friedl postulates that

in any society, status goes to those who control the distribution of valued goods and resources outside the family. . . . Only as managers, executives, and professionals are women in a position to trade goods and services, to do others favors, and therefore to obligate others to them. Only as controllers of valued resources can women achieve prestige, power, and equality. Within the household, women who bring in income from jobs are able to function on a more nearly equal basis with their husbands. (1990: 218)

Certainly these professional women confirm Friedl's hypotheses, both in the wider society and at home. Most reported that their marriages were extremely egalitarian, with their husbands putting in at least as many and sometimes more hours with their children than they:

> I don't think I could find a spouse anywhere in the world who has been more supportive in my career because I got my M.B.A. after getting married. . . . And then we had a child when I was halfway through my M.B.A., and therefore, you know, he made a real commitment. I think he views [my career] very much on equal footing with his, even though [he makes significantly more than I do]. . . . As a matter of fact, Don has often said, and I agree with him, that if I could make what he makes he would prefer, he would just as soon stay home with the kids. And he would. I mean, he's great with the kids.

Those women who often had to work late into the night on a regular basis especially counted on their husbands to provide the primary parenting for their children. One such woman, Janis, had been working "hundred-hour weeks" as acting head of a major city department. Offered the job on a permanent basis by the city council, she turned it down and resigned altogether as soon as she had trained a permanent replacement. She stated,

> I was burned out, exhausted, and I wanted to be home with my family. Although my husband had been great, just 100 percent with the house and the kid, I am forced to realize that a woman is the center of the home. Since I have been home for the last two months, my child's grades have gone way up in school, my husband and I are lovers again, and our house is a joy to live in. I know I will go back to work again, but I don't want to lose all the benefits we have gained from my being home. I don't want to go back to the way it was, when I left the house at 6:00 A.M. and didn't get home till 10:00. But when I do work, I have to be in charge. I am not willing to take a lesser job and let somebody else boss me. So I don't know what I am going to do. Sometimes I

fantasize about running a small clothing store, where I could provide excellent service, which I value, to my customers and still get home to meet Jeff when he gets off the bus.

Some women did actually rate their parenting at five or six. These women recognized that their work-to-home time ratio precluded them from being fully committed parents. They felt strongly that they had been sold a bill of goods by the women's movement, stating "you can't do it all," and feeling that the brave new world they had entered as pioneers had betrayed them in some fundamental way. Now locked into the need for two salaries, they longed to quit or slow down and spend more time with their children. Even though they too spent only two hours a day with their kids, they mocked the notion of quality time, calling it "a massive self-deception in which we all engage to rationalize our guilt." One, who had been heavily committed to work throughout her son's childhood, was now having to cope with a teen-ager, in and out of hospitals, suffering from severe emotional distress and various psychological disorders. Although she did not blame herself entirely for his troubles, she felt strongly that this might not have happened if she had been less committed to work and more to parenting. She wondered out loud if the emotional instability of her child was the price she paid for her career.

Kay and Janis had expected to leave their babies in day care early on. They were both suprised when they simply couldn't bring themselves to do that. Kay has so thoroughly integrated her work life with her children's lives that she has rented an office, right next to her husband's on the floor below hers, where her children spend the day with their nanny. Continued nursing and family lunches are regular parts of her daily routine. Janis is now at home with her six-year-old until further notice. Sharon and Liza are seriously considering chucking their management positions in a few years to teach school, so that they will have shorter hours and summers and holidays off to spend with their families. Susan is waiting until her husband completes a year of consulting work at an outstanding salary so that they can save up enough for her to quit work for a year or two and have their second child. Many of the women in my study were engaged in an intensive process of self-questioning and were seriously entertaining the possibility of getting off the fast track for a while, or permanently. These women feel that they have "made it in a man's world," proved that they can do it. (When I asked them to whom have they proved this, they answered, "To myself. I'm the only judge that matters.") Even some of those who actively seek defeminization in the business world are beginning to consider alternatives to the feelings of dehumanization and impoverished family life which accompany their high-powered, time-intensive careers.

Those women with no intention of giving up the fast track feel that they are doing their best to make it work. Carolyn said,

My husband and I just do the best we can every day to be terrific parents and terrific professionals. And if the kid gets left on the street corner for three hours because we each thought the other was supposed to pick him up—yes, that happened once!—we know better than to burden ourselves with guilt. We are giving him all we can—those two hours a day when we are with him are spent in close physical proximity. We don't waste time on the house or other stuff—we just focus on him.

The Dichotomies of Technocratic Life

The similarities in the desires, experiences, and perceptions of pregnancy and birth of these professional women raise many questions. For example, what happens when you can't control everything? Janis had uterine fibroids which made her pregnancy very difficult and dangerous. Carolyn, after not exercising for one very busy year, woke up one morning with such a severe pre-arthritic condition in her legs that she could not walk for days. Susan experienced a hormone shift toward the end of her pregnancy which resulted in intense and long-lasting anxiety attacks from which she did not recover until the proper medication was found five years later. Bewildered and angered by their out-of-control bodies, these women, rather than surrendering, intensified their commitments to control: Jan was determined to keep working until time for birth—and did; Carolyn embarked on a rigorous exercise program and is doing much better; and Susan fought her near-paralyzing anxiety so successfully that no one at work ever knew of her problem.

When the body works right, it is a vehicle for success. When it does not, it is an impediment to be overcome. As professional and personal are separate domains, so are mind and body, so are mother and baby (even when contained in one body), and so are self and children:

professional/personal
self/body
mind/body
mother/baby
parent/children

These dichotomies seem to encapsulate and express the divisions and tensions of technocratic life as most of these women experience it. To some degree, they appear to be mediated by the emotional and nurturent qualities through which these women see themselves as enriching both the workplace and the home.

Cross-Cultural Comparison: Home-Birthers

In recent research, Igor Kopytoff (1990) found that many aspects of women's work among the Suku of Zaire are not believed to be immanent in the role of women, but are circumstantial and pragmatic. Thus, women engage in horticulture and cooking because it is practical for them to do so, not because such work is intrinsic to being a woman, and when women choose to expand their role options they meet with few obstacles and no criticism, as they are not contravening any deeply held cultural notions that confuse who women are with what they do. Through his understanding of women's roles among the Suku, Kopytoff is able to highlight the fact that many aspects of American women's roles are culturally held to be immanent in the concept of womanhood, among these the notion that the mother herself is primarily responsible for the socialization of her children. So powerful is this idea that a mother, no matter what her other commitments, "cannot delegate entirely to others the rearing of her children . . . to do so would make her an unnatural mother in her own eyes no less than in the eyes of others" (1990: 94). Certainly we have seen the force of this notion at work in the tensions these women experience between the demands of the personal and professional realms.

Quite possibly many of the basic beliefs about self and body held by the professionals in my study feel familiar to the reader. A number of these notions are perhaps "immanent" in the American middle-class worldview; one of the most notable is the notion that birth should always take place in the hospital. For that reason, a group of equally middle-class home-birthers I am interviewing for another study present as useful a contrast to these professionals as do the Suku, for their values and beliefs differ radically, in spite of the fact that they live in the same cities and share many of the same concerns.

For example, instead of emphasizing mind/body separation, the home-birthers tend to see self and body as one. While pregnant, they see themselves as actively growing the baby. They say that mother and baby form one system, one "energy field" that can only be harmed by dissection into its individual parts. Far from interpreting the baby as a "separate entity," a "foreign body growing inside my body," as did a number of the professionals, these home-birthers believe in the reality of active communication and partnership with their unborn babies. They see labor and birth as hard work that a woman does and accept pain as an integral part of that process. They give birth at home because they believe that the safety of the baby and the emotional needs of the mother are one and the same, so the safest birth for the baby will be the one that provides the most nurturing environment for the mother. Many of them work in family enterprises centered around the home, and some of them also home school their children. Even those who work in the professional world do the best they can to minimize the separation of the personal and professional realms; for them, that separation is "just a cultural construct"—something they must put up with but place no value upon. One of these home-birthers, a stay-at-home mother, once told me that she often thinks of her children as little moons in constant orbit around her sun, with all of them together, including the big planet, her husband, encompassed within the body of one solar system.

But for most of the women in this present study, children are not little moons orbiting their sun, but asteroids crossing over to a different galaxy for most of the day. Husbands too tend to live in separate realms, although on good days the orbits of all three match up at night, and sometimes on weekends.

In *Lying-in: A History of Childbirth in America,* Dorothy and Richard Wertz (1989) describe the process by which many women in the 1920s and 1930s eagerly sought hospital birth because of the freedom it provided from their regular household work cycles. Hand in hand with this freedom went a redefinition of the roles of women in American society. In the 1800s, a woman's place was in the home. Her primary duties were childbearing, nursing, and child rearing. As the Wertzes point out, many women longing for emancipation from these burdens found the beginnings of that emancipation in the removal of the birthplace from home to hospital. For accompanying this shift in birthplace was a shift in society's definition of women's bodies, reflecting a cultural reconstruction of femininity and the female role. As long as women gave birth exclusively in the home, that home remained their excusive domain, excluding them by definition from participation in the wider world and its challenges. To reconceptualize birth as a mechanical process best handled by trained technicians and machines was to remove its feminine mystique and, in so doing, to remove the mystique from the feminine. When separated from the biological "earthiness" that had so long kept them down, women were to be freer than they had been for countless centuries in the West, finally given license to seek equal opportunity with men in the nonbiological arena of the workplace.

Pursuing this trend to its logical conclusion, we might well expect that today's highly competitive professional women would wish to identify with their earthy biological selves and the confines of the domestic realm even less than their turn-of-the-century sisters who paved the way for them. I sometimes give talks at childbirth education and midwifery conferences, and have come to understand well the worldview and rationale of those holistically oriented midwives and childbirth educators who make earnest and sincere efforts to help their clients both desire and achieve the kind of truly natural childbirth they believe will empower birthing women as individuals and as women. While many American women still find much of value in the ideal of natural childbirth, the women in this particular study do not want such services. They want plenty of education and personal attention, but not when it is framed under a holistic paradigm; in fact, they perceive the holism of the home-birthers described above as frightening, irresponsible, limiting, and disempowering. While home-birthers see the hospital as out-of-control technology running wild over women's bodies, these professionals experience the hospital and its technology as a liberation from the tyranny of biology, as empowering them to stay in control of an out-of-control biological experience.

I have seen many holistically oriented birth professionals shaking their heads in bewilderment as they speak of the 1990s as the age of the "epidural epidemic"—an apt metaphor. As the epidural numbs the birthing woman, eliminating the pain of childbirth, it also graphically demonstrates to her through her lived experience the truth of

the Cartesian maxim that mind and body are separate, that the biological realm can be completely cut off from the realm of the intellect
and the emotions. This microcosmic mirror of our technocratic society casts its reflection in ever-widening ripples in the pond of social
life. As the babies so birthed are carried off to the nursery and placed
in their separate bassinets, and spend much of infancy in their separate cribs and plastic carriers, so in later years they will be carried off
to day care and to school. Ours is a nation founded on principles of
separation, and we enact and transmit those principles to each other
in the spatial and interactional relational patterns we have developed
between mind and body, mother and baby, and parents and child.

Body Image as a Microcosm of Social Relationships and Worldview

In "The Ideology of Reproduction," Emily Martin (1990) contrasts
the beliefs and experiences of American middle- and working-class
women. She sees the efforts of the middle-class women's health
movement to regain control of birth as resulting in

> middle-class women's becoming controlled themselves, being
> the agents of exerting control over themselves, as silent, except
> for certain controlled forms of breathing they perform in the
> public arena of the hospital. In so doing they may be ignoring
> other aspects of their experiences, which are less easily articu-
> lated because they are (as our culture sees them) more physical
> and less controllable. Working-class women more readily articu-
> late precisely these kinds of experiences: I am in pain, this
> hurts, it is enough to make me scream; I am not really in control
> of this situation, and no one could be. (1990: 309)

Martin suggests that this situation mirrors social structures in the
workplace, where, "middle-class women more than working-class
women advocate and practice 'mind over matter' and seek mental
concentration that does not allow the body to dictate events," (1990:
310).

The professionals in my study insist on control, and they, like Martin's middle-class interviewees, tend to be silent in the hospital: they

do not scream out their pain; rather they anesthetize it away. But it is their words that bring the anesthesia. They do not experience that they are being controlled by the medical establishment, but rather that they are manipulating the technological resources of the medical establishment to control their own bodily experiences. Martin suggests that such feelings of being "empowered and in control" are illusory, and that "losing control" in birth "can mean having one's body physically penetrated, as the Cesarean section rate . . . is now over 20% in many states" (1990: 309). But for these professional women (one of whom scheduled her cesarean to take place between conference calls), having a cesarean is not losing control but gaining it—given the models of reality they individually hold. Regardless of how they came to believe in the value of technological control over their imperfect, mechanistic bodies, the fact that they do believe in and value such control is not an illusion, and their feelings of empowerment when they achieved such control through the agencies of the professionals they have hired for that purpose—their physicians—are not illusions either. Although my personal feelings may be more in accord with Martin's view, as an anthropologist I know that those who participate most fully in a society's hegemonic core value system, as these women do, are most likely to be empowered by and to succeed within that system, as these women have.

As feminists, we have fought for the right to make our bodies our own, to metaphorize, adorn, and technologize as we please. We are just beginning to guess at the cultural and individual impact of the symbolic messages today's professional women are sending through their symbolic placement of their bodies in relation to their families, and through their mental attitudes to the physical changes brought about by the biological processes of pregnancy, birth, and motherhood. The intensifying quest of many of these women for distance from these biological processes of pregnancy and birth leads inevitably to the questions: Will/should our culture still define these domains as primarily belonging to women? What do we want? As we move into the twenty-first century, will the options opened to us by technology leave equal conceptual room for the women who want to *be* their bodies as well as for the women for whom the body is only a tool? As researchers have shown (Ehrenreich and English 1973a, 1973b; Corea 1985; Rothman 1982, 1989; Spallone 1989), the patriarchy has been and is only too willing to relieve us of our uniquely female biological processes. To what extent do we desire to give up those processes that since the beginning of the species have been used to define us as women, in order to compete with men on their terms and succeed on their terms?

In the new society we are making, will the home-birthers and the home schoolers, the goddesses and the earth mothers, have equal opportunity to live out their choices alongside those who want to schedule their cesareans, and those who want their babies incubated in a test tube? Or will the paradigm of body conceptualization and placement vis-à-vis social relationships now being articulated by highly successful professional women like the ones in this study become *the* defining template for most American women? Certainly that paradigm—which I have elsewhere called the technocratic model (Davis-Floyd 1992)—is fully supported and further disseminated by the American medical system, which almost completely fails to take into account the alternative templates held by home-birthers and their ilk, and is only too willing to encourage scheduled cesareans and test-tube incubation. Indeed, Western biomedical researchers are actively trying to shape the future of the cultural treatment of the female body precisely through intensifying the above dichotomies of mind/body and mother/child separation. The phenomenon of surrogacy discussed by Nicole Sault in this volume is one result that is already with us. Other such options, from court-ordered cesareans to genetic engineering, abound. The cover story of the February 1989 issue of *Life*, titled "The Future and You," carries these dichotomies to their logical conclusion, predicting "Birth without Women": "By the late 21st century, childbirth may not involve carrying at all—just an occasional visit to an incubator. There the fetus will be gestating in an artificial uterus under conditions simulated to recreate the mother's breathing patterns, her laughter and even her moments of emotional stress" (p. 55).

The paradigm that makes such futuristic options seem not only possible but desirable presents real dangers to those who conceptually oppose it and act on their convictions. Across the country, would-be home-birthers and the lay midwives who attend them report harrassment and sometimes prosecution by the medical and legal establishment, as do women who attempt to refuse obstetrical interventions, including court-ordered cesareans. Such interventions are often ordered because the technocratic paradigm grants no legitimacy to women who value their own "inner knowing" more than technologically obtained information about what is "safe":

In a 1981 Georgia case, doctors told the court there was a 99% chance of fetal death and a 50% chance of maternal death unless a scheduled Cesarean section was performed, since two ultrasounds indicated a complete placenta praevia [a potentially life-threatening situation in which the placenta lies under the baby, blocking the entrance to the birth canal]. The mother steadfastly believed in her ability to give birth safely. After the court order was granted, a third ultrasound showed no praevia at all. Either the placenta had moved late in pregnancy or the ultrasound machine had been wrong. (Shearer 1989:7)

The mind/body::mother/child dichotomy that provides so much structural tension in the lives of the pregnant professionals in this study is, these days, a fulcrum for the swirlings of cultural change. Most of that change seems to be heading in the direction of intensified separation between these categories; but a vast cultural movement, which includes home-birthers and unnumbered others concerned with "holistic health," is organizing around the alternative concept of mind/body integration. In the oppositions between self and body that define the lives of the professional women in this study, we can read, writ small, the paradigmatic struggles that are defining opposing movements and trends within American society as we struggle, half blind, toward an uncertain future. As anthropologists engaged in tracking our cultural gropings toward that future, we would do well to recall that not only social relationships, but also the worldview, sense of purpose, and environmental relationships of the entire society are often encapsulated in the self and body images of its individual members.

ACKNOWLEDGMENTS

I thank Nicole Sault for her editorial assistance and her patience, Adela Popp for her outstanding tape transcriptions, and most especially the women in this study who so willingly took time out of their busy schedules to talk with me. All of them made it clear that they were motivated to do so out of a strong desire to help other women.

NOTES

1   Eleven of these interviews were conducted and transcribed by the following students: Kim Durham, Melody Hatfield, Courtney Hollyfield, Mark Thompson, and

Erin Rogers. I express my appreciation to these students for their hard work, their enthusiasm, and their continuing inspiration.

2   I find it curious that all these women had amniocentesis in an effort to ensure that they would have perfect babies and that all expected their babies to in fact be perfect. Yet not one who had anesthesia expressed any concern about what it might do to the child, in spite of mounting evidence of the possibility of long- and short-term damage (Brackbill et al. 1984, 1988:23; Golding et al. 1990; Iseroff 1980; Jacobson et al. 1987, 1988). While I would never question their—or my— right to the mind-body separation such drugs provide, I would suggest that this paradox provides fruitful ground for further study.

REFERENCES

Brackbill, Yvonne, Karen McManus, and Lynn Woodward. 1988. *Medication in Maternity: Infant Exposure and Maternal Information.* Ann Arbor: University of Michigan Press.

Brackbill, Yvonne, June Rice, and Diony Young. 1984. *Birth Trap: The Legal Low-Down on High-Tech Obstetrics.* St. Louis: C. V. Mosby.

Corea, Gena. 1985. *The Mother Machine: Reproductive Technologies from Artificial Insemination to Artificial Wombs.* New York: Harper and Row.

Davis-Floyd, Robbie. 1992. *Birth as an American Rite of Passage.* Berkeley: University of California Press.

Ehrenreich, Barbara, and Deirdre English. 1973a. *Complaints and Disorders: The Sexual Politics of Sickness.* Old Westbury, N.Y.: Feminist Press.

————. 1973b. *Witches, Midwives, and Nurses: A History of Women Healers.* Old Westbury, N.Y.: Feminist Press.

Friedl, Ernestine. 1990. "Society and Sex Roles." In *Anthropology: Contemporary Perspectives,* ed. Phillip Whitten and David Hunter, pp. 215–219. New York: Harper Collins. Article originally published in 1978.

Golding, J., M. Paterson, and L. J. Kimlen. 1990. "Factors Associated with Childhood Cancer in a National Cohort Study." *British Journal of Cancer* 62:304–308.

Handwerker, W. Penn. 1990. "Politics and Reproduction: A Window on Social Change." In *Births and Power: Social Change and the Politics of Reproduction,* ed. W. Penn Handwerker, pp. 1–38. Boulder, Colo.: Westview Press.

Iseroff, A. 1980. "Facilitation of Delayed Spontaneous Alternation Behavior in Adult Rats following Early Hydroxyzine Treatment: Differential Sensitivity in Late Infancy." *Psychopharmacology* 69:179–181.

Jacobson, B. G. Eklund, L. Hamberger, D. Linarsson, G. Sedvall, and M. Valvereius. 1987. "Perinatal Origin of Adult Self-Destructive Behavior." *Acta Psychiatrica Scandinavica* 76:364–371.

Jacobson, B., Karin Nyberg, Gunnar Eklund, Marc Bygdeman, and Ulf Rydberg. 1988. "Obstetric Pain Medication and Eventual Adult Amphetamine Addiction in Offspring." *Acta Obstetrica Gynecoliga* 67:677–682.

Kopytoff, Igor. 1990. "Women's Roles and Existential Identities." In *Beyond the Second Sex: New Directions in the Anthropology of Gender,* ed. Peggy Reeves Sanday and Ruth Gallagher Goodenough. Philadelphia: University of Pennsylvania Press.

McCarthy, Mary. 1954. *The Group.* New York.

Martin, Emily. 1990. "The Ideology of Reproduction: The Reproduction of Ideology." In *Uncertain Terms: Negotiating Gender in American Society*, ed. Faye Ginsburg and Anna Lowenhaupt Tsing, pp. 300–314. Boston: Beacon Press.

Rothman, Barbara Katz. 1982. *In Labor: Women and Power in the Birthplace*. New York: W. W. Norton. Reprinted in paperback under the title *Giving Birth: Alternatives in Childbirth*. New York: Penguin Books, 1985.

———. 1989. *Recreating Motherhood: Ideology and Technology in Patriarchal Society*. New York: W. W. Norton.

Shearer, Beth. 1989. "Forced Cesareans: The Case of the Disappearing Mother." *International Journal of Childbirth Education* 4(1):7–10.

Spallone, Patricia. 1989. *Beyond Conception: The New Politics of Reproduction*. Granby, Mass.: Bergin and Garvey Publishers.

Wertz, Richard W., and Dorothy C. Wertz. 1989. *Lying-in: A History of Childbirth in America*. 2d ed. New Haven: Yale University Press.

CONSTRAINING MEANING

T he last group of chapters in this volume focuses on how
control imposed by others redefines a person's body image,
either directly or indirectly. In the first example, Eugenia
Kaw examines cosmetic surgery among Asian American
women in California. Although in the United States the decision to
undergo cosmetic surgery is usually presented in terms of a woman's
"freedom of choice," the women Kaw interviewed believed that changing their faces was a requirement for achieving success in American
society. Whether they wanted to advance in the workplace or find a
husband, all these women felt that without surgery they could not be
happy with their faces. They had learned to view their own eyes negatively, as "small, dull, sleepy, slanted, and puffy," and their noses as too
"flat" or "broad." Up until the surgery, they used cosmetics to make
their eyes appear "bigger, more open, and awake," trying to attain the
"sharp look" that American women are "supposed to have." Unlike
Anglo women who seek cosmetic surgery to hide the signs of aging,
many of these Asian American women were young. Their goal was to
emulate the conventional Anglo-American features portrayed in fashion magazines and other mass media. Still, they insisted they were
proud of being Asian and did not want to look "white," just "better."
However, "better" is interpreted as changing a part of the face that
others stereotype as "Asian."

Kaw explores the political reasons for these Asian American
women's feelings and shows the complexity of their motivations.
The internalization of racist stereotypes is a long and sometimes
subtle process, and attempts at escaping the effects of racism can

take many forms. What experiences taught these women to see themselves as unattractive and made them willing to go beyond the camouflage of makeup to undergo costly and painful surgery, even at the risk of unpleasant side effects? The pressure is so powerful that even the law student who recognized the contradictions still planned to have her facial features surgically modified. While criticizing the effects of racism and working for political change, she still felt impelled to have her face re-figured in the likeness of an Anglo ideal.

In changing their bodies to more closely conform to the culturally accepted ideal, these Asian American women have much in common with the women described in the other chapters. Mimi Nichter and Nancy Vuckovic note that the mothers of adolescent Anglo girls in Arizona often encourage them to diet, and some mothers diet with their daughters. Kaw's research shows that in some cases, mothers, other relatives, and friends also influence Asian American women to undergo cosmetic surgery. Several mothers even accompanied their daughters to the medical offices, for the mothers themselves had had these surgeries performed on their own faces.

Adolescent Anglo girls in Arizona participated in "fat talk" by discussing dieting in order to show they are concerned about their looks, but the Asian American women in California tried to keep the surgery a secret, telling few people. Whereas "fat talk" can bond girls together as peers, there is no parallel "surgery talk" for young Asian American women to share the experience and form any kind of grouping among themselves. In this particular competition to look your best, there is no social group to turn to for support or advice, only a close female relative, a male surgeon, or the fashion magazines. In a sense, these women are on their own, which is the epitome of American culture.

Many of the chapters in this book address issues connected with negative body images, dislike of the body, and changes made to the body "to look your best." The added dimension of Kaw's chapter is that the Asian American women she interviewed described the ideal face in terms that are stereotypically "Caucasian." In this case, cosmetic surgery is a statement not only about gender issues or aging but about another form of disidentification in the relationship with one's own people. The psychologist Clarisa Estés asks if a woman "is taught to hate her own body, how can she love her mother's body that has the same configuration as hers? . . . In essence, the attack on women's bodies is a far-reaching attack on the ones who have gone before her as well as the ones who will come after her" (Estés 1992:203). Kaw's chapter is both painful and powerful, but she does not judge the women and their families; instead, she focuses on trying to understand the process of internalizing racism that results in re-forming the body image.

The violence of the forced change in body image is more overtly apparent in the chapter by Cathy Winkler, who provides a way to understand rape trauma and body memory. Rape is a violent physical act, but it involves more than the physical body, for rape is committed by and against social beings. It is not only an act of violence upon the body but an attack that assaults the person's body image and identity. As Winkler explains in describing her own rape trauma experience, the rapist was attempting to define himself and his own existence by redefining her and her existence. He wanted to "brand" her with his mark. His intention was to fragment her self-image and identity by imposing his own.

This book's thesis is that a mirroring occurs between body image and social relations, so an act upon either one affects the other. Women and men who are raped experience not only physical harm to their bodies but changes in their body images and social relationships. When others learn about a rape, some may view the person who has been attacked as a rape *victim* and interpret this term in a way that redefines the person's whole identity and all her or his actions as those of a victim. They assign to the person a body image dominated by the rape. Winkler describes this phenomenon as part of the *second assault* on the person who has been raped. For others, a person who is raped is a rape *survivor*, someone who has experienced rape but has moved beyond the role of victim to the role of an actor or activist who redefines what has happened and how this affects a sense of identity. Such a person has overcome the rapist's attempt to redefine her or his identity and fragment the sense of self.

Rape requires an adjustment in a person's body image and social relationships, but the degree of adjustment varies. Whether a person is viewed as a rape victim or a rape survivor, as a part person or as a whole person, depends on prior relationships to others and their body images, personal experiences, and sense of identity. All these influence their response, be it fear and anger toward the person who was attacked or understanding and support.

In response to the initial attack and the second assault, persons who are raped experience a variety of symptoms known as *rape trauma syndrome.* Although these responses are often interpreted as a sign of the rape victim's inability to function, Winkler explains how trauma serves as part of the body's protective and informative response mechanisms to safeguard against further assaults, such as those that occur when a person who has been raped addresses her social circle or encounters the legal and medical systems. The rape severs certain connections between parts of the mind and the rest of the body, so that painful or disruptive memories are blocked out. This blockage can create a numbness that enables the person to function while the mind secrets away these memories, which become embedded in the rest of the body memory. Events that signal danger will trigger a trauma reaction in the body, warning the victim to avoid that situation and seek protection.

Here we can see how the body image system applies. The distress of the rape experience creates a disjunction in the woman's body image, fragmenting her sense of self. A distancing of mind from body occurs, associated with body image distortion—feeling that one's body is a separate entity a world apart. What happened to that body can be mentally and emotionally removed for observation. But for healing to progress, the mind-body connections must be restored. Moving from rape victim to rape survivor means regaining a sense of wholeness, repairing not only the broken ties perceived between body and mind but mending the fragmented social relationships between oneself and others.

It is interesting to compare and contrast this example of body/mind separation to Davis-Floyd's description of women in childbirth who ask for drugs to anesthetize their bodies. While in both cases the body/mind separation protects the woman from pain and provides a pleasant sense of numbness, in the case of rape this separation of body and mind is something she cannot control and may not even understand or be able to verbalize easily. This disjunction is created when a man uses violent force against her body and her body image. She cannot suddenly terminate this body/mind separation at will, but as she recovers, these two aspects of self are reintegrated. From this junction she regains a sense of wholeness as well as power and control. The separation of body and mind is only a temporary protective measure.

For the woman in childbirth, however, the separation of body and mind reflects an ongoing division in her two worlds of home and work. She sees the world in terms of two selves represented by her mind and her body, and she wants control over the body to keep it from intruding upon her mind-self. Painkillers remove her from the physical experience of childbirth so that she can experience it intellectually. Integration of body and mind makes her feel powerless, for she fears the body will take over. Consequently, it is the act of separating body from mind that strengthens her sense of control and removes the conflict in her life.

The last chapter, by Nicole Sault, uses cross-cultural comparison to show how body concepts shape ideas about parenthood. By comparing two very different views of parenthood, namely "surrogate" mothers in the United States and godparents in Mexico, the key values of each cultural system are brought into relief and the contrast in body concepts becomes evident. In the United States, "surrogate" motherhood arrangements generally involve an agency that negotiates a contract between a married man or a couple who are unable to have a child and a young woman who agrees to be artificially inseminated with the married man's sperm in order to bear a child genetically related to the man. Surrogacy is often portrayed as an issue of technology, phrased in terms of individual choice, and justified in terms of personal freedom of access. However, surrogacy is also a practice that symbolically encodes deep-seated beliefs about the human body, parenthood, gender, individual ownership, and race. The development and use of surrogacy, and even the perception of a need for it, are all based on a particular set of cultural assumptions according to which the body is defined as mechanical, partible, and bounded, with male seed as the key to the life force.

In American culture the body is a machine, or at least the ideal body is as machinelike as possible, and the male body is the epitome of the finely tuned machine. In addition, the body is a collection of parts that can be removed and replaced by new and improved products made in factories from plastic and steel. The body has definite boundaries that must be maintained and protected, but especially the male body, for the female body is an inherently "leaky vessel." This view of the human body enables Americans to reduce a person to a specific part: a man is viewed as a brain that may be cryogenically frozen, whereas a woman is viewed as a uterus. In surrogacy negotiations, a woman who becomes a "surrogate" mother is reduced to a "substitute uterus," a part that can be "rented out" to others so that they may fulfill their need to be "real" parents who possess a child absolutely.

When we compare surrogacy in the United States with godparenthood in Mexico we see a very different understanding of *parent* and *body*. Procreation is highly valued in Mexico, but parenthood is not defined in a narrow biological sense that establishes ownership. Instead, the concept of parenthood is expanded to encompass spiritual ties and other social relationships based on nurturance and sharing. Among the Zapotec of southeastern Mexico, "real" parenthood includes the spiritual relationships established between godparents and godchildren during sponsorship ceremonies like baptism. The Zapotec view of parenthood exists in conjunction with a fundamentally different view of the body as indivisible, but with a boundary that is normally permeable. Concerns for health and well-being focus not on keeping boundaries rigid and separating individuals or their parts, but on maintaining balance within the individual and the community. Body boundaries are more fluid in Mexico, and the essence of an individual can pass from one person to another, particularly in the context of rituals for sponsorship and healing. Health means maintaining a balance within one's body and between oneself and others.

The cross-cultural comparison of parenthood raises an important question. As the body image is reciprocally connected to social relations, each reflecting upon and influencing the other, what does the development of surrogacy tell us about the nature of social relations in the United States today?

REFERENCE

Estés, Clarisa Pinkola. 1992. *Women Who Run with the Wolves*. New York: Ballantine.

"OPENING" FACES

The Politics of Cosmetic Surgery and Asian American Women

EUGENIA KAW

llen, a Chinese American in her forties, informed me she had had her upper eyelids surgically cut and sewed by a plastic surgeon twenty years ago in order to get rid of "the sleepy look," which her naturally "puffy" eyes gave her. She pointed out that the sutures, when they healed, became a crease above the eye which gave the eyes a more "open appearance." She was quick to tell me that her decision to undergo "double-eyelid" surgery was not so much because she was vain or had low self-esteem, but rather because the "undesirability" of her looks before the surgery was an undeniable fact.

During my second interview with Ellen, she showed me photos of herself from before and after her surgery in order to prove her point. When Stacy, her twelve-year-old daughter, arrived home from school, Ellen told me she wanted Stacy to undergo similar surgery in the near future because Stacy has only single eyelids and would look prettier and be more successful in life if she had a fold above each eye. Ellen brought the young girl to where I was sitting and said, "You see, if you look at her you will know what I mean when I say that I had to have surgery done on my eyelids. Look at her eyes. She looks just like me before the surgery." Stacy seemed very shy to show me her face. But I told the girl truthfully that she looked fine and beautiful the way she was. Immediately she grinned at her mother in a mocking, defiant manner, as if I had given her courage, and put her arm up in the manner that bodybuilders do when they display their bulging biceps.

As empowered as Stacy seemed to feel at the moment, I could not help but wonder how many times Ellen had shown her "before" and "after" photos to her young daughter with the remark that "Mommy looks better after the surgery." I also wondered how many times Stacy had been asked by Ellen to consider surgically "opening" her eyes like "Mommy did." And I wondered about the images we see on television and in magazines and their often negative, stereotypical portrayal of "squinty-eyed" Asians (when Asians are featured at all). I could not help but wonder how normal it is to feel that an eye without a crease is undesirable and how much of that feeling is imposed. And I shuddered to think how soon it might be before twelve-year-old Stacy's defenses gave away and she allowed her eyes to be cut.

The permanent alteration of bodies through surgery for aesthetic purposes is not a new phenomenon in the United States. As early as World War I, when reconstructive surgery was performed on disfigured soldiers, plastic surgery methods began to be refined for purely cosmetic purposes (that is, not so much for repairing and restoring but for transforming natural features a person is unhappy with). Within the last decade, however, an increasing number of people have opted for a wide array of cosmetic surgery procedures, from tummy tucks, facelifts, and liposuction to enlargement of chests and calves. By 1988, two million Americans had undergone cosmetic surgery (Wolf 1991:218), and a 69 percent increase had occurred in the number of cosmetic surgery procedures between 1981 and 1990, according to the ASPRS or American Society of Plastic and Reconstructive Surgeons (n.d.).

Included in these numbers are an increasing number of cosmetic surgeries undergone by people like Stacy who are persons of color (American Academy of Cosmetic Surgery press release, 1991). In fact, Asian Americans are more likely than any other ethnic group (white or nonwhite) to pursue cosmetic surgery. ASPRS reports that over thirty-nine thousand of the aesthetic procedures performed by its members in 1990 (or more than 6 percent of all procedures performed that year) were performed on Asian Americans, who make up 3 percent of the U.S. population (Chen 1993:15). Because Asian Americans seek cosmetic surgery from doctors in Asia and from doctors who specialize in fields other than surgery (e.g., ear, nose, and throat specialists and opthamologists), the total number of Asian American patients is undoubtedly higher (Chen 1993:16).

The specific procedures requested by different ethnic groups in the United States are missing from the national data, but newspaper reports and medical texts indicate that Caucasians and nonwhites, on the average, seek significantly different types of operations (Chen 1993; Harahap 1982; Kaw 1993; LeFlore 1982; McCurdy 1980; Nakao

1993; Rosenthal 1991). While Caucasians primarily seek to augment breasts and to remove wrinkles and fat through such procedures as facelifts, liposuction, and collagen injection, African Americans more often opt for lip and nasal reduction operations; Asian Americans more often choose to insert an implant on their nasal dorsum for a more prominent nose or undergo double-eyelid surgery whereby parts of their upper eyelids are excised to create a fold above each eye, which makes the eye appear wider.[1]

Though the American media, the medical establishment, and the general public have debated whether such cosmetic changes by non-white persons reflect a racist milieu in which racial minorities must deny their racial identity and attempt to look more Caucasian, a resounding no appears to be the overwhelming opinion of people in the United States.[2] Many plastic surgeons have voiced the opinion that racial minorities are becoming more assertive about their right to choose and that they are choosing not to look Caucasian. Doctors say that nonwhite persons' desire for thinner lips, wider eyes, and pointier noses is no more than a wish to enhance their features in order to attain "balance" with all their other features (Kaw 1993; Merrell 1994; Rosenthal 1991).

Much of the media and public opinion also suggests that there is no political significance inherent in the cosmetic changes made by people of color which alter certain conventionally known, phenotypic markers of racial identity. On a recent Phil Donahue show where the racially derogatory nature of blue contact lenses for African American women was contested, both white and nonwhite audience members were almost unanimous that African American women's use of these lenses merely reflected their freedom to choose in the same way that Bo Derek chose to wear corn rows and white people decided to get tans (Bordo 1990). Focusing more specifically on cosmetic surgery, a *People Weekly* magazine article entitled "On the Cutting Edge" (January 27, 1992, p. 3) treats Michael Jackson (whose nose has become narrower and perkier and whose skin has become lighter through the years) as simply one among many Hollywood stars whose extravagant and competitive lifestyle has motivated and allowed them to pursue cosmetic self-enhancement. Clearly, Michael Jackson's physical transformation within the last decade has been more drastic than Barbara Hershey's temporary plumping of her lips to look younger in *Beaches* or Joan Rivers's facelift, yet his reasons for undergoing surgery are not differentiated from those of Caucasian celebrities; the possibility that he may want to cross racial divides through surgery is not an issue in the article.

When critics speculate on the possibility that a person of color is attempting to look white, they often focus their attack on the person and his or her apparent lack of ethnic pride and self-esteem. For instance, a *Newsweek* article, referring to Michael Jackson's recent television interview with Oprah Winfrey, questioned Jackson's emphatic claim that he is proud to be a black American: "Jackson's dermatologist confirmed that the star has vitiligo, a condition that blocks the skin's ability to produce pigment . . . [however,] most vitiligo sufferers darken their light patches with makeup to even the tone. Jackson's makeup solution takes the other tack: less ebony, more ivory" (Fleming and Talbot 1993:57). Such criticisms, sadly, center around Michael Jackson the person instead of delving into his possible feelings of oppression or examining society as a potential source of his motivation to alter his natural features so radically.

In this chapter, based on structured, open-ended interviews with Asian American women like Ellen who have or are thinking about undergoing cosmetic surgery for wider eyes and more heightened noses, I attempt to convey more emphatically the lived social experiences of people of color who seek what appears to be conventionally recognized Caucasian features. Rather than mock their decision to alter their features or treat it lightly as an expression of their freedom to choose an idiosyncratic look, I examine everyday cultural images and social relationships which influence Asian American women to seek cosmetic surgery in the first place. Instead of focusing, as some doctors do (Kaw 1993), on the size and width of the eyelid folds the women request as indicators of the women's desire to look Caucasian, I examine the cultural, social, and historical sources that allow the women in my study to view their eyes in a negative fashion—as "small" and "slanted" eyes reflecting a "dull," "passive" personality, a "closed" mind, and a "lack of spirit" in the person. I explore the reasons these women reject the natural shape of their eyes so radically that they willingly expose themselves to a surgery that is at least an hour long, costs one thousand to three thousand dollars, entails administering local anesthesia and sedation, and carries the following risks: "bleeding and hematoma," "hemorrhage," formation of a "gaping wound," "discoloration," scarring, and "asymmetric lid folds" (Sayoc 1974:162–166).

In our feminist analyses of femininity and beauty we may sometimes find it difficult to account for cosmetic surgery without undermining the thoughts and decisions of women who opt for it (Davis 1991). However, I attempt to show that the decision of the women in my study to undergo cosmetic surgery is often carefully thought out. Such a decision is usually made only after a long period of weighing the psychological pain of feeling inadequate prior to surgery against the possible social advantages a new set of features may bring. Several of the women were aware of complex power structures that construct their bodies as inferior and in need of change, even while they simultaneously reproduced these structures by deciding to undergo surgery (Davis 1991:33).

I argue that as women and as racial minorities, the psychological burden of having to measure up to ideals of beauty in American society falls especially heavy on these Asian American women. As women, they are constantly bombarded with the notion that beauty should be their primary goal (Lakoff and Scherr 1984, Wolf 1991). As racial minorities, they are made to feel inadequate by an Anglo American–dominated cultural milieu that has historically both excluded them and distorted images of them in such a way that they themselves have come to associate those features stereotypically identified with their race (i.e., small, slanty eyes, and a flat nose) with negative personality and mental characteristics.

In a consumption-oriented society such as the United States, it is often tempting to believe that human beings have an infinite variety of needs which technology can endlessly fulfill, and that these needs, emerging spontaneously in time and space, lack any coherent patterns, cultural meanings, or political significance (Bordo 1991; Goldstein 1993; O'Neill 1985:98). However, one cannot regard needs as spontaneous, infinite, harmless, and amorphous without first considering what certain groups feel they lack and without first critically examining the lens with which the larger society has historically viewed this lack. Frances C. MacGregor, who between 1946 and 1959 researched the social and cultural motivations of such white ethnic minorities as Jewish and Italian Americans to seek rhinoplasty, wrote, "The statements of the patients . . . have a certain face validity and explicitness that reflect both the values of our society and the degree to which these are perceived as creating problems for the deviant individual" (MacGregor 1967:129).

Social scientific analyses of ethnic relations should include a study of the body. As evident in my research, racial minorities may internalize a body image produced by the dominant culture's racial ideology and, because of it, began to loathe, mutilate, and revise parts of their bodies. Bodily adornment and mutilation (the cutting up and altering of essential parts of the body; see Kaw 1993) are symbolic mediums most directly and concretely concerned with the construction of the individual as social actor or cultural subject (Turner 1980). Yet social scientists have only recently focused on the body as a central component of social self-identity (Blacking 1977; Brain 1979; Daly 1978; Lock and Scheper-Hughes 1990; O'Neill 1985; Turner 1980, Sheets-Johnstone 1992). Moreover, social scientists, and sociocultural anthropologists in particular, have not yet explored the ways in which the body is central to the everyday experience of racial identity.

Method and Description of Subjects

In this article, I present the findings of an ethnographic research project completed in the San Francisco Bay Area. I draw on data from structured interviews with doctors and patients, basic medical statistics, and relevant newspaper and magazine articles. The sampling of informants for this research was not random in the strictly statistical sense since informants were difficult to find. Both medical practitioners and patients treat cases of cosmetic surgery as highly confidential, as I later discuss in more detail. To find a larger, more random sampling of Asian American informants, I posted fliers and placed advertisements in various local newspapers. Ultimately, I was able to conduct structured, open-ended interviews with eleven Asian American women, four of whom were referred to me by the doctors in my study and six by mutual acquaintances; I found one through an advertisement. Nine had had cosmetic surgery of the eye or the nose; one recently considered a double-eyelid operation; one is considering undergoing double-eyelid operation in the next few years. The women in my study live in the San Francisco Bay Area, except for two who reside in the Los Angeles area. Five were operated on by doctors who I also interviewed for my study, while four had their operations in Asia—two in Seoul, Korea, one in Beijing, China, and one in Taipei, Taiwan. Of the eleven women in my study, only two (who received their operations in China and in Taiwan) had not lived in the United States prior to their operations.[3] The ages of the Asian American women in my study range from eighteen to seventy-one; one woman was only fifteen at the time of her operation. Their class backgrounds are similar in that they were all engaged in middle-class, white-collar occupations: there were three university students, one art student, one legal assistant, one clerk, one nutritionist, one teacher, one law student, and two doctors' assistants.

Although I have not interviewed Asian American men who have or are thinking of undergoing cosmetic surgery, I realize that they too undergo double-eyelid and nose bridge operations. Their motivations are, to a large extent, similar to those of the women in my study (Iwata 1991). Often their decision to undergo surgery also follows a long and painful process of feeling marginal in society (Iwata 1991). I did not purposely exclude Asian American male patients from my study; rather, none responded to my requests for interviews.

To understand how plastic surgeons view the cosmetic procedures performed on Asian Americans, five structured, open-ended interviews were conducted with five plastic surgeons, all of whom practice in the Bay Area. I also examined several medical books and plastic surgery journals which date from the 1950s to 1990. And I referenced several news releases and informational packets distributed by such national organizations as the American Society of Plastic and Reconstructive Surgeons, an organization which represents 97 percent of all physicians certified by the American Board of Plastic Surgery.

To examine popular notions of cosmetic surgery, in particular how the phenomenon of Asian American women receiving double-eyelid and nose bridge operations is viewed by the public and the media, I have referenced relevant newspaper and magazine articles.

I obtained national data on cosmetic surgery from various societies for cosmetic surgeons, including the American Society of Plastic and Reconstructive Surgeons. Data on the specific types of surgery sought by different ethnic groups in the United States, including Asian Americans, were missing from the national statistics. At least one public relations coordinator told me that such data is unimportant to plastic surgeons. To compensate for this lack of data, I asked the doctors in my study to provide me with figures from their respective clinics. Most told me they had little data on their cosmetic patients readily available.

Colonization of Asian American Women's Souls: Internalization of Gender and Racial Stereotypes

Upon first talking with my Asian American woman informants, one might conclude that the women were merely seeking to enhance their features for aesthetic reasons and that there is no cultural meaning or political significance in their decision to surgically enlarge their eyes and heighten their noses. As Elena, a twenty-one-year-old Chinese American who underwent double-eyelid surgery three years ago from a doctor in my study, stated: "I underwent my surgery for personal reasons. It's not different from wanting to put makeup on . . . I don't intend to look Anglo-Saxon. I told my doctor, 'I would like my eyes done with definite creases on my eyes, but I don't want a drastic change.' " Almost all the other women similarly stated that their unhappiness with their eyes and nose was individually motivated and that they really did not desire Caucasian features. In fact, one Korean American woman, Nina, age thrity-four, stated she was not satisfied with the results of her surgery from three years ago because her doctor made her eyes "too round" like that of Caucasians. One might deduce from such statements that the women's decision to undergo cosmetic surgery of the eye and nose is harmless and may be even empowering to them, for their surgery provides them with a more permanent solution than makeup for "personal" dissatisfactions they have about their features.

However, an examination of their descriptions of the natural shape of their eyes and nose suggests that their "personal" feelings about their features reflect the larger society's negative valuation and stereotyping of Asian features in general. They all said that "small, slanty" eyes and a "flat" nose suggest, in the Asian person, a personality that is "dull," "unenergetic," "passive," and "unsociable" and a mind that is narrow and "closed." For instance, Elena said, "When I look at other Asians who have no folds and their eyes are slanted and closed, I think of how they would look better more awake." Nellee, a twenty-one-year-old Chinese American, said that she seriously considered surgery for double eyelids in high school so that she could "avoid the stereotype of the 'oriental bookworm' " who is "dull and doesn't know how to have fun." Carol, a thirty-seven-year-old Chinese American who received double eyelids seven years ago, said: "The eyes are the window of your soul . . . [yet] lots of oriental people have the outer corners of their eyes a little down, making them look tired. [The double eyelids] don't make a big difference in the size of our eyes but they give your eyes more spirit." Pam, a Chinese American, age forty-four, who received double-eyelid surgery from another doctor in my study, stated, "Yes. Of course. Bigger eyes look prettier. . . . Lots of Asians' eyes are so small they become little lines when the person laughs, making the person look sleepy." Likewise, Annie, an eighteen-year-old Korean American woman who had an implant placed on her nasal dorsum to build up her nose bridge at age fifteen, said: "I guess I always wanted that sharp look—a look like you are smart. If you have a roundish kind of nose it's like you don't know what's going on. If you have that sharp look, you know, with black eyebrows, a pointy nose, you look more alert. I always thought that was cool." The women were influenced by the larger society's negative valuation of stereotyped Asian features in such a way that they evaluated themselves and Asian women in general with a critical eye. Their judgments were based on a set of standards, stemming from the eighteenth- and nineteenth-century European aesthetic ideal of the proportions in Greek sculpture, which are presumed by a large amount of Americans to be within the grasp of every woman (Goldstein 1993:150, 160).

Unlike many white women who may also seek cosmetic surgery to reduce or make easier the daily task of applying makeup, the Asian American women in my study hoped more specifically to ease the task of creating with makeup the illusion of features they do not have as women who are Asian. Nellee, who has not yet undergone double-eyelid surgery, said that at present she has to apply makeup everyday "to give my eyes an illusion of a crease. When I don't wear make-up I feel my eyes are small." Likewise, Elena said that before her double-eyelid surgery she checked almost every morning in the mirror when she woke up to see if a fold had formed above her right eye to match the more prominent fold above her left eye: "[on certain mornings] it was like any other day when you wake up and don't feel so hot, you know. My eye had no definite folds, because when Asians sleep their folds change in and out—it's not definite." Also, Jo, a twenty-eight-year-old Japanese American who already has natural folds above each eye but wishes to enlarge them through double-eyelid surgery, explained:

I guess I just want to make a bigger eyelid [fold] so that they look bigger and not slanted. I think in Asian eyes it's the inside corner of the fold [she was drawing on my notebook] that goes down too much. . . . Right now I am still self-conscious about leaving the house without any makeup on, because I feel just really ugly without it. I try to curl my eyelashes and put on mascara. I think it makes my eyes look more open. But surgery can permanently change the shape of my eyes. I don't think that a bigger eyelid fold will actually change the slant but I think it will give the perception of having less of it, less of an Asian eye.

For the women in my study, their oppression is a double encounter: one under patriarchal definitions of femininity (i.e., that a woman should care about the superficial details of her look), and the other under Caucasian standards of beauty. The constant self-monitoring of their anatomy and their continuous focus on detail exemplify the extent to which they feel they must measure up to society's ideals.

In the United States, where a capitalist work ethic values "freshness," "a quick wit," and assertiveness, many Asian American women are already disadvantaged at birth by virtue of their inherited physical features which society associates with dullness and passivity. In this way, their desire to look more spirited and energetic through the surgical creation of folds above each eye is of a different quality from the motivation of many Anglo Americans seeking facelifts and liposuction for a fresher, more youthful appearance. Signs of aging are not the main reason Asian American cosmetic patients ultimately seek surgery of the eyes and the nose; often they are younger (usually between eighteen and thirty years of age) than the average Caucasian patient (Kaw 1993). Several of the Asian American women in my study who were over thirty years of age at the time of their eyelid operation sought surgery to get rid of extra folds of skin that had developed over their eyes due to age; however, even these women decided to receive double eyelids in the process. When Caucasian patients undergo eyelid surgery, on the other hand, the procedure is almost never to create a double eyelid (for they already possess one); in most cases, it is to remove sagging skin that results from aging. Clearly, Asian American women's negative image of their eyes and nose is not so much a result of their falling short of the youthful, energetic beauty ideal that influences every American as it is a direct product of society's racial stereotyping.

The women in my study described their own features with metaphors of dullness and passivity in keeping with many Western stereotypes of Asians. Stereotypes, by definition, are expedient caricatures of the "other," which serve to set them apart from the "we"; they serve to exclude instead of include, to judge instead of accept (Gilman 1985:15). Asians are rarely portrayed in the American print and electronic media. For instance, Asians (who constitute 3 percent of the U.S. population) account for less than 1 percent of the faces represented in magazine ads, according to a 1991 study titled "Invisible People" conducted by New York City's Department of Consumer Affairs (cited in Chen 1993:26). When portrayed, they are seen in one of two forms, which are not representative of Asians in general: as Eurasian-looking fashion models and movie stars (e.g., Nancy Kwan who played Suzy Wong) who already have double eyelids and pointy noses; and as stereotypically Asian characters such as Charlie Chan, depicted with personalities that are dull, passive, and nonsociable (Dower 1986; Kim 1986; Ramsdell 1983; Tajima 1989). The first group often serves as an ideal toward which Asian American women strive, even when they say they do not want to look Caucasian. The second serves as an image from which they try to escape.

Asian stereotypes, like all kinds of stereotypes, are multiple and have changed throughout the years; nevertheless they have maintained some distinct characteristics. Asians have been portrayed as exotic and erotic (as epitomized by Suzie Wong, or the Japanese temptress in the film *The Berlin Affair*), and especially during the U.S. war in the Pacific during World War II, they were seen as dangerous spies and mad geniuses who were treacherous and stealthy (Dower 1986; Huhr and Kim 1989). However, what remains consistent in the American popular image of Asians is their childishness, narrow-mindedness, and lack of leadership skills. Moreover, these qualities have long been associated with the relatively roundish form of Asian faces, and in particular with the "puffy" smallness of their eyes. Prior to the Japanese attack on Pearl Harbor, for instance, the Japanese were considered incapable of planning successful dive bombing attacks due to their "myopic," "squinty" eyes; during the war in the Pacific, their soldiers were caricatured as having thick horn-rimmed glasses through which they must squint to see their targets (Dower 1986). Today, the myopic squinty-eyed image of the narrow-minded Asian persists in the most recent stereotype of Asians as "model minorities" (as eptimoized in the Asian exchange student character in the film *Sixteen Candles*). The term *model minority* was first coined in the 1960s when a more open-door U.S. immigration policy began allowing an unprecedented number of Asian immigrants into the United States, many of whom were the most elite and educated of their own countries (Takaki 1989). Despite its seemingly complimentary nature, *model minority* refers to a person who is hardworking and technically skilled but desperately lacking in creativity, worldliness, and the ability to assimilate into mainstream culture (Huhr and Kim 1989; Takaki 1989). Representations in the media, no matter how subtle, of various social situations can distort and reinforce one's impressions of one's own nature (Goffman 1979).

Witnessing society's association of Asian features with negative personality traits and mental characteristics, many Asian Americans become attracted to the image of Caucasian, or at least Eurasian, features. Several of the women in my study stated that they are influenced by images of fashion models with Western facial types. As Nellee explained: "I used to read a lot of fashion magazines which showed occidental persons how to put makeup on. So I used to think a crease made one's eyes prettier. It exposes your eyelashes more. Right now they all go under the hood of my eyes." Likewise, Jo said she thought half of her discontent regarding her eyes is a self-esteem problem, but she blames the other half on society: "When you look at all the stuff that they portray on TV and in the movies and in Miss America Pageants, the epitome of who is beautiful is that all-American look. It can even include African Americans now but not Asians." According to Jo, she is influenced not only by representations of Asians as passive, dull, and narrow-minded, but also by a lack of representation of Asians in general because society considers them un-American, unassimilable, foreign, and to be excluded.

Similar images of Asians also exist in East and Southeast Asia, and since many Asian Americans are immigrants from Asia, they are likely influenced by these images as well. Multinational corporations in Southeast Asia, for example, consider the female work force biologically suited for the most monotonous industrial labor because they claim the "Oriental girl" is "diligent" and has "nimble fingers" and a "slow-wit" (Ong 1987:151). In addition, American magazines and films have become increasingly available in many parts of Asia since World War II, and Asian popular magazines and electronic media depict models with Western facial types, especially when advertizing Western products. In fact, many of my Asian American woman informants possessed copies of such magazines, available in various Asian stores and in Chinatown. Some informants, like Jane, a twenty-year-old Korean American who underwent double-eyelid surgery at age sixteen and nasal bridge surgery at age eighteen, thumbed through Korean fashion magazines which she stored in her living room to show me photos of the Western and Korean models who she thought looked Caucasian, Eurasian, or had had double-eyelid and nasal bridge surgeries. She said these women had eyes that were too wide and noses that were too tall and straight to be on Asians. Though she was born and raised in the United States, she visits her relatives in Korea often. She explained that the influences the media had on her life in Korea and in the United States were, in some sense, similar: "When you turn on the TV [in Korea] you see people like Madonna and you see MTV and American movies and magazines. In any fashion magazine you don't really see a Korean-type woman; you see Cindy Crawford. My mother was telling me that when she was a kid, the ideal beauty was someone with a totally round, flat face. Kind of small and five feet tall. I guess things began to change in the 50s when Koreans started to have a lot of contact with the West." The environment within which Asian women develop a perspective on the value and meaning of their facial features is most likely not identical in Asia and the United States, where Asian women are a minority, but in Asia one can still be influenced by Western perceptions of Asians.

Some of the women in my study maintained that although racial inequality may exist in many forms, their decision to widen their eyes had little to do with racial inequality; they were attempting to look like other Asians with double eyelids, not like Caucasians. Nina, for example, described a beautiful woman as such: "Her face should not have very slender eyes like Chinese, Korean, or Japanese but not as round as Europeans. Maybe a Filipino, Thai, or other Southeast Asian faces are ideal. Basically I like an Asian's looks. . . . I think Asian eyes [not really slender ones] are sexy and have character." The rest of her description, however, makes it more difficult for one to believe that the Asian eyes she is describing actually belong on an Asian body: "The skin should not be too dark . . . and the frame should be a bit bigger than that of Asians." Southeast Asians, too, seek cosmetic surgery for double eyelids and nose bridges. One doctor showed me "before" and "after" photos of many Thai, Indonesian, and Vietnamese American women, who, he said, came to him for wider, more definite creases so that their eyes, which already have a double-eyelid, would look deeper-set.

In the present global economy, where the movement of people and cultural products is increasingly rapid and frequent and the knowledge of faraway places and trends is expanding, it is possible to imagine that cultural exchange happens in a multiplicity of directions, that often people construct images and practices that appear unconnected to any particular locality or culture (Appadurai 1990). One might perceive Asian American women in my study as constructing aesthetic images of themselves based on neither a Caucasian ideal nor a stereotypical Asian face. The difficulty with such constructions, however, is that they do not help Asian Americans to escape at least one stereotypical notion of Asians in the United States—that they are "foreign" and "exotic." Even when Asians are considered sexy, and attractive in the larger American society, they are usually seen as exotically sexy and attractive (Yang and Ragaz 1993:21). Since their beauty is almost always equated with the exotic and foreign, they are seen as members of an undifferentiated mass of people. Even though the women in my study are attempting to be seen as individuals, they are seen, in some sense, as less distinguishable from each other than white women are. As Lumi, a Japanese former model recently told *A. Magazine: The Asian American Quarterly*, "I've had bookers tell me I'm beautiful, but that they can't use me because I'm 'type.' All the agencies have their one Asian girl, and any more would be redundant" (Chen 1993:21).

The constraints many Asian Americans feel with regard to the shape of their eyes and nose are clearly of a different quality from almost every American's discontent with weight or signs of aging; it is also different from the dissatisfaction many women, white and non-white alike, feel about the smallness or largeness of their breasts. Because the features (eyes and nose) Asian Americans are most concerned about are conventional markers of their racial identity, a rejection of these markers entails, in some sense, a devaluation of not only oneself but also other Asian Americans. It requires having to imitate, if not admire, the characteristics of another group more culturally dominant than one's own (i.e., Anglo Americans) in order that one can at least try to distinguish oneself from one's own group. Jane, for instance, explains that looking like a Caucasian is almost essential for socioeconomic success: "Especially if you go into business, or whatever, you kind of have to have a Western facial type and you have to have like their features and stature—you know, be tall and stuff. So you can see that [the surgery] is an investment in your future."

Unlike those who may want to look younger or thinner in order to find a better job or a happier social life, the women in my study must take into consideration not only their own socioeconomic future, but also more immediately that of their offspring, who by virtue of heredity, inevitably share their features. Ellen, for instance, said that "looks are not everything. I want my daughter, Stacy, to know that what's inside is important too. Sometimes you can look beautiful because your nice personality and wisdom inside radiate outward, such as in the way you talk and behave." Still, she has been encouraging twelve-year-old Stacy to have double-eyelid surgery because she thinks "having less sleepy looking eyes would make a better impression on people and help her in the future with getting jobs." Ellen had undergone cosmetic surgery at the age of twenty on the advice of her mother and older sister and feels she has benefited.[4] Indeed, all three women in the study under thirty who have actually undergone cosmetic surgery did so on the advice of their mother and in their mother's presence at the clinic. Elena, in fact, received her double-eyelid surgery as a high school graduation present from her mother, who was concerned for her socioeconomic future. The mothers, in turn, are influenced not so much by a personal flaw of their own which drives them to mold and perfect their daughters as by a society that values the superficial characteristics of one race over another.

A few of the women's dating and courtship patterns were also affected by their negative feelings toward stereotypically Asian features. Jo, for example, who is married to a Caucasian man, said she has rarely dated Asian men and is not usually attracted to them, partly because they look too much like her: "I really am sorry to say that I am not attracted to Asian men. And it's not to say that I don't find them attractive on the whole. But I did date a Japanese guy once and I felt like I was holding my brother's hand [she laughs nervously]."

A Mutilation of the Body

Although none of the women in my study denied the fact of racial inequality, almost all insisted that the surgical alteration of their eyes and nose was a celebration of their bodies, reflecting their right as women and as minorities to do what they wished with their bodies. Many, such as Jane, also said the surgery was a rite of passage or a routine ceremony, since family members and peers underwent the surgery upon reaching eighteen. Although it is at least possible to perceive cosmetic surgery of the eyes and nose for many Asian Americans as a celebration of the individual and social bodies, as in a rite of passage, this is clearly not so. My research has shown that double-eyelid and nasal bridge procedures performed on Asian Americans do not hold, for either the participants or the larger society, cultural meanings that are benign and spontaneous. Rather, these surgeries are a product of society's racial ideologies, and for many of the women in my study, the surgeries are a calculated means for socioeconomic success. In fact, most describe the surgery as something to "get out of the way" before carrying on with the rest of their lives.

Unlike participants in a rite of passage, these Asian American women share little *communitas* (an important element of rites of passage) with each other or with the larger society. Arnold Van Gennup defined rites of passage as "rites which accompany every change of place, state, social position, and age" (quoted in Turner 1969:94). These rites create an almost egalitarian type of solidarity (communitas) between participants and between the participants and a larger social group. A body modification procedure which is an example of such a rite is the series of public head-scarification rituals for pubescent boys among the Kabre of Togo, West Africa (Brain 1979:178). The final scars they acquire make them full adult members of their group. Their scarification differs considerably from the cosmetic surgery procedures of Asian American women in my study in at least two of its aspects: (1) an egalitarian bond is formed between the participants (between and among those who are doing the scarring and those who are receiving it); and (2) both the event and the resulting feature (i.e., scars) signify the boy's incorporation into a larger social group (i.e., adult men), and therefore, both are unrelentingly made public.

The Asian American women who undergo double-eyelid and nasal bridge surgeries do not usually create bonds with each other or with their plastic surgeons. Their surgery, unlike the scarification rite of the Kabre, is a private event that usually occurs in the presence of the patient, the doctor, and the doctor's assistants only. Moreover, there is little personal connection between doctor and patient. Though a few of the Asian American women in my study were content with their surgery and with their doctors, most describe their experience on the operating table as one of fear and loneliness, and some described their doctors as impersonal, businesslike, and even tending toward profit-making. Annie, for instance, described the fear she felt being alone with the doctor and his assistants in the operating room, when her mother suddenly left the room because she could not bear to watch:

> They told me to put my thumbs under my hips so I didn't interfere with my hands. I received two anesthesia shots on my

nose—this was the only part of the operation that hurt, but it hurt! I closed my eyes. I didn't want to look. I didn't want to see like the knives or anything. I could feel like the snapping of scissors and I was aware when they were putting that thing up my nose. My mom didn't really care. They told her to look at my nose. They were wondering if I wanted it sharper and stuff. She said, "Oh no. I don't want to look" and just ran away. She was sitting outside. I was really pissed.

Elena described her experience of surgery in a similar manner: "I had no time to be nervous. They drugged me with valium, I think. I was awake but drugged, conscious but numb. I remember being on the table. They [doctor and nurses] continued to keep up a conversation. I would wince sometimes because I could feel little pinches. He [the doctor] would say, "Okay, Pumpkin, Sweetheart, it will be over soon." . . . I didn't like it, being called Pumpkin and being touched by a stranger. . . . I wanted to say Shut up! to all three people." Clearly, the event of surgery did not provide an opportunity or the atmosphere for the women in my study to forge meaningful relationships with their doctors.

Asian American women who undergo cosmetic surgery also have a very limited chance of bonding with each other by sharing experiences of the surgery, because unlike participants in a Kabre puberty rite, these women do not usually publicize either their operation or their new features. All informed me that apart from me and their doctors, few people knew about their surgery since at the most they had told three close friends and/or family members about it. As Annie stated, "I don't mind if people found out [that I had a nose operation], but I won't go around telling them." Jane explained: "It's nothing to be ashamed of, not at all, but it's not something you brag about either. . . . To this day my boyfriend doesn't notice I had anything done. That makes me feel pretty good. It's just that you want to look good, but you don't want them [other people] to know how much effort goes into it." In fact, all the women in my study said they wanted a "better" look, but one that was not so drastically different from the original that it looked "unnatural." Even those who underwent revision surgeries to improve on their first operation said they were more at ease and felt more effective in social situations (with boyfriends, classmates, and employers) after their primary operation, mainly because they looked subtly "better," not because they looked too noticeably different from the way they used to look. Thus, it is not public awareness of these women's cosmetic surgery or the resulting features which win them social acceptance. Rather, the successful personal concealment of the operation and of any glaring traces of the operation (e.g., scars or an "unnatural" look) is paramount for acceptance. Clearly, the alteration of their features is not a rite of passage celebrating the incorporation of individual bodies into a larger social body; rather, it is a personal quest by marginal people seeking acceptance in a society where the dominant culture's ideals loom large and are constraining. The extent to which the Asian American women have internalized society's negative valuation of their natural features is best exemplified by the fact that these women feel more self-confident in social interactions as a result of this slight alteration of their eyelids—that is, with one minor alteration in their whole anatomy—which others may not even notice.

Medicine and the "Disembodiment" of the Asian American Female Consumer

Some sectors of the medical profession fail to recognize that Asian American women's decision to undergo cosmetic surgery of the eyelid and the nose is not so much triggered by a simple materialistic urge to feel better with one more status item that money can buy as much as it is an attempt to heal a specific doubt about oneself which society has unnecessarily brought on. For instance, one doctor in my study stated the following about double-eyelid surgery on Asian American women: "It's like when you wear certain shoes, certain clothes, or put certain makeup on, well—why do you wear those? Why this brand of clothes and not another? . . . You can label these things different ways, but I think that it [the double-eyelid surgery of Asian Americans] is just a desire to look better. You know, it's like driving a brand-new car down the street or having something bought from Nordstrom." By viewing cosmetic surgery and items bought from a department store as equally arbitrary, plastic surgeons, like economists, sometimes assume that the consumer (in this case, the cosmetic surgery client) is disembodied (O'Neill 1985:103). They view her as an abstract, nonhuman subject whose choice of items is not mediated by any historical circumstances, symbolic meaning, or political significance.

With "advances" in science and technology and the proliferation of media images, the number of different selves one can become appears arbitrary and infinite to many Americans, including the women in my study. Thus, many of them argue, as do some plastic surgeons (see Kaw 1993), that the variation in the width of the crease requested by Asian Americans (from six to ten millimeters) is indicative of a whole range of personal and idiosyncratic styles in double-eyelid operations. The idea is that the women are not conforming to any standard, that they are molding their own standards of beauty. However, they ignore that a primary goal in all double-eyelid operations, regardless of how high or how far across the eyelid the crease is cut, is to have a more open appearance of the eye, and the trend in all cases is to create a fold where there was none. These operations are an instance of the para-doxical "production of variety within standardization" in American consumer culture (Goldstein 1993:152). Thus, there is a double bind in undergoing a double-eyelid operation. On the one hand, the women are rebelling against the notion that one must be content with the physical features one is born with, that one cannot be creative in molding one's own idea of what is beautiful. On the other hand, they are conforming to Caucasian standards of beauty.

The women in the study seem to have an almost unconditional faith that science and technology will help them feel satisfied with their sense of self. And the plastic surgery industry, with its scientific advances and seemingly objective stance, makes double-eyelid sur-gery appear routine, necessary, and for the most part, harmless (Kaw 1993). The women in my study had read advertisements of cosmetic surgery clinics, many of them catering to their specific "needs." In my interviews with Nellee, who had once thought about having double-eyelid surgery, and Jo, who is thinking about it for the near future, I did not have to tell them that the operation entailed creating a crease on the upper eyelid through incision and sutures. They told me. Jo, for instance, said, "I know the technology and it's quite easy, so I am not really afraid of it messing up."

Conclusion: Problem of Resistance in a Culture Based on Endless Self-Fashioning

My research has shown that Asian American women's decision to undergo cosmetic surgery for wider eyes and more prominent noses is very much influenced by society's racial stereotyping of Asian features. Many of the women in my study are aware of the racial stereotypes from which they suffer. However, all have internalized these negative images of themselves and of other Asians, and they judge the Asian body, including their own, with the critical eye of the oppressor. Moreover, almost all share the attitude of certain sectors of the media and medicine in regard to whether undergoing a surgical operation is, in the end, harmful or helpful to themselves and other Asian Americans; they say it is yet another exercise of their freedom of choice.

The American value of individualism has influenced many of the women to believe that the specific width and shape they choose for their eyelid folds and nose bridges indicate that they are molding their own standards of beauty. Many said they wanted a "natural" look that would be uniquely "in balance" with the rest of their features. However, even those such as Jane, who openly expressed the idea that she is conforming to a Western standard of beauty, emphasized that she is not oppressed but rather empowered by her surgical transformation: "Everything is conforming as I see it. It's just a matter of recognizing it. . . . Other people—well, they are also conforming to something else. Nothing anybody has ever done is original. And it's very unlikely that people would go out and be dressed in any way if they hadn't seen it somewhere. So I don't think it's valid to put a value judgment on [the type of surgery I did]. I'm definitely for self-improvement. So if you don't like a certain part of your body, there's no reason not to change it."

The constraints Asian American women in my study feel every day with regard to their natural features are a direct result of unequal race relationships in the United States. These women's apparent lack of concern for their racial oppression is symptomatic of a certain postmodern culture arising in the United States which has the effect of hiding structural inequalities from public view (Bordo 1990). In its attempt to celebrate differences and to shun overgeneralizations and totalizing discourses that apparently efface diversity among people in modern life, this postmodern culture actually obscures differences; that is, by viewing differences as all equally arbitrary, it effaces from public consciousness historically determined differences in power between groups of people. Thus, blue contact lenses for African American women, and double eyelids and nose bridges for Asian women are both seen as forms of empowerment and indistinguishable in form and function from perms for white women, corn rows on Bo Derek, and tans on Caucasians. All cosmetic changes are seen in the same way—as having no cultural meaning and no political significance. In this process, what is trivialized and obscured is the difficult, and often frustrated struggle with which subordinate groups must assert their difference as something to be proud of in the face of dominant ideologies (Bordo 1990:666).

With the proliferation of scientific and technological industries, the many selves one can become appear infinite and random. Like the many transformations of the persona of Madonna throughout her career or the metamorphosis of Michael Jackson's face during his "Black and White" video, the alteration of bodies through plastic surgery has become for the American public simply another means of self-expression and self-determination. As Ellen said, "You can be born Chinese. But if you want to look like a more desirable one, and if surgery is available like it is now, then why not do it?" She said that instead of having to undergo the arduous task of placing thin strips of transparent plastic tape over the eyelids to create a temporary crease (a procedure which, she said, many Asians unhappy with single eyelids used to do), Asians now have the option to permanently transform the shape of their eyes.

Thus, instead of becoming a battleground for social and cultural resistance, the body has become a playground (Bordo 1990:667). Like Michael Jackson's lyrics in the song "Man in the Mirror" ("If you want to make the world a better place, then take a look at yourself and make a change"; Jackson 1987), it is ambiguous whether political change and social improvement are best orchestrated through changing society or through an "act of creative interpretation" (Bordo 1990) of the superficial details of one's appearance. The problem and dilemma of resistance in U.S. society are best epitomized in this excerpt of my interview with Jo, the twenty-eight-year-old law student who is thinking of having double-eyelid surgery:

JO: In my undergraduate college, every Pearl Harbor Day I got these phone calls and people would say, "Happy Pearl Harbor Day," and they made noises like bombs and I'd find little toy soldiers at my dorm door. Back then, I kind of took it as a joke. But now, I think it was more malicious. . . . [So] I think the surgery is a lot more superficial. Affecting how society feels about a certain race is a lot more beneficial. And it goes a lot deeper and lasts a lot longer.

INTERVIEWER: Looking into the future, do you think you will do both?

JO: Yeah [nervous laughter]. I do. I do.

Jo recognizes that undergoing double-eyelid surgery, that is, confirming the undesirability of Asian eyes, is in contradiction to the work she would like to do as a teacher and legal practitioner. However, she said she cannot easily destroy the negative feelings she already possesses about the natural shape of her eyes.

Implications: Asian Americans and the American Dream

The psychological burden of having constantly to measure up has been often overlooked in the image of Asian Americans as model minorities, as people who have achieved the American dream. The model minority myth assumes not only that all Asian Americans are financially well-to-do, but also that those Asian Americans who are from relatively well-to-do, non-working-class backgrounds (like many of the women in my study) are free from the everyday constraints of painful racial stereotypes (see Takaki 1989; Hurh and Kim 1989). As my research has shown, the cutting up of Asian Americans' faces through plastic surgery is a concrete example of how, in modern life, Asian Americans, like other people of color, can be influenced by the dominant culture to loathe themselves in such a manner as to begin mutilating and revising parts of their body.

Currently, the eyes and nose are those parts of the anatomy which Asian Americans most typically cut and alter since procedures for these are relatively simple with the available technology. However, a few of the women in my study said that if they could, they would also want to increase their stature, and in particular, to lengthen their legs; a few also suggested that when safer implants were found, they wanted to augment their breasts; still others wanted more prominent brow bridges and jawlines. On the one hand, it appears that through technology women can potentially carve an endless array of new body types, breaking the bounds of racial categories. On the other hand, these desired body types are constructed in the context of the dominant culture's beauty ideals. The search for the ideal body may have a tremendous impact, in terms of racial discrimination, on patterns of artificial genetic selection, such as occurs at sperm banks, egg donation centers, and in the everyday ritual of courtship.

ACKNOWLEDGMENTS

I first thank the many women who generously gave their time and shared their thoughts in interviews with me. Without their contributions, this research project would not have been possible.

I continue to thank Cecilia de Mello, without whose encouragements I never would have even begun to formulate my research. I am also grateful to Nancy Scheper-Hughes, Aihwa Ong, Paul Rabinow, Lynn Kwiatkowski, and Steve Mc-Graw, as well as the various anonymous reviewers, for their insightful comments on earlier versions of this chapter.

This chapter appeared, in slightly different form, in *Medical Anthropology* 7:1(March 1993). Reproduced by permission of the American Anthropological Association.

I thank Nicole Sault for her patience, continual advice, and careful readings of the present chapter. Also, I am grateful to John Kelly and Rena Lederman for their willingness to read and provide helpful comments.

NOTES

1   I have not yet found descriptions, in medical texts and newspaper articles, of the types of cosmetic surgery specifically requested by Latinos. However, one newspaper article (Ellison 1990) reports that an increasing number of Mexicans are purchasing a device by which they can attain a more Nordic and Anglo-Saxon "upturned" nose. It requires inserting plastic hooks in the nostrils.

2   The shapes of the eye and nose of Asians are not meant in this chapter to be interpreted as categories which define a group of people called Asians. Categories of racial groups are arbitrarily defined by society. Likewise, the physical traits people in a racial group are recognized by are arbitrary (see Molnar 1983).

Also, I use the term *Asian American* to name collectively the women in this study who have undergone or are thinking about undergoing cosmetic surgery. Although I recognize their ethnic, generational, and geographical diversity, people of Asian ancestry in the United States share similar experiences in that they are subject to many of the same racial stereotypes (see Hurh and Kim 1989; Takaki 1989).

3   Cosmetic surgery for double eyelids, nasal tip refinement, and nose bridges are not limited to Asians in the United States. Asians in East and Southeast Asia have requested such surgeries since the early 1950s, when U.S. military forces began long-term occupations of such countries as Korea and the Philippines. Some American doctors (such as Millard) were asked by Asians in these countries to perform the surgeries. See Harahap 1982; Kristof 1991; Millard 1964; Sayoc 1954.

4   Ellen's mother, however, did not receive double-eyelid or nose bridge surgery. It appears that the trend of actually undergoing such surgeries began with Asian women who are now about forty to fifty years of age. Jane and Annie, sisters in their early twenties, said that though their mother who is about fifty had these

surgeries, their grandmother did not. They also said that their grandmother encouraged them to have the operation, as did their mother.

None of the women in my study mentioned their father or other males in their household or social networks as verbally encouraging them to have the surgeries. However, many said they felt their resulting features would or did help them in their relationships with men, especially boyfriends (Asians and non-Asians alike). We did not discuss in detail their father's reaction to their surgery, but those who mentioned their father's reaction summed it up mainly as indifference.

REFERENCES

American Society of Plastic and Reconstructive Surgeons (ASPRS). N.d. "Estimated Number of Cosmetic Surgery Procedures Performed by ASPRS Members in 1990." Pamphlet.

Appadurai, Arjun. 1990. "Disjuncture and Difference in the Global Cultural Economy." *Public Culture* 2(2): 1–24.

Blacking, John. 1977. *The Anthropology of the Body.* London: Academic Press.

Bordo, Susan. 1990. "Material Girl: The Effacements of Postmodern Culture." *Michigan Quarterly Review* 29:635–676.

Brain, Robert. 1979. *The Decorated Body.* New York: Harper and Row.

Chen, Joanne. 1993. "Before and After: For Asian Americans, the Issues Underlying Cosmetic Surgery Are Not Just Skin Deep." *A. Magazine: The Asian American Quarterly* 2(1): 15–18, 26–27.

Daly, Mary. 1978. *Gyn/ecology: The Metaethics of Radical Feminism.* Boston: Beacon Press.

Davis, Kathy. 1991. "Remaking the She-Devil: A Critical Look at Feminist Approaches to Beauty." *Hypatia* 6(2): 21–43.

Dower, John. 1986. *War without Mercy: Race and Power in the Pacific War.* New York: Pantheon.

Ellison, Katherine. 1990. "Mexico Puts on a Foreign Face." *San Jose Mercury News,* December 16, p. 14a.

Fleming, Charles, and Mary Talbot. 1993. "The Two Faces of Michael Jackson." *Newsweek,* February 22, p. 57.

Gilman, Sander L. 1985. *Difference and Pathology: Stereotypes of Sexuality, Race and Madness.* Ithaca, N.Y.: Cornell University Press.

Goffman, Erving. 1979. *Gender Advertisement.* Cambridge: Harvard University Press.

Goldstein, Judith. 1993. "The Female Aesthetic Community." Poetics Today 14(1): 143–163.

Harahap, Marwali. 1982. "Oriental Cosmetic Blepharoplasty." In *Cosmetic Surgery for Non-white Patients,* ed. Harold Pierce, pp. 79–97. New York: Grune and Stratton.

Hurh, Won Moo, and Kwang Chung Kim. 1989. "The 'Success' Image of Asian Americans: Validity, and Its Practical and Theoretical Implications." *Ethnic and Racial Studies* 12(4):512–537.

Iwata, Edward. 1991. "Race without Face." *San Francisco Image Magazine,* May, pp. 51–55.

Jackson, Michael. 1987. "Man in the Mirror."On *Bad.* Epic Records, New York.

Kaw, Eugenia. 1993. "Medicalization of Racial Features: Asian American Women and Cosmetic Surgery." *Medical Anthropology Quarterly* 7(1):74–89.

Kim, Elaine. 1986. "Asian-Americans and American Popular Culture." In *Dictionary of Asian-American History*, ed. Hyung-Chan Kim. New York: Greenwood Press.

Kristof, Nicholas. 1991. "More Chinese Look 'West.' " *San Francisco Examiner
and Chronicle*, July 7.

Lakoff, Robin T., and Raquel L. Scherr. 1984. *Face Value: The Politics of Beauty*.
Boston: Routledge and Kegan.

LeFlore, Ivens C. 1982. "Face Lift, Chin Augmentation and Cosmetic Rhinoplasty
in Blacks." In *Cosmetic Surgery in Non-White Patients*, ed. Harold Pierce.
New York: Grune and Stratton.

Lock, Margaret, and Nancy Scheper-Hughes. 1990. "A Critical-Interpretive Approach in Medical Anthropology: Rituals and Routines of Discipline and
Dissent." In *Medical Anthropology: Contemporary Theory and Method*,
ed., Thomas Johnson and Carolyn Sargent, pp. 47–72. New York: Praeger.

McCurdy, John A. 1990. *Cosmetic Surgery of the Asian Face*. New York: Thieme
Medical Publishers.

MacGregor, Frances C. 1967. "Social and Cultural Components in the Motivations
of Persons Seeking Plastic Surgery of the Nose." *Journal of Health and
Social Behavior* 8(2):125–135.

Merrell, Kathy H. 1994. "Saving Faces." *Allure*, January, pp. 66–68.

Millard, Ralph, Jr. 1964. "The Original Eyelid and Its Revision." *American Journal
of Opthamology* 57:546–649.

Molnar, Stephen. 1983. *Human Variation: Races, Types, and Ethnic Groups*.
Englewood Cliffs, N.J.: Prentice-Hall.

Nakao, Annie. 1993. "Faces of Beauty: Light Is Still Right." *San Francisco Examiner and Chronicle*, April 11, p. D-4.

O'Neill, John. 1985. *Five Bodies*. Ithaca, N.Y.: Cornell University Press.

Ong, Aihwa. 1987. *Spirits of Resistance and Capitalist Discipline: Factory
Women in Malaysia* Albany: State University of New York Press.

Ramsdell, Daniel. 1983. "Asia Askew: U.S. Best-sellers on Asia, 1931–
1980." *Bulletin of Concerned Asian Scholars* 15(4):2–25.

Rosenthal, Elisabeth. 1991. "Ethnic Ideals: Rethinking Plastic Surgery." *New York
Times*, September 25, p. B7.

Sayoc, B. T. 1954. "Plastic Construction of the Superior Palpebral Fold." *American
Journal of Opthamology* 38:556–559.

———. 1974. "Surgery of the Oriental Eyelid." *Clinics in Plastic Surgery* 1(1):157–
171.

Sheets-Johnstone, Maxine, ed. 1992. *Giving the Body Its Due*. Albany: State University of New York Press.

Tajima, Renee E. 1989. "Lotus Blossoms Don't Bleed: Images of Asian Women." In
*Making Waves: An Anthology of Writings by and about Asian American
Women*, ed. Diane Yeh-Mei Wong, pp. 308–317. Boston: Beacon Press.

Takaki, Ronald. 1989. *Strangers from a Different Shore*. Boston: Little, Brown.

Turner, Terence. 1980. "The Social Skin." In *Not Work Alone*, ed. J. Cherfas and R.
Lewin, pp. 112–114. London: Temple Smith.

Turner, Victor. 1969. *The Ritual Process: Structure and Anti-Structure*. Chicago:
Aldine.

Wolf, Naomi. 1991. *The Beauty Myth: How Images of Beauty Are Used against
Women*. New York: William Morrow.

Yang, Jeff, and Angelo Ragaz. 1993. "The Beauty Machine." *A. Magazine: The
Asian American Quarterly* 2(1):20–21.

THE CONTEXT OF MEANINGS BEHIND RAPE TRAUMA

CATHY WINKLER
with RENATA McMULLEN
and KATE WININGER

Unexplained Trauma

"He can't keep raping me with these feelings of terror, can he? He held me against my will last night, but can't I be free of him now? He's out of my life. I can beat him. He can't keep threatening me." These were the questions I asked the rape-survivor advocate at Grady Hospital in Atlanta, Georgia, immediately following the attack.[1] Believing that I could stand up to the trauma embedded inside me by the rapist and that I could beat those future bombshells of emotions was important for regaining my self-esteem. Yet the view of the advocate, a professional experienced in the field of victim-survivors' reactions, was discouraging:[2] "You can't deny what's there. It has to come out and you have to let it come out." To give up was not my strategy. "Yes," I replied, "but can't I control it as it comes out? Can't I handle it if I understand what it is?" Her response contained the same fatalism: "No, everyone suffers it, and everyone suffers the trauma as it comes out." The honesty in her response was a doomsday notice: my future would be a road of unpredictable cliffs and detours, bombardments of emotional reactions. The rapist had more than terrorized me for one night; he had planted a series of land mines that later would further destroy me.

In one sense, the advocate's perception of the aftermath of rape parallels our lack of understanding of the traumas experienced by rape victim-survivors. The types and sources of these trauma are a sundry list of symptoms and a fusion of disjointed, chaotic reactions. Advice on survival and on how to control the ongoing, dehumanizing effects of the trauma[3] remains minimal in the area of meaning, and in general, trauma needs further study.[4] As a result, the seemingly unexplained and inescapable trauma were my prescription for life. Preparation for the trauma rested in fear of the upcoming trip through the unknown. But a question kept surfacing: If I had to suffer the trauma, wasn't it possible to discover its forms and contexts and, by examining them, ready myself for the roller coaster ride?

My first difficulty was that I didn't know when I would start down the road of terror. The day after the rape, I did not feel upset about the brutal assault. My body rested in a pleasant state of numbness; I felt calm, cool, and collected. Actually admitting that I experienced those nonemotional feelings was an embarrassment. The slight jitters one feels before teaching class were missing. I was a person without nerves. The realization that this state was unnatural for me left me only one option—enjoy those nerveless and jitter-free moments. How long this numbness would continue was unclear.

Feelings of upheaval did occur during this time, but these feelings belonged to my friends, family members, and co-workers. These people had nightmares, crying spells, angry outbursts, and numerous disquieting feelings. The effects of the rapist's terror were extensive. Inexplicably, my body exuded a calmness unknown to me before, and my go-with-the-flow approach disconcerted many: with the victim in a state of survival, supporters were in state of upheaval.

Yet the focus of my numbed emotions was specific: the emotions tied to the rapist, his attack, and his threats were unfelt and unrealized. Those desensitized nerves were alien and temporarily transformed me into an emotionless, Mr. Spock-like state. My feelings about the attack were therefore untouchable. Discussion of the rape, by myself or others, left me unscathed. This respite from emotional pain gave me time to investigate further the literature and, unfortunately, to feel the wrath of the second assault as discussed later in this chapter.

According to Burgess and Holmstrom (1985:51), victims experiencing this numbness are in a state of disbelief and nonacceptance that the attack occurred; the authors describe numbing as reduced responsiveness and involvement with the environment. Unlike the victims in the data, I had no doubt that the rape had occurred, and answered any and all questions about the attack. My emotional numb-ness temporarily silenced only my feelings of rage; it did not induce behavioral restraints or denial. I did feel hate toward the rapist, but I did not yet feel the rage he had buried inside me during the attack.

An interesting result of this numbness was a separation between my mind and body. Previously when something disturbed me, it mani-fested itself in an interconnected manner. The rape temporarily severed—noticed only by myself and unrealized by others—a few of those connections between my mind and body. After the attack, I began to note reactions in my body as if it were a world apart from my mind.

The contexts of these trauma form the basis for this chapter, and examples of these contexts demonstrate the impact of the partial body-mind separation.[5] I discuss how I experienced, learned, and deciphered the meanings behind the different contexts of rape trauma. Important to my conceptualization is the insight gained from in-depth interviews with other rape survivors. Their words and experiences also form part of my perspective. I explain how our bod-ies activated sets of trauma when we found ourselves in threatening social/cultural contexts.

Rape Trauma Syndrome

Burgess and Holmstrom provide the foundational studies on trauma (1974a, 1974b, 1985). They conceptualized the feelings one experi-ences after rape with the term *rape trauma syndrome.* Their research demarcated the problem, legitimated the dysfunctional feelings of dis-equilibrium, and exposed the symptoms of malice which range from physical to emotional upheavals. A list of the symptoms or trauma-tophobia is extensive:[6]

flashbacks	nightmares	moodiness
irritability	guilt	self-blame
lack of concentration	fear	various phobias
depression	suicidal traits	anger
revenge	stuttering	fatigue

introversion   confusion   shaking

tenseness   restlessness   insomnia

paranoid   overreacting   sleeping disorders

decreased libido   psychotic behavior

intense exhaustion   paralyzing anxiety

lack of sexual desire   hysterical crying and screaming

feelings of worthlessness

addictive traits, e.g., alcoholism and/or drug addiction

obsessions from behavioral traits to thoughts

psychosomatic disorders, e.g., startled awakenings

Egad, this was to be my future! A compilation of symptoms leaves a victim with the impression of bewilderment and dismay: Which of these symptoms will take over? Would I find myself half crazed and wandering the neighborhood nude at three o'clock one morning? How dysfunctional a victim would I become? Moreover, stories of the trauma screaming out of the victim in front of a group of people, such as a classroom in my case, provided me with a repertoire of fears to which my friends added their horror stories. The studies on rape trauma repeat examples of detachment similar to mine and insist it is a foregone conclusion that trauma disrupts every victim's life. In other words, they stress that these traumas demonstrate the continued and all-pervasive control the rapist holds over the victim, despite the rapist's absence.

Most discussions of rape trauma syndrome place the source of these disruptive traits in the rape attack. While some mention other difficulties such as institutional response (Holmstrom and Burgess 1978) and social antagonisms from rape myths (Holmes and Williams 1981; Burt 1980; Winkler 1989), only infrequently are these separated out as the antagonizers that generate rape trauma. Researchers argue that other calamities such as police insensitivity and rape myths add to the trauma frenzy.

With a list of symptoms and in an initial state of numbness, I waited for those rape trauma disruptions to take over and pull my life apart. No specific guidance was available. In other words, when rape trauma symptoms grab us, our only possibility for survival is to stay on the roller coaster and cling to the bar of safety until the ride is over. Trauma is an unstoppable and unpredictable avalanche of pain, or so I was led to believe.

Attacklike Contexts

Attacklike contexts include features that parallel the attack, such as location, time of day, and words and movements that expose the wound of terror. When features from the attack are replayed in the life of the victim-survivor, hidden wounds become inflamed with pain. Attacklike contexts spark terrorizing trauma and, in capsule form, expose emotional trauma from the attack. In this respect, a set of meanings exists that explains some of the disquieting and unnerving feelings.

For example, one night my dog inadvertently hit my ankle at the same spot where the rapist had kicked me awake. With a frenzied reaction and a hypersensitized response, I jumped up in a state of agitation. Being able to decipher the meaning of my emotional flare-up helped me quiet my nerves and return to sleep.

With this knowledge, my ability to squelch the attacks of trauma as they surfaced became possible. As the octopuslike tentacles of terror (Sheffield 1987) began to surround me, I made the situation feel safe by turning on a light, checking the windows and doors, or calling a friend. Thus I prevented those tentacles from completely grabbing me and holding me down. While I felt the initiation of that terror, its intensity was stifled.

Meaning behind Attacklike Contexts

But why do similar contexts ignite the trauma? The answer that they are similar seemed insufficient, for it ignored the reasons for the surfacing. Why did my memory want to remind me of this horror?

After the stranger's assault, I had to face the possibility that the rapist would return, and this was an excruciating and real fear. Although initially numb from the attack, my self-preservation skills warned me that experiencing another rape would seriously jeopardize my ability to survive. These fears of the rapist's return are real fears, they are valid fears, and they are protective fears.

Contexts and characteristics of the contexts which correspond to the rape, rapist, and attack are *sources* of attacklike trauma. This trauma is the body's protective strategy to safeguard the survivor in order to provide space and time for her or him to heal in a situation of comfort and safety. This evidence gave me hope that by understanding the source and meaning of the types of trauma, one cannot delete it from one's life but put a check on its disruptiveness.

Second-Assault Contexts

The meanings and sources of trauma related to the rape are described in the literature as a fusion of pain coming from three sepcific areas: the rape attack, rape myths or statements in the form of a second assault, and institutional confrontations. This indiscriminate prescription for pain was disconcerting. Were the traumas from these sources one huge dark blob that enveloped a victim's life?

Forced to return to work to face colleagues and co-workers in shock, I began to feel traumatized by their negative statements: my facial muscles became tense, as if lined with age, and my legs quivered as if I were walking through a land of earthquakes. These two bodily feelings constantly infiltrated my existence, yet went unnoticed by others. These were not signs of trauma from the rape, nor did this trauma feel like the terrorizing trauma that surfaced later. Rather this was a part of a series of traumas whose source was the second assault.

Holmes and Williams (1981) define derogatory comments made about a person raped as the second assault. They point out that the accumulative negative responses by those around us can result in an attack more severe than the attack forced on us by the rapist. They point out that there are many types of constraints against us besides rape.

Another more common term used to describe the statements made in the second assault is *rape myth*. Rape myths, a type of sexual discrimination, are prejudicial statements that antagonize and aggravate victims (Burt 1980; Winkler 1989). Popular rape myths include such comments as "She was asking for it; she went to a bar," or "What do you expect? Look at what she wore." As Valerie Fennell notes in her chapter on aging terminology in this volume, terms vary extensively in emphasis, selection, and presentation. Categories alter and are in flux, and it is this characteristic of flexibility that likewise exists in the phrases that make up the second-assault statements. In my case, those stated, crass comments were not my lot.

Flexibility surfaced in the context of rape myths (Winkler 1989) about me in that the form altered as a result of what I call the *chameleon of disguises*.[7] These are discriminatory rape myths reformulated to attack a particular victim's characteristics. Instead of statements focused against the victim-survivor and her or his reactions at the time of the attack, prejudicial comments zero in on a victim-survivor who speaks against rape. "*My* rape," as some mistakenly called it, "was destroying *their* lives."[8] My ten-minute explanation to my students about my classroom absences and facial bruising became distorted—by those antagonists around me—into a supposedly full-length theme of my course. My favorite example: After an innocuous discussion on some issue unrelated to rape, two people listening to my conversation each pulled me aside to confer privately. Person A informed me: "You are too much in control and are denying the rape"; this person felt I should have discussed the rape at that time. On the other hand, Person B demanded: "You must take control because you are acting out of control due to the rape"; interpreting my actions inversely, the person perceived in my give-and-take conversation that my day-to-day abilities to function had caved in. These contradictory responses were not uncommon. Like the rapist, these people wanted to define my life, and define it only according to the rape. In her chapter on eating disorders, in this volume, Dixie King points out how others assume they have a right to take control and interpret the problems in a person's life, instead of employing a perspective of negotiation.

Thus the second assault became the first *source* of feelings in my body after the attack. Yet my denial of the second assault or the words of discrimination left no room for analysis. I couldn't believe some of my colleagues and some of my friends were not supporting me: Wasn't the act I had suffered rape? Instead, my strained face and pulsating legs expressed the pain caused by their comments.

Another example of a second assault was experienced by a friend, Suzanne (a pseudonym), whose female boss became angry at Suzanne's intermittent work absences due to the police investigation. As a result, the boss fired her, and for a while Suzanne could only find part-time work. While the part-time work paid poorly, the comforting conditions of this job replaced her aggravating experiences with her previous boss.

Later Suzanne found a full-time job. One day at this new job, her co-workers were discussing the disadvantages of part-time work. Suzanne fell silent immediately and experienced a momentary foglike condition. The state of her emotions was initially unexplainable. Later she pieced the connections together: the part-time-work discussion had exposed the trauma from the first boss's aggravations, which had forced her into a diminished work status. Unintentionally, her support group reopened the wound from the second-assault rape. In another yet similar way, this chapter topic and my discussion of the attack I experienced might cause this type of reaction in readers who have been raped and socially assaulted.

Second-assault context then is the *source* of negative statements against the victim. These examples demonstrate two types of statements. The first type consists of antagonistic and discriminatory comments intentionally directed against the person raped. The second type are indirect and unintentionally antagonistic statements that expose the pain from the rape or from others' second-assault statements. Second-assault trauma reactions can include foglike conditions that place us in a state of nonresponse, stifling our thoughts and words, or they can be other nervous conditions such as tight-muscled facial features and unsteadiness in the legs.

Meaning behind Second-Assault Contexts

As Holmes and Williams (1981) note, the accumulation of negative statements about a rape victim is another type of rape, and this second-assault rape can be far worse than the initial one. Physical rape is spatially, temporally, and individually confined. Second-assault statements, on the other hand, can surface *at any time, in any place,* and be made *by anyone.* This context generates a second type of rape and trauma.

Some persons would argue that second-assault statements are not intended to rape the victim and would object to my position that second-assault statements are another form of rape attack. But intention is not the issue. As Mimi Nichter and Nancy Vuckovic, and William Young demonstrate in their chapters in this volume, one must understand the meaning behind—not the intent of—a person's statements:

teenagers who repeatedly state "I'm fat" are not dieting but rather sharing a common set of meanings with their peers as expressed by that phrase; and Sudanese terms used to describe women's clothing, while similar to those having to do with camels, are not due to the Sudanese associating women with camels but rather to their meaning on body control. Holmes and Williams also state, and I emphatically agree, that the second assault is more than one statement: it is a *community* of harsh and antagonistic statements, which then create the force of a second rape on the victim. The meaning behind the second-assault context, then, is the terror of another form of rape. The body warns us through trauma to distance ourselves from those illiterate to the meaning of their rape statements.

Rapist-Identified Contexts

During my period of numbness, I worked with the police detectives.[9] We spent time on surveillance, watching men in subway stations and on the street. Although there is always an expectation of a break during a stakeout, those emotions tied to the rape remained silent except in one instance, an experience I at first discarded as a senseless response.

The police detective called a man over to the car. As usual, my mind worked to match that man's face to the mental image of the rapist. While his features fell within the realm of possibilities, I checked other parameters: facial recognition, voice response, and bodily movements and reactions. He registered no sign of familiarity—the sort one sees in a long-lost friend or even a long-lost foe. Moreover, his voice was meaningless to me, and his short retorts to the detective's questions were sounds of an unfamiliar and unrecognized enemy.

While my memory gave no spark of remembrance, feelings of terror like those experienced during the attack emanated from my body. For the first time in a month, I had feelings of trauma that matched those during the rape attack. As the man came within six to nine feet of the car, my body began to effuse the fear of that frenzied attack. In desperation, my arms wanted to reach out and cling to the detective for protection. Why was I reacting this way? My memory gave no recognizable signal that this man was the rapist. On the contrary, his eyes were relaxed and steady like a newcomer or stranger to that set of meanings.

The evidence was clear: Since I did not recognize the face of this man as that of the rapist, and since this man displayed no secondary evidence of guilt, then this man was not the rapist. Nonchalantly, the man walked away. Words of his innocence I gave to the detective, but other words followed: "That's not the man, but remember that body. That is the same body as the rapist, and the shape of his head is identical." These words of identification came as the man distanced himself from the car and I viewed his back—a side of the rapist I had not seen that night. My statement of the man's innocence held no doubts then, but later I learned from the police he was the rapist. Months later, upon reflection, I asked myself: Why couldn't I recognize his face? How could I point out the rapist by his back features, a never-before-seen side of him, and yet not discern his face?

No answer existed then, and none of the data matched legally acceptable information. A legally acceptable identification of a suspect as the rapist rests only on the memory of the person raped. My logical collection of visual data, the basis for legal evidence, which supported the man's innocence, stood in opposition to the supposed "illogic" of my body's trauma reaction. Data unrecognized are the reactions of the body of the person raped in the presence of the rapist.

The body is able to circumvent the protective mechanisms of the mind. When the person raped is within a short distance of the attacker, the victim-survivor's body provides information by duplicating the terrorized conditions. While the terror during that street surveillance episode matched the attack, the only meanings available to explain the re-experienced rape feelings were inadequate. These false meanings were that, first, I was another dysfunctional rape victim whose feelings of horror surface randomly and without reason; second, the intensity of the trauma had left me in an unstable condition and unable to distinguish my real feelings; and third, I was an unreliable witness and unable to make visual distinctions. Each of these three explanations for my street feelings were wrong. Bierwert (1990) provides a fourth explanation: the rapist was able to alter sufficiently his presentation of self in order to disguise himself from me. The closeness that occurred during the attack made me susceptible to these alterations in his body form. In other words, on the night of the attack, the man projected himself to me as a rapist; during street surveillance, the man projected his body image as one of innocence.

By the third month, I had hired a private investigator to further pursue the case, and he was confident he would find the rapist.[10] To prepare myself to handle the process of identifying the man who raped me—an experience frequently noted by victim-survivors as another form of rape—I questioned my friend Kate Wininger. In a police lineup, she had identified the rapist who attacked her. Initially I had intended to ask her the question, "What was it *like* to face the attacker?" Inadvertently I asked, "*How* did you identify the rapist?" The switch of questions from the experience to the mechanisms of identification revealed the database of information in my body. Kate explained:

> I had gotten a good look at the rapist in spite of the fact he had put clothing over my face. The presence of the gun, even though I didn't believe it was real, and being strangled until I became unconscious, along with the rapist's threats to come back and kill me and my husband, all made the trauma more real.
>
> Nevertheless, I still felt competent I could identify him. In the police lineup, the men singly walked into view. I was not afraid and had no reason to feel fear because these men were behind a one-way mirror. Yet one of them had an impact upon me. When he entered my vision, my body first identified him in the lineup. It was *a purely visceral response, a return of the fear and revulsion.* My body told me immediately that he was the rapist. After my body's split-second identification, I then visually recalled that man's face as that of the rapist. (emphasis added)

Her experience of body trauma explained mine.

In continuing to seek help from other women, I talked with Shelley (pseudonym), who told me of her experience identifying an assailant from a photo lineup. In that attack, the man had kidnapped her and beat her with the butt of a gun. To save herself, she had jumped from the car when it was traveling fifty miles per hour. Later, at the police station, she viewed a series of pictures and selected three. While she told the police that these men looked like the attacker, she told me, after the conviction, that she had selected those three photos because her body went into rape-attack shock as it viewed each photo. In the end, she had selected the same man whose pictures were taken over a period of years.

The information for the following case comes from Renata McMullen, a past student of mine. All of us agree that these data need to become public information, and identification of rape with our names is no cause for us to feel any shame.

A date rapist attacked Renata with such severity that she experienced piercing vaginal pain and bleeding. The rapist told her that "this was OK," and then he said, "I know what I'm doing." The following year Renata became interested in a number of other men. Yet each time, as she became friends with a man she considered a prospective lover, she felt the same vaginal pain she first experienced during the date rape. Due to her body's warning, she decided in each case against pursuing her interest in these men. Two years later, after therapy, when she again became interested in another man, she experienced no pain. Now analytically interested in understanding the information supplied by her body, Renata conducted her own study of those past prospective lovers at whose presence her body dictated disgust. She discovered that each of these men had some abusive characteristics or, in some cases, were children of an abusive parent. Their traits paralleled those of the date rapist, who was both a son of abusive parents and an abuser himself. Her body identified those rapists and protected her from further assaults.

Failure to understand the meaning of our body trauma rests in the people in our legal system and in our cultural misunderstandings of rape. Neither our legal system nor our culture accepts the trauma in our bodies as a mechanism for identifying the rapist. While acknowledging that rape as a crime is second in severity only to murder, the legal system denies its impact on the bodies and minds of the victim-survivors. As perceived by courts and police, persons raped are incapacitated by their emotions, but inversely I argue that victim-survivors are *interpreters* of those emotional traumas.

Meaning behind Rapist-Identified Contexts

Trauma reactions in rapist-identified contexts are those that parallel the repulsion and nausea experienced at the time of the attack, thus warning us of dangerous men. They are trauma markers of protection against the rapist(s). While the attacklike context signifies protection, rapist-identified trauma—more severe and more pronounced in intensity than the trauma in attacklike context—warns us of immediate, not just pending, danger.

The *source* of my street-surveillance trauma was the context in which the rapist was present and was a danger to me; the *meaning* was his presence as a threat to my life. Interestingly, when I saw Kenneth Redding in police custody, knew he was guilty, and knew the results of his DNA Fingerprinting (Lewis 1988), I did not feel this body fear. Police custody and the absolute certainty of evidence alleviated my body's need, in that context, to feel fear in order to protect myself.

While our minds are still paralyzed with fear, our bodies aid our mental and analytical abilities by taking on in a pronounced manner the responsibility of identifying the terrorists. In these cases, our bodies warn us: they scream at us by repeatedly duplicating, through feelings of terror, those same emotions experienced during the attack. Previously people had told me not to trust those body traumas because they were indeterminate and dysfunctional trauma responses to the rape, but now I know that my best protection is my body's built-in non-battery-operated alarm system.

Blame-Denial Contexts

Still I had not experienced the trauma from the attack. In a gradual way, it emerged. Intermittent crying, only when I was alone and not surrounded by others' constraints, began after three months. Yet the meaning of these five-to-ten-minute bouts of tears was a mystery. Had a part of me died? Was it a way of releasing bottled-up terror? Was it hatred for the rapist? What were my reasons for this trauma? What is it that defines rape? Why does our fear of rape block us from discussing it, block even those who have not experienced an attack? The meanings of the rape-attack trauma needed further explanation.

The literature explains rape as an act of control and power—words used over and over. If control and power are everyday issues embedded in our interactions, then how was the rapist's intention to gain control and power distinct? For myself, an explanation of that rape attack as an issue of control and power was insufficient, because in a context of conflict I would give up my contention for power and control in order to maintain myself in a peaceful state of existence. What happened then that made rape a far more severe experience of domination?

The answer didn't seem to speak out to me from the literature, and my feelings during the second three-month period focused only on those short but almost daily, meaningless times of crying. In order to discover the truth and confront the trauma, I read everything about rape, from research to reported accounts. On March 27, 1988, the

New York Times ran a lengthy article on the prep-school student rapist-murderer. Undaunted as usual, I read the details of the case. At a bar in New York City, the woman had accepted a ride from this man. He took her to Central Park to rape her, and then he killed her. The details in three-fourths of the article passed by me; I was unmoved by the facts of that rape and murder. What sparked a reaction were the words of the rapist:

> Mr. Chambers, who is 21, told the authorities after his arrest—in a written statement and a videotape that was played repeatedly at the trial—that Miss Levin died accidentally during sex. He said she had pursued him at an Upper East Side bar on the night of her death and had finally talked him into going to Central Park sometime after leaving the bar at 4:30 A.M. Once there, he said, she went "insane," scratching and biting him and finally squeezing his testicles so painfully that *he grabbed her "instinctively" from behind the neck to stop the pain.* He stressed on tape that he never meant her harm. (Johnson 1988: 32; emphasis added)

It was the meaning behind these words spoken by that rapist-murderer—they had the same meaning as those Redding had expressed to me six months earlier: "It's your fault that I hit you. I didn't want to do it, but you made me beat you up. I had to stop you." Chambers blamed the victim, and the rapist who attacked me likewise accused me of instigating the beating. But the crucial point was that I realized, through Chambers's words and actions, that if I had not quit fighting and had not completely and absolutely given in to the rapist at the time of the attack, he would have ended my life as Chambers ended the life of Jennifer Levin. Rape was my escape from death.

The recognition of this meaning, revealed in the rapist-murderer's words, set off an explosion by my body in which screams of terror left my mouth and my body evacuated its contents. Alone at the time, I was glad no one could hear those anguished screams, whose reality mimicked the horror of the attack far better than any acted-out scream in those popularized films on terror.

Denial of the *act* of rape had not occurred for me, but another type of denial—and those around me had joined in it—was denial of the attacker's threat to my social and physical life (Winkler 1990). The context provided by the words from the New York prep-school student rapist-murderer forced me to confront this truth. The bomb of emotions was my body's means of overriding my mind's protective barrier of denial. In this case, my body had channeled the truth of the attack into an explosion of meaning. This torrent of emotional pain, unlike the first three-month period of numbness, and unlike the second three-month period of crying, incapacitated me. Days of recuperation were necessary.

Yet I discovered later still another type of denial buried inside me. After the police received the results of the DNA Fingerprinting which confirmed the suspect as the rapist, I asked them when I would see the rapist in a lineup. They had hedged, not anwering this question for months. Avoidance was impossible now, and they told me the truth: There would be no lineup because during street surveillance and in a photo lineup, the rapist's face had been unrecognizable to me. Yet they admitted that the similarity between the artist's composite and the rapist was unquestionable, and my data describing the rapist's traits were 80 percent accurate, in contrast to the 30 to 50 percent accuracy rate common to most witnesses of crime.

My incompetence at visual identification juxtaposed against my description, which produced an unquestionably similar artist's composite, plus a significant array of accurate peripheral data was a contradiction. This was impossible, and the impossibility traumatized me, almost preventing me from working. At that time, the mixture of other types of trauma from the rapist, the second assault, and the legal system initially worked to obscure the meaning and source of that trauma. Days of crying and anguish eventually untangled the traumas, and strengthened me to accept this impossible contradiction. An aspect of my visual acuity, a part of my mind, had been impaired by the rapist.

Meaning behind Blame-Denial Contexts

The source of the trauma was the contradiction between my ability to identify the rapist from an artist's composite and my inability to identify the rapist in person. The trauma itself was a means of helping me accept this illogic. Terror had breached my ability to make this connection mentally, and trauma was my body's means of confronting this illogic, which is part of the terror. I would resolve this contradiction by understanding that my mind had protected me from the terror of the act—an attack whose intensity I could not now ignore.

The meaning behind this trauma took the form of another type of denial—denial that the magnitude of the rape had reached an intensity so severe that it severed part of my day-to-day abilities in visual identification. To transgress the trauma, I had to accept that the rapist had the ability to terrorize and incapacitate me in that way. The rapist had left his mark buried inside me. In order to define himself, the rapist had had to define me out of existence. He had wanted to brand me with *his* definition of myself; in other words, only his ideas about me should define my "existence," or as I felt it, nonexistence. I had to accept that his acts of raping me successfully embedded his brand inside me by partially impairing one of my mental abilities.

Legal Contexts

Almost one year after the rape attack, the pretrial motions began. At the time I had a dream involving the classic "light at the end of the tunnel" image, which reflected my desires for conviction of the rapist, legal recognition of the rape as a crime, and termination of the battle to stop the rapist. In one pretrial motion the defense attorney challenged the search warrant on which the DNA evidence had been obtained, leaving the prosecution in a tenuous position. While the DNA Fingerprinting had convinced everyone—even the family of the defendant—of his guilt, the search warrant contained legal problems. At the pretrial hearing the judge announced the trial would be delayed and that he had serious doubts about the validity of the search warrant. Only with this search warrant—the basis for collecting the blood for DNA Fingerprinting—would the state try the defendant.

This legal wrangling was another *source* of rape and trauma, and these feelings were a trauma of blind rage (Savage 1990; Barr 1979). The legal eagles, on the one hand, had admitted the guilt of the rapist and, on the other, had used the legal process to absolve the rapist (Winkler 1992). This was illogical. No legal reason should exist that vindicates these terrorists. In this case, my feelings of trauma were not those of confusion and lack of direction; rather, they were feelings of directed anger, a trauma in itself. Luckily for the rapist, the safety of the jail due to previous robbery convictions prevented me from acting on my rage against him.

Surrogacy exemplifies another form of legal incongruency, for a woman who enters a surrogacy agreement signs over to the agency complete legal and medical control not only over the fetus in her womb but over all her own behavior as well. Although the surrogacy agreement presupposes a separation of the fetus from the mother, the two do not have a separate existence until the day of birth (see Sault, this volume).

Meaning behind Legal Contexts

The legal system emphasizes process over and above evidence of the guilt of the rapist. The system that defines the crime also absolves the criminal. Conviction would mean that the rapist is legally recognized as having committed a crime. The *meaning* of rage is found in the legal context in which I came to recognize this chasm: although I believe in and accept the legal system, I could not reconcile my beliefs with the outcome of the rape case.

Reclamation Contexts

The most difficult trauma to explain was the one that occurred one and a half years after the attack. Until this time, my facial muscles had remained constrained, outlining my contour. In addition, a nervousness, slight at first, had invaded my whole body. During the first two weeks, it had been controllable and, as usual, unnoticed by others. By the third week, the tremors began to disrupt my ability to function, tearing me apart. Calling friend-counselors for help was futile in this case; they repeated the dried-out list of advisory statements, and only irritated and aggravated the shaking. They could not explain the meaning behind this sudden flair up. Instead, they blamed and became annoyed at me, assuming I was not employing therapy in my daily life.

Then it stopped. Those nerve-racking feelings disappeared, as did the facial constraints that had defined my life for one and half years. The feelings of agitation ended. My face once again was relaxed. The facial muscles that I had been unable to forget from day to day were now not felt, and their tenseness evaporated. Yet the dissipation of this trauma remained unexplained.

Meaning behind Reclamation Contexts

Nevertheless, a meaning did exist I discovered later: my body had refused to suffer further the attacks of rape. This occurred because I was in a context in which I felt safe—safe from the rapist and safer from the second assaulters. In protest, my body erupted in a volcanolike explosion to say, "this is enough."

The meaning behind this reclamation context was to reclaim, or begin to reunite the mutually interdependent interpretive connections between my mind and body. This disjunction between mind and body, initiated by the rapist, had to be reconstituted and reconnected. The terror that had separated my body and my mind was pushed out of existence by the trauma in order to reestablish some of those familiar mind-body connections. The meaning behind the reclamation context was restitution of the mind-body junctures along with my right to preside over myself.

Scrambled Trauma

Experientially, my rape trauma, like that of all rape survivors, is distinct. The lengthy numb period allowed me to differentiate the contexts of the second assaulters from the context of the rapist. DNA Fingerprinting, which provided positive identification of the defendant as the rapist, legitimized my reactions during street surveillance as not false or manufactured terror but as viable trauma inaugurated within the context of the rapist. The lack of guilt feelings—common for some rape victim-survivors but absent in my case due to self-education prior to the rape, self-counseling during the attack, and self-defense against the blamers—was not part of my trauma and did not then become intermixed with other types of trauma. Nevertheless, there were times when the meaning behind the disruptive feelings—whether brought on by the rapist, the second assaulters, or the legal eagles—was barely decipherable.

Deciphering Trauma

Rapists bury land mines in the bodies of their victims, and these emotional explosions—such as confusion, nausea, nightmares, tremors, depression, and shakiness—form the rape trauma syndrome. While some interpret rape trauma as a sign of the victims' inability to function and a somatic memory of the initial event, rape survivors learn that their visceral experiences of trauma are meaningful interpretations of the contexts into which they are subsequently thrust. In part, rape trauma is initially instigated by the rapist, but it is also a product of successive traumas unwittingly imposed by friends, acquaintances, and institutions.

The traumas result in a mind-body separation, and during this period of partial and temporary separation—usually unrecognizable and unseen by others—survivors' bodies aid their terrorized minds by shielding them from further pain or dangerous contexts and by interpreting contexts that are mentally unclear. The body's memory, by acting out different forms of trauma in dangerous or nonsupportive contexts, becomes a vehicle to help victims transform themselves into survivors.

The trauma of rape is a shock then both to the minds and bodies of people raped. The mind, in order to protect itself against the ravages of the attack, may block parts of the assault or, as frequently revealed in rape cases, the face of the rapist. Yet the body continues to carry an active memory of the attacker and his acts of terror. In order to access information embedded in the mind by terror from the rape, the bodies of persons raped become computers filled with data that guard them and supply wavelengths of information. Without an understanding of the meanings of these trauma reactions, persons raped are impeded from recovering and processing the meanings entrenched in the responses made by their bodies. Our bodies duplicate, transistorize, channel, and explain the pain and horror of rape; they interpret dangerous situations and threatening ideas, and they are able to defend us by identifying rapists and revealing disruptive situations that parallel the attack.

The body supplies data on the reality of the rape while the mind protectively covers up the torturous terror that threatened our lives. Moreover, similar contexts trigger reactions in the body of the person raped, and a replication of the trauma alerts us to potentially threatening contexts. Our bodies, traumatized by the rapist, continue to recreate the unnerving terror in order to warn us against the same or comparable contexts of danger.

Rape traumas have multiple forms which find expression in divergent contexts. While trauma cannot magically disappear, a mechanism that helps alleviate trauma is our deciphering of the meanings behind our body's reactions to contexts of terror and shock. These meanings stem from attacklike contexts, guilt and denial issues, second assaults, the rapist's presence, and legal failures at reclamation. On a daily basis, our mind and body work together to interpret and analyze our experiences. Yet rape is an attempt to sever the connections between mind and body. Since the trauma from rape—a road not regularly experienced—is without the routine map of familiarity, the meanings behind the contexts need to be analyzed and studied in order to provide us with directions for understanding the trauma. Discussion of the emotions and meanings in the body is an area as yet without a sufficient dictionary of terms for interpretation. In addition, the silencing of people raped has further enforced this lack of terms.

The discreteness of these traumas, as I have described them in this chapter, is an uncommon experience. Many times one finds an overlapping of trauma differently sourced, which compounds the problem of discovering the meanings conveyed by the body. Methodologically, an explanation of trauma through categories is part of our cultural style of presentation, understanding, and organization; as such it imposes, in part, a false discreteness. To understand an experience, we dissect it into parts, but one must remember that the parts do not always appear discrete.

Critical to the interpretation of trauma in this chapter is an understanding of the context. Initially, I had formulated a typology of traumas and, erroneously, ascribed the traits of the traumas as contextless. This perspective failed to explain a controversial point of data in which my body generated trauma at the sight of the rapist on the street, and was calm at the sight of the rapist during the arraignment and pretrial hearing. The rapist was the same man, but the context had altered from a threatening to a nonthreatening situation. Contexts, and not typologies, explain the source of the trauma.

In conclusion, this chapter uncovers the meanings embedded in our bodies after an assault. One means of understanding these trauma reactions is to study the contexts of traumas and their associated meanings. The context of attacklike trauma encapsulates our terror as a warning of danger. The second-assault context results from the assault by persons who attack the victim-survivor with statements of sexual discrimination in the form of rape myths; it places us in a foglike and silent condition. The rapist-identified context duplicates the initial terrorized feelings during the attack in order to alert us to the presence of the rapist or a man with similar abusive characteristics. The blame-denial context that stems from our culture's denial of the intensity of the terror can channel itself into a bombshell of emotional response. The legal trauma accentuates the anger against the people in the legal system, who use legal loopholes and their lack of a victim-survivor perspective to free rapists. The trauma in the reclamation context is an experience of nervous spells that kick out those severed barriers between the mind and body, and begin to reconstitute ourselves. Of great importance, the expression of the trauma is not prescriptive in form but is unique in manifestation.

If these contexts and sets of meanings are recognized and understood, then we can better help ourselves deal with the rocky road to recovery. For my particular interests, these contexts are not just an explanation to outsiders of the roller-coaster ride of emotions experienced by persons raped. Rather my perspective is a vehicle that helps us survivors deal with the trauma and, as such, enables us to overcome the difficulties of speaking out against rapists and rape-supportive persons. Understanding the meaning behind our traumas helps us make the transformation from victim-survivors to activists.

ACKNOWLEDGMENTS

The second and third authors are listed in alphabetical order, not by order of contribution, and are heroic for their pioneering efforts against rape. I thank John J. Winkler, David Braaten, and Stel Simonton for their comments on an earlier version, and Peggy R. Sanday and Carole Browner for their strong support of these ideas. Moreover, I express special thanks to Nicole Sault, a good friend, whose work on this volume was outstanding. Her and Peter Reynolds's multiple edits of this chapter have also helped crystallize my ideas and clarify my writing. Earlier versions were presented at the 1990 American Anthropological Association meetings in New Orleans and the 1991 American Ethnological Society meetings in Atlanta. See also Winkler with Wininger 1994.

NOTES

1   I thank the rape-survivor advocate in Atlanta whose approach helped me regain my sense of reality. She has asked to remain anonymous. I note that our memories differ on this time period.

2   While I believe and, I hope, have demonstrated that those of us victimized by rape do survive, use of the word *survivor* at times denies the multiple forms of victimization forced on us after the attack. For that reason, I use the word *victim* to stress the aggression and terror imposed on us, the word *survivor* to demonstrate our ability to work against rape and its distortions, and the word *victim-survivor* to incorporate both of these meanings.

3   Advice on survival centers on counseling theories of trauma as only in the rape attack (Kilpatrick et al. 1979a, 1979b, and 1983), on victim's mental disabilities (Hepper and Hepper 1977), displacement (Spring 1977), and avoidance through psychotherapy and hypnosis (Spiegel and Spiegel 1978). Other treatment methods are found in Holmes and St. Lawrence 1983; Ellis 1983; Frank et al. 1979; Kilpatrick and Calhoun 1988; Kilpatrick et al. 1981; Burkhart 1991; Myers et al. 1984; Turner and Frank 1981; and Spring 1977. Most literature on rape discusses the victim as an object—the how-to-treat-the-victim approach. I suggest that deleting the victim as a person disqualifies the therapy. My disagreement with some counselors of rape victim-survivors stems from their lack of direct knowledge of rape and thus their lack of understanding of the terror we suffered, their lack of information or experience in guiding victim-survivors who speak out against the attack, and their perception that all rape victims are candidates for counseling. I thank those who employed a "friend-counselor" perspective with me. Many thanks to Marti Loring, Linda Ronald, D. E. Dale, and Barbara Bullette.

4   Burgess and Holmstrom 1974a, 1974b, and 1985, and the Boston Women's Health Collective 1984 give a chronology of patterned responses for rape victims. Researchers who present studies on the phasic interpretation of rape trauma are Becker and Abel 1981; Sutherland and Scherl 1970; Ellis 1983; Kilpatrick et al. 1979a; Koss 1985; and Atkinson et al. 1982. Instead I argue that reactions to rape vary too extensively to categorize into phases. Rather we need to stress that each person's emotional responses are distinct and not necessarily correlated with categories. Moreover, even if categories do exist, they change over time. Historical time dimension needs to be built into our perceptions of rape survivors' reactions.

5   Special thanks to Peter Reynolds who suggested that I add the perspective of context to my interpretation and thus delete the constraints from a typologically, positivistic-based perspective.

Blacking 1977 takes the perspective that the mind and body work together uniformly. While there is a cooperative interactive process between the mind and body, I argue that in situations of crises and shock, the impact of trauma alters this interactive process; it is this reconstituted relationship that expresses the extent of the trauma.

6   Sources for this list are Burgess and Holmstrom 1974a, 1974b; Kilpatrick et al. 1979a, 1979b, and 1983; Kilpatrick et al. 1981; Sutherland and Scherl 1970; Atkinson et al. 1982; Frank et al. 1979; Nadelson et al. 1982; Ellis 1983; Seligman 1976; Veronen and Kilpatrick 1980; Koss 1985; Frazier 1990; Torem 1986; Stewart et al. 1987; Santiago et al. 1985; and Gidycz and Koss 1991. The word *traumatophobia* is itself sufficient to scare anyone. The American Psychiatric Association (1987) defines rape trauma as Post Traumatic Stress Disorder (PTSD).

7   I developed this term in a conversational ping-pong match with Stephen N. Butler (Winkler with Wininger 1994).

8   Since I had no part in the definition of the context of the rape attack

against me, I disagree with the use of the possessive adjective *my*. I was an unwilling victim of the attack. It was *his* rape against me; the attack belongs to the rapist in terms of authority of that terror.

9   I thank Detectives Rosser, Dawson, and Carpenter for their extensive work in the investigation process.

10   I thank Louis Ferguson and Marvin Dickson, both private investigators. Marvin Dickson provided the initial clues to find the rapist, and Louis Ferguson diligently verified these and other points. Both men are earnest in fighting such crimes. I also thank Louis Ferguson for his respect, and for teaching me that anthropology and private investigation have extensive similarities.

REFERENCES

Albin, R. S. 1977. "Psychological Studies of Rape: Review Essay." *Signs* 3(2):423–435.

American Psychiatric Association. 1987. *Diagnostic and Statistical Manual of Mental Disorders*. 3d ed. rev. Washington, D.C.

Atkinson, B. M., K. S. Calhoun, P. A. Resick, and E. M. Ellis. 1982. "Victims of Rape." *Journal of Consulting and Clinical Psychology* 50:96–192.

Barr, J. 1979. *Within a Dark Wood: The Personal Story of Rape*. Garden City, N.J.: Doubleday.

Becker, J., and G. Abel. 1981. "Behavioral Treatment of Victims of Sexual Assault." In *Handbook of Clinical Behavioral Therapy*, ed. S. M. Turner, K. S. Calhoun, and H. E. Adams. New York: John Wiley.

Bierwert, C. 1990. "Somatic Transformations: Shape Changing in Contemporary Native American Literatures and Practices." Paper presented at the American Ethnological Society Meetings, Atlanta, Ga.

Blacking, J. 1977. *Anthropology of the Body*. New York: Academic Press.

Boston Women's Health Book Collective. 1984. *The New Our Bodies, Ourselves*. New York: Simon and Schuster.

Burgess, A. W. 1988. *Sexual Assault*, Vol. 2. New York: Garland.

———, ed. 1985. *Rape and Sexual Assault*. New York: Garland.

Burgess, A. W., and L. L. Holmstrom. 1974a. "Rape Trauma Syndrome." *American Journal of Psychiatry* 131:981–986.

1974b. *Rape: Victims of Crisis*. Bowie, Md.: Prentice-Hall.

1985. "Rape Trauma Syndrome and Post-Traumatic Stress Response." In *Rape and Sexual Assault*, ed. A. W. Burgess. New York: Garland.

Burkhart, B. R. 1991. "Conceptual and Practical Analysis of Therapy for Acquaintance Rape Victims." In *Acquaintance Rape*, ed. A. Parrot and L. Bechhofer, pp. 287–303. New York: John Wiley.

Burt, M. R. 1980. "Cultural Myths and Support for Rape." *Journal of Personality and Social Psychology* 38:217–230.

Dewar, H. 1990. "Victims Back Biden Bill on Crimes against Women." *San Jose Mercury News*, June 29. Orig. pub in *Washington Post*.

Doyle, A. M. and C. Dorlec. 1978. "Treating Chronic Crisis Bearers and Their Families." *Journal of Marriage and Family Counseling* 4:37–42.

Dubois, W. E. B. 1967. *The Philadelphia Negro*. New York: Schocken Books.

Ellis, E. M. 1983. "A Review of Empirical Rape Research: Victim Reactions and Response to Treatment." *Clinical Psychology Review* 3:473–490.

Feild, H. S. 1978. "Attitudes toward Rape: A Comparative Analysis of Police, Rapists, Crisis Counselors, and Citizens." *Journal of Personality and Social Psychology* 36:156–179.

Foley, T. S. 1985. "Family and Legal Response to." In *Rape and Sexual Assault*, ed. A. W. Burgess. New York: Garland.

Frank, E., S. M. Turner, and F. Duffy. 1979. "Depressive Symptoms in Rape Victims." *Journal of Affective Disorders* 1:269–277.

Frazier, P. A. 1990. "Victim Attributions and Post-Rape Trauma." *Journal of Personality and Social Psychology* 59(2):298–304.

Gidycz, C. A., and M. P. Koss. 1991. "The Effects of Acquaintance Rape on the Female Victim." In *Acquaintance Rape*, ed. A. Parrot and L. Bechhofer, pp. 270–283. New York: John Wiley.

Hepper, P. P., and M. Hepper. 1977. "Rape: Counseling the Traumatized Victim." *Personnel and Guidance Journal* 56:77–86.

Holmes, K. A., and J. Williams. 1981. *Second Assault*. Westport, Conn.: Greenwood Press.

Holmes, M., and J. S. St. Lawrence. 1983. "Treatment of Rape-Induced Trauma." *Clinical Psychological Review* 3:417–433.

Holmstrom, L. L., and A. W. Burgess. 1975. "Assessing Trauma in the Rape Victim." *American Journal of Nursing* 75(8):1288–1291.

———. 1978. *The Victim of Rape: Institutional Reactions.* New York: John Wiley.

Johnson, K. 1988. "Chambers, with Jury at Impasse, Admits 1st Degree Manslaughter." *New York Times,* March 26.

Kilpatrick, D. G. 1983. "Rape Victims: Detection, Assessment, and Treatment." *Clinical Psychologist* 36:88–101.

Kilpatrick, D. G., and K. S. Calhoun. 1988. "Early Behavioral Treatment for Rape Trauma: Efficacy or Artifact? *Behavior Therapy* 19:421–427.

Kilpatrick, D. G., P. A. Resick, and L. J. Veronen. 1981. "Effects of a Rape Experience: A Longitudinal Study." *Journal of Social Issues* 37(4):105–122.

Kilpatrick, D. G., L. J. Veronen, and P. A. Resick. 1979a. "The Aftermath of Rape: Recent Empirical Findings." *American Journal of Orthopsychiatry* 49:658–669.

———. 1979b. "Assessment of the Aftermath of Rape: Changing Patterns of Fear." *Journal of Behavioral Assessment* 1:133–148.

———. 1983. "Rape Victims: Detection, Assessment, and Treatment." *Clinical Psychologist* 36:88–101.

Koss, M. P. 1985. "The Hidden Rape Victim: Personality, Attitudinal, and Situational Characteristics." *Psychology of Women Quarterly* 9:193–212.

Koss, M. P., and M. R. Harvey. 1991. *The Rape Victim: Clinical and Community Interventions.* Newbury Park, Calif.: Sage.

Lewis, R. 1988. "DNA Fingerprints: Witness for the Prosecution." *Discover,* June, pp. 42–52.

Loh, W. D. 1981. "What Has Reform of Rape Legislature Wrought?" *Journal of Social Issues* 37(4):28–52.

Metzger, D. 1976. "It Is Always the Woman Who Is Raped." *American Journal of Psychiatry* 133(4):405–408.

Myers, M. B., D. I. Templan, and R. Brown. 1984. "Coping Ability of Women Who Become Rape Victims." *Journal of Consulting and Clinical Psychology* 52:73–78.

Nadelson, C. C., M. T. Notman, H. Zackson, and J. Gornick. 1982. "A Follow-up Study of Rape Victims." *American Journal of Psychology* 139:266–270.

Ochberg, F. M., and C. R. Spates. 1981. "Services Integration for Victims of Personal Violence." In *Evaluating Victim Services*, ed. S. Salasin. Beverly Hills, Calif.: Sage.

Parrot, A. 1991. "Medical Community Response to Acquaintance Rape: Recommendations." In *Acquaintance Rape*, ed. A. Parrot and L. Bechhofer, pp. 304–316. New York: John Wiley.

Sales, E., M. Baum, and B. Shove. 1984. "Victim Readjustment Following Assault." *Journal of Social Issues* 37(4):5–27.

Sanday, P. R. 1981. "The Socio-Cultural Context of Rape." *Journal of Social Issues* 37(4):5–27.

———. 1986. "Rape and the Silencing of the Feminine." In *Rape: An Historical and Social Enquiry*, ed. S. Tomaselli and R. Porter. New York: Basil Blackwell.

Sanders, W. B. 1980. *Rape and Women's Identity*. Beverly Hills, Calif.: Sage.

Santiago, J. M., F. McCall-Perez, M. Gorcey, and A. Beigel. 1985. "Long-Term Psychological Effects of Rape in Thirty-five Rape Victims." *American Journal of Psychiatry* 142(11):1338–1340.

Savage, A. 1990. *Twice Raped*. Indianapolis, Ind.: Book Weaver.

Scheppele, K., and P. B. Scheppele. 1983. "Through Women's Eyes: Defining Danger in the Wake of Sexual Assault." *Journal of Social Issues* 39(2):63–81.

Schwendinger, J., and H. Schwendinger. 1974. "Rape Myths: In Legal, Theoretical, and Everyday Practice." *Crime and Social Issues* 1:18–26.

Seligman, M.E.P. 1976. "Phobias and Preparedness." *Behavioral Therapy* 2: 307–321.

Sheffield, C. J. 1987. "Sexual Terrorism: The Social Control of Women." In *Analyzing Gender: A Handbook of Social Science Research*, ed. Beth B. Hess and Myra M. Ferree. Newbury Park, Calif.: Sage.

Silverman, D. C. 1978. "Sharing the Crisis of Rape: Counseling the Mates and Families of Victims." *American Journal of Orthopsychiatry* 48:166–173.

Spiegel, H., and D. Spiegel. 1978. *Trance and Treatment*. New York: Basic Books.

Spring, S. 1977. "Resolution of Rape Crisis: Six to Eight Month Follow-up." *Smith College Studies in Social Work* 48:20–24.

Stewart B. D., E. Hughes, E. Frank, B. Anderson, K. Kendall, and D. West. 1987. "The Aftermath of Rape." *Journal of Nervous and Mental Disease* 175(2): 90–94.

Sutherland, S., and D. J. Scherl. 1970. "Patterns of Responses among Victims of Rape." *American Journal of Orthopsychiatry* 40:503–511.

Torem, M. S. 1986. "Psychological Sequelae in the Rape Victim." *Stress Medicine* 2(4):301–305.

Turner, S., and E. Frank. 1981. "Behavioral Therapy in the Treatment of Rape Victims." In *Future Perspectives in Behavioral Therapy*, ed. L. Nichelson, M. Herson, and S. Turner. New York: Plenum Press.

Veronen, L. J., and D. G. Kilpatrick. 1980. "Reported Fears of Rape Victims." *Behavioral Modification* 4:383–396.

Warshaw, R. 1988. *I Never Called It Rape*. New York: Harper and Row.

Weis, K., and S. S. Borges. 1973. "Victimology and Rape: The Case of the Legitimate Victim." *Issues in Criminology* 8:71–115.

Winkler, C. 1989. "Myths about Rape or Prejudices about Rape: DeFamiliarizing the Familiar." Paper presented at the 88th American Anthropological Association Meeting, Washington, D.C.

———. 1990. "Rape as Social Murder." *Anthropology Today* 1(3):12–14.

———. 1992. "Comparison of Legal and Physical Rape: The PS Game." Paper presented at the 91st American Anthropological Association Meeting, San Francisco, Calif.

————. N.d.a. "Rape Attack: Ethnography of the Ethnographer." In *Fieldwork in Crisis*, ed. C. Nordstrom and T. Robbens. Berkeley: University of California Press.

————. N.d.b. *Raped Once, Raped Twice, Raped a Third Time*. Beverly Hills, Calif.: Sage.

Winkler, C., with K. Wininger. 1994. "Rape Trauma: Contexts of Meaning." In *Embodiment of Knowledge*, ed. T. Csordas. Cambridge: Cambridge University Press.

Winkler, J.J. 1990. *Constraints of Desire*. New York: Routledge.

HOW THE BODY SHAPES PARENTHOOD

"Surrogate" Mothers in the United States and Godmothers in Mexico

NICOLE SAULT

Commercial surrogacy contracts have been fiercely debated throughout the world, but only in the United States are such arrangements legal and upheld by the courts (Kimbrell 1993:112). People from other countries who seek a child through surrogacy must make arrangements with agencies in the United States. How has this country become the center for such worldwide trade in children?

Surrogacy is generally portrayed as technological progress, but it is not simply a technical development, for it redefines the relationship between mother and child. Surrogacy involves either mechanically inseminating a woman with sperm or implanting a fertilized embryo in her womb, making her both gestational mother and birth mother of the child. In the first case, she is also the genetic mother; in the second case, she has no genetic connection to the child. The genetic father is the man whose sperm fertilized the egg and who arranged the surrogacy contract. If the man is married and one of his wife's eggs is used to create the fertilized embryo, then his wife is the genetic mother. The technology for these procedures is available in many countries where commercial surrogacy is not allowed, and turkey basters have been around for a long time. In addition, throughout history female slaves and concubines have borne children for others.

Although legal, medical, and religious experts have argued both for and against surrogacy, anthropologists have generally remained aloof from the controversy, with the exception of Ragoné (1994), Rivière (1985), Stolcke (1988), Strathern (1992), Whiteford (1989), and Cannell (1990). Yet the use of Western biomedicine to create "synthetic families" calls into question the core values of our society (Krauthammer 1987), and anthropologists can contribute to an understanding of the issues by examing the cultural meanings associated with parenthood, gender, and the body.

Any technology is created and sustained by a particular system of cultural values. What led people in the United States to envision surrogacy in the first place, before it had even been tested and developed? Why do so many people in the United States feel surrogacy is desperately needed, when it has been banned in Europe, Japan, and Australia? Conversely, why isn't it an important issue in other countries such as Mexico?

Since beliefs about parenthood and the use of technology vary from one society to the next, we cannot assume that the issues raised by surrogacy will be the same in each country or even that the technology will be used simply because it is available. This essay shows how surrogacy in the United States reflects a cultural system of values and concepts specific to late twentieth-century Anglo-American society. Core concepts in this system are biology, fatherhood, individual ownership, the partible body, the bounded body, and whiteness. This particular cultural system is contrasted with an alternative set of values and concepts exemplified in the Zapotec godparenthood system of Mexico, and analyzes both to discover what they can tell us about the way bodily understandings shape our ideas about parenthood.

Much of the debate on surrogacy in the United States revolves around the "needs" of childless couples who want to have "children of their own" and a woman's right to "control" her body. These topics are debated in terms of legal, medical, and religious values, while ignoring their underlying cultural significance. It is generally assumed that the words *mother, father, parent,* and *body* have the same meanings in every culture and that everyone agrees on those meanings. However, each of these words entails a host of underlying assumptions that vary from one culture to the next; even within a society, people may hold differing views on the meaning of each term.

Parenthood Is Biology

The first cultural assumption made by people in the United States is that parenthood is biological: we become parents through physical acts of procreation. As Schneider (1968) noted, biology is taken as the basis for kinship, using blood as the symbol to refer to "real kin." People in the United States often say, "blood is thicker than water," and adopted parents are contrasted with "real" parents, those connected to a child by "blood" (i.e., biologically). As Strathern observes, "natal kinship" is "biologised" (1992:19).

Anthropologists, however, recognize that parenthood and kinship in a broader sense are both cultural constructions. Delaney notes that paternity is not a physical entity, a natural fact, or a universal process (1986:495). A cultural understanding of parenthood "has to do with the symbols, meanings and beliefs by which life is thought to come into being. It provides a view of what life is, how and by what or whom it comes into being and for what purpose, what the person is (both male and female), how persons are related to each other, the non-human world and the cosmos" (1986:506). Parenthood exists as a concept embedded within a system of cultural beliefs, so it cannot be abstracted from its context without distorting the meaning (1986:495).

Cross-cultural studies show that societies differ in how they envisage parenthood and kinship, with some emphasizing biology and others emphasizing spirit (Meigs 1986; Wilbert 1970). In the United States, real parents are defined as biological parents, whereas adoptive or foster parents are considered a legal fiction. Since the biological model for kinship and parenthood prevails in the United States, people do not feel that they really have children of their own unless they are so defined biologically (Schneider 1968; Nelson 1990). The biological definition of parenthood ignores both the psychological attachment and care-giving aspects of parenthood recognized by many societies as well as by certain groups within the United States, such as African-Americans (Stack 1974).

In societies that do not emphasize the biological aspect of parenthood, people who raise and feed a child are considered the child's parents, whether or not they have conceived and given birth to the child. This is also the case in Papua New Guinea, where parenthood is more flexibly envisaged and can encompass a number of different people who share parenting roles (Meigs 1986). Shared parenting allows for greater flexibility. It places less burden on biological parents, who do not have sole responsibility for raising a child, and for those individuals who cannot conceive and bear children, there is always the opportunity to become parents by nuturing children born to others. In societies such as Papua New Guinea, Mexico, and Korea,

parenting itself is a highly valued and desirable activity which provides meaning to life and increases one's status (Cho 1978).

Fatherhood and the Body

In the United States, the great cultural distinction between motherhood and fatherhood is expressed in biological terms. One of the
arguments raised by critics of surrogacy is that it values fatherhood
over motherhood, as court decisions have given more weight to the
male contribution of sperm than to the female contribution of egg
and gestation in the womb (Pollitt 1987:686). In the famous court
case of Baby M, William Stern was always referred to as the baby's
father or natural father, while Mary Beth Whitehead was called the
"surrogate mother," implying that the real mother was Mr. Stern's
wife, Elizabeth Stern. As shown by transcripts from the court case,
only Mrs. Whitehead referred to Mr. Stern as the sperm donor (quoted
in Pollitt 1987:683).[1] In short, U.S. courts accept an asymmetrical
terminology that is biased toward the male genetic contribution.

Pollitt argues that in the Baby M case, Judge Sorkow's decision
"exalted male biology at the expense of female [biology]," as William
Stern's contribution of semen was seen to override Mary Beth Whitehead's contribution of ovum and gestation. The fact that Baby M had
Mr. Stern's genes was judged "more important than Mrs. Whitehead's
genes, pregnancy, and childbirth put together. We might as well be
back in the days when a woman was seen merely as a kind of human
potting soil for a man's seed" (Pollitt 1987:686).

This view of reproduction is strikingly similar to Delaney's description of contemporary views on paternity in Turkey, where women are
compared to a receptacle or a plowed field, ready for the farmer with
his seed (1986:496). Delaney notes that this language is not used
figuratively for decorative purposes alone. In this case, the metaphor
creates an image that influences the way people think about procreation and has behavioral and legal consequences (1986:497).

In the Turkish cultural system, paternity is *not* equivalent or comparable to maternity; the physiological contribution of each parent is
coded differently, and the connection between parent and child is
conceptualized according to the gender of the parent. Maternity
means nuturing the fetus and giving birth to the child, while paternity means begetting the child. The primary and essential creative

role is male (Delaney 1986:495). It is men who beget children, as in biblical chapters on the begetting of male lines. Women only nurture and bear children.

According to Delaney, Turkish culture has a "monogenetic" theory of procreation—holding that a child originates "from only one source" (1986:496). It is men who contribute the seed, the essential identity of the child, the spark of life (1986:497–498), and the principle of movement (Delaney 1991:48). In this system, men engender both males and females. Women provide only the perishable substances of blood and milk through nuturance in the womb or at the breast (1986:497).

Delaney also points out that this view of procreation, which so greatly values paternity over maternity, is not unique to Islam and the Koran. It is also central to ancient Greek understandings of the body, gender, and parenthood. As DuBois notes, in contrast to pre-Socratic society, which saw women's bodies as "fruitful, spontanously generating earth," Platonic philosophy emphasized a view of women as passive, a field that must be ploughed and planted with seed if it is to bear fruit (DuBois 1988:28, 68). Aeschylus supported Apollo's view that "the female body is not the source of life but, rather, that it is a receptacle, a temporary container for the father's seed" (DuBois 1988:71).

Western biomedicine has been greatly influenced by Greek ideas about the body and healing, including the works of Hippocrates and Aristotle. Both viewed male seed as engendering life in female vessels. Hippocrates speculated that the male seed contained a minature human being; Aristotle believed that the female state is one of deformity, requiring male semen to transform female menstrual blood into a human being (Corea 1985:295–296).

Delaney argues that "the theory and symbols permeate the attitudes, values, laws, and institutions that shape our everyday lives" (1991:8). These images of men creating life for women to contain are so deeply a part of our own culture that they have been ignored in cross-cultural discussions of kinship (Delaney 1986:497). In discussions of surrogacy among Euro-American societies, agricultural images are repeatedly used to describe parenthood, again without any analysis of their meaning.[2]

Pollitt has hit the mark by pointing out the implicit dominance of male seed over female soil in most American discussions of surrogacy. However, she implies that this kind of thinking is now outmoded, since we have progressed to a more modern and scientific perspective. Yet people in the United States still use this imagery of seed and field, for it underlies the American concept of parenthood. For example, in the American cult film *Raising Arizona*, a man reacts to the news that his wife is barren by saying: "At first I didn't believe it, that this woman who looked as fertile as the Tennessee Valley could not bear children. But the doctor explained that her insides were a rocky place where my seed could find no purchase" (Coen 1987).

This preeminence of male seed in American culture is further heightened by the development of "surrogate" motherhood, which amplifies the importance of men as life-givers who produce the spark that engenders creation, while reducing women to merely vessels that contain and nurture growing life. This imagery is dramatically expressed in the surrogacy industry, where the birth mother is described as the vessel for the man's seed (Corea 1985:221). The language of surrogacy refers to women as incubators, receptacles, a kind of hatchery, rented property, or plumbing (1985:222). These birth mothers have learned to speak of themselves this way, saying, "I'm not the mother, I'm the plumbing," or "It's not buying a baby—it's buying a receptacle" (1985:224).[3] The overriding ethic is that the man's bloodline be continued, or as talk show host Phil Donohue put it, "every man has a right to reproduce himself" (Corea 1985:223–224).

"Surrogate" motherhood gives men of means a way to assure that they have children of their own seed, regardless of whose womb is used as the nuturing receptacle. What is more, surrogacy contracts give men preemptory rights over the products of that seed. Although people are generally aware that surrogacy is open only to those who can afford it, they seldom notice that, in Pollitt's words, "contract maternity is not a way for infertile women to get children, although the mothers often speak as though it were. It is a way for men to get children. Elizabeth Stern's name does not appear on the contract" (1987:684). Only Mr. Stern's name appears on the contract. Mrs. Stern was Baby M's primary caretaker, who *adopted* Baby M. According to Pollitt, "rather than empower infertile women through an act of sisterly generosity, maternity contracts make one woman a baby machine and the other irrelevant" (1987:684).

Individual Ownership of Children

Those involved in surrogacy arrangements place great emphasis on contracts. The contract is drawn up by attorneys for the surrogacy agency, to ensure that the "surrogate" mother abides by the agreement but also to ensure the father's legal rights over the child. This documentation of rights over the child is crucial because in the United States parenthood is viewed as a relationship of ownership. Just as a man traditionally had rights over his wife, so he also has rights over his children. Individual accumulation of property is associated with private ownership of that property.

When people talk about wanting to have a child of their own, they mean that the child must be *born* to them to be real, and born to *them* to be theirs, their own, or *owned*. (And of course the child can be disowned.) Exclusivity is an important aspect of the desire to have children. "Their own child" is owned as a possession, which they alone raise without the help or interference of others. Those who assist are either paid child-care workers or are relatives who can be called on to provide child care for free because of their kinship relationship to the child.

People do not share ownership of a child, for the child is theirs exclusively. Witness the difficulties divorced couples face in sharing their "own" children. Each usually wants full custody, or complete ownership and control. Visiting rights are usually not awarded to the grandparents, aunts, uncles, or other members of either parent's kin group. The rights of ownership are also at issue in day care centers: "Motherhood confers the privileges of claiming, molding, and keeping; other people's children cannot be claimed, molded, and kept. To think that one can do so with other people's children creates a situation where one can only be disappointed" (Nelson 1990:595). The concern with exclusive ownership is highlighted in the contract disputes that have brought surrogacy arrangements into the courts and created headlines like "Contract Mightier Than the Womb" (Paddock and Lynch 1993). The contracting couple seek a child for themselves, not one they will be forced to share with the birth mother.

The ownership aspect of parenthood is often expressed by persons discussing surrogacy as the right of everyone to have a child. (People do not talk about the right to love a child.) By contrast, the 1987 Vatican document on reproductive technology states that couples do *not* have a right to a child, for such a right would make the child an "object of ownership" (quoted in Cook 1988:6). As Shannon notes:

The right to reproduce does not include the right actually to *obtain* a child. What is protected legally and morally is the right

to exercize a capacity, not the securing of the end of that capacity. It is not the obligation of law, philosophy, medicine, or theology to guarantee that one actually achieve that for which one
strives. . . . The right to reproduce does not ensure those exercising that right that they will receive a child. (Shannon 1988:164)

In a similar vein, Kamal observes that part of the enthusiasm for
reproductive technology is "fanned by the attitude" that certain people can't accept not having something (Kamal 1987:153).

American society emphasizes ownership by the individual. There is
no cultural emphasis on sharing one's children with those who help
raise and care for them; nor is there regard for the rights of grandparents, aunts, and uncles, as in other societies. In the United States relatives may help out, but without the strong cultural valuation for their
active role in child sharing that is expected in many other societies.

The emphasis on individual ownership is also biased toward male
ownership. Although in recent decades custody battles have been
fought between men and women over their children, throughout
most of European and American history, the husband, not the wife,
was clearly considered the owner of the children and his precedence
was codified in law. There was no need for a separate contract to
specify who had claim over the children born to the marriage. According to Corea:

We see man's appropriation of the child in the laws throughout
the world, which, until less than a century ago, gave fathers
sole guardianship of children. The father had an absolute right
to take the children away from his wife during marriage and,
upon his death, could bequeath that guardianship to another
male rather than to their mother. Fathers were routinely
granted custody of children upon divorce. It was not until 1886
in England that, under certain rare circumstances, a woman
could get custody of her children. All but five states in America
in the 1890s gave fathers sole legal guardianship of children.
(Corea 1985:288)

If a couple separated and divorced, the father automatically re-
tained custody of the older children born to the marriage, whereas
smaller children remained with the mother until they were older, at
which time they were transferred to their father. Whether or not the

mother could economically support the children, she did not have the same rights over them as her husband (Calhoun 1945).

The importance of property ownership today is revealed in the language used to discuss surrogacy arrangements. Those who attack surrogacy claim that it entails buying and selling babies; those who defend surrogacy counter that it involves only renting a womb. In surrogacy cases, real-estate terms are used in reference to the woman's body, as though she were a portable rental unit on legs. For example, an April 1981 editorial in the *New York Times* commented that surrogate baby Thrane was "residing in a rented womb," that the contract parents "lost the lease on the womb; their lawyer seems something less than a crack real estate agent; and Mrs. Thrane [the surrogate mother] is keeping her property" (Corea 1985:246).

While the womb of the birth mother is described as a rental unit, the child is described as a product or an investment (Corea 1985:219). Michigan attorney Noel Keane argues that "In a commercial society 'commercialization' is the usual way in which many individual needs are satisfied." The process of commercializing motherhood and babies is "simply generalizing what we do in almost all other sectors of our lives" (quoted in Shannon 1988:112).

As with other products, "quality control" is an important issue in surrogacy arrangements. Clients can review portfolios of prospective "surrogate mothers," complete with photographs and a list of such characteristics as eye color, intelligence, and personality (Shannon 1988:119). In addition, the contracts are drawn up with clauses to protect the client, who is the genetic father, against defective merchandise (Corea 1985:219). The child is thought of as a "custom-designed" product, a "perfect" baby (Rowland 1987:78).

It is generally accepted that women who become "surrogate" mothers are usually motivated by economic need. Both those who advocate surrogacy as well as those who oppose it, and also the courts, believe that if surrogacy were not financially compensated, few women would volunteer such a service (Shannon 1988:140; Corea 1985:229–230; also see quote by Michigan attorney general in Kimbrell 1993:112).

The Partible Body

The development of surrogacy also rests on the modern Western idea that the body is a conglomeration of parts that can be added and subtracted for various purposes. Surgery is performed to remove an appendix, tonsils, a gallbladder, or a uterus. One can donate blood to blood banks, semen to sperm banks, and milk to milk banks. Even body organs can be donated for a transplant, and a uterus can be signed away under contract. There are, however, laws restricting the donation of such vital body organs as kidneys, and these organs cannot be sold legally (Pollitt 1987:684). In fact, medical and public opinion against the commercialization of "vital body parts" is quite strong (Shannon 1988:11–15), although U.S. law prohibits the sale of many body organs, a woman's uterus is not granted such protection.

There has also been a marked increase in the number of hysterectomies, radical mastectomies, and cesarean sections performed in the United States, whose rates were already much higher than those of England, France, or West Germany (Payer 1988:24, 124–125).[4] Payer argues that this "aggressive" use of surgery is related to cultural attitudes toward medicine and the body, which is treated like a machine, often a well-running car (1988:148–150). As Rothman explains: "Problems in the body are technical problems requiring technical solution, whether it is a mechanical repair, a chemical rebalancing, or a 'debugging' of the system" (Rothman 1982:34; see also Kimbrell 1993:228–260; Featherstone 1990:182; Martin 1987:19, 54). O'Neill calls this a "mechano-morphic" or "prosthetic society" (O'Neill 1985:25).

Although American medicine portrays the human body as a machine, it is the male body that is the most machinelike, and the prototype for the smoothly functioning machine. By contrast the female body is perceived as hopelessly defective and dependent on technology for reproduction to be successful (Davis-Floyd 1987, 1992). Davis-Floyd asks, "Why is a birthing woman like a broken-down car, and whence comes this mechanistic emphasis in obstetrics?" (1987:163).

In American society a woman's uterus is considered a nonvital organ which can therefore be removed or rented out for surrogacy. The "surrogate" mother is then defined in terms of her uterus and treated as a body part rather than a complete human being. For example, in the case of Mary Beth Whitehead, child psychologist Lee Salk referred to her as a "surrogate uterus" (Pollitt 1987:683).

If the mother's body is partible, then her womb is only attached to her. When she rents out her womb to others it is no longer hers to do with as she wishes. Thus she must abide by all the surrogacy contract stipulations, which generally include the following: (1) that she not smoke, drink alcohol, or take aspirin, and that she follow a certain diet; (2) that she atttend regular psychological counseling by the contract parents' doctor and submit to any procedures the doctor deems necessary or advisable, including amniocentesis, a cesarean section, or an abortion; and (3) that she notify the agency of her whereabouts at all times as well as the particulars of her emotional life, such as job loss or family deaths (Shannon 1988:107; Corea 1985:241–242).

Advocates of surrogacy argue that the "carrying mother" has agreed to gestate and give birth to the child for payment, that she has rented her womb for a certain time period and purpose. This notion assumes that the body is partible, that the womb can be separated from the body and later reinserted after the contract has been fulfilled. It is the concept of the *partible body* that makes ownership of the child contingent, enabling people to argue that a baby "belongs" to the contract parents, since the carrying mother is merely rented plumbing or a receptacle and therefore has no rights to the baby. This concept of renting the woman's body is crucial if the child is to be clearly owned by the contracting couple and not by the carrying mother.

"Uterine environment" and "harvesting of eggs" are some of the new terms and phrases used to describe aspects of the surrogacy technology and procedures, indicating the extent to which, in Rowland's words, "women's bodies are dehumanized" (Rowland 1987: 77). Spallone and Steinberg point out that the new reproductive technologies are not really new at all, that there is a long history of women's bodies being treated as objects. What is new, they argue, "is the emphasis today on *parts* of women's bodies being used in unprecedented ways and to an unprecedented degree" (Spallone and Steinberg 1987:10).[5]

The Bounded Body

In the United States, where individual achievement is emphasized, independence and self-sufficiency are also encouraged. These are expressed in terms of a tension between maintaining one's body boundary and losing control of it to someone or something. These individual concerns, in turn, become the focus of industries related to diet and nutrition, bodybuilding and exercise, drugs and health care, beauty aids for youthfulness, sexuality and pornography, and personal security.

An essential feature of the *bounded body* is the equation of permeability with loss, violation, and ultimately, death. This view engenders a wide range of practices for maintaining a separation between self and other, and it underlies one of the major metaphors of Western medicine—that maintaining health involves an ongoing battle in which the body defends itself against disease by marshaling white blood cells to fight off invading microbes (Martin 1987). Also, many people consider attacks on the body boundary the ultimate kind of violence, as in torture or rape. Given this cultural framework, body mutilation and the donation of body parts have special significance.

In protecting body boundaries a gender difference occurs, for it is the male body boundary that society strives hardest to safeguard. Surrogacy does not contradict the cultural premise of protecting body boundaries because women's bodies are viewed as inherently permeable and therefore problematic. As Delaney notes in her discussion of Turkey: "Men's bodies are viewed as self-contained while women's bodily boundaries oscillate and shift, for example in developing of breasts and the swelling of pregnancy; they leak in menstruation and lactation, and are permeable in intercourse and birth" (Delaney 1986:499).

In Europe the contrast in the *boundedness* of male versus female bodies was forged during the sixteenth century and expressed as a difference between the "classical" versus the "grotesque" body. In Bakhtin's discussion of the Renaissance text of Rabelais, the classical body presents an image of "finished, completed" man, with "the border of a closed individuality that does not merge with other bodies and with the world" (Bakhtin, as quoted in Stallybrass 1986:124). The classical body, in contrast, "emphasizes the head as the seat of reason, transcending the 'merely' bodily" (Stallybrass 1986:124). The grotesque body is characterized by "extraterritoriality," "liberties," "obscenity and abuse." It emphasizes parts of the body "that are open to the outside world"—"the open mouth, the genital organs, the breasts, the phallus, the potbelly, the nose" (Bakhtin, as quoted in Stallybrass 1986:124). With an increasing emphasis on social and bodily purity, enclosing the body and purifying its orifices became associated with the surveillance of women, because a woman's body was assumed to be naturally "grotesque," as it is "unfinished, outgrows itself, transgresses its own limits" (Bakhtin, as quoted in Stallybrass 1986:126). This Renaissance view of men and women continues to influence contemporary Western cultural attitudes toward the body (Martin 1990).

Since women's bodies are characterized as permeable and unstable from within, they must be controlled from the outside through a variety of techniques that either reinforce the body boundary or remove the unstable body parts. When female reproductive organs no longer function properly, they become useless at best, or troublesome at worst.[6] Among a growing number of women, even healthy breasts, ovaries, and uteri are being removed as a prophylactic against cancer (Corea 1985:308; Bartimus 1991).

American society holds science and technology as core values. The ultimate compliment to the human body is to compare it to a machine, and the ultimate treatment for a broken human body is to repair it and re-make it into a machine. In a society in which human bodies can be disassembled into parts and women's bodies in particular are treated as objects or assemblages of parts, surrogacy simply carries this view one step further. As long as a woman's body is penetrated in the name of producing children for a man, traversing the woman's body boundary is considered acceptable.

In Search of Whiteness

Critics of surrogacy have been quick to point out the class-related aspects of the technology, which enables couples from upper socioeconomic levels to hire women of lower incomes to bear their children. John Stehura, president of Bionetics Foundation, a surrogacy company, is concerned that the cost "is too financially burdensome for middle-class American couples," but he thinks the current price of $10,000 will come down "once surrogate motherhood is more commonplace. The industry can then go to poverty-stricken parts of the country" where people will accept half as much to be "surrogates" (quoted in Corea 1985:214).

What has received much less attention is the color symbolism involved in seeking "the perfect baby" through reproductive technology. Prospective parents are preselecting babies of a certain gender, with a specific eye color, hair color, and skin color. One reason people choose surrogacy is that they do not want to adopt a child of "mixed" racial background (Corea 1985:218). For white middle- or upper-class couples, the perfect baby is a white baby (Rowland 1987:78).

This requirement limits the number of "surrogate" mothers available, since they must be white in order to donate an egg that will produce a white baby. But the agencies are responding by using already fertilized embryos which are then implanted into the wombs of nonwhite women, opening up whole new market areas for surrogacy. As Stehura has noted, once this technology is fully developed, the industry can look outside the United States for "surrogates," in places like Central America. Women of Third World countries could be paid one-tenth of the current rates, or work for just "rent and food" (Corea 1985:215, 245). Stehura explains that these Third World women wouldn't even need to be healthy: "if her diet is good and other aspects of her life are O.K., she could become a viable mother for a genuine embryo transfer" and earn money to raise her other children (quoted in Corea 1985:215).

Richard Levin's corporation, Surrogate Parenting Inc., has expanded internationally to include Australia, Canada, France, and Mexico (Corea 1985:225). Says Stehura: "We're bringing girls in from the Orient," including Korea, Thailand, and Malaysia, to serve as "surrogate" mothers. He also explored the possibility of initiating pregnancies in Asian countries and bringing just the babies into the United States (quoted in Corea 1985:245). In these examples, white couples are seeking white children, through the use of white women as birth mothers who donate their eggs, or women of color who are implanted with already fertilized embryos so that none of their genetic material is transmitted to the child (Paddock and Lynch 1993). There are also cases in which people of color from outside the United States choose to have a white woman from the United States as both the birth mother and the genetic mother for their child, hoping the child will have lighter coloring. In discussing the subject of internationally arranged surrogacy, a colleague from Mexico explained that, of course, certain wealthy people in Mexico would want Anglo women in the United States as "surrogates," for the couple's status would rise if their child was lighter skinned. As he phrased it: "You don't see them asking Mayan or Zapotec women to be surrogates, do you?" (Garcia Parra, 1989, personal communication).

Another growing and lucrative business involves Japanese couples who seek Asian American women as "surrogates" because the medical procedure must be done outside Japan and the couples "don't want to hire white women with blond hair, or blacks." Due to the public debate about whether surrogacy should be allowed in Japan, the only Tokyo service is "fiercely" anonymous. Arrangements are made through the

New York branch of Noel Keane's Infertility Center ("Japanese Seek U.S. Surrogates" 1992).

One of the guiding principles of the surrogacy industry is that only women who are defined as "appropriate," "worthy," and "fit" are selected. These terms are applied for the purpose of exclusion, to weed out those who are disabled, older, nonwhite, lesbian, or single (Spallone and Steinberg 1987:8; Kamal 1987:146). Although the melting pot is an important image in American ideology, not all colors are equally valued. According to the ideals of mainstream American culture, one's children should be as white as possible, so the lighter the "surrogate" the better.

In the preceding sections I have outlined some of the cultural assumptions central to understanding surrogacy in the United States: that parenthood is biological, that paternity takes precedence over maternity, that individual ownership includes rights over children, that the human body can be reduced to an assemblage of parts, that men's bodies are bounded while women's bodies are permeable, and that skin, hair, and eye color are important for defining the perfect child.

Having described some of the cultural assumptions that characterize parenthood and surrogacy in the United States, I now present an alternative view of parenthood in another society and discuss the underlying cultural assumptions.

Zapotec Godmothers in Mexico

In Mexico great emphasis is placed on parenthood, much more than in the United States (Velez Ibañez 1980). People are not considered full adults until they marry and have children. While this is openly recognized in rural agricultural villages, those who live in urban industrial sectors such as Mexico City also uphold this view. For example, an engineer in Mexico City explained to me that being unmarried and childless has held him back in his professional career. He will not be trusted as a mature, responsible adult until he marries and has a family. In rural villages in particular, young people talk about marrying and raising a family as their aspiration in life; the kind of job they have is secondary, for men and women alike. Despite industrialization and modernization, the values of the majority in this society still emphasize reproduction over production.

This emphasis on parenthood places a heavy burden on those who are infertile or childless, and we might expect that people would turn to surrogacy. However, the number of Mexicans who have done so is limited. This is not simply for reasons of technology or finance, but because parenthood in Mexico does not follow the same biological model of the United States. While biological parenthood is important in Mexico, there are several alternatives open to those who are physiologically unable to have children.

In Mexico, one way to experience parenthood is to become a godparent, a particular kind of ceremonial sponsorship common throughout Latin America. Sponsors of ceremonies for rites of passage can be found in societies throughout the world, including Africa, Asia, Europe, the Middle East, and Native American societies, but perhaps the best-known form of sponsorship is Latin American godparenthood or *compadrazgo*—a central aspect of Latin American social organization. This form has been particularly well-documented in Mexico (Foster 1969; Mintz and Wolf 1950; Nutini and Bell 1980; Sault 1985a; Stavenhagen 1959). Godparenthood is an important alternative form of parenthood, not only for childless couples but also for older people whose children have grown, especially widows, and also for couples to whom children have already been born. My discussion of godparenthood is based on research in an indigenous Zapotec community of the Oaxaca Valley in southeastern Mexico, but much of what I have to say about Zapotec society applies to godparent ties elsewhere in Mexico and Latin America. Santa Catalina is the name I use to refer to this village.[7]

In Santa Catalina, people can sponsor a variety of ceremonies, including baptism, confirmation, a wedding, sixth grade graduation, the funeral cross, a new house, or the rosary. Of all these ceremonies, baptism is the most important, for it is baptism that makes a child human, a person, Catholic, and legitimate (El Guindi 1983:98). By sponsoring a child's baptism, the sponsor participates in the social birth of the child into the community. The sponsor becomes the child's spiritual parent and acquires certain rights and responsibilities regarding the godchild.

During the baptismal ceremony, the godmother holds the child in her arms and the godfather places his hand on the godchild. These gestures are of particular importance because through this physical contact the godparents impart some of their essence to the godchild, which gives them a special ability to mediate with supernatural forces on behalf of the child (Sault 1985a). Godparents are expected to guide the child's religious development, to help in curing the child at times of sickness, and to assist financially with the child's schooling in terms of books, clothes, fees, or housing. Godparents also have a special role as counselors and go-betweens when the godchild marries. In the event of the godchild's death, the godparents buy the grave clothes. If the child's parents die, then the godparents take on responsibility for the child. People refer to the godparents as a second mother and father, and the godchild addresses and refers to the godparents using either the Spanish terms *madrina* (godmother) and *padrino* (godfather), or the Zapotec terms *nanmbál* and *dadmbál*.

For those couples who do not have children or who wish to have more, godparenthood is an important option. Most people hope to have several godchildren, and if they are not asked to sponsor a child then they may offer to do so. Godparenthood provides a flexible alternative to bearing children and is very prestigious. Both men and women seek godparenthood as a means of gaining status in the community, as it is important for acquiring political and economic power (Sault 1985a).

Through godparenthood people share in raising and caring for children, including the various rights and responsibilities this entails. Godparenthood is also used as a form of fostering children, in which the godchild goes to live with the godparents for a period of time, or as an alternative to adoption. In Santa Catalina, godchildren often go to live with their godparents for an extended period of time, sometimes permanently.

One reason a child might go to live with godparents is that households need to be gender balanced. The sexual division of labor is quite marked and social life in general is divided according to gender, so it is important for each household to have both boys and girls as well as adult men and women. If a family has only sons, they will ask around for someone to send a daughter to live with them, and they will send one of their sons to live with that family.

In other cases an older couple might ask that one of their godchildren come stay with them to run errands and do chores around the house and accompany the adults. When a child comes from a large family, the chance to live with godparents may represent a real opportunity.

There were also several cases in which grown children went to live with their godparents in order to finish school in another community or to take a job. Such fostering or adoption is common in other societies, but godparenthood gives special meaning to the relationship since it involves a permanent and sacred spiritual tie that continues on past death into the next world. When you die, your godchildren greet you at the heavenly gates and plead your case before God and the saints. Your godchildren explain that you performed an act of charity by sponsoring them, and they ask that the gates be opened.

In Mexico the strong emphasis on sharing includes not only material resources but also the responsibility for raising children and the benefit of their respect and affection. Villagers are emphatic about the advantages of having a second set of parents: the child benefits from the additional care the godparents can provide, in terms of counseling, financial support, and opportunities for education and job placement. Childless couples may in some cases leave an inheritance to a godchild, though godchildren have no legal claim to inheritance. The significant point is that sharing children is seen as natural and beneficial to children.

While the benefits to the parents and godparents are not as openly discussed, they are just as significant. Parents gain by sharing childcare responsibilities and the cost of raising a child. Godparents enjoy the emotional rewards of raising a child, as well as the child's labor contribution and care for them in their old age. For a childless couple, godchildren mean security in their later years, when concerns arise over finances, living alone, and burial costs and arrangements. Having godchildren, like having children, brings security by providing for needs that no welfare agency could handle as well, even if one were available.

Child Sharing in the United States

Ceremonial sponsorship is a flexible form of sharing parenthood that has a long history in pre-Christian Europe as well as in Mexico and Peru among the Aztec, Maya, and Inca. The institution of sponsorship has proved sufficiently flexible to endure into the modern age of industrialization and urbanization, adapting to life in cosmopolitan urban centers, even thriving in such places as Mexico City, New York, and Los Angeles. Immigrants to the United States who have maintained strong god parenthood traditions include people not only from Mexico but from Greece, Italy, Poland, Puerto Rico, and Yugoslavia (Sault 1985b).

There are so many advantages to this method of sharing parent-hood that in some U.S. families the godparent relationship has been adapted to a purely secular context. People who do not practice reli-gion can still organize sponsorship around ceremonial events and thus fulfill extraparenting needs. In the cases I have observed, cou-ples ask a close friend to be the "godparent" for their child. The par-ents make legal arrangements so that if both of them die before their child has reached eighteen, the child will be placed in the custody of the godparent. The friend is referred to as the baby's godfather or godmother.

Most often a woman is asked to be a sponsor. These godmothers are women who either have no children or have children who are grown. For these women, godmotherhood is a way to participate in motherhood in a special sense, with very real advantages to both the child and the parents as they cement their ties with the godmothers.

If godparenthood is so useful that it has been adapted to purely secular contexts in the United States, then why hasn't such a form of shared parenting become more common? Actually, in addition to god-parenthood, other forms of shared parenting are common among certain ethnic and racial groups in the United States. One example is the sharing of rights and responsibilities for children in African-American communities, as has been well documented by Stack (1974).

Stack found that in the suburban Black community she studied outside Chicago, families have adapted domestic strategies to insure the stability of kinship networks and the free exchange of goods within those networks (Stack 1974:27). People share parental responsibili-ties through temporary fosterage or what they call "child-keeping" (1974:29). They are proud of their children, and "child-begetting" is highly prized. However, what counts is not biological parenthood but social parenthood.

People acquire socially recognized kin ties as friends become incor-porated into the domestic circle (Stack 1974:29). If they live up to their obligations, "they may be called kin—cousins, sisters, brothers, daddies" (1974:30). The kin of the social parents also have claims to parenthood and extend help to the social parents. These kin have the right to request children to raise away from the parents (1974:67). All this means that "rights in children" are distributed over a network of people who are "entitled to assume parental roles" (1974:30).

Stack's research near Chicago shows that in the United States, alternative views of parenthood exist that value social parenting and child sharing. However, the dominant value system is quite different. For members of this larger group within the United States, surrogacy contracts are the alternative to godparenthood or child sharing. This choice reflects a different view of the world.

Contrasting Worldviews

In the United States the dominant worldview emphasizes the independent individual in opposition to the group, for individual needs and social obligations are often assumed to be in conflict. People are believed to exist as isolated physical entities who seek to control rather than be controlled. Thus, cooperation and sharing are frequently interpreted as a sign of subordination or submission. By contrast, for many people in Mexico, a person's sense of self is defined primarily by membership in a social group. An individual's needs are defined in terms of what is good for the group, and cooperation and sharing are encouraged.

In Mexico, interdependence among people is emphasized and expressed through cosleeping and "skinship." In the United States, sleeping alone is usually considered desirable and necessary for privacy, but in Mexico, particularly in rural areas, sleeping alone is considered lonely and unpleasant, even a little frightening. Generally, several people share the same bed or sleeping mat, either a couple with their small children or same-sex relatives. When visiting relatives and friends arrive, they join others of the same sex in sleeping together (Pader 1993:126). In Japan the term *skinship* is used "to characterize the value placed on parent-child cosleeping patterns and more general bodily contact as essential to the development of a sense of well-being and interdependence in the child" (Hendry and Lebra, as cited in Pader 1993:126).

A similar type of "skinship" also exists throughout Mexico—all one has to do is look at the way people walk or sit together. As Estés observed in Oaxaca, Mexico: "Tehuana women are always patting and touching not only their babies and not only their men, not only the grandmas and grandpas, not only the food, the clothes, the family pets, but each other as well. It's a very touching culture that seems to make people blossom" (Estés 1992:481). In rural Mexico a person is continually in contact with others and rarely alone (Pader 1993:128).

Unlike the situation in the United States, where nature is assumed to be subordinate to human technology, in Mexico the world is not preceived as ultimately controllable by human beings—the most one can do is to try to manipulate whatever power is available—one's relatives, patrons, the saints, or supernatural forces.

In Mexico, neither spiritual nor social values are subordinate to material ones, and although procreation is important, socialization and godparent ties are equally significant. Parenthood is not defined in a narrow biological sense as male seed and female receptacle but encompasses the whole web of nurturance that surrounds the child. Not only parents but also godparents and other group members participate actively in raising a child. It is not that biology is unimportant but that parenthood is based on spiritual ties, and other social relationships are equally important and just as real.[8]

The view that parenthood entails multiple roles performed by different people is related to the emphasis on sharing and cooperation characteristic of the Zapotec (Williams 1979) as well as other rural groups of Mexico. People do not "have" children in the sense of private, individual ownership. For the Zapotec, children exist as part of the larger kinship group, and they are seen as part of the village community. (For a Jamaican example, see Sobo, this volume.)

Many households are composed of several generations, and grandparents have considerable authority over how their grandchildren are raised. People from other households also contribute to feeding, disciplining, teaching, and counseling them. Godparents and consanguines feel that they have both the right and the responsibility to participate in raising children, while most people in the United States would perceive such behaviors as interfering. For the Zapotec, having children means sharing children.

Although some observers have argued that in Mexico paternity takes precedence over maternity, this characterization reflects Anglo views of parenthood, power, and authority. Others have observed that maternity takes precedence, both in family organization and in the role of The Virgin. Among the Zapotec, the importance of motherhood is ritually expressed in various ways, including the elaboration of godmother roles (El Guindi 1983, 1986; Sault 1985a, 1985b).[9] Although Zapotec baptisms usually involve a godfather and a godmother, they can take place with two godmothers or a godmother alone. Male participation is not required for a socially binding relationship (Sault 1985a, 1985b).

The ritual elaboration of Zapotec women's roles is grounded in a concept of the body quite different from that of mainstream society in the United States. Zapotec society emphasizes balance over boundary maintenance. While much behavior focuses on protecting and reinforcing collective boundaries, as in defending against other villages or the outside world, within the community individual body boundaries are seen as fluid. Health for the individual as well as the community means striking a balance within one's body and between oneself and others in the community. Like the !Kung San of southern Africa and the Meratus Dayak of Indonesia, among the Zapotec, healing means regaining balance rather than strengthening or repairing body boundaries (Katz 1982:210, 246, 297; Tsing 1988).[10] One manifestation of this emphasis on balance is that people seek communion with others in this world and the next, and characteristically Anglo-American concerns with privacy and solitude are downplayed.

Conclusion

At the beginning of the chapter I asked why surrogacy is accepted in the United States but not in Mexico. My conclusion is that people in these two cultures have radically different concepts of the body which influence their understanding of parenthood. Because parenthood in Mexico is not defined biologically, there is room for creating kinship ties through the sponsorship of ceremonies like baptism. The Zapotec emphasis on cooperation and sharing is reflected in the many ways parents and godparents share the rights and responsibilities of raising children. People expect to share in raising children, whether those children live with them or in another household, regardless of whether or not those children were physically born to them. The ritual kinship relationship of godparenthood provides a social alternative to biological reproduction by enabling childless adults to participate in parenting and nurturing children. Godparenthood is a means of maintaining a balance among those who have many children and those who have few, and also a way for redistributing children so that each household has children of both sexes. The flexibility of individual and household boundaries enables a strengthening of the larger village as a community.

By contrast, the American definition of parenthood is preeminently biological and associated with exclusive rights of ownership over children. Couples feel that they have a "right" to have children "of their own." Surrogate *parent*hood is seen as a "solution" for childless couples living in a society that emphasizes the biological connection between parent and child. Surrogate *mother*hood is seen as a "solution" for childless couples (or single men) when fatherhood is preeminent and defined by the male seed.

American society is oriented toward controlling individual boundaries to maintain a rigid seperation between self and other (see Martin 1990:411). Moreover, the focus of concern is men's bodies, furthering male procreation while also protecting men from being controlled by others. Because the human body is conceptualized as partible and women's bodies are considered inherently permeable, female bodies can be divided up and rented out to further the goal of male procreation and reaffirm male control. Originally surrogacy procedures were accepted because they fulfilled the goal of male reproduction. When male procreation is preeminent and women's bodies are defined as containers for nuturing male seed, one womb-container can be substituted for another. After all, it is the male seed that engenders life and the male bloodline that must be continued.

The dominant values of American society emphasize a view of parenthood that is biological, individual, and androcentric. Surrogacy was developed in the United States and is enforced legally (Paddock and Lynch 1993) because it expresses features central to the dominant worldview of the United States. The cross-cultural comparison of parenthood in the United States and Mexico shows that we need to look beyond the conventional framework of debate on this subject. Arguments about "surrogate" motherhood are made within a specific cultural context which entails a particular view of the body, gender, parenthood, and social relations. These terms can only be fully understood in light of their cultural context.

NOTES

For their comments, support, and encouragement, I thank all those who contributed to this chapter, especially Peter Reynolds, Cathy Winkler, Peggy Sanday, Carole Browner, Camilo Garcia Parra, Robbie E. Davis-Floyd, and Holly Mathews.

    1   Regarding the term *surrogate mother,* Pollitt argues: "if anyone was a surrogate mother, it was Elizabeth Stern, for she was the one who substituted, or wished to substitute, for the child's actual mother. . . . In this article I will use the term 'contract mother,' 'maternity contract' and their variants, except where I am

directly quoting others" (Pollitt 1987:682). Instead of *surrogate mother,* Corea uses the term *breeder* (1985).

    2   Note that agricultural imagery is embedded in the derivation of the words *seed, semen,* and *sperm* in English: *seed* meaning "to sow," *semen,* "to cast or let fall," and *sperm* meaning "seed, germ, to sow, scatter, or spark" (*Webster's New World Dictionary*). For another example of agricultural images of parenthood, see the poem *Song of Lawino* by Okot p'Bitek (1966:99) from Uganda:

> "Periodically each woman/Sees the moon,/And when a young girl/Has seen it/ For the first time/It is a sign that/The garden is ready/For sowing,/And when the gardener comes/Carrying two bags of live seeds/And a good strong hoe/ The rich red soil/Swells with a new life."

    3   In the literature on cloning, women are "viewed as passive physical material for the cloning process: ovaries, eggs, uteri. Meanwhile, men are seen as 'parents' of clonal offspring—simply by donating a set of chromosomes" (Murphy 1985:87).

    4   According to Corea: "In 1977, hysterectomy became the nation's most commonly performed operation and remains so as I write. In 1969, Dr. R. C. Wright, publishing in *Obstetrics and Gynecology,* advocated removal of the uterus routinely after the last planned pregnancy on the ground that the uterus is potentially cancer-bearing. Wright claimed: 'the uterus has but one function: reproduction. After the last planned pregnancy, the uterus becomes a useless, bleeding, symptom-producing, potentially cancer-bearing organ and therefore should be removed' " (quoted in Corea 1985:308).

In a 1971 article for the *American Journal of Obstetrics and Gynecology,* Dr. Eleanor Easley encourages the use of hysterectomies, arguing: "It is an excellent procedure for sterilization. A woman is a more reliable worker after she's had one. It is advantageous at the menopause if only to simplify estrogen therapy. For some time I've been telling women that in another twenty years I expect hysterectomy to have become almost routine at the menopause" (quoted in Payer 1988:185–186).

    5   In addition to using body parts for "surrogate technology," the number of body parts used for general research is even greater. In the 1970s, for example, human fetuses were imported from South Korea for use in biological weapons research, along with twelve thousand pairs of kidneys from human fetuses. During this time the number of abortions in South Korea increased to three times the number of births (Bullard 1987:114).

    6   According to Shorter: "Of all male fears of women, most wrenching was the fear of the uterus. Ever since Hippocrates, academic medicine had assigned to the uterus bizarre qualities, such as the ability to wander about the abdomen or to send women into hysterical fits. . . . In much of Europe's popular culture, the uterus was thought to be alive, not just part of a living body, but a separate animate creature housed inside a woman. And an elaborate body of folklore existed for feeding or appeasing this animal once it became aroused, causing 'colic' or 'macica.' Some people thought of the uterus as a frog 'with many legs that is supposed to stay in the body because you have to die when the colic [or frog] creeps out to your throat.' . . . The point is that any organ to which such life-threatening, life-saving qualities were assigned could not help but take on a fearsome aspect in the eyes of men. If the demonic bodies of women had to be controlled, it was first because of the uterus inside them" (Shorter 1982:286–287).

    7   Funding for my research in Mexico was provided by a Fulbright-Hays Research Scholarship and also travel and research grants from the regents of the University of California. The material presented on godparenthood is based on research in a Valley Zapotec village of Oaxaca, beginning in 1977.

8   In contemporary Mexico, the emphasis on biological connections may be partly related to the history of Spanish conquest and colonization. To this colonial society the Spaniards brought with them an emphasis on "purity of blood" to distinguish "true" Christians from those "tainted by Jewish or Muslim affiliation" (Helms 1975:168; Wynter 1983).

9   Some observers have characterized the Zapotec as an example of a matriarchal culture, though Chiñas and others describe this society as egalitarian, or matrifocal, based on the complementarity of female and male roles (Chiñas 1973:93).

10   In two neighboring Indonesian cultures, Tsing found contrasting models for healing that parallel the differences between Mexico and the United States regarding attitudes toward the body and social relations. Among the Meratus Dayak, healing restores the fluidity of body boundaries that was lost because of "the patient's narrow-focused definition of self-interest and personal space." The shaman cures with chants that "open and expand social and somatic boundaries; they open up the pores to let in healthy cosmic flows." Among the Banjar Muslims, healing "fortifies" the body boundary against "intrusions" from outside, like "poisoned winds" and "messy extrusions" (Tsing 1988:829).

REFERENCES

Bartimus, Tad. 1991. "Cancer Fears Spur Healthy Sisters into Mastectomies." *San Jose Mercury News*, December 22, 1991, pp. 1A, 19A.

Bullard, Linda. 1987. "Killing Us Softly: Toward a Feminist Analysis of Genetic Engineering." In *Made to Order*, ed. Patricia Spallone and Deborah Steinberg. Oxford: Pergamon.

Calhoun, Arthur C. 1945. *A Social History of the American Family*. New York: Barnes and Noble.

Cannell, Fenella. 1990. "Concepts of Parenthood: The Warnock Report, the Gillick Debate, and Modern Myths." *American Ethnologist* 17(4):667–686.

Chiñas, Beverly. 1973. *The Isthmus Zapotec*. New York: Holt, Rinehart.

Cho, Haejong. 1978. "Burden or Joy? A Study of Child Care Based on the Ethnography of a Female Diver's Village in Korea." Paper presented at the American Anthropological Association.

Coen, Ethan. 1987. *Raising Arizona*. Circle Films, CBS Fox Films distributors.

Cook, Martin L. 1988. "Reproductive Technologies and the Vatican." *Issues in Ethics* (Center for Applied Ethics, Santa Clara University), Spring, pp. 1, 6.

Corea, Gena. 1985. *The Mother Machine: Reproductive Technologies*. New York: Harper and Row.

Davis-Floyd, Robbie. 1987. "The Technological Model of Birth." *Journal of American Folklore* 100(398):93–109.

———. 1992. *Birth as an American Rite of Passage*. Berkeley: University of California Press.

de la Fuente, Pat. 1989. "Beyond Baby M: The Controversy over Surrogate Motherhood." *Utne Reader*, May/June, pp. 118–123.

Delaney, Carol. 1986. "The Meaning of Paternity and the Virgin Birth Debate." *Man* 21(3):494–513.

———. 1991. *The Seed and the Soil: Gender and Cosmology in Turkish Village Society*. Berkeley: University of California Press.

DuBois, Page. 1988. *Sowing the Body*. Chicago: University of Chicago Press.

El Guindi, Fadwa. 1983. "Some Methodological Considerations for Ethnography." In *The Future of Structuralism*, ed. Jarich Oosten and Arie de Ruijter. Amsterdam: IUAES-Intercongress.
———. 1986. *The Myth of Ritual: A Native's Ethnography of Zapotec Life-Crisis Rituals*. Tucson: University of Arizona Press.
Estés, Clarisa Pinkola. 1992. *Women Who Run with the Wolves*. New York: Ballantine.
Featherstone, Mike. 1990. "The Body in Consumer Culture." In *The Body: Social Process and Cultural Theory*, ed. M. Featherstone et al. London: Sage.
Foster, George. 1969. "Godparents and Social Networks in Tzintzuntzan." *Southwestern Journal of Anthropology* 25:261–278.
Helms, Mary W. 1975. *Middle America*. Garden City, N.J.: Prentice-Hall.
"Japanese Seek U.S. Suggogates." 1992. *San Francisco Chronicle*, October 12. Associated Press.
Kamal, Sultana. 1987. "Seizure of Reproductive Rights? A Discussion on Population Control in the Third World and the Engineering of the New Reproductive Technology in the West." In *Made to Order*, ed. Patricia Spallone and Deborah Steinberg. Oxford: Pergamon.
Katz, Richard. 1982. *Boiling Energy: Community Healing among the !Kung*. Cambridge: Harvard University Press.
Kimbrell, Andrew. 1993. *The Human Body Shop: The Engineering and Marketing of Life*. San Francisco: Harper and Row.
Krauthamer, Charles. 1987. "The Ethics of Human Manufacture." *New Republic*, May 4, pp. 17–21.
Martin, Emily. 1987. *The Woman in the Body: A Cultural Analysis of Reproduction*. Boston: Beacon.
———. 1990. "Toward an Anthropology of Immunology: The Body as Nation State." *Medical Anthropology Quarterly* 4(4):410–426.
Meigs, Anna. 1987. "Blood Kin and Food Kin." In *Conflict and Conformity*, ed. James Spradley and David McCurdy. Boston: Little, Brown.
Mintz, Sidney, and Eric Wolf. 1950. "An Analysis of Ritual Coparenthood (Compadrazgo)." *Southwestern Journal of Anthropology* 6:341–365.
Murphy, Jane. 1985. "From Mice to Men? Implications of Progress in Cloning Research." In *Test-Tube Women: What Future for Motherhood?* ed. Rita Arditti, Renate Duelli Klein, and Shelley Minden. London: Pandora.
Nelson, Margaret. 1990. "Mothering Others' Children: The Experiences of Family Day-Care Providers." *Signs* 15(3):586–605.
Nutini, Hugo, and Betty Bell. 1980. *Ritual Kinship: The Structure and Historical Development of the Compadrazgo System in Rural Tlaxcala*. Princeton, N.J.: Princeton University Press.
O'Neill, John. 1985. *Five Bodies: The Human Shape of Modern Society*. Ithaca, N.Y.: Cornell University Press.
Paddock, Richard C., and Rene Lynch. 1993. "Contract Mightier Than the Womb." *San Jose Mercury News*, May 21, p. 1A.
Pader, Ellen J. 1993. "Spatiality and Social Change: Domestic Space Use in Mexico and the United States." *American Ethnologist* 20(1):114–137.
Payer, Lynn. 1988. *Medicine and Culture*. New York: Holt, Rinehart.
p'Bitek, Okot. 1966. *Song of Lawino*. Nairobi, Kenya: East Aftrican Publishing.
Pollitt, Katha. 1987. "The Strange Case of Baby M."*Nation*, May 23, pp. 682–688.
Ragoné, Helena. 1994. *Surrogate Motherhood: Conception in the Heart*. Boulder: Westview Press.

Rivière, Peter. 1985. "Unscrambling Parenthood: The Warnock Report." *Anthropology Today* 1(4):2–6.

Rothman, Barbara Katz. 1982. *In Labor: Women and Power in the Birthplace.* New York: Norton.

Rowland, Robyn. 1987. "Of Woman Born, But for How Long?" In *Made to Order,* ed. Patricia Spallone and Deborah Steinberg. Oxford: Pergamon.

Sault, Nicole. 1985a. "Baptismal Sponsorship as a Source of Power for Zapotec Women in Oaxaca, Mexico." *Journal of Latin American Lore* 11(2):225–243.

Sault, Nicole. 1985b. "Zapotec Godmothers: The Centrality of Women for Compadrazgo Groups in a Village of Oaxaca, Mexico." Ph.D. diss., University of California, Los Angeles.

Schneider, David. 1968. *American Kinship: A Cultural Account.* Garden City, N.J.: Prentice-Hall.

Shannon, Thomas A. 1988. *Surrogate Motherhood: The Ethics of Using Human Beings.* New York: Crossroad.

Shorter, Edward. 1982. *A History of Women's Bodies.* New York: Basic Books.

Spallone, Patricia, and Deborah Lynn Steinberg. 1987. *Made to Order: The Myth of Reproductive and Genetic Progress.* Oxford: Pergamon.

Stack, Carol. 1974. *All Our Kin: Strategies for Survival in a Black Community.* New York: Harper and Row.

Stallybrass, Peter. 1986. "Patriarchal Territories: The Body Enclosed." In *Rewriting the Renaissance,* ed. Margaret W. Ferguson, Maureen Quilligan, and Nancy J. Vickers. Chicago: University of Chicago Press.

Stavenhagen, Maria Eugenia. 1959. "El compadrazgo en una comunidad zapoteca (Zaachila)." *Ciencias Políticas Y Sociales* 5(17):365–402.

Stolcke, Verena. 1988. "New Reproductive Technologies: The Old Quests for Fatherhood." *Reproductive and Genetic Engineering* 1(1):5–19.

Strathern, Marilyn. 1992. *Reproducing the Future: Essays on Anthropology, Kinship, and the New Reproductive Technologies.* Manchester, England: Manchester University Press.

Tsing, Anna Lowenhaupt. 1988. "Healing Boundaries in South Kalimantan." *Social Science and Medicine* 27(8):829–839.

Velez Ibañez, Carlos. 1980. "The Nonconsenting Sterilization of Mexican Women in Los Angeles." In *Twice a Minority: Mexican American Women,* ed. Margarita Melville. St. Louis: Mosby.

Whiteford, Linda M. 1989. "Commercial Surrogacy: Social Issues Behind the Controversy." In *New Approaches to Human Reproduction,* ed. Linda Whiteford and Marilyn Poland. Boulder, Colo.: Westview.

Wilbert, Johannes. 1970. "Goajiro Kinship and the Eiruku Cycle." In *The Social Anthropology of Latin America,* ed. Harry Hoijer and Walter Goldschmidt. Los Angeles: University of California Press.

Williams, Aubrey. 1979. "Cohesive Features of the Guelaguetza System in Mitla." In *Social, Political, and Economic Life in Contemporary Oaxaca,* ed. Aubrey Williams. Vanderbilt University Publications in Anthropology, Nashville.

Wynter, Sylvia. 1983. "New Seville and the Conversion Experience of Bartolomé de Las Casas." *Jamaica Journal* 17(2):25–32.

CONCLUSION

Ransoming the Body

NICOLE SAULT

Mirroring of body image and social relations exists in all human societies. But as chapters in this book show, some societies view the person as a whole, including body, mind, and spirit as integrated aspects of the self. Other societies view the person as fragmented into a self that is separate from the collection of parts called the body. Societies that conceive of the self as integrated emphasize the connection between the individual and the larger community, and they conceptualize sickness and health in terms of group integration and solidarity. They define sickness in terms of loss or imbalance, and healing requires a restoration of unity among community members by reinforcing the sick person's ties to everyone. For example, in Morocco, when a woman has *baraka* or "divine blessing," she has "sufficiency; she has all that she needs. In corporeal terms, the woman's body is in balance with her surroundings and her society" (Kapchan 1993:9).

Spatial and emotional distance are of crucial importance for healing. In contemporary cross-cultural psychology, Katz found that among the !Kung San of the Kalahari Desert in southern Africa, the healing power of *num* energy flows across individual boundaries during trance. Fluidity of body boundaries is especially marked among the !Kung healing specialists when they are in the *kia* trance. Even the boundaries between camps of people are permeable, for the !Kung San want everyone to have access to the healing power of *num* (Katz 1982:206–208, 235).

This permeability of body boundary is recognized in many other societies and understood to be characteristic of holy people or saints, whose healing power flows out from them into others, even after death. For example, in modern Luxor (the site of ancient Thebes), a sheikh may be "endowed with a divine energy or life-force known as *baraka,* which may radiate from him in life and in death and be absorbed and ingested by others" (Wickett 1993:185).[1]

The chapters on communities in Jamaica and Mexico show how this understanding of the reciprocal relationship between the individual and the larger community is promoted by an emphasis on the need to share with others and show concern. A person does not choose to share; sharing within the community is expected. A refusal to share either food or children reflects poorly on the person and raises doubts about the person's physical and social health. Fennell's chapter on a southern community in the United States provides another example of social unity that is embodied. In this case, people are characterized using age as a symbol to express transient or permanent characteristics. Despite their verbal emphasis on *physical* characteristics for defining age, in everyday life these people take into account a number of factors. Individuals are portrayed as "old" according to a combination of activity levels, knowledge about the person, and context. For these southerners, body is not understood as separate from self or community, but acquires meaning in relation to a person's history within a set of social relations.

By contrast, societies that view the self as fragmented emphasize the isolation of the individual into particular body parts. Sickness is defined in terms of a malfunctioning body part that requires medication or removal. Patients are socialized to see the body as separate from, and even antagonistic to, the self. Kugelman (1992) tells us this fragmentation is particularly important for understanding stress. The perception that a separation of the self from the body is not only normal but desirable is bourne out in Davis-Floyd's chapter, which shows that in American hospitals many women seek anesthesia to distance themselves from their own birth experiences and to gain control over their bodies. They are not simply avoiding pain but trying to ensure that they will be present at the birth only intellectually, not physically. The self as "other" also appears in the chapter by Winkler as well as my own. Rape trauma leads to a fragmenting of the body, but healing brings a restoration of wholeness. American surrogacy arrangements require that the birth mother "give up" her uterus and hand over control to others. She becomes fragmented into rentable/nonrentable body parts.

The chapters that discuss dieting and eating disorders describe an ongoing separation of body and self, one that is upheld by the body values of the United States in the twentieth century. Anorexia demonstrates the power of the culturally accepted opposition between body/self taken to the point of death. In this view of the body, the whole person is lost, for anorexia is "a disease in which the concept of the whole person is so confused, so dialectically divided, that 'I' can at the same time be choosing to live, as the self, and choosing to die, as the body" (MacLeod as quoted in Turner 1984:185).

Eating disorders are fundamentally a representation of social isolation. Vincent explains that "binging is by nature isolating—it takes time and is not feasible socially or in public places. But the binger is mentally as well as physically isolated" (Vincent 1979:72). More important, however, the bulimic (or the anorexic) is socially isolated from herself as well as from others. The fragmentations in body image and in social relations reflect each other.

Young, Beausoleil, Kaw, and Klein all address the tension between self-image and social relations—changing oneself or redefining the context in order to bring self and social relations into alignment. In Young's description of the tattoos worn by the Rashaayda of Sudan, the body is altered as an expression of social relationship and control over the relationship.

According to Beausoleil's findings, makeup practices in the United States vary greatly in relation to the perception of self. For some women, being oneself requires makeup; for others makeup masks the true self. Still other women describe makeup practices in terms of enhancing the self or bringing out its varied aspects. They use makeup to be someone different for each occasion. The women Beausoleil interviewed felt that the self may be either expressed or hidden with makeup: the unadorned body may not represent who a woman really is, or it may say too much. Are we more ourselves when clothed or naked, with or without glasses, or watches, or jewelry? If we recognize the cultural aspect of being human, then our adornments are clearly part of who we are. Yet clothing reflects both cultural norms and individual taste, so how do we weigh the influence of each?

Kaw describes Asian American women who undergo surgery to look their "best," for whom looking good means having a less "Asian" face. It is as though the women's core selves have acculturated to the American worldview and lifestyle, but their bodies have not kept pace. Once "the self" assimilates, surgery is used to align the body with the new image.

Bodybuilding reflects the self/body split in another way. Women bodybuilders find that controlling their bodies is a way to gain self-mastery and a general sense of control in life. Building the body works to create a better sense of self. Although body and self are still separate, in bodybuilding culture they are not so much in opposition as in alliance, for the muscled body protects the "self" inside. Rebellion as well as control are expressed by the muscled body that resists convention.

The opposition of body and self is visible throughout American culture. Simply pick up a newspaper or magazine and you see such headlines as "Body Wars" or "Your Body: Friend, Foe, or Total Stranger?" and articles about Americans "fighting a long-term battle with their bodies" (Kimbrell 1992; Lamb 1992; Walker 1993). Many people have so internalized a sense of their bodies as "other" that they feel separated from their bodies, believing that the self can exist independently from the body, which is a collections of parts, or something that each of us must drag around every day, a burden from which we long to be freed. The belief that the body is a primitive object that science will one day transform into radiant energy or starlight is one of the defining features of modern technocratic culture (Reynolds 1991).

This view of the body as "other" has engendered a reaction, so that people now talk about getting back "in touch" with their bodies, "reclaiming" their bodies, and becoming "reembodied" after years of disembodiment. In *Giving the Body Its Due*, Sheets-Johnstone states that "loss is recovered only by recovering the body that was once integrally present but now remains unattended or left behind" (1992a:14). She goes on to explain that "materialization of the body, as epitomized in the prevalent twentieth-century Western view, eventuates in both an eroded sense of self and an eroded sense of responsibility" (1992b: 134). In the same book, Romanyshyn goes on to say that

> items of information are not the real issue and that in isolating our focus upon them we relieve ourselves of the responsibility to recognize that in our objectification of food and eating we are revealing that attitude of distance which separates us from each other, from our bodies, and from the material world of nature. In the anorexic's symptomatic behavior toward food, there is remembered for us our terror of intimacy, and that destructive exploitation of animals and nature that allows us to separate ourselves from the world and to treat is as a consumable thing. (Romanyshyn 1992:174–175)

Sheets-Johnstone suggests that our bodies offer us a way back, for "bodily understandings have the possibility of ransoming us, as much from insulated arrogance as from indifferent violence" (1992a:4–5).

Part of the difficulty lies in the way we talk about the body as a separate entity that we own or disown. Our use of language presumes disembodiment, accepting that the phrase "reach out and touch someone" means picking up a telephone or that "networking" is done via computer. We need to recognize that interactions mediated by machines are not personal. We need to get back to talking and acting as whole people, with "I" or "me" understood to include a self with physical as well as mental and spiritual dimensions.

Modern medicine is supposedly derived from Hippocratic practice, but the healing arts of the ancient Greeks were quite different from the mechanistic model of the body and depersonalized technique of scientific medicine. If we look at what the ancient Greeks thought, we find that "Hippocratic medical theory was anchored in the concept of the proportionality of the elements—in the concept of harmony or disharmony," and proportionality also figured in the various relationships of a person to surrounding people and the environment (Sheets-Johnstone 1992b:140–141). When the Greeks talked about a patient, it was in terms of the whole body as a *living* body, and this meant a *person* (1992b:147). As Bohm points out: "It is instructive to consider that the word 'health' in English is based on an Anglo-Saxon word 'hale' meaning 'whole': that is, to be healthy is to be whole, which is, I think, roughly the equivalent of the Hebrew 'shalem.' Likewise, the English 'holy' is based on the same root as 'whole' " (Bohm 1980:3).[2]

We use the body to symbolize the self, society and social relationships, but in doing so, we affirm either fragmentation or wholeness. If we believe our "selves" exist in opposition to our "bodies," then we will experience this opposition in the fragmentation of our lives and the deterioration of our social relationships. But if we believe that we are whole people who understand our social experience as embodied, then our everyday actions will reflect this worldview, and our relationships with the people around us will mirror a sense of integrity. When we refuse to accept the objectification of our bodies as "other," then we can refuse to tolerate the objectification of societies as collections of objects that are "other." This embodied understanding also entails a sense of being connected with the surrounding world, rather than viewing the environment as an abstract entity from which we stand apart, or as a cluster of resources to exploit. By recognizing the embodied character of our social relationships, we discover that our bodies were never lost in the first place, and we regain a sense of wholeness both within ourselves and with the people around us.

NOTES

1   Applying henna to the skin is an example of healing through permeability. Due to its association with the Prophet Mohamed, henna has *baraka,* and when a person is painted with henna it purifies as it penetrates the skin (Kapchan 1973:7–8).

2   Bohm goes on to argue that "wholeness is what is real, and that fragmentation is the response of this whole to man's action, guided by illusory perception, which is shaped by fragmentary thought. In other words, it is just because reality is whole that man, with his fragmentary approach, will inevitably be answered with a correspondingly fragmentary response" (1980:7). Yet when we look at other societies we find examples of wholeness that continue to be valued, so fragmentation is not an inevitable characteristic of human society.

REFERENCES

Bohm, David. 1980. *Wholeness and the Implicate Order.* London: Routledge and Kegan Paul.

Carstensen, Jeanne, and Richard Kadrey. 1989. "Is the Body Obsolete? Introduction." *Whole Earth Review,* no. 63 (Summer):2–3.

Kapchan, Deborah. 1993. "Moroccan Women's Body Signs." In *Bodylore,* ed. Katherine Young. Knoxville: University of Tennessee Press.

Katz, Richard. 1982. *Boiling Energy: Community Healing among the !Kung.* Cambridge: Harvard University Press.

Kimbrell, Andrew. 1992. "Body Wars." *Utne Reader,* May/June, p. 52–64.

Kugelman, Robert. 1992. "Life under Stress: From Management to Mourning." In *Giving the Body Its Due,* ed. Maxine Sheets-Johnstone. Albany, N.Y.: SUNY Press.

Lamb, Lynette. 1992. "Your Body: Friend, Foe, or Total Stranger?" *Utne Reader,* May/June, p. 51.

Reynolds, Peter C. 1991. *Stealing Fire: The Atomic Bomb as Symbolic Body.* Palo Alto, Calif.: Iconic Anthropology Press.

Romanyshyn, Robert. 1992. "The Human Body as Historical Matter and Cultural Symptom." In *Giving the Body Its Due,* ed. Maxine Sheets-Johnstone. Albany, N.Y.: SUNY Press.

Sheets-Johnstone, Maxine. 1992a. "Charting the Interdisciplinary Course." In *Giving the Body Its Due,* ed. M. Sheets-Johnstone, pp. 1–15. Albany, N.Y.: SUNY Press.

———. 1992b. "The Materialization of the Body: A History of Western Medicine, A History in Process." In *Giving the Body Its Due,* ed. M. Sheets-Johnstone, pp. 132–158. Albany, N.Y.: SUNY Press.

Turner, Bryan S. 1984. *The Body and Society.* Oxford: Basil Blackwell.

Vincent, L. M. 1979. *Competing with the Sylph: Dance and the Pursuit of the Ideal Ballet Figure.* New York: Andrews and McMeel.

Walker, Chip. 1993. "Retreat from the Battle of the Bulge." *San Francisco Chronicle/Examiner,* February 14.

Whiteford, Linda M. 1989. "Commercial Surrogacy: Social Issues Behind the Controversy." In *New Approaches to Human Reproduction,* ed. Linda Whiteford and Marilyn Poland. Boulder, Colo.: Westview.

Wickett, Elizabeth. 1993. "The Spirit in the Body." In *Bodylore,* ed. Katherine Young. Knoxville: University of Tennessee Press.

CONTRIBUTORS

Natalie Beausoleil is currently an assistant professor of sociology at Memorial University, St. Johns, Newfoundland, Canada. She was a postdoctoral fellow at the Ontario Institute for Studies in Education, funded by the Social Sciences and Humanities Research Council of Canada. She received her doctorate in sociology from the University of California, Los Angeles. Her current research interest is an ethnographic approach to theory and popular culture, including the sociology of personal appearance and the production of gender, race, class, femininity, sexuality, and self.

Robbie E. Davis-Floyd, a cultural anthropologist who specializes in medical and symbolic anthropology, gender studies, and futures planning, is a research fellow at the University of Texas at Austin and lectures widely on ritual, gender, and birth. Her publications include *Birth as an American Rite of Passage* (University of California Press, 1992), the revised and updated edition of Brigitte Jordan's classic work, *Birth in Four Cultures* (Waveland Press, 1993), as well as numerous articles. She is currently writing a book entitled *The Technocratic Body and the Organic Body.*

Valerie Fennell received her Ph.D. in anthropology from the University of North Carolina at Chapel Hill and is an associate professor of anthropology at Georgia State University in Atlanta. Her research focuses on age and gender relations in southern communities. Her work appears in *Women in the South: An Anthropological Perspective* (University of Georgia Press, 1989). Currently she is examining the influence of age and gender on the mediation process in the U.S. legal system.

Eugenia Kaw is doing doctoral work in anthropology at Princeton University. A graduate of the University of California at Berkeley, she received the Steven Polgar Prize from the Society for Medical Anthropology. She plans to do fieldwork in Thailand to study how Theravada

Buddhists perceive modernization. Her broad interests include local concepts of race, ethnicity, and sexuality in Southeast Asia, with an emphasis on the postcolonial context.

Dixie L. King is the Student Assistance Programs coordinator for the Kern County Superintendent of Schools Office in California. She designs intervention programs for at-risk youth in 220 schools and 47 districts in the county and trains school staff in how to expand services for students and their families, working with the Kern County Healthy Start Collaborative. Previously she served as an independent consultant in evaluating programs for health education throughout California, focusing on substance abuse, early childhood neglect, HIV education, and smoking. King has authored publications on women and immigration as well as evaluations on the effectiveness of tobacco education media. She is completing her doctorate in anthropology from the University of California, Los Angeles.

Alan M. Klein is a professor of anthropology at Northeastern University in Boston. He is the author of *Sugarball: The American Game, the Dominican Dream* (Yale, 1991), and *Little Big Men: Bodybuilding Subculture and Gender Construction* (SUNY Press, 1993). His forthcoming book, *The Owls of the Two Laredos: Culture and Baseball on the Border,* will be published by Yale University Press.

Mimi Nichter is the project coordinator for the Teen Lifestyle Project, a longitudinal study on body image, dieting, and smoking among adolescent females, funded by the National Institutes of Health, at the Department of Anthropology at the University of Arizona. Her work (coauthored with Mark Nichter) was awarded the 1992 Rudolph Virchow Prize for Critical Medical Anthropology. She has conducted extensive anthropological fieldwork on women and health in India, Sri Lanka, and the Philippines. Her articles have appeared in *Human Organization, Medical Anthropology,* and the *International Journal of Adult Education.*

Peggy Reeves Sanday is a professor of anthropology at the University of Pennsylvania. She is the author of *Female Power and Male Dominance* (Cambridge University Press, 1981), *Beyond the Second Sex* (University of Pennsylvania Press, 1990), and *Fraternity Gang Rape* (New York University Press, 1990). She is currently writing a book on acquaintance rape and American sexual culture.

Nicole Sault is an anthropologist who has studied indigenous approaches to kinship and healing among the Zapotec of Oaxaca, Mexico. Her research also includes a cultural analysis of breast implants and reproductive technology in the United States. She received her doctorate from the University of California, Los Angeles, and teaches at Santa Clara University in California. She is presently writing *Zapotec Godmothers: Kinship Rituals in Mexico*, based on her field research.

Elisa J. Sobo is an assistant professor in the Department of Sociology and Anthropology at New Mexico State University. Her recent book, *One Blood: The Jamaican Body* (SUNY Press, 1993), concerns traditional health beliefs in Jamaica. She is involved in HIV/AIDS prevention research with youths and women in the United States. Her book, *Not My Man: Women, Relationships, and AIDS-Risk Denial*, is forthcoming.

Nancy Vuckovic is research associate for the Teen Lifestyle Project, a longitudinal study on body image, dieting, and smoking among adolescent females, funded by the National Institutes of Health. Her other areas of anthropological research include studies on gender and language, media influences on health behavior, and self-medication practices in the United States. She is affiliated with the Department of Anthropology at the University of Arizona.

Cathy Winkler received her doctorate in anthropology from Indiana University for her work on the role of gender in the acquisition and expression of economic authority in the lacquer industry of Olinalá, in Guerrero, Mexico. Her current research uses an investigator-victim perspective to comprehend the meanings of rape, trauma, myth, and legal barriers to conviction. She is working on a book titled *Raped Once, Raped Twice, and Raped a Third Time*, which analyzes the rape attack, the social antagonisms, and the six-year legal battle to stop the rapist. She is an assistant professor of anthropology at Tuskegee University in Alabama.

William C. Young is a Fulbright Lecturer in anthropology at Yarmouk University in Irbid, Jordan. He has published work on gender and pilgrimage in the *International Journal of Middle East Studies*, and also on Islam among nomadic pastoralists. His case study *The Rashaayda Bedouin: Arab Pastoralists of Eastern Sudan* will soon be published by Harcourt and Brace, College Publishers.

INDEX

aborigines, 12

abortion, 150, 302, 315n5

abstinence, from eating, 186–188, 193–194, 201, 202n7

abuse, xii, 184, 195, 199, 202n6, 210, 277, 303

academics, 15

adolescents, 168, 171, 173n7, 176; girls, 105–106, 109–127, 136, 236, girls/boys, 120–121, 137; homogeneity of, 119

adoption, 308–309

adulthood, 170–171, 306; established by having children, 142, 152n5; markers of, 256

advertising, 8, 122, 252, 259. *See also* media

Aeschylus, 296

aesthetics, 248; of food and clothing, 59

Africa, 225, 307, 313, 319; East, 22–23n8; West, 2, 13, 134, 136, 256. *See also individual countries*

African Americans, 16, 111, 159, 161, 163, 168, 252, 294, 310; and cosmetic surgery, 243; heritage, 151n2; women, 260

age, 246, 306; categories, 106; chronological, 157–158, 169–171, 173n6; defining, 320; hierarchies, 166, 172n2; labels, 156–158, 171–172; middle age, 157–158; old age, 157–158

aging, xi, 15, 87–88, 100, 106, 150, 155, 159–161, 170–171, 198, 220, 235–236, 250, 254, 320; and appearance, 158–160; bodily indicators of, 159–160; cultural symbols of, 155–157, 160, 170–171; and gender, 162–169; gerontology literature, 155–156; as metaphor, 155, 169; negative/positive categories, 155,

157–158, 162, 167, 170–172; and poor health, 170; psychological traits of, 160–162; rewards of, 162; stereotypes of, 155, 162, 171; and strength, 167–168; "old talk," 164; terms for, 272; wrinkles as marker of, 158–159, 164 (*see also* hair)

agricultural images of parenthood, 296, 315n2

alcohol, and pregnancy, 212, 301

alcoholism, 269; alcoholics, 183–184, 187, 194, 198–199; Alcoholics Anonymous, 176, 181–182, 194, 201n3, 202nn3–4

alienation, 101, 199, 211

Amazon, Peruvian, 5

American: beauty ideals, 180, 192, 194, 196, 250; concept of parenthood, 297; culture, 239, 245, 322; definitions of body, 189; Dream, 262; girls, 236; ideal, 236, 254; look, 235, 252; paradigm, 200; society, 293, 314; values, 314; women, 179–180, 199, 235, 305; worldview, 8, 312–313

Americans, *see* African Americans; Asian Americans; Blacks; European Americans; Latinas/Latinos; Native Americans; United States

amniocentesis, 212, 232n2, 302

ancestors, 10, 13, 236–237

Andes, 11

androcentrism, 8, 314

anesthetics, 177, 213–216, 227, 229, 232n2, 238, 244, 256–257, 320

anger, 81, 181, 193, 195, 199, 237, 268, 281–282

anorexia, 179–180, 201, 320–322; "pills," 146

anthropologists, 22n4, 82, 197, 229, 231, 246, 292–294

godparenthood, 239–240, 293, 306–
313; godchildren, 240, 307–301;
godfathers, 307–309, 312; godmothers, 239, 292, 306–310, 312
Goffman, Erving, 39–40, 45–46
Goldstein, Judith, 249, 259
Gordon, Daniel, 22n5
Gorman, Peter, 5
Gottman, J., and G. Mettetal, 113
grandparenthood, 144, 159, 161, 170,
299, 311, 312; grandchildren, 312;
grandmothers, 264n4
Greece, Greeks, 21n3, 296, 309, 323;
aesthetic ideal, 249
guilt, 115, 268, 275, 281–283, 285
Guisewite, Cathy, 179

hair, 38, 58, 146 ,151n2, 179, 243,
260; binding, 66; color, 158–159,
167–168, 201, 304–306; women's
styles, 163, 172n4, 210
Handwerker, W. Penn, 220
happiness, 235
hard/soft, 148–149
harmony/disharmony, 137, 323
hate, 268, 278
healing, 2, 10–11, 238, 240, 271,
308, 313, 319–320, 324; chants,
316n10
health, 2, 8, 11, 15, 92, 106–107, 192,
195, 220, 228, 240, 313, 319–320;
associated with plumpness, 140; associated with vitality, 132–133; 137,
147–149; associated with youth,
171; beliefs about, 132–139, 148,
150–151; care, 302; etymology of
term, 323; problems, and aging,
165, 168–171; research, 23n10;
symbolism, 133. See also medicine
Hebrew, 323
hegemony, physical and cultural, 98–
103; and core value system, 229
Helms, Mary, 316n8
henna, 324
Herber, J., 58–59,
Hershey, Barbara, 243
heterosexuality, 40, 164, 172n5, 184
hierarchy, and age, 166
Hippocrates, 296, 315–316n6, 323
Hispanic girls, 111
holistic paradigm, 227, 231

Hollywood celebrities, and plastic surgery, 243
Holmes, K. A., and J. Williams, 271,
273–274
holy, 323
home, 177, 221, 226–227, 312–313;
home vs. work, 223, 225, 238;
housekeeping, 220
homosexuality, 80, 91, 172n5, 184–
185; gay men, 184–185; lesbians,
40, 81, 90, 306
honor, 72
Hope, C., 112, 115
hormones, see steroids
hospitality, 59
hospitals, 7, 140, 225, 320
hot, 148; vs. cold, 10
Hotz, Robert Lee, 15
household, 134, 221, 312–313
Huckshorn, Kristin, 23n10
hunger, 105; as metaphor, 98; sexual,
148
Hurston, Zora Neale, 144
husbands, 40–42, 58, 163–164, 194,
204–205, 208–209, 212, 220, 222–
223, 226, 235, 276
hysterectomies, 301, 315n4

ideal images, 35, 37
identity, 237
illness, see sickness
images, 177, 199, 251; constructed,
253–254; cultural, 244; distortion,
245; normalizing, 34; in media, 242
immigration, 251, 252, 309
Inca, 309
incense, 4, 23n11
incest survivors, 184
independence, 196, 208, 302, 311
India, Indians, 109
individual, 311–314; achievement,
302; ownership, 293, 298–299, 306;
individuality, 303; individualism,
86, 97, 260
Indonesia, Indonesians, 253, 313,
316n10
industrialization, 306, 309
infertility, 140, 144–146, 294, 297,
306–307. See also fertility
inheritance, 309
insecurity, 95, 97, 101

sexuality, 98–99, 106, 175, 186, 197, 204, 206, 302; and aging, 164–169; control of, 194–195, 198; as ripeness, 138
shaman, 316n10
shame, 149, 175, 185, 199, 277
Shannon, Thomas, A., 298–302
shape, 149–159, 210
shape-changing, 275
sharing, 96, 240, 311–313; of bodily substance, 142–148; of children, 309–311; of children or food, 320; of children and goods, 310; of food and money, 132–133, 136, 140–142; of sleeping arrangements, 311
Shearer, Beth, 231
Sheets-Johnstone, Maxine, 11, 132, 322–323
sheikh, 319–320
Shorter, Edward, 315–316n6
sickness, 10, 11, 17, 140, 169, 171, 319–320. See also health
silence, 228, 268, 274, 286; silencing, 285
Simmons, D. R., 23n11
size, 95, 97, 102, 105, 119; and age, 170; body, 176, 180, 182; concern over, 107, 127; control over, 186, 194–195; of eyes, 248; large, 135–136; and reproductive success, 136
skin, 23n11, 29, 250, 324; color, 52, 151, 201, 253, 304–306; darkening/lightening, 151n2, 243–244, 261; light, 140, 148; "skinship," 311
slavery, 134, 136
sleeping arrangements, cosleeping, 311
Smith, Dorothy, 33, 36–37, 46, 55
smoking 110–111, 128, 216, 301
Sobo, Elisa, 106–107, 137, 139, 152n5, 312
sociability, 132–133, 151
socialization, 15, 114, 183, 187–190, 225, 312
social: bonding, 89, 96; group, 6; mirrors, 1; networks, 133, 142
social relationships, 1, 10, 18–19, 30, 53, 95, 106–107, 120, 137, 175–176, 178, 204–206, 231, 237, 240, 244, 264n4, 312, 314, 319–321,

323; dysfunctional, 185, 187–188; embodied, 324; as separation, 228
Socrates, 296
song, 3; communal, 16
sons, 41–42, 191, 223, 308
soul, 10–11, 17, 186, 210, 212, 247. See also spirit
South, U.S., 106, 155–173
space, 8; sexual division of, 60, 62
Spallone, Patricia, and Deborah Lynn Steinberg, 302, 306
Spanish, 316n8
speech, 106–109, 195, 198, 200. See also discourse; language
Spencer, Paul, 22–23n8
sperm, 142–144, 149, 239, 292, 295; banks, 263; donors, 295, 301. See also semen
spirit, 9, 11, 294, 319. See also soul
spiritual: awakening, 183, 202n3; distress, 176, 186; health, 189; parents, 307–309; solution, 187–188; ties, 240, 308–309, 312; understanding of body, 21n3
Spitzack, Carol, 195–196, 201n2
sponsorship, 197, 306–310, 313; ceremonies, 240
sports, 16, 76, 83, 92, 99, 102–103
Stack, Carol, 310
Stallybrass, Peter, 303
Steele, Valerie, 15
Stehura, John, 304–305
Steiner-Adair, Catherine, 114
stereotypes, see racial stereotypes
sterilization, 315n4
Stern, William, and Elizabeth Stern, 295, 297, 314n1
steroids, 31, 91–93, 101
stinginess, 107, 132, 141–142, 150. See also sharing
Strathern, Andrew, and Marilyn Strathern, 23n11
Strathern, Marilyn, 294
strength, 87–88, 92, 95, 167–168
stress, 136, 230
Striegel-Moore, R.,121
success, 221, 224, 235, 241, 254–256
Sudan, 58, 61–74, 274, 321. See also Rashaayda Bedouin
Sullivan, H., 114
supernatural forces, 307–308, 312

violence, 183, 237, 303, 323. *See also* assault; rape; torture
Virgin, the, 312
virility, 144
visual evidence, 275, 276; in identification, 280–281
vitality, 137, 140–141, 144–151, 168–169
Vuckovic, Nancy, 23, 176, 273

warfare, 74
Wax, Murray, 54
weakness, 200
weddings, 65–67
weight, 105, 107, 109–115, 118–127, 146–147, 176, 191, 210, 254; control, 186, 189, 194–195, 197; loss, 136–137; morality of, 127; obsession, 183; perfect, 116; problem, 180, 185. *See also* fat; thinness
Weir, Shelagh, 59–61
Wertz, Dorothy, and Richard Wertz, 226
Western: body image, 5, 9, 25, 133, 252; categories, 4; countries, 179; culture, 1; perceptions of Asians, 253; world, 227; worldview, 12, 20–21n2, 29, 128n3, 300–301, 322
whiteness, 293, 304–306; emulating, 52, 151n2, 235, 244
Whitehead, Mary Beth, 295, 301
whites, 198, 245, 304–305; academics, 15; adolescent girls, 119; as beauty models, 36, feminists, 36; men, 159, 172n4; women, 37, 40–42, 53, 109, 112, 249, 260, women tourists, 148
wholeness, 320, 323–324, 324n2. *See also* person
Wickett, Elizabeth, 319–320
wives, 59, 205, 207; rights over, 298
Wilbert, Johannes, 294
Wilbert, Werner, 3
Wild, Helga, 14
Wilson, Bill, 202n4
Wilson, P. J., 146
Winfrey, Oprah, 244
Wininger, Kate, 266, 276
Winkler, Cathy, 20, 237–238, 320
Wintu, 13
Wolf, Naomi, 242

woman as: container, 212, 296–297, 302; earth, 296; egg harvest, 302; plowed field, 295–296; uterus, 239, 301
womb, 292, 295–296, 305; as container, 314; renting, 300, 302. *See also* uterus
women, xi, xii, 7, 8, 15, 23n10, 29–30; aging, 163–169; behavior of, 196; bodies of, 227, 304; and childbearing and nurturing, 296; of color, 36, 52; competitive bodybuilders, 76–104; control of bodies of, 71–74; costume of, 58; definitions of, 95, 225; domain of, 227, 229; and feminism, 98; and health, 189, 228; imitating men, 101; and makeup, 33–55; modern, 214; professionals, 8, 177, 204–232; roles of, 313; status of, 60–62; surveillance of, 303; white and non-white, 254; and work, 225. *See also* femininity; mothers; wives
Wong, Suzy, 251
Woodman, Marion, 180
work, 177, 222, 225–226; corporate ladder, 207; work force, 252, workplace, 219, 227–228, 235
worldview, 12, 105, 198, 200, 204, 321; dichotomies, 177, 225, 230–231, 311–314; dominant, 314; and language, 13
World War I, 242
World War II, 251
Wynter, Sylvia, 316n8

Yang, Jeff, and Angelo Ragaz, 254
young, 195, 198, 302; appearance, 163–164, 235, 250, 254; as healthy, 171; vs. old, 105; symbols of, 165, 170; "young blood," 165
Young, William, 20, 29–30, 61, 87, 273, 321
Yugoslavia, 309

Zaire, Suku, 225–226
Zapotec, 240, 293, 305–309, 311–313; complementary gender roles among, 316n9; Tehuanas, 311
Zimmerman, Francis, 4

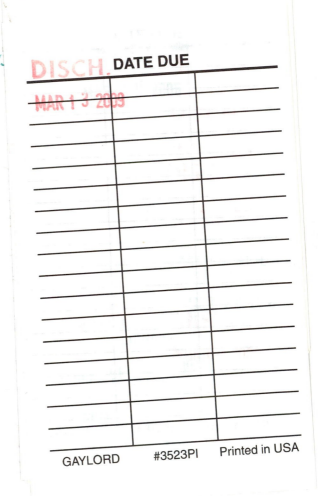

GAYLORD   #3523PI   Printed in USA